D1269328

WORKS ISSUED BY

THE HAKLUYT SOCIETY

THE TROUBLESOME VOYAGE
OF CAPTAIN EDWARD FENTON
1582–1583

SECOND SERIES
No. CXIII

ISSUED FOR 1957

HAKLUYT SOCIETY

PATRON

H.R.H. THE DUKE OF GLOUCESTER, K.G., P.C., K.T., K.P.

COUNCIL AND OFFICERS, 1958

PRESIDENT

J. N. L. BAKER, Esq., M.A., B.Litt.

VICE-PRESIDENTS

Professor E. G. R. TAYLOR, D.Sc.   JAMES A. WILLIAMSON, Esq., D.Lit.

Sir ALAN BURNS, G.C.M.G.

COUNCIL (WITH DATE OF ELECTION)

K. R. ANDREWS, Esq., Ph.D. (1958)
Professor C. F. BECKINGHAM (1958)
Professor C. R. BOXER (1955)
G. R. CRONE, Esq. (1955)
E. S. DE BEER, Esq., D.Litt., F.S.A. (1956)
Sir MAURICE HOLMES, G.B.E., K.C.B. (1957)
Sir GILBERT LAITHWAITE, G.C.M.G., K.C.B., K.C.I.E., C.S.I. (1956)
Professor C. C. LLOYD (1958)
Sir HARRY LUKE, K.C.M.G., D.Litt. (1954)
Commander R. D. MERRIMAN, R.I.N., D.S.C. (1957)
J. V. MILLS, Esq. (1956)
GEORGE NAISH, Esq., F.S.A. (1955)
N. M. PENZER, Esq., Hon.Litt.D., F.S.A. (1958)
Professor D. B. QUINN (1957)
Royal Geographical Society (General Sir JAMES MARSHALL-CORNWALL)
HELEN M. WALLIS, D.Phil. (1957)

TRUSTEES

J. N. L. BAKER, Esq., M.A., B.Litt.
E. W. BOVILL, Esq., F.S.A.

TREASURER: FRANK MAGGS, Esq.

HON. SECRETARY

R. A. SKELTON, Esq., B.A., F.S.A., F.R.Hist.S.,
British Museum, W.C.1

HON. SECRETARIES FOR OVERSEAS

Australia: G. D. RICHARDSON, Esq.
Canada: Professor J. B. BIRD
New Zealand: C. R. H. TAYLOR, Esq., M.A.
South Africa: DOUGLAS VARLEY, Esq.
U.S.A.: W. M. WHITEHILL, Esq., Ph.D., F.S.A.

Publisher and Agent for Sale and Distribution of Volumes:
CAMBRIDGE UNIVERSITY PRESS,
Bentley House, 200 Euston Road, London, N.W.1

I. The promoter of Fenton's voyage: Robert Dudley,
Earl of Leicester

Engraving by Hendrik Goltzius, 1586

The
Troublesome Voyage of
Captain Edward Fenton
1582-1583

Narratives & Documents

edited by

E. G. R. TAYLOR

Emeritus Professor of Geography
in the University of London

CAMBRIDGE
Published for the Hakluyt Society
AT THE UNIVERSITY PRESS
1959

PUBLISHED BY

THE SYNDICS OF THE CAMBRIDGE UNIVERSITY PRESS

Bentley House, 200 Euston Road, London, N.W. 1
American Branch: 32 East 57th Street, New York 22, N.Y.

©

THE HAKLUYT SOCIETY

1959

*Printed in Great Britain
by Robert MacLehose and Company Limited
at the University Press, Glasgow*

Our English Nation may seame to contend even with the Spaniard and Portugall himselfe, for the glory of Navigation. And without all doubt, had they but taken along with them a very reasonable competency of skill in Geometry and Astronomy, they had by this gotten themselves a farre more honourable name than they . . .

ROBERT HUES, *Tractatus de Globis*, 1594
(in John Chilmead's translation of 1639)

PREFACE

THE explosive entry of England into world affairs in the mid-years of the first Elizabeth has captured every imagination. That Drake sailed round the globe in 1577–80, that Lord Charles Howard defeated the Spanish Armada in 1588, and that in the following years Richard Hakluyt first published the sea-saga of the *Principall Navigations*, are among familiar matters upon which every Englishman prides himself. But not every sea-captain had the resolution—or the ruthlessness—of a Francis Drake. Not every commander under the Lord Admiral was of the first-rate calibre of a Hawkins. While, of Hakluyt's informants, there were many who held back facts as 'unfit to be told', and he himself considered that there was much which it would be indiscreet to make public. The story of Edward Fenton, who with his associates set out to emulate, even to outdo, the exploits of Drake, has never been told in full. For Fenton was one of the unsuccessful Elizabethans, his voyage a failure; and although he later helped to defeat the Spaniards in the Channel, Hakluyt considered him sufficiently remembered by the shortened narrative of his second-in-command. Yet the adverse circumstances which, equally with his character, made the voyage of 1582 abortive are well worth recording, for they too were typical of the times. While it is also important to remind ourselves that Hakluyt did not hesitate to use the editorial blue pencil.

The present volume contains all the surviving records of the voyage that can be discovered. These should be of special interest to the general reader, for they include two private diaries and a number of personal letters besides the somewhat austere Sea Journal of Edward Fenton himself. The latter (together with Fenton's Journal of his Arctic Voyage with Frobisher in 1578) has not apparently hitherto been noticed.

vii

The pair form part of the great collection of sea books and manuscripts brought together—and read—by Samuel Pepys. The 'China Voyage' is here published by the kind permission of the Master and Fellows of Magdalene College, Cambridge.

The professional bleakness of Fenton's Journal is set off by the very different character of that of his chaplain Richard Madox. Madox's nature shines through his Private Diary—a perceptive observer of his fellows, and keenly interested in the springs of human action; a man of firm Christian principle, who could yet relish seaman's humour and tell a broad anecdote with zest; outspoken in his judgements of others, but generous and peace-loving; an intelligent, curious, and articulate man, with a trained and well-stored mind; an admirable observer, indeed one who may be fairly called scientific. These are qualities which go to make a great diarist, and Madox was one. It is a matter for regret by the present editor that she can offer here no more than about a quarter of Madox's Diary, since to print the whole would have unbalanced her book. It may be hoped that some other scholar will undertake a complete edition of this vivid and circumstantial document that so clearly displays the diverse humours of the Elizabethans—in university, in capital city, in sea-port, and on shipboard.

No portraits of Fenton or his fellow-voyagers are known, although Madox tells us that on 28 February 1582 'Mr Betts of Moorgate made my picture and had 12s. for it.' Most of the illustrations in this volume are taken from the sketches (charts or pictures) in Madox's Diary, all of which—with one omission—are reproduced; they indicate the range and variety of his interest in natural science. The title of the book is borrowed from the words with which Captain Luke Ward closed his narrative of the expedition: '. . . and thus I ended a troublesome voyage.'

The present editor is deeply indebted to Mr R. A. Skelton for much information, many references, and unsparing help and advice in preparing a somewhat awkward collection of manuscripts and illustrations for the press. Her grateful thanks are also due to many who have provided information or answered enquiries with great kindness, notably many colleagues at Birkbeck College, University of London; Mr Evan James, Clerk of the Merchant Taylors' Company; the Rev. K. C. Francis, Vicar of St Nicholas, Deptford; Dr A. L. Rowse, Fellow of All Souls College, Oxford; Dr R. W. Ladborough, Pepysian Librarian; Professor D. B. Quinn; Dr J. A. Williamson; Dr K. R. Andrews; Mr G. P. B. Naish, of the National Maritime Museum; Miss M. A. Bennet-Clark, of the Ethnographical Department, British Museum; Dr D. W. Tucker, of the Department of Zoology, British Museum (Natural History); and Miss Margaret Holmes, County Archivist of Dorset. Permission to reprint copyright material has been generously given by Mr Francis P. Farquhar, for Document 49, and by Messrs John Murray Ltd, for Document 72.

Ralph's Ride, Bracknell   E. G. R. T.
August, 1958

Postscript (*February* 1959)

While this book was in the Press Mr Keith Short, a member of the Society resident in Brazil, drew the editor's attention to a document in the Spanish archives concerning the events at St Vicente. Mr Short generously supplied a microfilm and summary of the document, besides valuable notes on the personalities concerned. Excerpts have been printed as Documents 59A and 81.

CONTENTS

Part II: THE VOYAGE

Part III: THE AFTERMATH

ILLUSTRATIONS AND MAPS

Plates

Figures in text

Sketch Maps

Acknowledgements

Reproductions have been made by courtesy of the Trustees of the British Museum, the Trustees of the National Maritime Museum, the Master and Fellows of Magdalene College, Cambridge, the Director of the Science Museum, and the Director of the Biblioteca da Ajuda, Lisbon. The sketch maps were drawn by Mrs A. M. Huhtala.

BIBLIOGRAPHY

(The 'documents' cited in brackets are those printed
in this volume)

I. *Original sources: manuscript*

BRITISH MUSEUM

Cotton MS Otho E. VIII. (Various papers relating to Fenton's
expedition. Mutilated by fire. Ff. 130-143 until 1894 bound
in MS Sloane 2496, ff. 74-87. Documents 8-14, 16, 19,
21-23, 25, 26, 29-31, 33, 36, 39-44, 47, 48, 50-56, 58-67.)

Cotton MS App. XLVII. (49 ff., vellum; sometime Add. MS
5008. Richard Madox's Private Diary, 1 Jan.-15 Sept. 1582.
A prefixed note, signed F[rederic] M[adden], Jan. 1854,
states that 'the contents of this volume were formerly kept
with the unbound Papers of Dr John Dee (Cott. App. XLVI)'.
Documents 38, 77, 78.)

Cotton MS Titus B. VIII. (ff. 179-221, continuation of
Madox's Private Diary, 14 Sept.-31 Dec. 1582; f. 280, the
trial of Ralph Crane. Documents 38, 45, 77, 79.)

MS Harl. 167. (ff. 39-72, English translation of a Portuguese
manual of navigation. Document 75.)

MS Harl. 6993, arts. 6-8. (Papers of Arthur Atye relating to
Fenton's expedition. Documents 15, 17, 20.)

MS Lansdowne 31, arts. 81-83; and Lansdowne 102, art. 104.
(Documents on the abandonment of the First Enterprise,
20-29 August 1581.)

MS Lansdowne 100, art. 1. ('The doinges of Captayne
Furbisher, amongest the Companyes busynes', by Michael
Lok. Document 1.)

PUBLIC RECORD OFFICE

State Papers, Domestic, Elizabeth. S.P. 12/85; 12/143; 12/148;
12/150; 12/152; 12/153; 12/161. (Documents 3, 4, 6, 24, 27, 64.)

MAGDALENE COLLEGE, CAMBRIDGE

Pepys MS 2133. (Unfoliated. Edward Fenton's Sea Journals in
the *Judith*, 1578, and in the *Galleon Leicester*, 1582-3.
Documents 34, 37, 74.)

xxi

ARCHIVO GENERAL DE INDIAS, SEVILLE
2.5.2/21. (*Relación* of Juan Perez alias Richard Carter; letter of
Fray Juan de Rivadeneyra, 1583; inquiry at St Vincent, 1583;
depositions of John Drake, 1587. Documents 49, 59A, 72, 81.)

II. *Original sources: printed*

BEST, GEORGE. *The Three Voyages of Sir Martin Frobisher*, ed.
Sir R. Collinson. (Hakluyt Society, ser. I, no. 38.) London,
1868. (Document 1.)

*Calendar of State Papers, Colonial Series. East Indies, China and
Japan, 1513–1616.* London, 1862. (Nos. 155–233, abstracts
of documents in the B.M. and P.R.O. relating to Fenton's
expedition.)

Calendar of State Papers, Domestic, 1547–80, 1581–90. 2 vols.
London, 1856–65.

Calendar of State Papers, Foreign, 1578–9—1583–4. 4 vols.
London, 1904–14.

Calendar of State Papers, Ireland, 1574–85. London, 1867.

Calendar of State Papers, Spanish, 1580–1586. London, 1896.
(Despatches of Bernardino de Mendoza, Spanish Ambassador
in London, to King Philip II. Documents 2, 7, 18, 28, 32, 68,
69.)

DEE, JOHN. *The Private Diary of Dr John Dee*, ed. J. O.
Halliwell. London, Camden Society, 1842.

HAKLUYT, RICHARD. *The Principall Navigations, Voiages, and
Discoveries of the English Nation.* London, 1589. (pp. 160–2,
letter of Thomas Stevens from Goa, 1579; 644–7, instructions
to Fenton; 647–72, narrative of Luke Ward; 673–4, report of
Lopez Vaz. Documents 35, 46, 57, 70, 71, 76.)

—— *The Principal Navigations . . . of the English Nation.* 3
vols. London, 1598–1600. Modern reprint in 12 vols.,
Glasgow, MacLehose, 1903–5 (Hakluyt Society, extra series,
vols. 1–12).

HAWKINS, RICHARD. *The Observations of Sir Richard
Hawkins*, ed. J. A. Williamson. London, 1933.

MADOX, RICHARD. *A Learned and a Godly Sermon, to be read
of all men; but especially for all Marryners, Captaynes, and
Passengers, which travell the Seas, preached by John Madoxe
[sic], Maister of Arte, and fellow of All soules in Oxforde, at
Waymouth and Melcombe Regis . . . the 3. day of October
. . . 1581.* London, J. Charlwood, [1583?].

MARKHAM, C. R. (ed.) *The Hawkins' Voyages.* (Hakluyt Society, ser. I, no. 57.) London, 1878. (pp. 353–63, 'Journal of William Hawkins, lieutenant-general in Fenton's voyage . . . 1582'.)

— — *Narratives of the Voyages of Pedro Sarmiento de Gambóa to the Straits of Magellan, 1579–80.* (Hakluyt Society, ser. I, no. 91.) London, 1895.

MURDIN, W. (ed.) *A Collection of State Papers . . . 1571 to 1596 . . . left by . . . Lord Burghley.* London, 1759. (Document 5.)

NUTTALL, Z. (ed.) *New Light on Drake.* (Hakluyt Society, ser. II, no. 34.) London, 1914.

PACHECO PEREIRA, DUARTE. *Esmeraldo de Situ Orbis,* ed. G. H. T. Kimble. (Hakluyt Society, ser. II, no. 79.) London, 1936.

QUINN, D. B. (ed.) *The Voyages and Colonising Enterprises of Sir Humphrey Gilbert.* 2 vols. (Hakluyt Society, ser. II, nos. 83–4.) London, 1940.

TAISNIER, JEAN. *A very necessarie and profitable Booke concerning Navigation . . . named a treatise of continuall Motions. Translated into Englishe, by Richarde Eden.* London, [1579].

TAYLOR, E. G. R. (ed.) *The Original Writings & Correspondence of the two Richard Hakluyts.* 2 vols. (Hakluyt Society, ser. II, nos. 76–7.) London, 1935.

VAUX, W. S. W. (ed.) *The World Encompassed by Sir Francis Drake.* (Hakluyt Society, ser. I, no. 16.) London, 1855.

WARD, LUKE. 'The voiage intended towards China, wherein M. Edward Fenton was appointed Generall: Written by M. Luke Ward his Viceadmiral'. In: Hakluyt, *Principall Navigations* (1589), pp. 647–72.

III. *Secondary material*

ANDREWS, K. R. *English Privateering Voyages to the West Indies, 1588–95.* (Hakluyt Society, ser. II, no. 111.) London, 1959.

BURROWS, M. *Worthies of All Souls.* London, 1874.

CLARK, ANDREW (ed.) *Register of the University of Oxford.* vol. II: 1571–1622. Oxford, 1889.

CORBETT, Sir JULIAN S. *Drake and the Tudor Navy.* 2nd ed. 2 vols. London, 1899.

ELIOTT-DRAKE, E. F., Lady. *The Family and Heirs of Sir Francis Drake*. 2 vols. London, 1911. (Appendix II prints the depositions of John Drake, Spanish text and English translation. Document 72.)

FALCONER, WILLIAM. *An Universal Dictionary of the Marine*. London, 1769.

HERODOTUS. *History*, trans. G. Rawlinson. (Everyman's Library.) 2 vols. London, 1910.

NAISH, G. P. B. 'Ships and ship-building [*c.* 1500–*c.* 1750]', in *A History of Technology*, ed. Charles Singer *et al.*, vol. III (1957), pp. 471–500.

ROWSE, A. L. *The Elizabethan Age*. vol. II: *The Expansion of Elizabethan England*. London, 1955.

SOMERVILLE, Rear-Admiral BOYLE T. *Ocean Passages for the World*. 2nd ed. London, Hydrographic Dept., Admiralty, 1950.

TANNER, J. R. *Bibliotheca Pepysiana. A descriptive catalogue of the library of Samuel Pepys. Part I.—'Sea' manuscripts*. London, 1914.

TAYLOR, E. G. R. 'More light on Drake'. *M.M.*, vol. XVI (1930), pp. 134–51.

—— *Tudor Geography, 1485–1583*. London, 1930.

—— *Late Tudor and Early Stuart Geography, 1583–1650*. London, 1934.

—— 'Early empire building projects in the Pacific Ocean, 1565–85'. *Hispanic American Historical Review*, vol. XIV (1934), pp. 296–306.

—— 'Instructions to a colonial surveyor in 1582'. *M.M.*, vol. XXXVII (1951), pp. 48–62.

—— *The Mathematical Practitioners of Tudor and Stuart England*. Cambridge, 1954.

—— *The Haven-finding Art*. London, 1956.

WAGNER, H. R. *Sir Francis Drake's Voyage around the World*. San Francisco, 1926. (pp. 213–25, 398–403, 445–52: the Fenton expedition. Document 49.)

WALKER, GEORGE. *Puritan Salt, the Story of Richard Madox*. London, 1935. (Fictional biography; mainly conjectural.)

WILLIAMSON, J. A. *The Age of Drake*. 2nd ed. London, 1946.

—— *Hawkins of Plymouth*. London, 1949.

—— *Sir John Hawkins*. Oxford, 1927.

WOOD, ANTHONY À. *Athenae Oxonienses*, ed. P. Bliss. 4 vols. London, 1813–20.

ABBREVIATIONS

B.M.	British Museum.
Cal. S.P., Col., E. Indies.	*Calendar of State Papers, Colonial Series. East Indies, China and Japan.*
Cal. S.P., Dom.	*Calendar of State Papers, Domestic, Elizabeth.*
Cal. S.P., Foreign.	*Calendar of State Papers, Foreign Series.*
Cal. S.P., Ireland.	*Calendar of State Papers, Ireland.*
Cal. S.P., Span.	*Calendar of State Papers, Spanish.*
D.N.B.	*Dictionary of National Biography.*
J.I.N.	*Journal of the Institute of Navigation.*
M.M.	*The Mariner's Mirror.* Quarterly Journal of the Society for Nautical Research.
O.E.D.	*Oxford English Dictionary.*
P.R.O.	Public Record Office.
Pr. Nav.	Hakluyt, *Principall Navigations.* (If no date is given, the reference is to the first edition, 1589.)
Taylor, *Hakluyts.*	E. G. R. Taylor, *The Original Writings & Correspondence of the two Richard Hakluyts* (1935).
Wagner, *Drake's Voyage.*	H. R. Wagner, *Sir Francis Drake's Voyage around the World* (1926).

NOTE ON PRESENTATION OF THE DOCUMENTS

The Sea Journal of Edward Fenton (Document 37) has been transcribed as closely as possible from the original, with contractions extended, and supplied letters printed in italic. In the remaining documents transcribed from manuscript originals, extended contractions are not typographically indicated. Conjectural interpolations by the editor are enclosed in square brackets.

In Richard Madox's Private Diary (Document 38), from which only extracts are printed, dates have been inserted as required to inform the reader. In the original, the names of Sundays and Saints' Days are usually given as they appear in the Prayer Book Calendar, while the days of the week are shown by astrological symbols. Cipher passages are introduced by the word '*cipher:*', and enclosed in square brackets. Translated passages (from Latin), introduced by the contraction '*transl:*', are similarly enclosed.

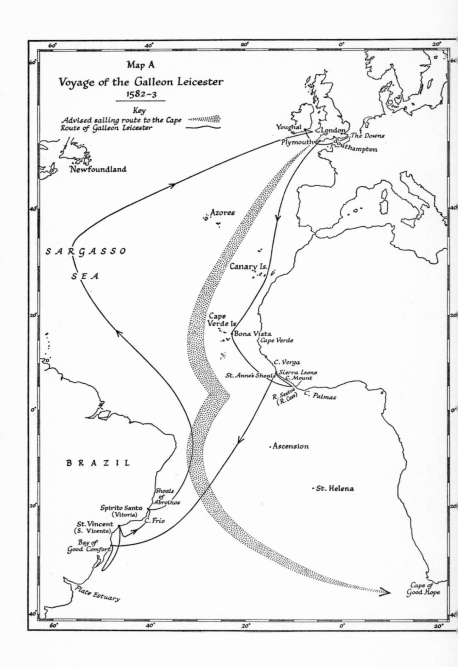

Map A

Voyage of the Galleon Leicester
1582–3

Key

Advised sailing route to the Cape
Route of Galleon Leicester

Youghal   *London*
Plymouth   *The Downs*
Southampton

Newfoundland

Azores

S A R G A S S O

S E A

Canary Is.

Cape
Verde Is.
Bona Vista
Cape Verde

C. Verga
St. Anne's Shoals   Sierra Leone
C. Mount
R. Sestos   C. Palmas
(R. Cess)

· Ascension

B R A Z I L

· St. Helena

Shoals
of
Abrolhos
Spirito Santo
(Vitoria)
St. Vincent   C. Frio
(S. Vicente)
Bay of
Good Comfort

Cape of
Good Hope

Plate Estuary

INTRODUCTION

EDWARD FENTON's voyage of 1582 'for China and Cathay', sponsored by the Privy Council, was officially intended to establish the first English trading base in the Far East, but since it was a signal failure it has attracted little attention from historians. It is generally known, moreover, only from the narrative of the vice-admiral, Luke Ward, which Hakluyt printed in 1589. This he subsequently cut to barely half its original length for inclusion in the *Principall Navigations* of 1599–1600, and it is from the latter version that modern reprints have been made. Fenton's own Sea Journal has never been published—the manuscript was one of those collected by Samuel Pepys—and it alone records the last six months of the voyage. For early in 1583 Ward 'lost company' with his General off the coast of Brazil, while two months earlier still young John Drake had taken himself off with the *Bark Francis*, to the consternation of the mariners in the two great ships. For as he vanished, so there vanished also their dream of sharing out another shipload of Spanish treasure such as Sir Francis had brought home, and in the secret hope of which so many of them had embarked.

Plan and preparation of the voyage

It might well be asked what prospect there could have been of taking Spanish treasure in the course of a voyage to the Moluccas which, as the official Instructions laid down, was to be made both outward and homeward by the Portuguese route round the Cape of Good Hope. But, once at sea, who is to hold a man? Drake's return, loaded with spoils, had set every young gentleman in England (so the Spanish Ambassador said) agog for the Pacific. Hence in the preparatory notes for the organization of the Fenton voyage there is to be found a warning that if young William Hawkins was to be given a command, someone 'trusty' must be associated with him to keep the venture to its purpose. That purpose was, in fact, expressed only very vaguely, but it was presumably to take advantage of the good relations established by Drake with the native rulers at Ternate in the Moluccas and purchase cloves. A landing party was to be left at some unspecified point in the East, and since we know that the Earl of Leicester (then Chancellor of Oxford University) had asked for up to three years' leave of absence for the man who was to be its chaplain, Richard Madox, Fellow of All Souls, this suggests at least a year's stay.[1]

It was definitely the Earl of Leicester's voyage, and he put all the business of organization into the hands of his recently appointed secretary, Arthur Atye, another Oxford man. His own investment in it was a sum of £2,200, while he invited his friends to take shares at a mere £100 or £200 apiece.[2] Nor had the venture, in fact, originally been planned in any relation to Drake's success in the Moluccas. It was the relatively insignificant aftermath of a more grandiose scheme to reap advantage for England from the claim made by Don Antonio, Prior of Crato, to the throne of Portugal. A year before Drake's return it had become obvious that the Pope's Line would shortly disappear, and the whole colonial empire of the world, whether it lay East or West, would fall into the single hands of King Philip of Spain. An English cosmographer, possibly Richard Hakluyt, had suggested three counter measures: colonizing Magellan Strait; seizing S. Vicente ('St Vincent'), then the most southerly Portuguese settlement in Brazil; and immediately searching out the north-east passage to Cathay, which was believed to run south-east after passing the mouth of the River Ob. Thus new trade approaches to the Far East, outflanking Spain, might be secured.[3]

Meanwhile the old Cardinal King Henry of Portugal died, and Queen Elizabeth committed herself cautiously to

[1] P. 151, n. 2.
[2] Document 6.
[3] E. G. R. Taylor, *The Original Writings & Correspondence of the two Richard Hakluyts* (Hakluyt Society, 1935), pp. 139–46.

the support of the Pretender. The returning Drake, understandably full of self-confidence, declared himself ready to lead a fleet back by the Cape route and secure the Portuguese Indies, and in the New Year of 1581 the Spanish Ambassador Mendoza reported to his master that the nation's hero was indeed about to sail on this adventure.[1] Actually, however, Don Antonio had already been defeated in Portugal, and the only territory acclaiming him as its King was Terceira, the large central island of the Azores group. This, however, for reasons of wind and weather, was at the very hub of Atlantic sea-traffic, and upon it the policy-making trio of the Privy Council, Burghley, Walsingham and Leicester, now formulated a supporting 'Enterprise'.[2] A fleet of two great ships (one the *Galleon Oughtred*), with six small vessels or pinnaces in support was to establish a fortress on Terceira with a garrison of two hundred (originally a thousand) men, and there cruise about to await the coming of the Spanish treasure fleet from the West Indies. If this were missed then they would range and spoil the Caribbean coasts. This last purpose, however, must have been too much for Lord Burghley, whose notes are on the relevant document, for it is heavily scored through. But letters of marque from the 'King' of Portugal would give legal cover to the seizing of the Spanish ships in the Azores. The same English fleet could also sail round the Cape to Calicut, and there in friendly cooperation with the Portuguese (it was assumed that these colonials would be in favour of King Antonio) they would establish an annual English spice trade.

On the back of the page, Burghley made a list of names of proposed captains for the double 'Enterprise'. Drake's naturally came first, but almost at once the Queen forbade his employment. Next was that of Richard Bingham, a notable soldier and a 'servant' of Sir Francis Walsingham, followed by those of Edward Fenton, Gilbert Yorke, and Luke Ward, who had all three been on Frobisher's second and third Arctic voyages. These voyages had enjoyed the financial support of Leicester and his brother, the Earl of

[1] P. 5.   [2] Documents 3, 4, 5.

Warwick, as well as of Burghley and Walsingham. Don Antonio, who was expected to put down £2,500 for the 'Enterprise', was to receive half the proceeds 'gotten from the enemies of the King', and (says the plan) the Queen 'may' provide the like sum. Drake and his friends were also expected to take shares in the adventure, to the tune of £5,820, and so make up the total estimated cost.

But no fleet sailed. Evidently the money was not forthcoming, and there were political complications besides. The Queen had no wish to embroil herself with her 'brother' Philip, while the cooperation of France in Don Antonio's affairs hinged upon her decision whether or no she would really marry the French King's sickly brother. However that might be, by August 1581, the Portuguese Pretender was being fobbed off with vague assurances,[1] while Leicester had developed quite different ideas for using the *Galleon Oughtred*, which had already been fully furnished and armed to lead the 'Enterprise'. His plan was to secure the partnership of the Muscovy Company, and send the ship (ostensibly at least) on a peaceful merchant voyage to the Moluccas. She was to have a consort and one or two small supporting barks or pinnaces.

Immediately, the Earl began writing round to his friends to take shares in this venture,[2] while his secretary Atye jotted down notes of various decisions and arrangements that would have to be made. John Hawkins, Treasurer of the Navy Board, on being approached sourly refused to contribute, saying that his credit had been exhausted by provision made by him on the Queen's behalf for the 'Enterprise', but now left on his hands. This, however, as will appear, was a mere pretence. He did not like the parties concerned. The Earl of Shrewsbury on the other hand was eager to send his *Bark Talbot*, but the partners who ran her on his behalf made unacceptable conditions with regard to prize-money, and the suggestion fell through. Atye jotted down a long list of names of possible subscribers, including many (those for example of Horatio Palavicini, the elder William Hawkins and Alderman

[1] See p. 9, n. 1.   [2] Documents 8–10, 15–17.

Martin) which he subsequently struck out. Shrewsbury eventually put up £200. The *Galleon* was bought from Sheriff Oughtred for £2,800 as she stood, and of this sum £800 was to represent her owner's investment in the voyage, the Earl of Leicester undertaking to pay him the £2,000 in a series of instalments spread over a year or more. Drake, who was supposed now to possess a bottomless purse, put in a thousand marks, all the other shares being small. A third of the proceeds was to be divided among the crew who actually sailed, at a standard rate according to their status, which explains why a suggestion, made by the military commander during the voyage, to bestow the rank of lieutenant and corporals upon some of his men was firmly rejected by Fenton.[1]

The merchandise carried was valued at no more than £2,000, and although this was to be sold for not less than three times its cost, a return of £6,000 could not make the voyage profitable. Other sources of gain, in particular from the purchase of spices, must have been expected. It is worth noting however that English merchants were already awake to the fact that Portuguese colonials in Brazil were hungry for manufactures, especially textiles and hardware, and could offer in return quantities of cheap sugar.[2] In West Africa, too, there was an unsatisfied native demand for salt as well as European manufactures, and an exportable surplus of pepper, slaves, ivory and perhaps gold. A voyage there might be worth £100,000.[3]

The voyagers

Command of the China voyage was at first given to Frobisher, with Captain Christopher Carleil (Walsingham's stepson), Edward Fenton, Luke Ward, and probably young Hawkins, in subordinate positions. But for reasons unexplained, after he had attended to the preparations for over five months, Frobisher was suddenly replaced by

[1] A typical Spanish scheme of division is given by Antonio de Herrera, *Historia General* (1601), dec. III, lib. viii, cap. 6.
[2] See pp. l, 106, 195, 280, 282.
[3] Randall Shaw (p. xxxv) to Edward Cotton (S.P. 12/143, art. 46).

Fenton, who had been his lieutenant in the Arctic voyages.[1] This was to exchange a sailor for a soldier, and was greatly resented by the mariners, some of whom repudiated their engagements and turned pirate.

Fenton came of a Nottinghamshire family.[2] His elder brother Geoffrey was to become well known as an administrator and writer, and Edward himself in 1567 produced a book (a translation from the French) which he dedicated to Lord Lumley (son-in-law to the Catholic-sympathizing Earl of Arundel). But he turned to soldiering, which qualified him in those days for taking command at sea. During 1580–1 he fought in the Irish Wars, as did Captain Bingham and Martin Frobisher, the two last-named in command of ships before Smerwick.

Carleil, jealous of young Hawkins, never sailed. He backed out at the last minute, pleading an ague, so that a colourless and nervous young gentleman, Nicholas Parker, who had also fought in Ireland, was promoted to replace him as commander on land. As already mentioned, Leicester chose the senior chaplain from Oxford, and it is Richard Madox's private diary[3] which lends such colour and human interest to the story of this voyage, although regrettably the diarist did not survive it. The second parson, also a diarist,[4] was John Walker, a simple pious man (not without his weaknesses) and one of Leicester's own chaplains. He, too, died at sea.

Both chaplains were profoundly shocked when, once past the Lizard, they discovered themselves to be part of a would-be pirate crew. Their General, they learned, was pondering wild schemes for self-aggrandizement among which a simple merchant voyage intended for the exchange of drapery and haberdashery for spices was quite lost sight of. That he sailed, moreover, under commission of the Broad Seal (as Frobisher had done in 1577 and 1578) went to Edward Fenton's head. It gave him powers and privileges which prompted him to arrogant behaviour and self-glory.

[1] P. 151; Documents 24, 27.
[2] D.N.B., s.vv. Fenton, Edward, and Fenton, Sir Geoffrey.
[3] Document 38.
[4] Document 39.

As a consequence he expected and demanded a humble submission and subservience as though he had been the Queen in very person. Madox declared that Fenton's evil genius during the voyage was the Portuguese renegade and ex-pirate, Simon Ferdinando (Simão Fernandes) 'Mr. Secretary Walsingham's man'. This fellow, a native of Terceira, was shipped as co-pilot with Thomas Hood, one of Drake's crew, although his knowledge and skill (without doubt considerable) were limited to navigation in the North Atlantic. A Protestant convert, he was all for robbing the Spaniard, and when Madox challenged him, since the Queen was at peace with Spain, he declared that he had a mandate to do so from five Privy Councillors.[1]

Ward, the vice-admiral, is rather a baffling figure. We do not know who his patron was (Fenton was a 'gentleman of the Earl of Warwick's'), and it was a mother, not a wife, who came to see him off when the *Edward Bonaventure* left Blackwall in April 1582. But he owned a ship, and (it is safe to say) was a professional sailor. The last we learn of him is that he was captain of a ship, the *Tramontana*, which was one of those assembled to meet the Spanish Armada in 1588, while in 1591 he commanded the Queen's ship *Swallow*.[2] Madox thought well of him at first, and indeed he was assiduous in the care of his men, in improving his maritime knowledge and in seeking the prosecution of the voyage as planned. But when he offered to keep the parson's private diary from prying eyes, Madox actually denied that he kept one, while writing in it that no one would care to put himself under an obligation to a man of that sort. Certainly Ward lacked self-control. Incensed at some order of Fenton's he made a painful scene at dawn one day in the cabin of his own chaplain Walker, then barely recovered from a dangerous attack of fever. And more than once he threatened privately that he would desert his commander. It was as Fenton's lieutenant that he had been chosen to overwinter in the Arctic in 1578, and it is perhaps fortunate that the exceptional ice conditions, and the loss of half the prefabricated building

[1] P. 197. [2] *D.N.B.*, s.v. Warde, Luke.

that the party was to occupy, caused that scheme to be abandoned. Michael Lok, who, as treasurer of the Cathay Company, found himself in the Fleet prison through no personal fault, declared that Frobisher had deliberately wrecked the plan lest Fenton's fame should outshine his own. Such back-biting and jealousy was typical of the day, and marred Fenton's own voyage. It is welcome to find in Richard Madox a man who could be critical without being spiteful, and one of whose integrity his Diary leaves the reader in no doubt.

There were about a dozen of Drake's men aboard, who included the pilots of the two principal ships (the renamed *Galleon Leicester* and the *Edward Bonaventure*), Captain John Drake commanding his cousin's little *Bark Francis*, and young William Hawkins (nephew of John Hawkins), whose rank was Lieutenant to Fenton. It had seemed a sensible step to carry mariners who had at least once sailed over the Cape route, hitherto completely unknown to English sailors, but in fact these men had one ambition only, namely to reach the forbidden Strait of Magellan, and once more plunder off the coast of Peru. And this in spite of the clear indications that since Drake's raids the Spaniards were taking precautions against any repetition of the earlier exploit, which had taken them unawares.[1]

A small committee of leading members of the Muscovy Company looked after details of the furnishing and manning of the ships. They were Alderman Barnes (son of old Sir George), William Towerson (who had traded to Guinea in Queen Mary's days), and John Castlyn.[2] They placed some of their own men aboard, notably Nicholas Chancellor (son of the famous Richard), who was purser in the *Edward*, Christopher Hall, the steady, reliable Master of the *Galleon*, and Richard Fairweather, who although he had held the rank of Master in the Arctic voyages now shipped as mate. He was advanced to Master of the *Bark Francis* when William Markham, a Drake man, died in Sierra Leone. Thus he was one of those ship-wrecked in the Plate estuary with young

[1] P. 161.   [2] P. 66.

xxxiv

Drake, and was later reported to have married in the country, while his captain was carried off to Peru. Chancellor, who had gone through the three dangerous North-West Passage voyages, died after the shock of getting separated from his companions in the West African forest: a 'nervous man', said Madox.

The total casualties in this affair were in fact well over one-third of those who set out, not all the deaths being reported. Captain Thomas Skevington, who had been with Frobisher in the north-west, died of the scurvy when within sight of home. He had originally been in command of the *Elizabeth*, a ship a little larger than the *Bark Francis*, bought to carry supplies. But from the outset he was discontented and had trouble with his men. Fenton suspected him too of an intention to slip away in company with the *Bark*, and decided to have the *Elizabeth* broken up. In the event, however, she was sold to the Portuguese in West Africa. The rebellious merchant, Miles Evans, satisfied that they were not bound for China, arranged to return home in her. He was one of five merchants aboard, a group which became very obnoxious to Edward Fenton, since they naturally wished to carry out the voyage in accordance with the official instructions, that is to say for trade, not piracy. Among them was Randall Shaw, who during the first two weeks aboard wrote at great length to Edward Cotton of Southampton about the prospects of a trade voyage to 'Bynney' (West Africa), which he believed would prove very profitable. The youngest was Peter Jeffery, chosen for his knowledge of Spanish and Portuguese.[1] There were also three gentlemen in the company who had secured coveted places as 'travellers', a fourth being left behind, in farcical circumstances, in the Isle of Wight.[2] A name that does not appear on the sailing list is that of John Wilkes, apparently an expert in dyeing. He was on board the *Elizabeth* at first (behaving very offensively to Captain Skevington), and then transferred to the *Edward*, in which he died on the homeward journey. It will be recalled that English cloth merchants were very anxious to improve

[1] P. 63, n. 1.   [2] P. 86, n. 3.

the finish of their goods, and the elder Hakluyt (in his role of economic adviser) pressed the importance of sending dyers abroad to study foreign methods and materials.[1] The physician carried was John Banister, licensed by Oxford University, a boastful man who had been in attendance on Leicester and 'Monsieur' when the latter was being escorted to the Netherlands in February 1582. Madox, for reasons that will become obvious, referred to him in his Diary as 'the hypocrite'.

Madox and his Diary

The parson produced *noms de plume*[2] for all his leading companions once he discovered that his Diary was being read, and that in any case it would be confiscate at the end of the voyage. He therefore resorted to writing in Latin, and for particularly intimate passages used his private cipher, which has proved not very difficult to break.[3] The Diary is complete for the year 1582, but there is no evidence as to whether or no the writer had started a new 'book' (as he called it) during the remaining two months of his life. All we learn of him during that period is Fenton's curt entry in the margin of his Journal, on 27 February 1583, 'my father Madox died'.[4] This phrase suggests, however, that in spite of the poor opinion that the chaplain had formed of his General (one that he expressed to himself very plainly in private) he continued to serve him with that loyalty and dignity which Fenton's office demanded.

Madox was, indeed, in receipt of many confidences, so that he can often tell us what Ward, or young Hawkins, or Parker or Master Hall, was secretly feeling and thinking. And by referring to them respectively as Hypothalasticus, Glaucus, Pyrgopolinices, and Palinurus he could safely add his own, sometimes caustic, comments. Fenton was Clodius, Ward was occasionally Milo. Ferdinando was Cornicola, or Verres (the swine). Madox says that these were the names of the characters in what he describes as a witty comedy about

---

[1] Taylor, *Hakluyts*, pp. 137–9, 184–95.
[2] See below, pp. 183, 319.
[3] Document 80, and Plate XV.
[4] P. 137.

which he had read in Aulus Gellius. Perhaps his memory was at fault, but more probably he was bent on confusing the surreptitious reader, for no such comedy is mentioned in that writer's *Noctes Atticae*.[1] The chaplain was, however, widely read, alike in the classics and in English and foreign literature (he quotes, for example, from Thevet, Cardanus, Chaucer and Edmund Spenser). His age was 36 at the time of the voyage, and he had come up to Oxford in 1567, taking his B.A. degree in 1571 and obtaining a Fellowship in 1573. He later became a University lecturer and Member of Convocation. In 1580 he took orders, and was elected Junior Proctor in 1581, a post from which he had to secure leave of absence. He had earlier been absent from the University for nearly three years between 1576 and 1579, when he had some employment at Dorchester and spent a few months in Paris.[2] He then evidently came to know the Dorsetshire sea-port of Weymouth and Melcombe Regis, for after his death his friend Thomas Martin had a 'learned and godly' sermon printed which the 'learned and vertuous young man' (Madox) had preached there on 3 October 1581.[3] This sermon was particularly directed to sea-farers and is full of homely sea-imagery: the speaker is clearly familiar with the sailors' instruments, with the balestilha (cross-staff) and nocturnal, and he can speak eloquently of sea-hazards. Madox proved a wise choice as ship's chaplain, for unlike those around him, he had a trained mind and understood self-discipline and self-restraint.

Navigation

In fairness to Edward Fenton it must be said that his voyage to the East Indies and the Moluccas was foredoomed

[1] P. 183.

[2] Madox jotted down the salient facts of his life at the end of his Diary. (Document 79.)

[3] His editor mis-names the preacher as 'John' Madox, but describes him correctly as Master of Arts and Fellow of All Souls, Oxford. The publication bears no date, but refers to the Chaplain's death in the words 'hee, now having reaped the fruits of his faith, is made coheir with his, and our Christ, in the kingdom of our good God', which appear in Thomas Martin's dedication to the Mayor, Bailiffs and Aldermen of Weymouth and Melcombe Regis. See Bibliography, p. xxii above.

to failure not only by the late start but also by the unusual weather experienced that spring in the English Channel. The proposed sailing date had been the end of February. This was the correct one, for to avoid headwinds in rounding the Cape of Good Hope it is necessary to pass it during the winter of the southern hemisphere, that is to say between June and August. But the fleet was not ready to leave Southampton until the end of April, and throughout May, when a high proportion of easterly (i.e. down-Channel) winds may normally be expected, such favourable winds failed and the ship did not lose sight of the Lizard until the first of June. During that month, however, they had following winds and made remarkable progress, and it is just possible that with a skilled East India pilot they could yet have made the voyage. Drake, it will be recalled, seized pilots as he went. But Drake's men in the *Galleon* and the *Edward* for all their talk and boasting, did not have, and could not have, the necessary years of experience of the winds and currents likely to be encountered to enable them to give good advice. And the Muscovy Company's sea-men, of course, were at home only in high latitudes. A few years earlier a Portuguese pilot-book for the shores of West Africa and Brazil had been translated into English[1]—whether for Drake or for the new trade with S. Vicente (Brazil) that some London merchants were attempting, cannot be decided. But for the Cape route the only information available was that given by a young English Jesuit who in 1578 had sent home a careful account of his voyage to Goa.[2]

It is necessary for a sailing ship to stand well away from Africa in order to cross the 'doldrums' and then work down into the 'brave west winds' which carry ships past the Cape, and it was this necessity that gave their opportunity to those who wished to divert the voyage. For coming so near (they said) to the South American shore, it would be best to water there. And so they would be well on their way (but this they did not add openly) to Magellan Strait, or if not, they would come within reach of St Vincent, where Captain Fenton

[1] Document 75. [2] Document 76.

secretly believed he might make himself conqueror and king. The government of all doubtful questions on the voyage had been carefully committed in the Instructions to majority decisions made by a nominated Council.[1] But the masters and pilots were to be called in when some matter of sea causes arose, and so they could soon silence any protests about the course made by the chaplains or the merchants either with technical talk, or by declaring that the matter was outside their province.[2]

As a matter of fact Richard Madox was familiar with the most up-to-date navigation methods of the day as laid down by William Borough, Treasurer of the Queen's Ships and a leading contemporary expert, who in turn (as a young man) had received instruction from Dr John Dee. As part of his equipment, too, the chaplain brought an 'Ephemerides' (a book of astronomical tables) and had with him 'a very perfect instrument', perhaps an astrolabe, for taking the height of sun or star. He also records some careful observations which he made from time to time of the variation of the compass, using a method which did not become routine until the following century.[3] And it is worth noting that during the long west-east run following a parallel of latitude which was necessary for rounding the Cape of Good Hope, it was on the variation that Portuguese pilots relied to give them their position. It was 'the greatest and best industry of all', wrote Thomas Stevens, the young Jesuit already mentioned, since there was no means of determining the longitude at sea at that time. It is tempting to believe that Madox had read Stevens's newsletter (which Hakluyt later printed), but what we do know is that in company with his Oxford contemporary, the brilliant young mathematician Nathaniel Torporley, he had been down to Ratcliff to see Robert Norman, the well-known compass-maker, on 19 February 1582.[4] Norman worked in close contact with William Borough, and both had written books on the mariners' needle, which were published under one cover in 1581. Madox mentions that on April 8 he

[1] Document 35. [2] P. 77.
[3] Document 77. [4] P. 151.

read over the sea-manual entitled *The Regiment of the Sea* which he says was 'made' by William Borough, 'a very proper man for sea-matters'.[1] It is just possible that this was the unauthorized edition of William Bourne's well-known *Regiment* about which that author had complained.

Madox, like others of the gentlemen aboard, worked out the ship's run daily from the figures chalked up in the steerage. The helmsman pegged on the traverse board the number of half-watch periods sailed along each compass rhumb, i.e. in each direction, and the ship's way (or rate per hour) was either estimated, or measured with the log. From these figures the distance travelled was reckoned to the nearest league. Since, however, a ship had frequently to 'traverse', i.e. follow a zig-zag course athwart the desired direction according to the wind, the daily 'course made good' had to be calculated in terms of northing or southing (i.e. change of latitude) and easting or westing (change of longitude). The calculated latitude could be checked (when the sky was clear) by observation of the Pole Star (until the equator was approached) or by the height of the noon sun, but there was then no practicable means of checking longitude. When Fenton's fleet was in mid-ocean the masters' and pilots' reckonings were very greatly at variance.[2] Allowance has to be made for leeway and unknown currents, and Madox points out how errors of judgement in this respect had probably led to the faulty reckonings of their latitude off Guinea in July, when for two weeks no astronomical observations could be made. It is worth noticing that the chaplain showed knowledge not only of the elements of practical navigation but also of coastal survey.[3] Among his London friends was Cyprian Lucar,[4] one of the 'mathematical practitioners' (as they called themselves) who were promoting such rapid technical progress in England at this period. Despite the absence of any Reader or Professor in the mathematical field, Oxford too was alive to the importance of the subject, and Madox's University contemporaries

[1] B.M., Cotton MS Appendix XLVII, f. 12.   [2] P. 113, 186.
[3] See Pl. XIII, and note thereon.   [4] P. 152.

included Dr Richard Forster, Thomas Allen, Thomas Hariot, and Robert Hues, as well as Torporley.

Privateering

Before considering the events of the voyage, a word should be said about piracy and privateering, the latter being simply a licensed form of sea robbery. A privateer was a shipmaster who had secured 'letters of marque' (as they were termed) from some ruler (or claimant to a throne), giving him commission to prey upon the merchant shipping of the 'king's enemies'. Many Englishmen, including Drake and Sheriff Oughtred (the owner of the *Galleon* sold to Leicester), were given letters of marque by Don Antonio. The Azores thus became currently known as the 'Isles of Pickery' among people who remembered the injunction in the Catechism against 'picking and stealing' and considered that even licensed theft was theft. Such letters might be granted, even where no state of war existed, so as to enable the holder to make a reprisal and recompense himself for some previous piracy or wrong. Francis Drake claimed that he held the Queen's license to recover from the Spaniards the money lost by John Hawkins through Spanish treachery at San Juan de Ulloa in 1568. It may well have been so, although he never showed his Commission, and Edward Fenton was not the only man who plainly called him 'thief'. In any case the treasure he secured in reprisal was more than twenty-fold the value of what had been lost, and it seems reasonable to suppose that it was because Master Fletcher (his chaplain) denounced the Captain to the crew, when all faced death as the ship struck a rock, that he was immediately punished and humiliated in public by Drake on *The Golden Hind*. This would explain why it was whispered that Richard Madox wanted to 'play the Fletcher' when his opposition to Fenton's plans for pickery began to be known.[1]

Records of the voyage

The Documents included in this volume fall into three

[1] P. 174, n. 1.

groups, those relating to the inception of the voyage and the preparations made, those dealing with the voyage itself, and those which belong to its aftermath of recrimination and enquiry. All save Edward Fenton's formal Sea Journal are incomplete: in particular the letters and memoranda put together by Arthur Atye are fragmentary. These passed into Sir Robert Cotton's library, and the volume in which they are contained (MS Otho E. VIII) was one of those seriously damaged by the fire of 1731. Madox was appointed official Registrar of the voyage, and his fair copy of the Instructions and account of subsequent events is complete as far as it goes,[1] but it breaks off on 21 July 1582, perhaps because the writer continued in poor health throughout the voyage. He had the difficult task of keeping the Minutes of the Councils held in accordance with the Instructions when matters of moment had to be decided. Such fragments of these Minutes as remain have been transcribed. Extracts only have been taken from the two chaplains' diaries, these being selected for their relevance to the voyage itself, or to the many dissensions which arose among the company. Madox's cipher passages[2] have been decoded word for word where possible (he was far from consistent in the use of his symbols), and a free translation is given of his Latin entries where they are sufficiently legible. Vagaries of spelling and punctuation have raised some difficulties as to his meaning, and modern punctuation has occasionally been added to help the reader. Luke Ward's narrative has been used only where it throws additional light on the voyage, since it can be read in full in Hakluyt's printed version of 1589.

First phase of the voyage: to Sierra Leone

After the ceremonial send off of the fleet by the Muscovy Company's commissioners and the civic worthies of Southampton, the frustrating delays encountered in the Solent and in the Channel must have frayed all nerves. This prepared the way for the angry clash between Fenton and Drake's party that occurred at Plymouth. The crew became

---

[1] Documents 35, 36. [2] See Document 80.

mutinous but the tact of shipmaster Hall saved the situation. He had known how to put up with Frobisher's rages in the Arctic, and already he had taken Fenton's measure. But he could do nothing to heal the fierce enmity between the General and young William Hawkins, or to lessen the crew's greed for prize or 'purchase' (a word which at that date was a euphemism for forcible seizure of other men's goods). When letters were sent home from the Canaries by the *Bridget*,[1] Miles Evans informed Leicester that already the talk was of the forbidden Strait of Magellan, while Madox wrote to Arthur Atye of 'all things' among which he included 'our bad headpiece', i.e. Edward Fenton. Poor Walker still believed that the sailors were wonderfully delighted with sermons, and generously praised Captain Ward who within the next few days (but perhaps unjustly) was incurring the anger of his General.

On June 24 the first Council was held, when it was agreed to water at Bona Vista in the Cape Verde Islands. The pilots, called in to advise on the next place for refreshment, all insisted that they knew of none other but the River Plate. Thus the fleet was at once committed to crossing to the American coast. Another point that demanded discussion was the furnishing of the two small Barks. Fenton had already tried to get his vice-admiral to agree to breaking up the *Elizabeth*, where there was constant trouble, and both ships had been kept short of supplies so that they should not desert the fleet. Sufficient evidence of Fenton's failure in leadership! But the danger of accidental separation was so obvious that the Council voted them not only three months' provisions, but also copies of all necessary charts and plats. A few days before this the first death had occurred—an old sailor from Ratcliff was buried at sea.

But no watering at Bona Vista took place: the General suddenly left the island, and the rest despite 'great displeasure on al sydes' were under obligation to follow him. In Madox's opinion, Ferdinando was responsible, having persuaded Fenton to act so that 'for want of water we myght robb'. This

---

[1] Documents 40, 41, 42.

was probably true enough, but as the event proved, after a month of misery, beating up and down against contrary winds, the rest of the summer was spent in West Africa where there was plenty of water. For by the end of June the following wind was lost, and the weather, hitherto cool, became hot and clammy. The reason was that in the Gulf of Guinea a south-west monsoonal air stream replaces the north-east trade wind as the sun declines to the north. It was therefore to replenish their stock of wine that Fenton now planned to return to the Cape Verde Islands. There he could seize plenty.

His alternative project, confided first to Walker and then to Madox, was to make for St Helena and establish himself there as King, with the ships' crews as colonists. This island was quite uninhabited, but every year the Portuguese carracks from the East Indies called at it for water and refreshment. Their cargoes, he suggested, could be seized and sent to England in Luke Ward's ship, there to be sold.

This scheme was not quite so ridiculous as it sounds. The *Galleon Leicester* was a newly built warship framed on the lines of the *Revenge*. She carried over 40 guns on her upper and lower decks, and the gunners' room had been furnished at a charge of nearly £400. The *Edward Bonaventure* was also of modern construction and strongly armed, so that it is easy to understand the alarm of the inhabitants of S. Vicente in Brazil when six months later these two war-like vessels appeared, announcing themselves as 'peaceful merchants'.[1] According to Madox, Fenton's newest plan in fact was to seize that town, but the appearance of three armed Spanish ships dispelled any such notion, although he actually sent one of them to the bottom. The three were part of a great fleet sent out from Spain in 1581 to block the Strait of Magellan, of which there had been news before ever Fenton left England. But nobody cared a fig for the King of Spain's ships while they were at a distance. It was not until the fateful Council which Fenton called on December 20 that the ultimate decision had to be made: whether to sail east or sail

---

[1] P. 128; and Documents 59A, 81.

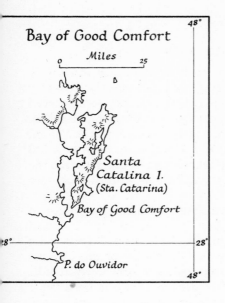

Bay of Good Comfort

0   Miles   25

48°

Santa
Catalina I.
(Sta. Catarina)

Bay of Good Comfort

28°   28°

48°

P. do Ouvidor

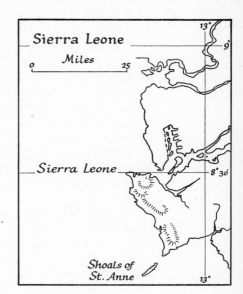

Sierra Leone

13°

9°

0   Miles   25

Sierra Leone   8° 30′

*Shoals of
St. Anne*

13°

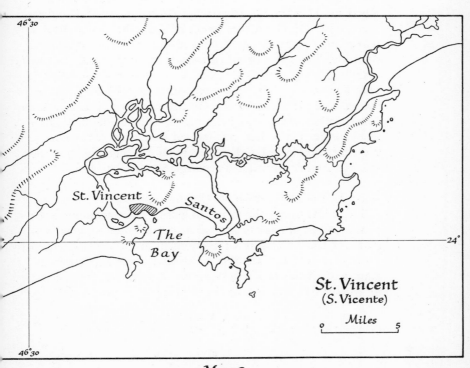

46° 30

St. Vincent   *Santos*

The
Bay

24°

St. Vincent
(S. Vicente)

Miles

0   5

46° 30

Map B
Ports of call

west or whether to go back north. Drake's men alone were prepared to run the gauntlet of the mile-wide track that lay beyond reach of gun-fire from twin forts which were believed now to be guarding the Narrows of the Strait of Magellan. Actually there was no one there. Don Diego Flores de Valdes, the great Spanish Admiral, had turned back when he heard that there were English ships about, and he did not reach the Strait's mouth until February 1583, only to turn back once more.[1]

This, however, is to anticipate. The last few pages of Madox's official narrative (July 21) show the English fleet in waters unknown to them, quite at a loss, their dead reckoning at fault. Their pilots were familiar with but one African harbour—Sierra Leone, where modern Freetown stands. This had been a land-mark since the early days of Portuguese discovery, but despite the noisy and mistaken affirmations of Hood and Hawkins (on the strength of having spent two days there with Drake) it was eventually reached only after a hazardous voyage in soundings across the dreaded Shoals of St Anne. The ships dropped anchor on August 10, and the many sick men aboard the *Edward* (it was 'only the scurvy', said Fenton) quickly recovered on a diet which included lemons and plentiful oysters. On this subject of health at sea Madox makes many sensible remarks.[2] The General, because of his secret plans, had not wished to land in West Africa, pressing the alleged unhealthiness of the climate, but the majority in the Council had been against him.

Second phase of the voyage: to Brazil

There was now little chance of getting away again until the next seasonal change of the wind, but an abortive start was made at the beginning of September from which Fenton quickly returned, ostensibly to effect further repairs to his mainmast. It was now that he made his piratical plans known to Walker and Madox, and subsequently to Captain Ward,

[1] C. R. Markham (ed.), *Narratives of the Voyages of Pedro Sarmiento de Gambóa* (Hakluyt Society, 1895), pp. 250 ff.
[2] P. 166.

but the shocked chaplains withstood him so stoutly as to carry Ward with them into opposition. On September 30 a Council was held (from which the merchants were excluded), when it was agreed to go through Magellan's Strait. The wind for the Cape, of course, had now long been lost. On the following day, the first of October, the dissatisfied Bristol merchant, Miles Evans, was dismissed from the company. He was only too anxious to leave, and took ship in the *Elizabeth* which had been handed over to the Portuguese in exchange for ivory and rice. This purchase of rice may have been made to allay the growing discontent of the crew, who suspected that there had been sharp practice over provisioning the ships, so that they were likely (they thought) to perish one and all.

Two events during the long stay in West Africa may be chosen to illustrate the incompatibility of soldier and sailor aboard ship. Captain Skevington had his Master court-martialled for some incautious (if true) words spoken about Fenton at the mess-table. As a result the Master was disgraced by being put in the bilboes, although within half an hour Captain Ward had him out. Fenton in his turn wanted to humiliate his own Master by making him kneel before him in front of the whole ship's company at divine service and beg his pardon for an alleged offence. Christopher Hall had indeed been stung into retort when the General threatened to deprive him of his office. But the good sense of members of the Council prevailed. He apologized but did not kneel. For, as Captain Ward said, Fenton had her Majesty's commission, but he had not her royalty.[1] The General claimed, however, that he had martial law, and Madox reports his threat to hang the steward, Esdras Draper. A study of the Instructions indicates how anxious the Privy Council had been to circumscribe their commander's powers at sea without actually forbidding him the extreme of the death penalty.[2] The execution of Thomas Doughty by Drake had caused very grave concern, for Plymouth gossip had seen it as an act of mere personal revenge.

[1] P. 206.   [2] Pp. 52, 58.

About a month passed before the three ships crossed the line, and on November 1 a Council was held in mid-ocean as to their course.[1] Simon Ferdinando openly suggested making for the Gulf of Mexico and the Spanish treasure fleet, but the Brazil coast was agreed upon, and as far south along it as possible. It was another month's sail in a south-westerly direction before land was sighted, and meanwhile Walker had fallen so dangerously ill of dysentery that Madox spent a few days aboard the *Edward* to be with him. There he learned from the sick man that Fenton had actually prepared to turn his guns on the *Edward* and the *Francis*, which he constantly feared would desert him, and that Blacoller (Ward's pilot) had in fact urged his Captain to 'depart' from his leader, but Walker's entreaties had prevailed.[2]

A few days in harbour restored everyone to health. Ward as usual had out his fishing net and had secured a great draft of mullets. Fenton named the place the Bay of Good Comfort; it lay in nearly 28° S, and was known to the Portuguese as Dom Rodrigo. On December 6 a small ship was sighted and, amid great excitement, was seized. It contained a party of Spanish Franciscan friars bound for the River Plate, and led by Fray Juan de Rivadeneyra, Commissary for the Plate region. To the crew at large this was a prize at last, and Fenton's disposition of the prize-crew which he put aboard set Captain Parker and Captain Ward bitterly at variance. The unfortunate Spaniards were at first to be left on the shore, which was uninhabited save by Indians believed to be cannibals, and their ship alone was to be carried away. After a heated debate, however, this cruel suggestion was rejected, but it was then argued that shortage of provisions forbade carrying the whole party off as prisoners.[3] In the end they were merely looted of some useful nails and small luxuries— to the value of £10, according to Madox—and allowed to sail away. Of much more importance than this spoil was the detailed information which Fray Juan and a young Spanish gentleman were able to give of the Spanish fleet. To their knowledge it had actually passed south of Dom Rodrigo for

[1] P. 187.　　　[2] P. 187.　　　[3] P. 212, and Document 50.

the Strait; they were unaware that Don Diego Flores had already turned northward again.[1] A few days later, Fray Juan was to meet the Spanish admiral and give him news of these heavily armed English intruders. It would be difficult to decide which party was the more alarmed! For at two points the Strait is little more than a league wide, so that if both were to be there an armed encounter seemed inevitable, the first arrival having the advantage.

Captain Fenton, nevertheless, continued on his way south for nearly two weeks, thinking matters over. The old friar, under interrogation, had given details of the overland route to Peru and of the unlimited supply of horses from the pampas which made travel along it so easy. This would allow news of the presence of English warships to reach Lima long before they could arrive by sea. On the other hand, a letter to the Governor of Peru which had been intercepted indicated that the Spanish fleet was short of both provisions and munitions.[2] On December 20 the Captain General summoned his Council. They were then in lat. 33° S, still well north of the Plate estuary.

The documentation of this Council meeting is abundant,[3] for it had become plain to all the members that they were neither going to make a voyage eastwards to China nor to amass treasure by piracy, and each had much to say. The question actually put to them in turn was in effect: the Spaniards being in the Strait, could the English ships pass through? But there was a further complication. Provisions were short (there was very little beer or beef left) while it was also necessary to repair the ships and their equipment on land, where the smiths' forges could be set up. Peter Jeffery might argue for the Cape route and for the Instructions. William Hawkins and John Drake were for the South Sea at all costs. Richard Madox set out all the alternatives in an academic essay. John Walker concurred in his own Captain's opinion that they should first provision themselves by the

[1] Markham, *Voyages of Sarmiento*, p. 252.
[2] Document 50.
[3] Documents 51–57.

sale of trifles of merchandise to the Portuguese, and only then consider how to make their voyage.

The General withheld his own opinion until a later hour, and then announced that they were to provision themselves on the hither side of the Strait and for the purpose must make their choice between the River Plate and St Vincent. The masters and pilots rejected the dangerous and unknown pilotage waters of the Plate estuary, and Fenton later made everyone sign the agreement they had given to going to St Vincent.[1] Hawkins signed, but not Drake. The document was presented on 22 January 1583 for signature, and John Drake had 'departed' in anger a month before, when first the new order to turn back was given.

When the ships' prows were turned northwards,[2] the disappointed and murmuring sailors were quietened with the assurance that it was only a turning aside for provisions. It was asserted by some of the gentlemen, nevertheless, that Fenton had spoken of seizing St Vincent and making himself King, or (and this was probably now true) of selling the whole of their merchandise to the Portuguese at a profit and going home. On arriving at St Vincent, however, he learned that the colonists had accepted the announcement that they were now under the Spanish crown, and had been specially warned by King Philip not to trade with the English on account of Drake's raids. It seems clear that they might have been ready to do this surreptitiously, had it not been for the Spanish fleet in their waters. A secret visit from John Whithall (an Englishman well married there, who had initiated a trade with London a few years earlier) raised English hopes, but the sudden appearance of three Spanish ships led to a fight and a hasty departure.[3]

Pedro Sarmiento, narrating the events, admits that the first attack was made by the Spaniards.[4] The *Begoña* threatened to board the *Galleon*, whereupon she was sunk by the English

---

[1] Document 58.   [2] Pp. 121, 218.
[3] For John Whithall's relations with the London merchants and the voyage of the *Minion* in 1580–1, see Hakluyt, *Principall Navigations* (1589), pp. 638–43. See also p. 195 below.
[4] P. 130, n. 1.

ship's lower-deck guns. This was at night, and the fight was renewed during the next forenoon, when it appears that the crew of the *Edward* considered that the Admiral did not play her due part.[1] Certainly the *Galleon* drew away first and put to sea. The Spaniards then withdrew to Santos,[2] and the two English ships rode in the Bay for another day until the wind served to carry them a few leagues southwards to Burnt Island (Queimada Grande), where they took in wood and water. Here the *Edward* 'departed' through stress of weather (so the vice-admiral maintained), and made for home.[3] She reached Plymouth on May 29, and Ward went ashore to bury Captain Skevington and one of the ship's boys who had both died the night before of the scurvy. He sent off, besides, the customary letter to the owners to announce his arrival, addressing it to the Earl of Leicester.[4] In this letter he explained briefly why, on the information given by the Spanish friars, the fleet had turned back in lat. 33° S, and had then 'lost company' with the *Francis*. He described, too, the fight at St Vincent and the circumstances of his own loss of company with the Admiral by force of weather.

Third phase of the voyage: return to England

Edward Fenton, meanwhile, seems not to have regarded the incidents at St Vincent as fatal to English trade with Brazil. He went north to Spirito Santo (Espírito Santo), a settlement in lat. 20° S, where the modern Vitória stands. Here he entered into negotiations with the Governor, but becoming seriously ill was obliged to entrust them to Simon Ferdinando. It was at this point that Madox died, on February 27, and a few days later, when the General was in the very act of signing a trade treaty, a small Portuguese vessel arrived from the more southern port. The news of the sinking of the *Begoña* (he judged) was out, and at dawn the next day the *Galleon* incontinently set sail. All through March the captain was troubled by an unlocated leak in the ship, while on April 1 a survey of remaining victuals shewed

---

[1] Pp. 260, 265, n. 1. [2] See Map B, p. xlv.
[3] Pp. 129, 130. [4] Document 60.

that they had neither beer nor beef, while 20 barrels of peas were written off as 'rotten'. A month later there were only five barrels of pork left, which had all disappeared by the first of June.[1]

During May the *Galleon* skirted the Sargasso Sea, and the astonishing thing is that, in spite of all, course was set, not for home, but for Newfoundland![2] This was only altered on May 19 'by the consente of the whole Companie' because water was very short. It would seem that, frustrated in one scheme after another, Fenton had now hoped to seat himself in command of the Grand Banks and of the entry-gate to Canada. It was a step which had been strongly urged by Anthony Parkhurst (who had been prospecting the region) in letters to the elder Hakluyt and another.[3] And in fact, Humfrey Gilbert was to assume authority at St John's that very summer. But there is no other mention of Newfoundland in documents concerning Edward Fenton (although Oughtred raided there). In his homecoming letter to Leicester and Burghley[4] he ascribed his failure to attempt the Cape route to the lateness of the season, and claimed that he might have made forty or fifty thousand pounds by the trade he was about to establish in Brazil, had not the Spanish ships attacked him.

Before the General entered the Downs, which was on June 29, the men of the *Edward Bonaventure* had been put under interrogation, for a fortnight earlier the *Galleon* had turned aside to Youghal in Ireland, desperately in need of men and provisions, and her arrival must have become known. Peter Jeffery's report (obviously based on a Journal) is dated June 20,[5] and gives the straightforward view of a young merchant who had expected the voyage to proceed according to the Instructions, which everyone had carefully studied. The shipmaster, Thomas Percy, set down from his journal the events leading to the parting from the *Galleon*.[6] This departure, if deliberate, would have been a very grave offence but he ascribes it (as agreed) to the adverse weather conditions.

---

[1] Pp. 140, 142. 145. [2] P. 144.
[3] Taylor, *Hakluyts*, pp. 123–34. [4] Document 64.
[5] Document 63. [6] Document 62.

In his answers to other interrogations he gives us one or two fresh points about the attitude of the men outside the ship's Council. They had queried, for example, the purpose of the delaying visit to West Africa, since the correct course (as Hall stated) would have been to proceed due south (or rather, a little west of south) from Bona Vista. He makes clear, too, why the crew of the *Edward* thought ill of the behaviour of the *Galleon* in the fight at St Vincent.[1]

From Edward Fenton's ship comes only the passionately indignant testimony of William Hawkins,[2] which does little more than underline his General's temperamental unfitness for leadership. It contains, however, a vivid picture of John Walker's reaction to the St Helena scheme and some further details about the events at Spirito Santo, these confirming Fenton's belief that there was treachery afoot among the Portuguese. But more than once Hawkins complains that he was not taken into his senior officer's confidence, although in view of his attitude this was not surprising. Drake's exploits were only made possible by his single-minded determination. He was not to be thwarted by the majority decisions of a Council, certainly he would not have brooked a Council of such disparate elements as faced Fenton—clergy, merchants, headstrong young men, a timid soldier and (as vice-admiral) a professional sailor.

Aftermath of the voyage

According to Ambassador Mendoza both the returning Captains were put under arrest,[3] and there survives a fragment of a letter from Fenton to Leicester apparently written from his place of confinement.[4] In this he begs humbly for his clothes, which had been taken away to Muscovy House, and complains of ill-health. Nothing more is known of the voyage. From the captured 'Discourse' written by Lopez Vaz,[5] Richard Hakluyt read and published an account of what became of John Drake and the *Bark*

[1] P. 260.
[2] Document 67.
[3] Document 68.
[4] Document 66.
[5] Document 70. Lopez Vaz was taken by the Earl of Cumberland's fleet in the River Plate in 1587.

Francis, as well as a Portuguese version of Captain Fenton's actions in Brazil. Five years after his return the Captain was commanding the old *Mary Rose*, one of the larger ships that fought against the Spanish Armada, so that clearly he was not disgraced. Nor was young Hawkins, who also captained a ship in this famous encounter. Fenton married Thomasine Gonson, niece of Sir John Hawkins' wife, and grand-daughter of a former Treasurer of the Navy Board. Perhaps it was these family connections that made Sir John Hawkins, then very overworked, ask for his appointment as Deputy Treasurer of the Board during 1589. He lived at Deptford until 1603 and died childless. A monument was erected to him in St Nicholas Church by the Earl of Cork, who had married his niece, and although there was no career of great distinction to record upon it, mention is made of his service against the Irish rebels, his Arctic and subsequent voyages, and his prowess against the Armada.[1]

The complete failure of Fenton's voyage was fortunately no deterrent to further ventures, and it must be assumed that on balance the monetary gain of participators in such adventures exceeded the losses.[2] In November 1582 Mendoza reported to his master that Oughtred (who had retained a share of £800 in the *Galleon Leicester*) had fitted out a ship for Newfoundland, while in a letter to Burghley (November 9) he complains that twenty Spanish ships had consequently been robbed there.[3] And whereas (he continues) Sir Francis Walsingham had referred the matter to the Court of Admiralty, Burghley had ordered the Judge to hand over the plundered goods and a captured ship to Oughtred. On 19 August 1583, again, he mentions to King Philip and to another correspondent that a new expedition 'for the Moluccas' is being prepared, in which the Queen's new favourite (presumably Ralegh) has a good share.[4] It is from Mendoza, too, that we hear of the return of an earlier

[1] Document 73.
[2] Cf. K. R. Andrews (ed.), *English Privateering Voyages to the West Indies*. (Hakluyt Society, 1959), pp. 31–34.
[3] P. lii, n. 3.
[4] *Cal. S. P., Span., 1580–6*, nos. 355, 356.

expedition (of which little is known) led by the elder William Hawkins. The company now lay at Plymouth, so the Ambassador wrote in a letter dated 26 November 1583,[1] 'and would not leave their ships until they had a general pardon signed with the Queen's own hand, which is sufficient proof that they have done something wrong and captured a great booty'. Fenton was probably not alone in thinking a like success might have been his, had he not been frustrated by the consciences of his two chaplains. Yet it was his own action, in sinking the *Begoña*, that was to turn William Hawkins aside from his intention of carrying merchandise to Brazil. With his brother John and Sir Francis Drake he had furnished four ships for a southern voyage, which were ready late in 1582.[2] They fell into trouble at Santiago (Cape Verde Islands), so that they were not ready to leave for the Atlantic crossing until April 1583. On their way across they took a prize, only to be informed of the Spanish alert on the Brazil coast. So they turned aside to unlawful business in the Caribbean Sea and brought practically all their merchandise home.[3]

But legitimate trade too was being fostered. The Levant

---

[1] *Cal. S. P., Span., 1580–6*, no. 362.

[2] See J. A. Williamson, *Hawkins of Plymouth* (1949), pp. 218–25; but Dr Williamson has failed to note MS Harl. 167, f. 201, and names the ships from Mendoza's first report (*Cal. S.P., Span., 1580–6*, no. 294). They were actually the *Primrose*, owner John Hawkins and two partners, the *Bark Bonner*, sole owner William Hawkins, the *Bark Hastings* and the *Matthew*, sole owner Sir Francis Drake. The document reviews 'The charges of the voyage'. John Hawkins's book stood at £3,367 12s. 10d. and his ship at £2,000, William's book at £3,819 8s. 2d., and his Bark at £700. Drake's charges are left blank, save that the *Bark Hastings* is valued at £1,000. 'The merchants booke of ye Comp. of Discovery amounteth in all to £1648. 3. 3.,' runs the entry, of which merchandise only a barrel of pewter was sold, besides some linen and woollen to the ship's company. The rest was returned. Four reasons for 'not proceeding to Brasilia from Santiago' are given, namely the late season (April), the decay of victual and merchandise (altered to 'caske'), the loss of men (there had been treachery and murder), and '4. fear of Spaniarde set to garde Brasile as a prize advised'.

[3] Young William Hawkins was apparently engaged by his father to bring into Milford Haven a prize which had been taken in the West Indies on the latter's 'late viage to Brasill', and which had possibly been left in Ireland. This is the subject of two letters from Leicester and Walsingham addressed respectively to William Hawkins of Plymouth (the father), 23 December 1583, and to the Judge of the Admiralty, 17 April 1584 (P.R.O., H.C.A. 14/22, nos. 95, 94).

Company was founded in 1582, and in May 1583 Edward Cotton, the same prominent Southampton merchant who had collected information about West Africa, sent out a ship to exploit the seals (for their hides and oil) reported to be so abundant in the Plate Estuary.[1] Unfortunately, she became a total wreck on the dangerous West African shoals, for competent English shipmasters and pilots were still only in the minority, although the next generation was to do better. The Earl of Leicester, again, was still interested in new trades. He and his brother head the list of patentees of the Company of Barbary Merchants incorporated in 1585, in which Arthur Atye also had a share.[2]

Nor did the English dread the Strait of Magellan, for the Spanish colony, not planted until 1584, quickly withered away. Thomas Cavendish, passing through in January 1587, took prisoner one of a mere score of survivors. They discussed the subject of Drake's puzzling discovery that the Strait did not run between two continents. Mendoza also knew about this.[3] He had not actually seen Drake's own chart, prepared for Fenton, but a spy had tried to explain it to him, and he had then tried clumsily to explain the matter to his master. Madox saw the map, and expressed the opinion that, considering the short time that the *Golden Hind* had been in the Strait the details must have been either copied or invented.[4] Yet there is no doubt that Drake had proved the absence of the great Southern Continent as mapped by Mercator and Ortelius, as well as the fact that Tierra del Fuego is an archipelago. But it was to be a generation before anyone actually rounded Cape Horn, and it is understandable that Drake was not generally believed, nor the world map immediately altered.

In spite of the failure of the 'China voyage', the trade of the Spice Islands remained an objective of English policy. Barely a year after Fenton's return, John Hawkins was writing to Burghley about Drake's offer of a projected

[1] *Principall Navigations* (1589), pp. 187–9.
[2] *Principall Navigations* (1589), p. 234.
[3] P. 39, n.1.
[4] P. 189.

expedition which (as Dr Williamson has shown) was designed for the Moluccas, and in all probability for conquest rather than commerce.[1] But the fleet and armament provided for this were (it seems) diverted to the great raid on the West Indies in 1585–6; and twenty-six years were to elapse between Drake's visit to Ternate in 1579 and the next English expedition—that of Captain Thomas Middleton—to trade in the Moluccas. But by 1605 Drake's scent was cold.

What is important, when we review this voyage, is to realize that the generation to which the younger Hakluyt, Richard Madox, Edward Fenton, Francis Drake, Walter Ralegh, Humfrey Gilbert, and many another pioneer of English expansion belonged, was the first English generation to have had the opportunity to become world-minded and take world views. The 'sweet study of cosmography' and the use of maps had only now become freely open to them. They were the first generation, too, that had heard John Dee preach the doctrine that technical skill and progress rest upon mathematics. Robert Dudley, Earl of Leicester, had chanced to come under Dee's influence as a very young man, while Lord Burghley kept himself well informed at all times about the advances made by the mathematical practitioners. Of course it is true that there were other factors—political, economic, social, personal—all helping to bring about the amazing English expansion which dated from the late 1560's onwards. But the first English Euclid and the first modern Atlas (Ortelius' *Theatrum*), as well as the first English log, typify some of the new tools which were becoming available. Technical leadership in seafaring was passing from the Spaniards and the Portuguese to the English and the Dutch. Nor were the men wanting.

[1] J. A. Williamson, *Sir John Hawkins* (1927), 410–12, citing MS Lansdowne 43, ff. 20–1 (Hawkins to Burghley, 20 July 1584) and MS Lansdowne 41, ff. 9–10 (endorsed by Burghley 'The charge of the navy to the Moluccas', 20 November 1584). The principal adventurers were the Queen, Drake, Leicester, the Hawkinses, Hatton, and Ralegh. Dr Williamson suggests political expediency as the motive for calling off the expedition; in the circumstances of 1585 it would have been highly imprudent to detach fifteen ships and many experienced commanders on a distant voyage, perhaps for two years and beyond urgent recall.

Part I

THE PREPARATIONS
(Documents 1–33)

Document 1

Frobisher and Fenton, 1577–8[1]

(i) [May 1577] When as the Commissioners had devised articles for his [Frobisher's] commission and Instructions for the direction and government of the voyadge[2] which were confirmed by her Maties honorable pryvie Councel, even by his owne advice: and for casualtye of deathe would have joyned unto him Capt. Fenton and some others of the gentillmen that went with him, he utterly refused the same, and swore no smale oathes, that he would be alone, or otherwise he woold not goe in the voyadge, for he had alredye a higher Commission under the broad seale than they coold give him anye, and badd them make what commission they woolde for when he weare abroade he woold use y^t as he lyst, and afterwardes because he coold not be furnished wth all things to his will, Therew^thall he flonge out of the doores and swore by gods wounds that he would hippe my m^rs the venturers for yt, at wch woordes Captayne Fenton plucked him secretly, and willed him to be modest. And so at length he had all the aucthorytye of the whole voyadge in his owne handes . . .

ii) [August 1577] He [Frobisher] misused Christopher Hawlle M^r of the *Ayde*[3] in the second voyadge at the newe lande, callinge him aloude cullerablye to goe searche Beare sounde, where beinge in a furyous humo^r of Tempier, he openly revyled him wth outrageous speaches and swore by gods bludd he wold hang him, and offered to stryke him on the

---

[1] Extracts. (*i*, *ii*) Michael Lok, 'The doinges of Captayne Furbisher', 1581. B.M., MS Lansdowne 100, art. 1. (*iii*) Narrative of Edward Sellman, in G. Best, *Voyages of Frobisher* (Hakluyt Society, 1868), p. 306.
[2] The second voyage, 1577.
[3] Master of the *Galleon Leicester* in 1582.

3

face with his fyst which Captaine Fenton did defend [prevent] and Hawlle did quietly putt upp, and all this wthout anye cause but onely upon vayne suspicion of hawlles dewety full service because he spake to him wth his cappe on his heade. [*margin:* He misuseth Ch. Hawll, M^r of the *Ayde* for a cappe reverence.]

(*iii*) The 19 said [August 1578], Captain Fenton came to make complaint to the Generall [Frobisher] of the boatswayn, and others of the Aydes mariners for disobeying him in certain service to have byn don for the furderance & dispatche of the ships lading at two severall tymes, his speches tending to dire punishment for same and after long recital of their abuses did like that the generall shold have ayded him therein, and to have commanded due punishments for their deserts. The Generall not taking order therefore Master Fenton and he did grow to hoat speeches, by whome eche others credit came by him and he denying the same, left their former matter, and fell to reason uppon the same with many hoat woords in somuch that in the end, the Generall affirming he preferred Master Fenton to be the Queen's servant, and he denying, alledging that the General did not well to rob them that did prefer them both to that service: and then at Master Fenton's departure, he said he had offered him great disgrace in that he would not punish the offenders which he complayned of but rather did animate them against him in neglecting of yt, which he could not take in good part, being his lieutenant generall, and recommending them to do nothing but their duties in her Majesties service . . .

The 23 said the Generall, Captain Fenton (his lieutenant), Gilbert York, and George Beste, gentlemen, assembled themselves together, Christopher Hall and Charles Jackman, masters, with them, for cause touching their Instructions, and amongst other matters, did call in question the abuses of the boteswayn and one Robinson[1] used towards the Generalls said Lieutenant, and after yt had been agreed of amongst the said Commissioners, the General referred the punishment

[1] Later an insubordinate quarter-master on board the *Galleon* (see p. 147).

4

thereof to them to determine; then they called the said offenders before them, who acknowledged their abuses, and upon their submission, as allso affirming they did not know Captayn Fenton to be the Generalls said lieutenant, they were pardoned and forgiven.

Document 2

Despatches from Bernardino de Mendoza to Philip II, December 1580–April 1581[1]

) London, 20 December 1580. The Queen has sent a small ship to the Azores to tell them to stand firm by Don Antonio. The islands are of utmost importance to the English in view of the designs they have to send ships to the East and West Indies & to the Moluccas by the route taken by Drake on his homeward voyage. Ships are being made ready so that they can leave in February. The business is in the hands of Leicester.

) London, 9 January 1581. Drake is to take 10 ships to the Isles of Moluccas by the same route as that along which he returned, which is to go almost in a straight line to these islands from the Cape of Good Hope, sighting only the island of San Lorenzo.[2] They expect to find the same winds as they encountered before, the Portuguese pilots having discovered that only two winds blow in those seas, east and

---

[1] Abstracts. *Cal. S.P., Span., 1580–6*, nos. 58, 59, 82. On June 26 (op. cit., no. 31) Mendoza had reported that the Queen had had a letter from Don Antonio, the Portuguese Pretender, asking help. It was dated May 10. The despatches here summarized give the first news of the proposed 'Enterprise' (Documents 3–5) in his support. Writing on October 16 (op. cit., no. 44) to describe Drake's return, Mendoza had said that the latter was to take six ships back to the Portuguese Indies, and 'there is hardly an Englishman who is not talking of undertaking the voyage'. Meanwhile Don Antonio was defeated in Portugal, and enthusiasm for him cooled.

[2] Madagascar.

5

west, so that if the weather does not serve for doubling the Cape of Good Hope when they arrive there, they will run before the wind and winter on the coast of Brazil.[1]

Knollys, who fitted out a piratical expedition to the Indies two years ago, is to go to Port S. Julian and thence to the South Sea. Humfrey Gilbert is to go with six ships to Cuba and there fortify. They are also pressing Frobisher to renew his attempt (in spite of late unsuccess) to discover a Passage to Cathay, which Drake is of opinion must exist there.

(iii) London, 16 April 1581. No resolution has yet been taken with regard to the Indies project,[2] but a meeting has taken place between Walsingham, Leicester, Drake, Hawkins, Winter, Frobisher and Bingham, all the latter being experienced mariners.

Document 3

Captains for the 'Enterprise'
April 1581[3]

The estymate of the charges of 8 shipes, and 6 pynaces, to be furnyshed to the sees in warlyke maner. & victualled for iiij[or] monthes for a thowsand men [*Endorsed, in Burghley's hand:*] Apryll 1581. The estymate of 10,320 li. The names of y[e] Caps. 1. Fra. Drake 2. Ry. Bingham[4] 3.

---

[1] This crude notion of the monsoons influenced Fenton's pilots (pp. 110, 113).

[2] Drake was knighted on 6 April 1581, and the Queen forbade him to leave the country. Richard Bingham and Frobisher had both served in the fleet sent to Ireland in 1580 under Winter as Admiral. It was Bingham who at first was chosen to take Drake's place, later given in succession to Frobisher and to Fenton. Bingham himself was to become military governor of Connaught.

[3] P.R.O., S.P. 12/148, art 46. The shipping was to be ready by the end of June (art. 43).

[4] Captain Bingham had commanded the *Swiftsure* at the siege of Smerwick in Ireland in 1580 (see below, p. 7, n. 1). He was a cousin of

Ed. Fenton. 4. Gil. Yorke. 5. Luke Warde. 6. Brewer. 7. Gregorye.[1]

Document 4
The 'Enterprise', June 1581[2]

i) The First Enterprise as followethe. June 1581.

There would be viii shippes, tow barks & vi pynnaces . . .
That ys to saye the Swyftsure w[t] her takle, sayles, cables, ankers, her ordenance of yron & her ordynary furnyture wylbe at charge of   3000. 0. 0.
The Gallyon Owtred furnyshed in lyke sort   3000. 0. 0.
The Primrose in lyke sort wylbe a charge of   2200. 0. 0.
[*margin:* The Swiftsure 170 men. The Galyon M. Hood, 170 men]
[*Details of supplies follow, including:*]
victual for viii monthes for 810 men for xv s per
month.   4850. 0. 0.
For this fyrst enterpryse there must be sett aland in the terseras the tow hundrethe goners and soldyers & a smale fortyfycacion made ther so as that Ilond may be a sucker for any of our shipes upon any occasyon.

    This company of shipes may spend the tyme abowt the

Edward Cotton, merchant of Southampton, who now had 'a ship of 300 ton a home and mete', i.e. for the 'Enterprise'.
[1] Geoffrey Fenton, writing to Walsingham on 15 August 1581, says that Bingham, Yorke, Ward and Fenton were 'put from the Portugal voyage by Sir Francis Drake' (S.P. 12/85, art. 19); see also Document 5. On May 4 Mendoza had reported to his master that the English Seville merchants had sent news to London that he (King Philip) was raising a fleet to protect the Indies.
[2] Extracts. P.R.O., S.P. 12/148, art. 47. Endorsed: June 1581. On June 5 Mendoza reported that, according to Sir James Crofts, Walsingham and Leicester were the principal adventurers in a plan to lie in wait at Terceira for the fleets from the two Indies, under letters of marque from Don Antonio.

Ilonds untyll thend of September waytyng the comyng of the flete from the west Indies, yf those shold be myssde then maie the hole fleete range all the cost of the west Indyes [and sacke all the townes and spoyle whersoever they fynd them by sea or land].[1]

(ii) *For the second enterprise*[2]

The same ships w^t ther fornyture & vitalls are a fytt proporcyon to go to the Callycutt & ther to establyshe the trad of spyce in her Maties ryght as a party w^t the Kyng of Portyngall.

That wch dothe lode one of the great caraks wylbe suffycyent to lade all the flote so as yf the trad be substancyally settlyd & determyned betwixt her Matie & the Kinge, our owne shipes may come home loden w^t spyce, & whaftt home any of the caraks that shal be thought meete to come w^t our shipes.

Yf this enterpryse take effect then the next yere ther wilbe fyvetie sayle of shipes imployed for this trade both to utter our commodytes & to serche the taradis [trades] of the malocos & the Chyna to the infynyte comodytye of this reallme.

It wylbe mete in this Jorney to settell a force in the terseras goyng outward, for that homeward yf any shipe scatter, ther they are to be relyved & suckeryd.

It were allso mete that some quantytye of mete merchandyzes were caryed in this flote to Callycutt. We shal find our lodynge the more willyngly delyveryd & we shalbe better wellcome.

The ylands of cape de verde, the cost of geney, the myne [El Mina], & S^t tome & Brasyll wilbe open for our men to traffique into as to Callycutt.

---

[1] The words in square brackets are deleted in the manuscript.
[2] Printed by Wagner, *Drake's Voyage*, p. 444.

Document 5

Letter from Paris to Robert Beale
30 August 1581[1]

. . . For the Matter of Portugal, sorry I am that a Cause importing her Majesty so greatly as that doth, should be overthrown, wherein surely the French king is greatly to be blamed, and I would to God that some there also werc not falty, seeing the Preparations were so forward, the Enterprise was not to have been given over . . .

---

[1] Extract. W. Murdin (ed.), *A Collection of State Papers . . . left by Lord Burghley* (1759), p. 355. The letter is unsigned. Beale was Secretary to the Privy Council. On June 15 Mendoza had reported that the English merchants trading in Spain had become anxious about what was going on in respect of Terceira. They had offered Walsingham 10,000 marks, of 26 reals each, to desist. 'This has somewhat slackened their fury, and the ships are not to leave until the end of August.' As late as August 20 Drake drew up 'advis for yᵉ ships for Azores' (MS Lansdowne 31, art. 82); but at a council held on the following day, for which we have Burghley's minutes (original, August 21, MS Lansdowne 102, art. 104; copy, August 23, MS Lansdowne 31, art. 81) a sober strategical assessment led to the conclusion that it could not be attempted without assurance of French support, although the suggestion ('whereunto Drake and Hawkins assent') was made that three ships and a bark be 'presentlie sent to the Iles' and the rest of the ships 'remaine in readines uppon knowledge from France.' The Queen accordingly countermanded the First Enterprise, and the consequent orders, signed by Drake, Hawkins and Francis Mills (Walsingham's secretary), provided for the discharge of men and sale of supplies (MS Lansdowne 31, art. 83); letters were to be written to 'Mʳ Owghtred and Luke Warde to sell awaie all provisions and victells . . . at the best prises.' (See also Corbett, *Drake* (1899), I, 325–31.)

This is the last we hear of the 'Enterprise', and the documents now deal with the active preparations for the alternative voyage 'for China and Cathay' under Leicester's auspices.

Document 6

The Adventurers in the Voyage[1]

The whole charge of the Galleon	6035.	10.	0d.
The whole charge of the Edwarde[2]	3457.	5.	0d.

The names of the Adventurers & how myche they adventure

Item the Erle of Lecester	2200.	0.	0.
The Erle of Warwick	200.	0.	0.
The L. Treasorer	200.	0.	0.
The Earle of Shrewsbury	200.	0.	0.
The Earle of Pembroke	200.	0.	0.
The L. Hunsdon	200.	0.	0.
The L. Howarde	200.	0.	0.
The Earle of Lyncoln	100.	0.	0.
Sir Fraunces Walsingham	200.	0.	0.
Sir Christofer Hatton	250.	0.	0.
Sir Fraunces Drake	666.	13.	4d.
Sir Thomas Heanege	200.	0.	0.
Sir Edward Horssye	100.	0.	0.
Mr Ughtred	800.	0.	0.
Mr Burde	100.	0.	0.
Mr Bowland	100.	0.	0.
Mr Carlile	300.	0.	0.
Mr Frobisher	300.	0.	0.
Mr Fenton	300.	0.	0.
Mr Warde	200.	0.	0.

7016.	13.	4.

The Muscovia Company amonge[2]

[1] P.R.O., S.P. 12/150, art. 96.

[2] The charge of the *Francis* 'with her furniture' is elsewhere given as £66 13s. 4d. She is called a 'frigate'. The burden of the *Galleon* is given as 400 tons. The 'sea-store for the guns' was inventoried at £375 13s. 4d. for the *Galleon* and £165 5s. 0d. for the *Edward*. This included equipment for the longbowmen and pikemen, but the heaviest item was for gunpowder ('powdercorne') which cost £200 for the larger and £45 for the smaller ship.

Document 7

Bernardino de Mendoza to Philip II
7 September 1581[1]

Leicester says that the Queen will fit out 3 ships to sail about
Christmas under Frobisher, and if the adherents of Don
Antonio are found numerous in the East Indies they will
effect a landing, otherwise they would carry merchandise
for trade, and go to the Moluccas.

Document 8

Earl of Shrewsbury to Leicester
24 September 1581[2]

'To the right honorable my very good L. & cousin the Earl of
Leycester.'
Thanks him for information about his setting forth 2 or 3
ships for the East Indies. Is contented to be one of the
adventurers and will furnish his part of the *Bark Talbot* and
send his man [Robert] Jolly with her. Reckons this will be
about £1000 adventure.[3]
From Sheffield, 24 September 1581.

[1] Abstract. *Cal. S.P., Span., 1580–6*, no. 134.
[2] Abstract. B.M., Cotton MS Otho E. VIII, f. 95. Also in *Cal. S.P.,
Col., E. Indies, 1513–1616*, no. 155.
[3] A number of letters from the Earl of Shrewsbury on this matter are
preserved (Cotton MS Otho E. VIII, ff. 96, 97, 101), and on November
22 Robert Jolly was supervising the fitting out of the *Bark Talbot* (f. 114)
in association with Frobisher (p. 30, n. 1).

Document 9

Advice of Drake to Leicester
[September (?) 1581][1]

. . . [satisfie] the same.

But myne opinion is that if [I were entered] into the like action I would [seek my] traffic from 18 degrees until . . . Taprobane[2] to the northward of [the line] Equinoctial until I came to Ja[va] wch distance of places they shall not [pass in] my judgment, and partlie that I have [myself] learned, wthout finding great store [of spices] of great price.

If the wind will not suffer them to pass [to the] East and north partes of Mallacca [Strait] then do I thincke it best to make their traffiique in the great baie from Taprobane to the westwards towards the Island [Seylon] in wch baie there are princes and [much] people of great wealth.[3]

For their traffiique of spices I am of this opinion that the Molucas will furnish them sufficientlie as cloves especiallie.

Whereas they are desirous to know the fittest places of watering and the best meanes to preserve their helthes, it shalbe sufficient in that they shall have in their companie divers of my men wch were in my late viage who can more effectuallie instruct them both of the places & of the order that is necessarie to be observed.

---

[1] B.M., Cotton MS Otho E. VIII, f. 61. This fragment is unsigned, but from internal evidence it must be a reply from Drake to a request for advice from Leicester.

[2] This name (originally applied to Ceylon) was used in the sixteenth century for Sumatra.

[3] The Bay of Bengal. The suggestion appears to be that they should follow the Portuguese route to the East by the Malacca Straits, when the route to Chinese lands would be north and east.

Document 10

Preparatory Notes by Arthur Atye[1]

(*i*) *Matters for consideration*

Order to be taken for Sir Fr. Drake his bark

Ordre for the generall his Commission

      for the Counsaile to be appointed him

      for their instruccions

      for Auditors for all accomptaunts

      for assurances for the Adventurers

Above all thinges ordre to be taken for amitie and good obedience amongest the Generall, Captaines, gentlemen and the rest

Your adventurers monye ariseth to 11600 marks[2] there abowtes. So yf the charges increase to 3 or 400 li more it is to be considered howe this is to be had. Sir Fr. Drakes Barcke is not accompted in these former charges. it is to be considered how it shalbe victualled: and manned. and the . . . to be certainly appointed when she shalbe re[ceived]

Your merchandise are £2000, and are wished might be more yf there were more money.[3] You are to consider herein also, whether it be convenient to take for dying of popingaye greenes Mr Wilkes[4]

---

[1] Extracts. B.M., Cotton MS Otho E. VIII, ff. 85–7, 105–7. Abstract in *Cal. S.P., Col., E. Indies, 1513–1616*, no. 183. Atye's notes are too rough and confused to be transcribed in full, apart from the mutilation of the document.

[2] A mark was 16s. 8d. The subscription list in Document 6 adds up to rather less than 11,600 marks.

[3] A list of merchandise, endorsed as 'Mr Fenton and Luke Ward's voyage', but headed in another hand: 'A note of wares fit to be sold in Brazil. 12 May 1582' (i.e. a date after the expedition had departed), is to be found in S.P. 12/153, art. 43. The total value given is £2,000, the bulk of the consignment being drapery. The two largest items are 'sorting cloths of diff^t sorts & colours £300', and 'Hollands, £300'. Apart from the various types of cloth, no item had a greater value than £50, while there was a £5 parcel of 'Red Scottish or French caps of a low price for slaves', besides some hardware.

[4] Wilkes was at first in the *Elizabeth*.

13

For the men you are to consider of the
Nomber of them all
Nomber of idle men.
Nomber of officers as captaines, marchants, ministers } & their men
surgeons
maisters
pursers etc.

Notes of sailors
of their generall enterteignments
How they are to be lodged in the shippes
Item what consideracion is to be given to every man that has taken paynes and must travaile before the setting furthe of the shippes . . .
The cost of theşe. The Mary Edwardes to be sett fourth by alderman Martin[1] and his con . . .
The Galeon Oughtrode 5000 allway [furnished]
The newe Barcke by estimat, furnished, victuall & all 400li
Allowance more for 100 quarters of mele 100^{li}
The Mary Edwards ut sub.
The cost to be defrayed thus
Therle of Leycester & Mr Ughtrede £3000^{ti}. Earle of Oxforde £500. E. of Lincoln 100. E. of Pembroke 200. E. of Warwick 200. L. Howarde 200. L. Hunsdon 200. Sir Chr. Hatton 200. Sir Fr. Walsingham 200.
The speciall men Mr Frobisher desireth
Cust: Smythe 200. Cust: Burde 100. Capt. Frobusher 300. Ed. Fenton & his frendes 300. Sir Fr. Drake 700.[2]
The appointing Cap. Lieuetenantes and especyally one that shall suceade him yf ought otherwyse then well betyde him.

(*ii*) *Organisation and instructions*

First we agree to laye together our porcions [at the] severall rates underwritten wch. amount to . This

[1] She did not sail. Madox reports dining with Sheriff Martin on 11 March 1582.

[2] Compare Document 6. On the latter list Customer Smith's name does not appear, but he actually paid £200 to Frobisher (see Document 15).

money to be delivered to A.B. who [is] o^r Treasorer of this voyage, by him [received] upon warrant from   .

We promise and bynde ourselves eche to other to make [division of] the gayne at retourn according to every mans adventure etc.

With this mony we agree to sett out the 2 good shippes the one called the Galeon Ughtred, the other called the Bark Hastinges,[1] whereof the Galeon to be admirall, both to be furnished wth victualls for 13 monethes wth named munition and other necessaries: wth marchandize for exchange: wth 140 men in the Galeon, wth 60 in the Barcke.

We appoint Generall of the voyage Cap. Frobusher, whom we will all others to obeye etc. And yf he fayle we appoint to succeede in his place A.B.

[We appoint] chefe merchant of eche shippe [C.D.] the Galeon and yf he fail [then] C.F. of the Barcke, and yf he [fayle] G.H. etc. [*margin:* or one good chiefe merchant for bothe shippes]

We appoint a Counsaile for this voyage to consist of the gentlemen A.B. etc. to whome we reserve in cases not provyded for in these Instructions to consult & debate during the time of the voyage of suche thinges as [are] for the wele of the voyage etc. whereof 2 partes to prevayle [*margin:* The general having voyces 1 or 2]

We appoint A.B. Register or public Notarye of ye voyage, to sett down as well the Actes of Counsaile; as also all other thinges to be noted in the voyage, whome we will to deliver up his book to the companye at his returne. This officer the Spanyardes had allwayes w^t them in every voyage, which serveth specially to restrayne partiall dealing either in ye generall or others, when every man shall knowe his doings must come to light and judgement at retourne.[2] Besides an orderly knowledge y^t he shall geve of all thinges happening in the voyage.

---

[1] *The Bark Hastings* belonged to Drake. It was perhaps the ship in which Frobisher later planned to sail when he decided on a separate voyage (pp. 40, 192); but see also p. lv, n. 2.
[2] The Spaniards were still considered the exemplars for the whole seafaring world.

In the appointment of all these or some of them or any other officer it shalbe requisite (yf younge Hawkins be Cap. of ye Barcke) y^t some other trusty, not alltogether to be ruled by him, be joyned in shippe wth him, as also y^t of Hawkins company, especially of those that have been wth Sir Fr. Drake on the last voyage, some be [trusty] etc. . . . We enjoyne the Generall etc. departing [from England] to take his course to the East Indias by [the east and if the] tyme of yeare be so spent before he [can return by] Buena Esperanca that he may not go easterly, that he do not retourne by the w[est], for that yf the strait of Magellanes be fortified, [as no] doubt the Spanyards may and will lay f[orces there], Sir Fr. Drake do probably thincke it to be [well that] he not so trye it (as farre as I can learne), he doth affirme it; and to put the hazarde of this adventure when the other way is sure were not good, [and the more] there be danger in this the more charge is to be [given the] generall of it, for y^t perhaps he will have some hum[our] to do as muche as Sir Fr. Drake in going & returning his course [and] thincke to do more then any man yet hathe done in going by este and retourning by west.[1]

[*margin:* Certain degree to be named +] We enjoyne the Generall etc. not to passe Chyna to the northeastwarde: so will the traffique be better made, and the reason of this charge to be given him is, least perhaps he showeth some desire to searche out his formerly pretended passage N.W. and so hinder this voyage wch is only for trade.[2]

Item y^t they deale lyke marchants traffiquing & purchasyng wares for wares, wth all courtesie to the nations they deale with, settling y^e . . .

We enjoyne the Generall etc. in any wise and as they answer the contrarye at their coming home by the law, that

---

[1] The spirit of emulation was a powerful incentive. Michael Lok described Frobisher's proud bearing as he set off for his third voyage to the Arctic: 'as already by discovery of a new worlde he was become another Columbus, so allso nowe by conquest of a new world he would become another Cortes.' But when he heard praise of Fenton's bravery in taking charge of the first party that was to winter in the Arctic 'he began then to suspect the yssue of this matter, and to feare that the fame of this enterprise of Cap. Fenton would dashe the glory and fame of his former doinge' (B.M., MS Lansdowne 100, art. 1).

[2] See p. 54, n. 3.

they [take] not any thinge from any her ma^ties frendes or w^tout paying justly for the same nor use any [violence] agaynst any suche except in their own defense yf they shal be sett upon, but that in all [things] they use themselfes lyke marchants etc.

Item that the [General, Treasurer][1] chief Purser give up, before his departure severall Inventoryes of the victualles, marchandises, ordinance & other furniture of bothe shippes to the Treasurer of the company, and the lyke at his coming home. At coming home not to lande any wares w^thout further order from the Companye. [*margin:* Take 2 or 3 or 4 payre of wheeles [to carry] any their pinases from Ryvir to Ryvir]

Document 11

The Merchants' Proposals for the Voyage[2]

[here are to] be had two good shipps [well] furnished and knowen to be strong, bothe of them to be sheathed for the [sum of li . . .], Whereas the Edward of Hampton sheathed [will cost] 2400 li and yet wante of the burden [. . . tons] at the least.

Also those two shippes are heere ready in [London] to take in there provisions and may also searve to transporte ye merchandize and other necessaries to be [carried] from hence to the Gallion Owtred whereby [both] the danger of transportacion as also the charge thereof wch woulde not be smale may be avoyded.

[1] The two words in square brackets are deleted in the manuscript.
[2] B.M., Cotton MS Otho E. VIII, f. 251. This fragment has no endorsement or clue to its origin, but it clearly belongs to the early stage of preparation, and by its cautious tone and general tenour it may fairly confidently be ascribed to the Muscovy merchants adventuring in the voyage.

That noe other gentlemen be appointed to goe on the voiage but the three captaines specified, the rest to be Factors and meere Seamen: for avoydance of superfluous Charge and hinderance of ye voiage, and those to be appointed by soche as are committes for the voiage.

That priviledge be procured for soche only as shall adventure in this voiage.

That the Captaines and merchants appointed to the charge for settinge forthe the voiage may be aucthorised by their Lordshippes and the rest of the Adventorers.

It is thought Convenient that at the retourne of ye Adventure the whole charge of ye voiage be first deducted, the rest beinge the gaine, to be devyded into thre partes, whereof two partes to be allowed to ye Adventorers. The other third parte to be allowed for the wages and allowances of the Captaines, factors, and Masters and Maryners, by wch meanes the Adventorers shalbe at no further charges, then the first settinge fourthe of ye voiage whatsoever shall happen thereof.[1]

And that at there retourne home wch god graunte in saffety, that the merchandize and hole retourne may be ordered by soche as there honnors and the merchants shall appoint.

Document 12

Frobisher to Leicester
1 *October* 1581[2]

. . . if it plese your honowr . . . I have agrede withe Mr Outerede the pryse of [the Galleon] as twente eyghte

---

[1] This explains the near mutiny of the sailors at Plymouth (p. 164), for 'ech man went upon his venter'.

[2] B.M., Cotton MS Otho E. VIII, f. 86. Abstract in *Cal. S.P., Col., E. Indies, 1513–1616*, no. 156.

hondrethe poundes with all thinges [belonging] to her and as muche plank as shall shethe her and . . . sakers, xx targites of proufe, and xxx calivars & iiij[ty] peces of ordinanse with all nesesseties belonging to the shepe & forniture.

Of the 2800 li your honour is to paye the fourthe [part in] Decembar, a thousande markes, and the ferste of Decembare 1582 a thousande pounde, and at medsomer after three hundrethe & sexte vi wheche is towthousande poundes, and for Mr Outrede is contentede tow adventare the othare eyght hondrethe poundes with your honour if it pleese you[r].

So I have lefte M[r] Bacare[1] there wth Mr Outrede to shethe the shepe whiche I hope in xv dayes welle be redye. Here is no answer come from my L. of frends here, as yet I have note mor need Sir Francis Wallsingham, noe any of the reste bute my L. of Oxforde, who bares me in hand he wolle beye the Edwarde Boneaventar, and Mr Bowland & I have offrede feyftene hondrethe poundes for here, bute they howlde her at eyghtene hondrethe.[2] We shall not go throwe w[t] anethyenge tille your honores retorne, for here is evre mane expectenge Fraynche newes so as thai have smalle denotions to aparte wth moni.

Thus wth my prayer for your providence and your arrivelle afte to gods pleasar. The ferste of octobar 1581 your honors most homble to comand

Martin Frobisher

[*Endorsed:*] To the reyghte honorabelle my sengulare good L. The Eyerll of Lesetare geve these

[1] Matthew Baker was the most notable shipwright of the day, who had 'moulded' the *Galleon* (see p. 154, and Pl. II). Ships were still usually sheathed with thin planks nailed over oakum, although lead sheathing was not unknown.

[3] Both the Earl of Oxford and Mr Bowland are named as adventurers, the former in Atye's notes (p. 14) and the latter in the list on p. 10. On October 20 Mendoza reported the transaction to King Philip (Document 18).

Document 13
Agreement Concerning the Galleon
[October (?) *1581]*[1]

For and concerning the Gallyon Ughtred.

Fyrst the sayd shypp beinge valued by Henry Ughtred and Marten Furbisher gentleman [employed in the] affayre for the sayd Earle at the pryce of 2 thousand [eight] hundred pownde the sayd Henry Ughtred ys to sell [to the sayd] Earle so much of the sayd shipp in partycypacion as amounteth unto two thousand powndes reserving to himself the said Henry so much of the same shipp in partycypacion . . . as amounteth to thother eyght hundred powndes. So as [the sayd] Earle and the sayd Henry may be partners in proffitt [as] god shall appoint to the same shypp: the Earle for his parte for two thowsande pownds and the sayd Henry for eyght hundred powndes.

And the sayd Earle ys to gyve the sayde Henry suffycyent assurance to paye the sayd two thowsande powndes in manner followinge. That ys to say Syxe hundred threscore fyve pownds att or before the last daye of November next ensuinge and one thowsand powndes the last of November 1582 and thother thre hundred thirtyefoure powndes to make up the two thowsande before bargained uppon the xxiiijth daye of June in the same yeare 1582 in full paym[t].

Item. The sayde Earle ys to case or sheathe the same shipp at his proper costes & charges wth all manor of thinges thereunto requysyte, towardes the doinge whereof the sayd Henry Ughtred ys to gyve at his charges so much yacht planke readye sawed as wyll case or sheathe the said shypp.[2]

[1] B.M., Cotton MS Otho E. VIII, f. 120. Abstract in *Cal. S.P., Col., E. Indies, 1513–1616*, no. 180. This agreement is preceded (ff. 118–19) by a list of stores for the *Galleon* to the value of £3,248 4s. 4d. endorsed by Atye as to be furnished by 'Ughtred'.

[2] See p. 19, n. 1.

Item. All thordynance accustomablye used in the sayd shipp wth rounde shott, crossbarres & chayned shott to them belonginge, also calyvers, targetts, maste, yards, standing tackle & runnyng roapes, pulleys, shyvers, cables, ancres, sayles, bootes, toppes.

. . . the lesser named shypp in every entente . . .

Item The sayd Earle at his costes & charges ys to [provide and] supply the roapes and sayles fullye & in all [points] for the performance of a voyage to the East Indyas

The present furniture delyvered by the sayde Henry to [the said Earl] wth powder suffycyent to all intentes towards the [sayde voyage]

The sayd Henry ys to delyver such new sayles [over & besides the] sayles of the shypp before bargayned as the sayd Henry provyded for the Stoart of the sayd shipp in the late pretended voyage to the Azores in the servyse of Don Anthonyo [King] of Portingale¹ as by an Inventory also appeareth. Albeit [the] supply is to remayne styll in the shypp to be used [in] the shipp in partycypacion, as the shypp and her former furnyture.

Item the sayd Earle ys to gyve for an earnest of this bargain so much velvet good and new as wylbe syffycyent to make a gowne for dame Elyzabethe wyffe of the said Henry Ughtred.

Item the sayd Earle ys to procure if he maie the Kynge of Portingals Commyssyon² for the sayd Henry auctorysynge the sayd Henry to send out two other shyppes of the sayd Henryes to the seas in warlyke maner to take & spoyle the Spaniardes or the Portingales enemyes to the sayde Kinge Don Anthonio gevinge unto the sayd Kynge the fyrst part of all that shalbe taken by vertue of that commyssyon

Henry Ughtred
Martin Frobisher

¹ The *Galleon* had been ready furnished and armed for the intended 'Enterprise'.

² I.e. letters of marque. Oughtred was an active privateer. For privateering in general, see K. R. Andrews, *English Privateering Voyages to the West Indies, 1588–95* (Hakluyt Society, 1959).

Document 14

Simon Ferdinando to Frobisher
[October (?) 1581][1]

. . . for assone as . . . was dyscharged savynge . . . sett nother w^t in board nor with [out]
. . . nor all the knees[2] as it in . . . it as fast as they came off . . . [m]en at worke I must fynd them meat . . . and wages for here is nothynge butt what . . . comands to be done expresslye named . . . saies plainlye that the breadcaske shall [be] rosned drye. Mr Utredge doe commande . . . I have undertaken to doe it upon me . . . is not att lyke butt a monday next god [willing] it is apoynted to be done. Here is not yet . . . mend aour sailes, the chayne pompe is bespooken [by my] self and what I cane doe I will doe but [to] conclud I would yor worshype would seand a pur[ser] to doe y^r busynes or else when yow thynke [to be] redye you maye lacke manye thynges, for as [now] matters goes here it is not currantt where the fawlte is, it will be knowen. I am sorye to write so muche butt, but iff I could endytt 3 chests of paste ware to lyttell turpynge,[3] you will be here verrye sone, for iff you come I thyncke it will be the beatter. I praye bespeacke 4 topsailes, shortt poolkes, with yrone shevirs,[4] for the yard armes, as by the byggnes of the shoots you knowe,

Thus in haste I end
your worshyps to comand
Simon Fernandez[5]

---

[1] B.M., Cotton MS Otho E. VIII, f. 103. Abstract in *Cal. S.P., Col., E. Indies, 1513–1616*, no. 167. This undated and mutilated fragment indicates that Simon Ferdinando was overseeing the final fitting out of the *Galleon* on Leicester's behalf.
[2] Knee-shaped timbers.
[3] This may be a proverbial saying, 'if I had my wish'.
[4] The reels inside the blocks over which the ropes run.
[5] The anglicized form of his name, 'Ferdinando', was generally used.

II. Draught of a ship compared with a fish, by Matthew Baker, the 'moulder' of
the *Galleon Leicester, c.* 1586

Pepysian Library, Pepys MS 2820

III. The *Revenge* in her last fight, September 1591

Detail from a tapestry woven in 1598; in the collection of M. Hippolyte Worms,
formerly on loan to the National Maritime Museum

The *Revenge*, a four-masted ship, was the prototype of the *Galleon Leicester*, and the picture shows some of the features of this class, e.g. the open stern- and quarter-galleries, the forecastle set back from a long beak, the gunports on the lower deck, and the capstan.

[*Direction:*] To the right worshypfull Mr Forbysher thes be d^ld in London

Document 15
Arthur Atye to Thomas Smith
10 *October* 1581[1]

Sir, the two hundred poundes whereof my L. my master wrote unto you yesterday to delivir to me as your adventure in the voyage to the Este indias wth Mr Frobusher and willed me to deliver over to him, because I canot come agayne to daye to you for it, I pray yor W. to deliver it to Mr Frobusher himselfe, and to take some note of his hande of the receipt of it, and to send that note to me at yor leysure; and so, I commit yor w. to the allmyghtye from the Court the xth of october, 1581.

yor W. at commande
Arth. Atye

xiith of October 1581
M^d. that I Marten Furbusher
gent. have receaved and had of
Thomas Smithe of London esquier } ccii:
accordinge to the tenor of this
letter the some of two hundred
pounds onely Recd.

[signed] Martin Frobiser.

[*Direction:*] Mr Customer Smith

[1] B.M., MS Harl. 6993, f. 10. Abstract in *Cal. S.P., Col., E. Indies, 1513–1616*, no. 158.

Document 16
Drake to Leicester
14 *October* 1581[1]

Yo[r] Lordship . . . I am well pleased [to pledge myself] to any adventure that yo[r] [L.ship sets forth] so farre forth as myne abilitie [will allow] and this especiallie both for y[t] yo[r] h[r] is [setting forth] so famous an accion, but also for y[t] in [Mr Frobisher is] on whom I judge (by gods permission) is [likely] to bring it to good effect: Wherein there shalbe [no] will wantinge in me to be assistant both w[th] [what money I] am able to geve and also, if M[r] Frobisher will, wth such sufficient men of my late companie [as have] som experience y[t] waie. Wherefore I will referre [him] to y[r] L[rs]. election & do here make offer of my [services] 3 severall waies to yo[r] best contentment. If yo[rs] good L. [will is] to have the adventure I shall beare in money, I will desburse valour of 1000 marks for the w[ch] Thowsand markes [I will] make som triall of my credit to furnishe this action [accordingly] notw[th]standinge as now greatlie indeted: yet shall they . . . S[r]vant see yo[r] thereof furnished. If yo[r] L. thincke better to have me provide a shippe I think I have for her burden, being at least 180 tonnes, a shipp as fit for that viage as maie be had, for her sufficiencie every waie, where I will baire the adventure of on thowsand poundes & furnishe her verie sufficientlie in verie short time, so that there may be order geven for the overplus of her charge: but if y[r] L. wth M[r] Frobusher thincke best to have the little new Barcke and the 2 pinaces I will bestowe the like adventure theron and uppon yo[r] sancsion geven will have them shethed, prepared & furnished wth sufficient provisions to yo[r] good likinge. Whereuppon I will gladlie attend yo[r] awnswer therin for that I am verie desirous to

---

[1] B.M., Cotton MS Otho E. VIII, f. 98. Abstract in *Cal. S.P., Col., E. Indies, 1513–1616*, no. 159.

show that dutifull service I can possiblie do in any accion yor good L: vouchsafith to use me. And for y^t I am willinge to follow the direction of yor L^s. and Mr Frobisher in any respect I shall pray y^t some one maie be sent doone . . . all necessary promises . . . your L. Yo^r shall understand I [hope] upon my coming into the Hampton to the services wch I promised here . . . to do. purposelie with newes from the [Bark], I look for her return wthin these [few days] at furthest: mynding to give your L. first advertisement thereof.[1] Thus humblie I [take] my leave, do commit yor L. to the preservation of the Almightie. Plymouth the 14 of October 1581 Yo^r Hono^rs alwaies most assured to comand

Fra. Drake

Document 17

John Hawkins to Atye and Others
20 October 1581[2]

[*Direction:*] To the right worshipfull Mr Thomas Smythe, Mr Atye, & Mr Rychard Bollond[3] Esq.^s or to any of them gyve this in haste at London.

I have reseaved yor letter of the xixth of this present, together w^t a letter inclosed from Sir Francys Drake of the 14th of the same.[4]

I wold be glad my abyllytye and state were soche as I might be an adventer in this Jorney: but I assure you I had so great a borden layd upon me in this last preparacion that w^t

---

[1] Drake had a ship in the 'Isles of Pickery', or Azores, with Don Antonio's commission to spoil his enemies. Mendoza wrote on November 7 that a multitude of Englishmen who possessed ships were asking the Pretender's agent for letters of marque.
[2] B.M., MS Harl. 6993, f. 11. Abstract in *Cal. S.P., Col., E. Indies, 1513–1616*, no. 160.
[3] Bowland. See p. 19, n. 2.
[4] Document 16.

all the means I can make I ame hardly able to overcome the dett I ower her Matie, & kepe my creddytt. Yt ys well knowen to you Mr bolland to whome I dyd at large declare my losses & borden besyde the shipyng & other dead provicions wch lay upon my hondes[1]

My syknes dothe contynewally abyde w^t me, and every second day I have a fytt. If I loke abrode in the ayre but one ower, I can hardly recover yt in vii days w^t good order, so as I am hertely sory that I cannot attend upon my very good Lord, whome I am desyrowes to sattisfye accordynge to my abyllytye if I had strengthe, for I ame more lyke to provyd for my grave, then to incomber me w^t worldly matters.

Ther cannot lake neyther adventerers nor any thyng that ys good, to the fortheraunce of so good an attempt, wch enterpryse I have had allwayes a very good lykyng unto for the further benyfyttyng of oure contry, wch God I hope wyll send to a good & prosperowes end, and so I hartely take my leve from Chattham the 20th of October 1581.

Your assured & lovyng friend
John Hawkyns

Document 18

Bernardino de Mendoza to Philip II
20 October 1581[2]

Leicester has bought a ship of 250 tons for £2,000,[3] to accompany the one which I said was in Plymouth for Frobisher to take to the Moluccas. They think of sending

---

[1] When the 'Enterprise' was abandoned two months earlier. But both Hawkins and Drake may already have had in mind the voyage of 1582–3, for which see p. lv, n. 2.

[2] Abstract. *Cal. S.P., Span., 1580–6*, no. 150.

[3] See Document 12. The *Edward Bonaventure* was priced at £1,800. Mendoza's figures are often exaggerated.

£3,000 of merchandize in them on account of private individuals, the shares being £100 & £200 each, at Leicester's request. He sent to ask Drake for sailors for the voyage, which he promised to send, and to contribute £400 to the risk, as well as giving a pinnace of 40 tons, which was built on the Queen's stocks here.[1]

Document 19

Fenton to Frobisher
31 *October* 1581[2]

. . . one yesternight I [learned from . . .] that his brother will not be h[able to provide in] readie moneye one θ^d li[3] But in[deed only] 4 or 500 li so that I gather . . . [the] whole burthen and charge for fur[nishing my] Shipp (wch. in marchandize & all [necessaries what]soever will not exceede 2600 li mus[t be found] by Sir Fr. Drake, who (his wife affirmeth & supposeth) will not adventure above . . . attendeth from hence to be supplied [with the sum] of 1000 li towardes the finishing and [furnishing] of the same.

I would wishe therefore, that before y[oung Mr] Hawkins departe, all things might be so by [him] considered of, as those ymperfections be not [caused] in this plott wch often happen and fall owt [by the] humors of younge men and so greater matters [are spoiled] by the lesser. For as hitherunto younge [Mr] Hawkins hath been of opinion that the charge

---

[1] The *Bark Francis*.
[2] B.M., Cotton MS Otho E. VIII, f. 82. Abstract in *Cal. S.P., Col., E. Indies, 1513–1616*, no. 163.
[3] £1,000. This letter presumably refers to the *Edward Bonaventure* (see Document 12), since the financing of the *Galleon* had already been agreed, while the small *Bark* supplied by Drake was reckoned at under £100. (But see next note, p. 28.) The brothers are possibly John and William Hawkins.

of the Barke fullie furnished would growe more nigh 4,000 £ than 3000 £. So confereinge throughlie thereof wth M^r Jo. Hawkins I finde (allowinge 500 li for merchandize) the charges cannot exceede the former some of 2600 li and sett her Royallie owt,[1] So that I gather the younger gent. more desirous of charge and to be ymployed than hable (w^tout spetial helpe) to sett furthe so greate an action as he taketh in hande.

I praye yor ynsist thus muche wth Mr Atye to lett things be carried wth a sounde foundacion and young Mr Hawkins so ymployed as he maie have both countenance and creditt and the accion not hindered or be disceaved by over much trust in his friendes. So salute yor and good Mr Atye very hartelie Besechinge the Lorde to guyde & blesse yor in all yor actions, From London the last of October.

By yo^rs and his own assured [friend]
Edward Fenton

[*Direction:*] Mr Martin Frobiser Esquire and in his absence to Mr Atye secretary of the Earl of Leicester at Courte wth haste.

Document 20

Frobisher to Atye
7 November 1581[2]

[*Direction:*] A warrant to Mr Atye for 300 li. viith November 1581.

Mr Atye there is presentlie to be paide for provisions alreadie bought and to give ernest of the some of three hundreth

---

[1] If the transaction relative to the *Edward* had not yet gone through, it is possible that the *Bark Hastings* was still under discussion, for which young William Hawkins had been suggested as Captain (see p. 16).

[2] B.M., MS Harl. 6993, f. 13.

poundes, wch we praye you furnishe Cap^{en}. Fenton according the ordre sett downe for that purpose. Do [bid] you hartelie farewell from London the viith of November 1581.

your very loving friends
Martin Frobiser
Luke Warde. Edward Fenton[1]

[*Endorsed by Atye:*] From Mr Frobiser, Fenton, Warde Payde to Ed. Fenton as appereth by his bill of 9th November.

Document 21

Drake to Leicester
7 November 1581[2]

. . . [I am willing] to forward [the adventure] the rather for y^t yor L. [is a] doer and dealer therin, [and I have] moved divers in this Country [to make] som adventure therin but I [have] not certentie of any: for mine [own part I] have entred so farre into the adventure for yor good L. sake as mynne ability [can] well endure, if I might otherwise [be able] in any steed to forward it my desire is to shew myne endevor to the utter most. I have here come downe to staie for [certain] shippinge set forthe in warlike manner wch maketh o^r [merchants] more doubtfull of adventuring than otherwise they would be. The Barcke wch I sent of late to the Iland Tresera is returned,[3] by whom I have received certain letters

---

[1] Fenton and Ward had presumably been chosen to serve under Frobisher from the outset, as they were to have served on the abortive 'Enterprise' (see p. 7, n. 1 and p. 9, n. 1).

[2] B.M., Cotton MS Otho E. VIII, f. 102. Abstract in *Cal. S.P., Col., E. Indies, 1513–1616*, no. 166. Drake had evidently been applied to for further funds; see Document 19.

[3] This *Bark* and the *Willoughby* were presumably on privateering ventures.

29

whereof some are directed to yor good L: wherein yor shold understand the state of that place more effectuallie then I can signify by writinge. The Willowghby of Bristoll I perceave is [returned] thence but not greatlie stored with wealth. What yor good L: is willinge to comand and to do ether in this or any other cause I rest most redie to the uttermost of my power to accomplyshe the same, as knoweth godd, to whose merciful preservacion I comit yor L: Plymothe the viith of November 1581. Your L.'s most humble & assured to command

Fra. Drake.

Document 22

Earl of Shrewsbury to Leicester
22 November 1581[1]

. . . Mr Chester and thothers partenors of my shipp have [taken upon] them to furnishe theire parte for this voyage and [have] promised in lyke sorte as they do to furnishe my [shipp] in all respects as royally as shall be thought mete and [proper]. The said Cester and my servauntes whom I have appoynted to deale therin have offered unto y^r L. the shipp so [also] wth theire bodies to serve in the same as a consorte of [the Galleon] promysinge to acknowledge Mr Frobisher as theire admirall, to [look] on him as theire leader, to assist

[1] B.M., Cotton MS Otho E. VIII, f. 104. Since his letter of September 24 (Document 8), further correspondence had passed between the Earl of Shrewsbury and the Earl of Leicester, but the latter apparently accepted the sum of £200 (see Document 6) as offered in this letter in lieu of the *Bark Talbot*. An illegible fragment of a letter endorsed by Atye 'Robert Jolly to me touching the *Bark Talbot*' is in Cotton MS Otho E. VIII, f. 114. It bears the same date, 22 November 1581, as Shrewsbury's letter. The words 'of the Muscovy Company. Tomorrow morning I mind to attend' can be distinguished, with a few others which suggest that the *Bark* was rejected.

him in all assays, not to [depart] from him duringe the voyage and to be directed by him [in all] actions honest and reasonable: so as the said Mr Frobisher [do] suffer them indyfferently, at suche tyme and place as [any] marte is to be made, or any prize lawefully to be gotten, to deale for theire share thereof accordynge to theire proportion, and will not intermedle wth the disposition of theire [merchandize] furniture nor vittayles w^thout theire consent. W^ch theire offer they are yett (as I thinke) ready to accomplishe yf [so] if please yor L. to accept the same. And for that the said Chester and others adventures wth him utterly refuse to deale in any other sorte for sundrye respects and good reasons them moving. And I understanding the said Chester to be a man very sufficient bothe for experience, conduct & abilitie, am willing to adventure my half wth him in forme before declared for the better performance of this expedition whatsoever the charges thereof amount unto, and otherwise not to adventure any thing therein unless it be the half of my ship if your L. can buy the other half of my partners, which I promised your L. I would adventure, though the same hath sithence been refused. Or else the sum of £200 in money whether shall better like you, to be disposed & employed as your L. shall think convenient. And so to leave my ship for some other voyage as I doubt not but that we shall shortly provide for her. And so wishing your L. health . . . I commit you to God. Sheffield the XXIIth of Nov. 1581.

> your L. ever assured lovinge cousyn
> Shrewsbury.

Document 23

John Barker to Leicester
23 November 1581[1]

[Yr L. has requested me the names] of fitt men to go on ye voyage . . . intended. I have dilligentlye considered [of those] travelers thatt are belonge to this Cittie [none fitter for y^r] L.spps purpose butt this berer who is [ready to do y^r] honor soche service as he can. His bringen up hath ben att sea thes xviij yere & dothe specke his f[rench] very well & his portegus & is well seene & hathe experience in the art of navigasion.[2] I hoope he will [acquit] him selfe thatt y^r L.spp. will licke well of him. He is ready to tacke a longe viadge in hand for thatt he hathe nought [to] care for butt him selfe. I have nott moved the matter [w^t] other for thatt I found none else fitt for thatt purpose & [there is] com downe 30 and od thowsand of the staves of the wch M^r   hathe shipped viii thowsand & this weecke god willing I mean to ship viii thousand more for provision of wines for yor L.shipp . . .

Bristoll ye 23 of November a.d. 1581
Your L.sppes. umble servaunt
John Barker

[*Direction:*] To the R.H. my singular good lord & master the Earl of Leicester [give these] at the Court.

[1] B.M., Cotton MS Otho E. VIII, f. 83. Abstract in *Cal. S.P., Col., E. Indies, 1513–1616*, no. 172.

[2] This description fits what is known of Miles Evans, the merchant who left the voyage in Sierra Leone (see pp. 110, 185). The writer is apparently a merchant dealing in barrel staves requisite for ships' stores.

Document 24

Burghley to Walsingham
11 February 1581/2[1]

Sir, this sonday I have receaved twoo depeches from you, on[e] in ye morning, the other this evening, w^t the first you sent me ye Instructions for furbiser[2] and a letter from Sir H. Cobham, and another from bungy (?). ye Instructions I do reteyne to consider, ye other ij lres I do retorn . . .

    this xj of feb. 1581

              Wm Burghley

[*Direction:*] To Sir Francis Walsingham

Document 25

Henry Oughtred to Leicester
17 March 1581/2[3]

. . . Mr Hawkyns a manne of . . . [is the chief] hoope of the viyage, butt wthall I [find you have] made him an underlyng to one who ys [without] knowledge, which att the

---

[1] P.R.O., S.P. 12/152, art. 42.

[2] Discussed in footnotes to Document 35. Madox reports the change of leadership a fortnight later (p. 151).

[3] B.M., Cotton MS Otho E. VIII, f. 127. Abstract in *Cal. S.P., Col., E. Indies, 1513–1616*, no. 188. Save for the brief note in Document 24, there is a gap of over three months in the dated papers relative to the voyage. The sudden appointment of Edward Fenton to the command, which followed Leicester's return from the Low Countries (see p. xxxi), appears to have been the occasion of this letter. The contents suggest that Sheriff Oughtred looked upon the voyage as an opportunity for repeating Drake's exploits, for young William Hawkins was bent on such an action. See also p. 16.

sea will make great dis[content,] his experience is verye small his mynd hyghe, his [temper] of the manne colerick, thrall to the collycke and st[ubborn,] which matters shall commence into those whoate cuntreyes. I [think] his service wil be verye small and yett his mynde [ho]te as not to be overruled, wh^{ch} woll make great dyscord in owr [company]. For the cawses abovesayd (and some other necessarye matters to longe to trouble y^r L. wth) I rather wyshe Mr Hawkyns to have the place of governement wch wollde yeald me a more assured hoape for a gaynefull returne. Besides ther ys an honeste gentleman, all so prepared for this vyage, son in law to Mr Secretarye Walsingham named Mr Carleyle, a proper manne of better experyence than Mr Fenton a manne also sober and tractable, whome yf yt myght like you^r to joyne wth Mr Hawkyns I perswade myeself they wolld agree well and dooe good servyse as menne bothe of mylder natures and more equall condycyons. yf y^r l. cold lyke of this motyon I knowe yt woolde be beste lyked of the merchaunts and yett nothing hynder the vyage. for they be all in equall readyness and surelye I thinke this course wold best lyke the maryners. For I fynde theme hardly bent agaynste Mr Fenton and trewlye none here woold goe if Mr Hawkyns lead theme nott.[1] Now my good . . . we might have bene on the vyage long synce [at less] charges and a muche speadyer retorne had [not been the] lyngeryng convocations of the Moskovia Howse [who] have over greate speech as many of judgement. [sobe]rlie, *Quot capita tot sensus*, makyng a great confusion [as] hathe bene noryshed wth owr emulows captaynes who [nourishing] theyre owne pryde, forgett our profett and the honour of the voyage, wch self course was observed in the vyage to the Azores [intended and] this feedethe the expectatyon of the Spaniard and robbethe us of [good &] richer prises which y^r wisdome I trust woll preavent.

By Mr Hawkyns his retorne y^r honowre shall understand what is done for the pacefyeng of the maryners who be much trubled [using] mutynous speaches and readye to continuall brawles.

[1] For the desertion of some of the men, see p. 153.

34

I wold no more be tedyous butt refer the hole to y^r honourable wysdome & satesfye myeself therewth. Godde long keepe you^r and I woll serve youe Humblye takyng mye leave Nettleye the 17th of march 1581 y^r honowres to command

Henry Ughtred

Document 26

Report of the First Council Held on 20 March 1582[1]

Hereafter followeth the nomber of those that are appointed to goe in the shipps besyde the Marrinors

In the Gallione		In the Edward Bonaventure	
Mr Edward Fenton ⎫		Mr Luke Warde ⎫ Gentillmen	
Mr William Hawkins ⎬ Gentellmen		Mr Skevington ⎭	
Mr Christofer Carlell ⎬		Randall Shawe ⎫ marchauntes	
Mr Edmonde (*sic*) Parker ⎭		Peter Jeffereye ⎭	
Mr Madox a preacher		Lewis a Surgeon	
Mathewe Tailboise ⎫		An appoticarye	*Evans*
Thomas Bayname ⎬ Marchants		A Jewiller	
— Evans ⎭		A Garbler	
Mr Banester a surgeone		A Smythe	
ij pursers		A Showmaker	
a Jewiler		A Taylor	
A Garbler		ij mewsitiones	
A distillor of freshe water		ij pursers	*some good*
A smythe		iij men Mr Warde	*ship-wryth*
A showmaker		i man for the surgen	

[1] B.M., Cotton MS Otho E. VIII, f. 151. Madox in his Diary (p. 152) reports a meeting of the officers, chaplain and Commissioners in London on March 20 to consider the personnel of the ships. This document is presumably a copy of an ensuing report. It lays down the number of 'idle men', whom the Muscovy merchants wished kept to a minimum. The 'travellers', Richard Cotton, Edward Gilman, Samuel Symbarb and Mr Bowes, are not mentioned.

A Taylor
iii mewsitiones
An appoticarye
iij men Mr Fenton
ij men Mr Carlell
ij men Mr Parker
i man Mr Madoxe
i man for the marchauntes
ij men Mr Bannester
And all the rest to be Saylors
to the number of lxxxviii
And in all for this ship
is cxx

i man for the marchauntes
And all the rest to be
Saylors to the nomber
of lx
Some in all for this
ship l[xxx]

We moste humblye desyer your Lordshippe to have the warrants for the ffree Custome and the . . . In [London] the shippe Edward doth only stay for the . . . This xxiiijth march 1581[1]

yr L. most . . .

Document 27
Walsingham to Burghley
9 April 1582[2]

Ap. 9. 1582. My verie good Lord. My L. of Leicester and I have now herewth sent you the Instructions for Mr Fenton praying y^r L. to signe the same for his speedier dispatche, as lykewise that it would please you to joine wth us in the signing of our other letter here inclosed unto Mr Owtred, Mr Barnes & Mr Towerson for certayne speaches to be by them used generally to all the mariners of this voyage, for

[1] The list was apparently sent to the Earl of Leicester with a request for warrants for the free custom of any goods brought home from the voyage. The total of 180 persons is that originally in the first draft Instructions (p. 50, n. 2).

[2] P.R.O., S.P. 12/153, art. 4. Abstract in *Cal. S.P., Col., E. Indies, 1513–1616*, no. 191. The writer urges haste, for the expedition was now over five weeks behind time. The Queen's Commission was signed on April 2 (p. 59).

yealding due obedience to Mr Fenton & the rest that have the chief charge . . .

yor L. to commande

Fr. Walsingham

[*Endorsed:*] 9 April 1582 Mr Secret. Walsingham, wth ye Instructions for Mr Fentons viage.

Document 28

Bernardino de Mendoza to Philip II
20 *April* 1582[1]

On the 4th [April] Alderman Barnes of London left here for Southampton, charged with the despatch of the 4 ships I have so often mentioned as going to the Moluccas. The ship which left the Thames, called the Edward Buenaventura, is of 300 tons, armed with 30 great cast-iron pieces & carrying 100 men, and the other ship is of 500 tons & takes 200 men, being armed with 70 cannon.[2] There is a pinnace also of 40 tons given by Drake, & which carries 35 men:[3] in addition to which there is a small craft of 14 tons.[4] Amongst these 300 and odd men[5] are some gentlemen and excellent sailors, as the Council gave licence to press the most suitable men for the voyage. Some of those who went with Drake accompany them, whilst six men who go have already been to the

---

[1] Abstract, *Cal. S.P., Span., 1580–6*, no. 248.

[2] The *Galleon* had 120 men and forty-two cannon (see pp. 157, 158, 154). Fray Juan reported her as having eighty pieces of ordnance (Document 49).

[3] The *Bark Francis* had a complement of seventeen (p. 160).

[4] A small ship, the *Peter*, which was carrying stores from London to Southampton (p. 153).

[5] The agreed complement of 200 was increased to 231 when the *Elizabeth* was bought (p. 44, n. 4).

Moluccas,[1] and having lived for eight years in the Portuguese Indies are well acquainted with the coast.

The pilot of the principal ship is a Terceira Portuguese, called Simon Fernando, a heretic who has lived here for some years, and is considered one of the best pilots in the country. They take victuals for two years & the cost of the expedition will reach £12,000, in addition to £4,000 or £5,000 worth of merchandize.[2]

Their intention is to sail from here to Cape Blanco in Barbary, where they will water and then continue their voyage. From what I have heard lately from persons who have been in communication with Drake and others, and have seen the secret chart of the voyage, I infer that their course is to be different from that which they originally intended, which was to go to the Cape of Good Hope and thence start for the Moluccas. The intention is now to run down the coast of Brazil to Port St Julian and the Strait of Magellan,[3] which Drake discovered not to be a strait at all, and that the land which in the maps is called Tierra del Fuego is not part of a continent, but only very large islands with canals [channels] between them. When Winter, who was one of those who went with Drake, returned hither, I wrote your Maj[y] that he with the other three ships had entered the Straits, but after he had proceeded eighty leagues therein, he was separated from the other ships by a storm on the 6th of September, which storm he says was the greatest that ever he had experienced. He then steered south with a north-west wind towards Tierra del Fuego which is in the Strait itself, and was seeking a port until the 28th of October, without being able to find one. At the end of this time, in order to find out where he was, he took observations and found that he was in the same latitude as the mouth of the Straits.[4] He therefore concluded that what

---

[1] These cannot be identified.

[2] The value of the merchandise is exaggerated, but in general Mendoza was well informed.

[3] This was undoubtedly the intention of the men who had been with Drake. Fenton had no clear plan.

[4] The entry and exit mouths of the Strait are in approximately the same latitude, but Mendoza, as he admits, was no geographer. It was already known that Tierra del Fuego was an archipelago, but this was thought to

Magellan described as Straits, and the continent, were really channels and islands all the way from Porte Grande to Cape Deseado, and from Cape Bona Senal to that of Maestro as they are marked on the maps, since he had run for 54 days without finding a port. Drake, who had a fair wind & fine weather, ran back to reconnoitre in the same direction as that in which he had been drawn by the storm, and then sailing north outside the islands which look like a strait and entering the South Sea, proceeded to Panama, from whence after he had committed the robberies, he sailed to the Moluccas, & returned by the Cape of Good Hope.

That the Straits are really formed by islands is proved by what happened to Winter, because after having proceeded for 80 leagues the storm carried him back to Port St Julian without his again passing out of the opening by which he entered:[1] which made cosmographers here think that Winter had not entered the Straits at all. Although he affirmed that the straits were formed by islands, he was not believed until Drake himself returned, who has not explained the secret to anyone but some of the Councillors, and the chief of this expedition,[2] who placed before him the danger that would be run by sending these ships whilst your Majesty had so large a fleet in the Strait of Magellan. Drake replied: So much the better: as they were thus assured that your Majesty's vessels

border a great Southern Continent, an idea disproved by Drake's run along the south-west margin of the islands.

[1] For Winter's narrative on his arrival home see E. G. R. Taylor, 'More light on Drake', *Mariner's Mirror*, vol. XVI (1930), pp. 134–51.

[2] This must refer to Leicester, and it may be inferred that Drake himself had discussed with members of the Privy Council the question of going by the Magellan or the Cape Route. It cannot be assumed, however, that Drake's argument was accepted. Cavendish in 1586 made no attempt to round Cape Horn; and from the examination of Tomé Hernandez, a survivor of the Spanish settlement, in 1620 it appears that the English Captain had given as his reasons the higher latitude that would have been involved, and the danger of getting among the islands (C. R. Markham (ed.), *Narratives of the Voyages of Pedro Sarmiento* (Hakluyt Society, 1894), p. 369). Pedro Sarmiento himself had been ordered in 1579 to examine all the mouths leading from the sea into the Strait, 'for it will be of little use to discover one if another is left for the pirates' (op. cit., p. 12). But Drake's assertion that the enemy assumed to be established at the Narrows in the Strait could be avoided by passing round in the open sea finds no echo in the arguments used by the participators in Fenton's voyage when debating whether to advance or return (see pp. 239–45).

would stay there and keep guard to prevent anyone entering the South Sea: but after all they would find themselves deceived, as it was not continents but only very large islands, and there was the open sea beyond Tierra del Fuego. The person who has given me this statement, although he saw Drake's chart,[1] and discussed it with him, does not understand navigation & cosmography sufficiently to tell me exactly the degrees of latitude, but only asserts the point that the land consists of islands and not continent . . . These ships expect to bring back 500 tons of spices, & they have already calculated the amount which will accrue to each adventurer. They are so confident about it that they are fitting out other ships for a similar voyage,[2] and it would be very desirable that wherever these ships are encountered, they and every man on board of them should be sent to the bottom and these expeditions stopped, as their effrontery has reached such a pitch that the Councillors speaking, say that they will send to these islands or wherever else they think proper, to trade & conquer. As it seems to be highly important to discover the truth of these statements, which are made by Drake in all confidence and believed by the Councillors, I would suggest that your Majesty's fleet, which was sent to the strait of Magellan, should be ordered to explore thoroughly their position.

[1] For Madox's comments on Drake's chart, see p. 189.
[2] This may refer to the voyage of the *Bark Hastings* (see p. 15). The captured Spanish friars were given a letter of safe conduct to 'Frobisher or Acres', of whose expedition they had been informed (see p. 192). Captain Acres had fought in Ireland and was the bearer of a letter from the Lord Deputy to Walsingham in February 1582, when Frobisher's plans were changed (S.P. (Ireland) 12/89, art. 55).

Document 29

Fenton to Leicester
22 *April* 1582[1]

. . . with my self . . . companies as com in . . . number, xxxvi persons[2] whereof [two pilots] with xii more were such as passed [with Sir] Frances Drake in his last voyage [to the Moluccas]. The Commissioners and I conferred for them [to go] in this viyage and fownd them (after [hearing] of o^r proportions which they verie well liked) willinge to enter the action wth us; Only [they] refused to come to agreement wth us [until they] had spoken wth Sir Frances Drake [and had] ended some matters wth him, wch I (in regarde of the losse of time) unwillingly yelded unto. But before we had resolved [the matter] (unlooked for) Sir Frances cam unto us[3] wherby all cawses tooke the better ende wth them, and have through his owne liberalitie and the ympreste allowed them by us, entortaigned the same xiiij persons for this voyage. Albeit I dare assure yor L. (in truthe) that the nombers before entretaigned for the voyage were both compleit and verie sufficiente men to undertake the same. So as nowe (if winde and weather serve) I truste (god willinge) to sett saile wthin thees v daies and leaves the reaport of all other matters to Sir Frances Drake whom I am well assured will acquaint yor L. what his opinion is towchinge the Beare Gallion,[4] the other Shippinge and Companies appointed for them, till suche time as the Commissioners repaire unto yor L. whose paines & cares hath been greate: Sithence their coming hither to

---

[1] B.M., Cotton MS Otho E. VIII, f. 144. Abstract in *Cal. S.P., Col., E. Indies, 1513–1616,* no. 194.

[2] Extra crew had been admitted, after the purchase of the *Elizabeth,* over and above the total of 200 persons originally agreed upon (see pp. 36, 156).

[3] See p. 155. Drake was at Southampton on the day this letter was written.

[4] The *Galleon Oughtred,* later *Galleon Leicester.*

provide for all things necessarie and to be [furnished] . . . One thynge sithence my departing [from London] hath much greeved me wch is the [departing from] the jorney of Cap^{en}. Carlile, whose [discontent] growes (chieflie) by placinge before him in thinstructions younge Mr Hawkins, who is offended wth me in that I did not [take action] wth your L. to have them reformed.[1] [But indeed] yor L. can best witnesse what care I had [to make him] contented, wch yor tolde me he should receive [with] good likinge and accordinge to an agreement [before set] downe betwixte yor L. and Sir Frances [Walsingham] so as (I trust) yor L. will discharge me and leave the   gentleman satisfied of my [good will] towards him. Whom I beseche yor to send me wth that contentment that the vertuous gentleman deserveth, and whose companie I most [desired] in this voyage, aswell for that I love him, [as for] menie other good thinges I have noted in him.

Thus receiving pardon for my boldness [do send] my humble dutie to yor L. restinge wholy at yor disposition and service. Prayinge that [our] Lorde maie conducte & guide yor in all yor actions and give yor much encreese of hono^r

From Netley in haste the xxiith of April

yor honors to commaund duringe life

Edward Fenton

I humbly besech yor ho: to be thankefull to Sir Frances Drake for his good counsaile used towardes me & persuacons to his Companies for their obedience to that effect.

---

[1] The official excuse was an ague (see p. 64). Carleil now turned his attention to North American ventures. Young Hawkins was clearly a fire-brand, and one with Oughtred's backing—and presumably Leicester's also.

Document 30
John Walker to Leicester
22 April 1582[1]

. . . Alderman Barnes wth . . . [received] me with great frendlynease . . . [& I am] ever bounden unto yor L. for sendinge [me hither]. Synce my departure from Courte I have byn [to &] have taken my institutyon & inductyon unto the [benefice of] fyllacke[2] whyche her M^{atie} bestowed upon me, and [was paid] for, to Sir John Arundel. The Byshopp showed [that] curtesy he myghte: and assured me of his friendship, be knowethe that it was her m^{aties} to geve, whe[resoever was] it graunted: my most humble sute unto yor good L. if yor L. woolde be a meanes unto her ma^{tie} that I [may be] dyspensed wth to keepe my lyvinges untyll I returne from the indyans: Mr Cudworthe wyll bringe yor L. the . . . to be assigned, wch Mr Secretary wyll procure at yor L. fyrste motyon, for yf I may have my poore lyvyngs [until] my cominge agayne, I shall thinke my selfe well satisfyed, I am now somewhat in debte and the profytts thereof (the tyme of my absence). will dyscharge the same, to the greate quyettness of my conscyence: And for my selfe bothe hearte & hande I wyll contynue and ever remayn as faythfull a servante as ever yor L. had in servyce, wheareof I hope yor L. shall have good experyence yf ever I returne. The almyghtye god preserve y^{or} L. in most happye estate to his glorye & yor L. hartes desyre

Southehampton this xxijth day of apryll 1582
yor honorable L. most bounden servante
John Walker.

May it please yor L. to geve me leave further to advertyse

---

[1] B.M., Cotton MS Otho E. VIII, f. 145. Abstract in *Cal. S.P., Col., E. Indies, 1513–1616,* no. 195.
[2] Phyllack, a parish in Cornwall, nine miles south of Redruth.

y^{or} L: that the ryghte worshyppfull Sir Francys Drake hathe used me wth the greateste frendshippe that any might desyre bothe in instructinge me for the voyage and in dealinge lyberallye with me & my fellowe preacher for the whyche [I besech y^r L. geve him] thankes.[1]

[*Direction:*] To the ryghte honorable my synguler good L. and master[2] the Erle of Leycester geve these.

Document 31
The Adventurers to Leicester
22 *April* 1582[3]

. . . theyre provisions in generall . . . abyletye. The captains & their ser[vants do] fynde all readye and well furnished [save for] the travayle of fyve or syxe dayes for [certain] matters to be embarked, the wch in their [hope soon] shalbe accomplyshed, reservynge godds blessing [of o^r] favourable wynde. Yt maye please your [L. to] understand thatt wth good advisement (and your allowance thereof as we hoope), and by the [consent of] the owner we have agrede to [allow the frigate] proferred by Captain Ward to be sold bye . . . and have accepted in lyewe thereof a bark[4] [which is] apter for the vyage to goe in this accstyon wherein upon her surrender we humblye crave yor honourable consente . . . the further relation bye letter, for thatt we hoape the more [fully to] satisfy yor honourable expectatyon in alltering the

---

[1] See p. 155.
[2] Mr Walker was presumably one of Leicester's chaplains.
[3] B.M., Cotton MS Otho E. VIII, f. 115. Abstract in *Cal. S.P., Col., E. Indies, 1513–1616*, no. 193.
[4] The *Elizabeth*. Ward's frigate had been sold to Sir Humfrey Gilbert (p. 156).

former dysposytyon of the sayd frygate, and we are [bold] to adventure of yor honowrable acceptance and in dutifull manner take our leave. Nettlye the 22th of Aprill. We humblye beseech yor honours to imagine we wrote in haste by this our blotted letter.

Your honowres to command

Henry Oughtred   Ed. Fenton   Nicholas Parker
George Barnes Alde^r.   H^{ry} Towerson   John Castelyn
Luke Ward   Wm Hawkins

[*Direction:*] To the R. Hon. owr verye good Lord the Earle of Leicester etc.
[*Endorsed:*] 22 aprl. Mr Ughtred, Mr Alderman Barnes etc. voyage.

Document 32
Bernardino de Mendoza to Philip II
26 April 1582[1]

I have today learnt that the ships which were ready to sail for the Moluccas have now left and also that Humfrey Gilbert is fitting out three more for Florida . . . Frobisher is also pushing forward the fitting out of three more ships for the Moluccas, affirming that he means to arrive in the South Sea by the islands that form the Straits of Magellan before these ships which have sailed.[2]

[1] Abstract. *Cal. S.P., Span., 1580–6,* no. 254.
[2] Frobisher and presumably Acres (p. 192) were going direct to the Strait of Magellan, but nothing is known of the voyage, if indeed they sailed.

Document 33
Henry Oughtred to Leicester
1 May 1582[1]

. . . to bear the name of [Gallion Leicester] . . . the reste of the companye dyd se . . . of the vyage and so styll dothe proceed, I trust with gods good favoure to retorne wth prosperous safety [to the] honour of the realme and and the profett of the adventurers [which may god] grawnt. Butt in the fornoone before theyr departure Mr Maddox your honowres chaplayne made a goddlye and eloquente sermon in the shippe before 300 people as I think therin trewlye he shewed himselfe to be a chapleyne worthye of so honowrable a patronne. Trewlye, Sir, Mr Alderman Barnes, Mr Towerson & Mr Castlyne have taken great paynes & travayle to further the despatche wch cowlde not [else] so sone have bene procured, amongste theyr unrewlye maryners who be as well voyde of reason as of obedyence. Butt godde be thanked now all y^s fynysshed and the shippes in the sea wth a prosperows wynde, under gods good protectyon. May godde keepe them for a safe retorne (And I wishe all the Kynge of Spayne his gold in theyr bellyes)[2] to temper the pryde of such a tyrawnte. Mye good lord I have nothing els whereof to advertyse youe butt to assure yor Lordshippe thatt I doo rest as hollye yor honours as anye poor gentle manne in Englande. And I will praye for you^r untyll you^r commawnd my servyce wth yor, ever readye.

I humblye take mye leave. Netleye the first of maye 1582
Your honowres to commawnd Henry Ughtred.

---

[1] B.M., Cotton MS Otho E. VIII, f. 122. Abstract in *Cal. S.P., Col., E. Indies, 1513–1616*, no. 199.
[2] Oughtred's mind was bent on the spoiling of the Spaniard.

Part II

THE VOYAGE
(Documents 34–59)

Document 34

Mariners' Provision Allowance[1]

A proportion for the diett of one man for vij daies at the sea and on Lande. sett downe the viij[th] of Marche 1577. by M[r] fforbisher, M[r] Dee, M[r] Younge, M[r] Lok and M[r] Edw. fenton and others Commissioners[2] appointed for thordringe of such cawses as were to be Dealt in for the new discoveries made by Cap*tai*n fforbisher to the Northweste   viz.

In Biskett breade for vij daies vij poundes   viij[d] ob q[a].
Beare at iij quartes le daie for vij daies v gallons j quarte xiij d
Beife, for iiij daies in the Weike iiij pounde   viij d
Habardine or stockfishe one fish & di for iij daies   ix d
Cheze for iij daies in the Weike iij quarters of a
         pownde at ij[d] le pownde   I[d] ob
Butter for iij daies in a Weike di pownde at 4[d] le pownde   ij[d]
Peaze for vij daies, ij quartes at ij s Le strike[3]   j[d] ob
Otmeale for vij daies, one pinte at iiijs Le strike   j[d]
Sweete oyle after the rate of a pinte for a monthe,
         amounteth for a daie   I[d] ob
Vinegar, after the rate of a pinte for a monthe,
         amounteth for a daie to   q[r]
Salte, after the rate of di pinte for a monthe,
         amounteth for a daie   q[r]
Muster seede, after the rate of a pinte for
         a monthe, amounteth in th weike to   q[r]. Sm[a] iiijs xjd.[4]

[1] Magdalene College, Cambridge, Pepys MS 2133 (unfoliated).
[2] This schedule of provision allowance for a ship's company was set down by a committee, in preparation for the scheme of wintering Edward Fenton, with one hundred men, in Meta Incognita in 1578–9. The items agree very closely with those of the ship's stores detailed by Fenton as remaining in the *Galleon* from 1 November 1582 onward, save that there is here no mention of honey. See p. 114.
[3] A denomination of dry measure usually identical with the bushel (*O.E.D.*).
[4] This is about 21s. a month. The estimate for the men taking part in

Document 35

The Instructions, as Issued on 9 April 1582[1]

Instructions given by the honourable the Lordes of the Counsell, to Edward Fenton Esquire, for the order to be observed in the voyage recommended to him for the East Indies and Cathay. Aprill 9. 1582.

First you shall enter as captaine Generall, into the charge and government of these shippes, viz. the Beare Gallion, the Edwarde Bonaventure, the Barke Francis, and the small Frigate or Pinnesse.

2 Item, you shall appoint for the furnishing of the vessels in the whole, to the number of 200, able persons, accompting in that number the Gentlemen and their men, the Ministers, Chirurgians, Factors, etc. which said number is no way to be exceeded,[2] whereof as many as may be, to be seamen, and shal distribute them into every vessell, as by advise here before your going shall be thought meete: Provided that you shall not receive under your charge & governement, any disordered or mutinous person, but that upon knowledge had, you shall remove him before your departure hence, or by y[e] way as soone as you can conveniently avoide him, and receive better in their places.

3 Item, for the more and better circumspect execution, and

the 'Enterprise' was only 15s. a month (S.P. 12/148, art. 47). The sailors expected to supplement their diet by fishing, and lines were trailed overboard, while near land Captain Ward (for example) was assiduous with his net (pp. 103, 118).

[1] Hakluyt, *Principall Navigations* (1589), pp. 644–7. The first draft of the Instructions, addressed to Frobisher (Cotton MS Otho E. VIII, ff. 88–90), was submitted to Lord Burghley on 11 February 1582 (Document 24), and some marginal notes are in his hand. Some preliminary notes are transcribed in Document 10. The first draft is abstracted in *Cal. S.P., Col., E. Indies, 1513–1616*, nos. 187, 192.

[2] The number 180 in the first draft was deleted and 200 substituted. The Muster Roll as given by Madox (pp. 157–60) contains 231 names, but from it some of those known to have been on board are missing. Fray Juan de Rivadeneyra said that the fleet carried 350 people. See pp. 334–6. Mendoza had reckoned much this number (p. 37).

determination in any waightie causes incident in this voyage, we will that you shall take unto you for assistances captaine Hawkins, captaine Ward, M. Nicholas Parker, M. Maddox, M. Walker, M. Evans, Randolph Shaw, Mathew Talboys,[1] with whom you shall consult and conferre in all causes, matters, and actions of importance, not provided for in these instructions touching this service nowe in hand. And in all such matters, so handled, argued, and debated, we thinke it convenient alwayes to be executed, which you shall thinke meetest with the assent also of any 4. of them, the matter having bene debated, and so assented unto, in the presence of your said Assistants. And in case that if such conference and debating the opinions of the aforesaide Assistants be founde in effect any way to differ, then it is thought meete, that all such matters so argued upon, shall rest to bee put in execution in such sort as you shall thinke most meetest, having the assent of any 4. of them as aforesaid. And if any of these Assistants shal die, then the number of the one halfe of the Survivours to joyne with the General Captaine for consent in all things aforesaid

4 Of all which your assemblies and consultations, for the matters aforesaid, we thinke it very convenient, that a particular and true note should be kept, for which cause we appoint master Maddox minister,[2] and if he shuld decease, then the Generall with halfe the Assistants Survivours, to name one to keepe a booke of all such matters as shall bee brought in consultation, and of all such reasons as shall be propounded by any person, either on the one side, or on the other: what was resolved on, and by whose consent, who dissented therefrom, and for what causes. In which booke he

---

[1] The list of assistants originally appointed for Frobisher was as follows: Fenton, Ward, Carleil, Parker, Randall Shaw, Baynham, Talbois, Madox. This is struck through, which suggests that this actual draft was used in drawing up the new one. The absence of Hawkins's name will be noted. Peter Jeffery's name was accidentally omitted from Fenton's appointed Council, and was added later (p. 63). John Drake was only occasionally called to a Council meeting and questioned.

[2] As originally entered, the name of the man who was to keep the 'true note' of the voyage was that of Captain Carleil, but this was deleted and a marginal note inserted: 'We reserve the nomination of this to your honors', i.e. to the members of the Privy Council concerned.

shall in the beginning of the note of every such assemblie set downe particulerly the day, and the place, if it may be, the names of the persons then present, and upon what occasion the said consultation was appointed or holden, and shall have to every acte, the hands of the Generall, and of all, or so many of the said Assistants as will subscribe; which booke the said master Maddox, or the other upon his decease appointed in his place shall keepe secrete, and in good order to be exhibited unto us, at your returne home.

5 Item, if there happen any person or persons imployed in this service, of what calling or condition he or they shall be, should conspire, or attempt privately or publikely, any treason, mutinie, or other discord, either touching the taking away of your owne life, or any other of authoritie under you, whereby her Majesties service in this voiage might thereby be overthrowne, or impugned: we will therefore, that upon just proofe made of any such treason, mutenie, or any other discord attempted as aforesaid, the same shalbe punished by you, or your Lieutenant, according to the qualitie and enormitie of the facte.[1] Provided alwayes, and it shall not be lawfull neither for you, nor for your Liuetenant to exceede the punishment of any person, by losse of life or limme, unlesse the partie shall be judged to have deserved it by the rest of your Assistants, as is before expressed, or at the least by foure of them. And that which shall concerne life[2] to be by the verdict of twelve men, of the companie employed in this voyage, to be impanelled for that purpose, with the observation of the forme of our Countrie lawes in that behalfe, as neere as you may. Provided, if it shall not appeare, that the forbearing of the execution by death, shall minister cause to increase the facte of the offendour, then it were better to convince the partie of his facte, by the othes of 12. indifferent persons, and to commit him to hard imprisonment, untill the returne. And aswell of the factes committed by any, as also of the proofe thereof, and of the opinions of you, and

---

[1] Fault (*O.E.D.*).

[2] This part of Item 5 is not in the draft, where there is a marginal note: '[It] shall be necessary to set down some form of proceeding according to martial law.'

your Assistants, and the maner of the punishment, the Register shall make a particuler and true note, in the booke of your consultation, as is before appointed.

6 Item, you shall not remoove captaine William Hawkins your lieutenant, master captaine Luke Ward your Viceadmirall, or captaine of the Edward Bonaventure, nor captaine Carlile from his charge by land, whom we will not to *M. Carlile* refuse any such service as shall be appointed to him by the *upon occasion* Generall and the councell, nor any captaine of other vessels *voyage.* from their charges, but upon just cause dulie prooved, and by consent of your Assistants, or of 4. of them at the least. *went not in the*

7 Item, for the succesion of the Generall governour of this whole voyage, if it should please God to take him away, it is thought meete that there should bee the names of such Gentlemen secretly set downe to succeed in his place one after the other, which are severally written in parchment, included in bals of Waxe, sealed with her Majesties signet, put into two coffers[1] locked with three severall locks, whereof one key is to be in the custodie of captaine Luke Ward, the other of William Hawkins, the third of master Maddox the minister,[2] and the same two coffers to bee put into two severall shippes, *videlicet*, the one coffer in the Gallion, in the custodie of the Generall, the other in the Edward Bonaventure, in the custodie of the Viceadmiral, the same two coffers upon any such casualtie of the Generals death by consent of the Assistants which shall overlive, to bee opened, and the partie therein named to succeed in the place, who shall thereupon take upon him the charge in the said voiage according to these instructions, in such sort as if they had bene specially directed unto him, and the rest of the companie so to take and repute him in every respect, as they will answer to the contrarie. But if it shall so fall out, (as we hope it will) that

[1] Only one was actually provided (p. 65).

[2] In the first draft the holders of keys were to be Frobisher, Fenton and Carleil. The last name was deleted in favour of Randall Shaw, while for that of Fenton that of Thomas Baynham was substituted, and this in turn deleted, so that Christopher Carleil could be put back. The selection of names suggests the influence of the Muscovy Company's commissioners as well as that of Walsingham, who was Carleil's step-father. Alderman Barnes was his uncle.

there shall bee no such need, but that the Generall doe continue still, then shall you at your returne deliver backe the said coffers and bals of waxe sealed in such sorte as they be, without opening them, unlesse it be in the case aforesayd.

8 You shall make a just and true inventorie in every ship and vessell appointed for this voyage of all the tackle, munition, and furniture belonging to them at their setting foorth hence, and of all the provisions whatsoever, and one copie thereof under your hand, & under the hands of your Viceadmirall and lieutenant, to be delivered to the Erle of Leicester, and the other to the Governour of the companie[1] for them before your departure hence, and the like to be done at your returne home of all things then remaining in the sayd shippes and vessels, with a true certificate how and by what meanes any parcell of the same shall have bene spent or lost.

9 Item, you shal use all diligence possible to depart from Southampton with your said ships and vessels, before the last of this present moneth of Aprill, and so goe on your course by Cape de bona Sperança,[2] not passing by the streight of Magellan, either going or returning, except upon great occasion incident, that shall be thought otherwise good to you, by the advise and consent of your sayd Assistants, or 4. of them at the least.

10 Item, you shall not passe to the Northeastward the fortie degree of latitude at the most, but shall take your right course to the Isles of Molucas, for the better discoverie of the Northwest passage, if without hinderance of your trade, and within the same degree you can get any knowledge touching that passage, wherof you shal do well to bee inquisitive as occasion in this sort may serve.[3]

---

[1] Alderman Barnes.

[2] According to the first draft the start was to be made 'before the last of February next', i.e. the document was drawn up in January 1582, but since it was already February when the paper reached the Privy Councillors, 'before the last of the present month' was substituted. When the change of leadership took place, there was delay before the second draft reached Lord Burghley. The phrase 'of April' had become necessary in consequence.

[3] Item 10 was made superfluous by Frobisher's departure from the voyage. It originally ran: 'You shall not pass to the north-eastward of the 40 degrees of latitude at the most, because we will that this voyage shall be

11 Item, you shall have speciall regard after your departure from the coast of England, so to order your course, as that your shippes and vessels loose not one another, but keepe company together both outward and homeward. And least they happen to sever the one from the other by tempest or otherwise, it shal not be amisse that you appoint to the captains and masters, certain places wherein you will stay certaine daies. And every ship passing aforehand, and not knowing what is become of the other ships to leave upon every Promontorie or Cape, a token to stand in sight with a writing lapped in lead to declare the day of their passage. And if any wilfulnesse or negligence in this behalfe shall appeare in any person or persons that shall have charge of any of the ships or vessels aforesayd, or if they or any of them shall doe otherwise then to them appertaineth, you shall punish such offenders sharply to the example of others.

12 Item, we do straightly enjoine you, and consequently all the rest imploied in this voiage in any wise, and as you and they will answere the contrary at your coming home by the lawes of this realme, that neither going, tarying abroad, nor returning, you doe spoile or take any thing from any of the Queens Majesties friends or allies, or any christians, without paying justly for ye same, nor that you use any maner of violence or force against any such, except in your owne defence, if you shall be set upon, or otherwise be forced for your owne safeguard to do it.

13 Item, we wil that you deale altogether in this voiage like good and honest merchants, traffiquing and exchanging ware for ware, with all curtesie to ye nations you shall deale with, as well Ethniks as others, and for that cause you shal instruct al those y^t shal go with you, that whensoever you or any of you shal happen to come in any place to conference w^t the people of those parts, y^t in all your doings and theirs, you and

only for trade and not for the discoverie of the passage by the northeast to Cataya, otherwise than if without hinderance to your trade and within the said degree you can get any knowledge', etc. The drafter of the clause was understandably confused over finding a north-west passage by the northeast. Frobisher, who swore he had in 1576 seen the 'capes' (extremities) of Asia and America on his right hand and on his left was justifiably suspected of a wish to view them from the Pacific side (see p. 16).

they so behave your selves towards the said people, as may rather procure their friendship & good liking toward you by courteousnesse, then to move them in offence or misliking, and especially you shal have great care of ye performance of your word, & promise to them.

14 Item wee will, that by the advise of your Assistants, in places where you and they shall thinke most fitte, you settle if you can, a beginning of a further trade to be had hereafter: and from such places doe bring over with you some fewe men, and women, if you may, and doe also leave some one or two, or more, as to you and your Assistants shall seeme convenient of our nation with them for pledges, and to learne the tongue, and secrets of the Countries, having diligent care, that in delivering, and taking of hostages, you deliver not personages of moe value then you receive, but rather deliver meane persons under colour of men of value, as the Infidels doe for the most part use. Provided that you stay not longer to make continuance of further trade, then shalbe expedient for good exchange of the wares presently caried with you.

Strange people to be brought home

15 Item you shall have speciall care, and give generall warning, that no person of what calling soever he be, shall take up, or keepe to himselfe and his private use, any stone, pearle, golde, silver, or other matter of commoditie to be had or found in places where you shall come, but he the said person so seased of such stone, pearle, golde, silver or other matter of commoditie, shall with all speede, or so soone as he can detect the same, and make deliverie thereof to your selfe, or your Viceadmirall, or your Lieuetenant, and the Factor appointed for this voyage, upon paine of forfeiture of all the recompense he is to have for his service in this voyage by share, or otherwise: and further to receive such punishment, as to you, & your Assistants, or the more part of them shal seeme good, & otherwise to be punished here at his returne, if according to the qualitie of his offence, it shal be thought needfull.

16 Item, if the Captaines, Merchants, or any other, shall have any apparell, jewels, chaines, armour, or any other thing whatsoever, which may be desired in Countries where they

shall traffique, that it shal not bee lawful for them, or any of them to traffique, or sell any thing thereof for their private accompt: but the same shall bee praysed by the most part of those that shall be in commission in the places where the same may be so required, rated at such value, as it may bee reasonably worth in England, and then solde to the profite of the whole voyage, and to goe as in adventure for those to whom it doeth appertaine.[1]

17 Item you your selfe shall in the Gallion keepe one booke, and the Factors appointed for the same ship another, wherein shalbe a just accompt kept, aswell of the marchandize carried hence, as of those you shall bring home. And aswell at your setting foorth, as from time to time, as exchange shalbe made, you shall set your hande to their booke, and they theirs to yours, and the like order shal you see that the Captaine and Factors in the Edward Bonaventure, shall use in their shippe and the other Captaines and Factors in eache other vessell.

18 Item you shall give straight order to restraine, that none shal make any Cartes, or descriptions of the said voyage, but such as shalbe deputed by you the Generall, which sayd Carts and descriptions, we thinke meete that you the Generall shall take into your hands, at your returne to this our coast of England, leaving with them no coppie, & to present them unto us at your returne: the like to be done if they finde any Cartes or Mappes in those Countries.

19 Item you shall at your returne so direct your course, that all the shippes under your government may come home together, and arrive here in the river of Thames, if it may conveniently be. And wheresoever in this Realme you, or any of the shippes shall arrive, you shall give special and straight order, that no person of what condition soever he be, shall unlade, or bring on lande, or foorth of the vessels for which it came, any part or parcell of marchandize, or matter of commoditie brought in any of the said vessels, untill we being certified of your, or their arrivall, shall give further order and direction therein, under the penalties and forfeitures

---

[1] This item, an injunction against private trade, does not appear in the Frobisher instructions. See p. 204.

expressed in the 15. article, against such as shall retayne any thing to their private use, as in the saide article is further expressed.

20 Item to the intent that all such persons, as shall goe with you in this voyage may better understand, what they ought to doe, and what to avoyde, we thinke it requisite, that aswell out of these, as otherwise with the advise of your Assistants, and masters, of the ships, you shall call some convenient order to be set downe in writing for their better government both at Sea, and land, if they shall happen to goe on land any where. And the same to bee openly read, and made knowen unto them, to the intent they may understand how to behave themselves, and upon any fault committed, not to have any excuse to pretend ignorance, and so to avoide such punishment, as it is requisite to have ministred, for the keeping of them in good order.[1]

21 And to the end God may blesse this voyage with happy and prosperous successe, you shall have an especiall care to see that reverence and respect be had to the ministers[2] appointed to accompanie you in this voyage, as apperteineth to their place and calling, and to see such good orders as by them shall be set downe for reformation of life and maners, duely obeyed and perfourmed, by causing the transgressours and contemners of the same to be severely punished, and the Ministers to remouve sometime from one vessell to another.

22 Provided alwayes, that the whole direction and government of the people, life and limme excepted, as in the fifth article, and the course of this voyage, shalbe wholy at your disposition, except in the course by the Streight of Magellan, either outward or homeward, and in your passage by the Northward of 40. degrees in latitude, wherein you shall followe direction set downe in the 9. and 10. articles, as also in the displacing of the Captaine of the Edward Bonaventure, & other captaines, wherein you shal followe the order appointed in the 6. article: Provided that we meane not by this article to derogate any thing from the authoritie of your

---

[1] See p. 67 for the further Instructions issued by Fenton.
[2] The first draft only referred to a single minister.

Assistants established in the third article, or in any other article of these instructions.

23 Item, in all occasions and enterprises that may fall out to be upon the lande, wee will that captaine Carlile shall have the generall and chiefe charge thereof.[1]

24 And finally wee require you and every of you to have a due regard to the observation and accomplishment of these our instructions, and of all such other things, as may any kind of way tend to the furtherance and benefite of this service committed to your charge.

Document 36

Official Narrative of Richard Madox[2]

A copie of her Maties broade seale graunted to our Generall [2 April 1582][3]

Elizabethe by the grace of God queen of England, France and Irland, defender of the fayth etc. to all & singuler our Justices of peace, mayres, sherifs, baylifs, constibles, head boroughes & to all other offycers, mynisters & subjectes to whome these presents shall come, greeting. Forasmuche as we have appoynted our trusty and well-beloved servant Edward Fenton esquyre, to have ye rule & government of such ship, shippinge & vessel, whatsoever in his company for

---

[1] The phrase 'and therein to command and dispose as by him shall be found most expedient', found in the earlier draft, has been omitted. The final Instructions were signed before Carleil's resignation from his office, and their curtailment of his powers and duties may have influenced him.

[2] B.M., Cotton MS Otho E. VIII, ff. 130–43, 173. Various passages of this document are abstracted in *Cal. S.P., Col., E. Indies, 1513–1616*, *passim*. Richard Madox was appointed Registrar of the voyage, and in the course of his duties assembled and copied a number of relevant documents before commencing the actual narrative. This unfortunately breaks off on 21 July 1582. He drew upon his Private Diary (Document 38), but naturally used his discretion in doing so.

[3] Printed by Wagner, *Drake's Voyage*, pp. 445–6.

ye viage w^t ye favour of almyghty god to be made into foreyn parties to the southeastwards as well for ye discovery of Cathaia & China, as all other lands & yslandes alredy discovered, & hereafter to be discovered by Edward Fenton. And to the intent he may be furnyshed of all & all maner of such necessaries as therunto shal appertayne, We therfore let you wyt y^t we have auctorized & appoynted and by these presents doe give ful power & authorytie unto our sayd servaunt Edward Fenton & to his suffycient deputye or deputyes, to presse, levye & take up for us & in our name for owre only servyce in all place or places of this our realme of Englande and other our Dominions as well wth in the franchyse and liberties as w^t out, all maner of shippe & shipps, vessele & vessels, mariners, soldiers, gunners, shipwryghts, smiethes, & carpenters, and all other needful artificers, workmen & labourers, such as shal be thowght meet and expedient by ye said Edward Fenton to furnyse ye sayd ships & shipping & vessels for the viage afforsayd. And also all maner of cariages as well by sea as by land or freshwaters, post horses or horses, for our reasonable wages and payment to be made in y^t behalf. And further we doe give suffycient and absolute power and auctoritie unto ye sayd Edward Fenton his lawful deputye or deputyes, to receave and take into his or their charge, ordre, rule & government, aswell of the sayd ships, shipping & vessels, as allso his whole company to be appoynted for his servyce, and them and every of them to order, rule, governe, correct and punyshe by imprisonment & violent meanes, & by death[1] yf the greatnes of the fawlt and necessytie shal so deserve, upon obstinate w^t standing suche orders and articles as are delivered by us or by owr Councell; and also them and every one of them, to conduct, employ and lead by himself, his lawful deputye or deputies unto every such place or places as to his or their discretion or discretions in the said viage & ye said land of Cathaia, China and other ylands, to be discovered by hym or them shall be thowght meet & expedient, for this our sayd servyce: and so many of

---

[1] The power of execution which Fenton possessed under the Broad Seal was carefully hedged about in the Instructions (see p. 52), but he more than once threatened to hang men out of hand (see pp. 72, 183).

the sayd companyes, of what nature & qualytie soever they bee shall leave to enhabyt and dwell in and uppon the same land by hym discovered, according to such orders & articles, as in y^t behalf shall be delyvered unto him, by us or by our Councell yf yt shall happen y^t our sayd servant Edward Fenton should dye, which god forbyd, before the full accomplyshment of this our servyce, y^t then our wyll & pleasure is y^t such person or persons as shall be by us or our Cowncell nominated and appoynted to succeed in his place, shal have the full power and lyke auctorytie hearby, for ye execution & government of this our servyce, as to ye sayd Edward Fenton in all respects as now commytted by vertue of this our Commyssion. Provided always y^t our sayd servant Edward Fenton or his deputye or such as shal succeed hym as aforesaid, shall not by vertue hearof take up any principal man y^t is very meete & expedient for our own servyce in ye warres, nor to presse levye or take any more parsons than suche and as many as shal be necessarye for our sayd viage. Wherefore wee wyll & commaund you & every of you by these presents to be w^t all care and diligence ayding helping & assysting to our sayd servant, & to his sayd deputye ye berer hearof, in ther due execution of this our commyssion as you & every of you shal tender our plesure and will answer to the contrary at y^r peril. In witness hearof we have caused these our letters to be made patents. Witnesse ourself at Westmynster ye second day of Aprill in ye four and twentyth yere of our regne. *Per breve de privato sigillo.* Powle[1]

On ye back yt was thus endorsed: A Commission granted, unto Edward Fenton Esquire. Powle.

Additional Instructions[2]

. . . for ye navigation outwards and [to China it is] thought convenient by their honno^rs that some [may be] expresslye appointed to remayne behinde under the g[overnment of Mr] Carleile. yt may therefore please their honno^rs to provide

---

[1] Powle was presumably Thomas Powle, one of the Chancery clerks.

[2] As the Endorsement (p. 62) indicates, this note was a request by the Commissioners for more explicit directions about Carleil's powers as governor of the party to be left in the Far East.

[what number to] them maye seeme most expedient, and of y^t number wch shall [be chosen] to be added to the abovesaid 200 to sende their expresse [promise] unto the Commissioners being at Southampton viz. Mr Ughtred [Alderman] Barnes & Mr Towerson: y^t accordinglye the same maie be very [ready to the] performance of this intended discoverie by land.

Item to ye ende y^t the said Capt. Carleile may with the better order [and good] government procede in this action, yt maye likewise please their [Honours to] geve ye said Carleile such direction, commission & aucthoritie as unto [officers] in the like affaires is ordinarily prescribed & graunted, whereby he maye [be able to] kepe his owne people comitted to his charge in so muche ye bettar discipline & good order of living. As also to know howe to employe and behave hymself in ye said action to the full liking & satisfaction of ther Honn^{ors} desires in this behalf.

Furthermore y^t yt will please their Honn^{ors} to send their letters of direction addressed to Mr Fenton and the whole nomber of his Assistantes and to every one of them that they shall geve all helpe and furtherance possible to the advauncing of this intended voiadge and discoverie by land of the East partes of the world, in assisting the said Carleile and his company w^t all suche necessaries as by them maie be convenientlie spared, as w^t shipping, victualls, armes, munition of powder & shott, merchandize and any other suche like thing as shalbe fytt to be used in this action, but in suche competent quantitie as the two greater shippes maye well spare w^{t}owt putting them selves in the wante or neede of any thing of importance that maye [serve] for their spedie and safe retorne homewards.

[*Endorsed:* A note of certayne defects in the instructions & preparations for the viage to Chyna etc. to be supplied.]

[*Leicester and Walsingham to Fenton, 11 April 1582.*]^1

To thes instructions when they fyrst cam to my syght was annexed an other letter, the coppy wherof folowth.

^{1} This was in answer to the previous note, but could hardly have satisfied Carleil.

To our verie loving frend Mr Edward fenton captaine and generall of the companie in the viage to China and those parts, . . . [A] matter very requisyte is [to make nomin]ation of some fyt persone in yor [company to be] left at y^r returne behynd you in China [and Cathay] and to remayne ther not only as an [agent to] vent such commodyties, as carrid now w^t you be distracted at y^r departure from thens home, and in steed of them to receave other commodyties of that countrey, to ye use of al the adventurers, but also to acqueynt hym self w^t ye language & cond[ition] of y^t people, as also w^t ye commodyties wch those cun[tries] ther about do yeld. whereby ye successe of this viage hearafter may prove more prosperous. Wee doe now in this behalf sygnify unto you, y^t Mr Christopher Carliel is by us thowght a meet man for this purpose and therefore we doe nomynate hym to be lefte behynde in maner & sort afforsayde, w^t whom also we think meet, y^t some others, such and so many of y^r company be left as ye sayd Carlyl hym self w^t the assent of you ye general of this viage and of the greater part of ye assistants shal make choise of to the ende y^t they also may lerne ye language maners etc. of y^t cuntrey.

Moreover wher in ye sayd instructions wee had forgotten to appoynt Peter Jefferie & Thomas Baynem of y^r cumpany to be of ye number of y^r assistants in this viage for y^t we doe understande them to be able men to serve in the viage, as well for language as for other experiences,[1] being also themselves adventurers each one of them in good portions in this jorneye we do nomynate them in so ample sort assystants unto you as any of ye other before expressed in the instructions, requyring you to accept and use them. And albeit ye L. Tres. hand be not to this letter by reason of his absence at this present from this place yet that the whole contents hear of be not lesse since and regard w^t you and all others joyned in assystance w^t you in this viage, then yf ye same had been conteyned in ye body of y^r instructions: for soe yt is her ma^{tyes} pleasure you sold account of this o^r letter and

---

[1] Peter Jeffery had some knowledge of Spanish. Baynham did not sail, owing to ill-health.

soe we commend you hartely to god from the Court at Greenw^{ch} the xith of Apl. 1582.

Y^r loving frends

R. Leicester

Fra. Walsyngham.

Accidents of alteration[1]

For the performance of all things aforesayde our General and ye merchants were very careful so to deale in ye execution of the busyness y^t nothing shold be in anye poynt swarving from thes directions, and yet notwithstanding on addition of ye fourth barque, so great was ye provision of all things y^t myght ether serve for o^r comfort by ye way or for our credyte at the journey's end, y^t all our ships were very deeply laden, espetially ye admirall, and yet some of the saylers complayned y^t she had not y^t shifte of cabling and cordage, as to ye length of hir viage and greatness of hir burden was convenient, this being a thing of all other carfully to be provided, synce all other necessaryes as they say & myght be boroed by ye waye, but as for ropes, a man wold not impart them to his own father when at ye sea.

Whyle thes things were a doing by hampton, word came y^t capten Carleyl was kept back by an ague,[2] whereof very many were sory, but espetially the tydings did troble mee, because I reposed more comfort of ye viage in ye hope of his good curtesy, than I did in many other lykelyhoodes of advantage, and had determined w^t my self also to have remaynede w^t him wherever he had stayd whyle god wold geve me leave, but yet I trust all for ye best. Upon ye notyce of his refusall, Mr Generall, & m^r Alderman Barnes did appoynt Mr Nicholas Parker to all suche preferments & charges wch by commysion wer to Mr Carleyle assygned. And also wher our admyral ship was in ye Commission called the Beare Galleon they thowght it wold be a name more sownding & significative to cawl her the Galleon Leicester, according to the honorable title of hir Lord & owner. Farther where there is mention

---

[1] This note is a personal one by Madox himself.
[2] See p. 42.

made in ye instructions of 2 chests, one to be kept in ye Galleon the other in the Edward, Mr Alderman Barnes told us that he had receaved of the Councell but one box, and therfore prepared but one chest w^t three loks, wherunto openly he put ye box & locking ye same agayn delyvered yt to o^r generall, and M^r sheriff Owtreed gave ye 3 keys to Capten Ward, Capten Hawkins & to mee.

1582. April 29. The fyrste weyinge of anchors[1]

These things being ernestly in hand Mr Sherif Owtreed (whom we fownd bothe wth curtesy of entertaynment and otherwyse to pleasure us) according as by ye Cowncel he was requyred,[2] mustered ye whole cumpany at his howse and receaving every mans frank promyse of wylling endeavour in ye service, commended ye action unto us, and yn a shortt and good pythy exhortacion dyd declare unto us, the favour of hir Ma^{tye}, ye bent of her Cownselors, our dutyes by the way, and hope of our returne, and then delyvred ye whole charge to Mr Edward fenton o^r generall, yn presens of Mr Alderman Barns & Mr Towrson who did also take noe smal paynes to see all things in ordre dispatched w^t noe lesse hast for ye preparation & tyme, than w^t advised care for ye safety and well ordering of the whole cowrse. So y^t on Sonday the 29th of April 1582 the rather to get all our men together aboord wch notw^{t}standing the straigte looking to of our generall, were ever slynking w^t back errands to ye shore, they thowght not amysse yf conveniently yt might be, to waye anchor & faul somewhat lower from ye towne, where fore our generall, whose care was y^t fyrst in all thinges gods name myght be blessed, and next y^t noe good opportunytye shold be overslacked, invited both them & Mr Owtered, ye Mayre of hampton and ye whole fleet to dynner aboorde the Galleon wher he appoynted me to preach and to handle such matter as I thowght meatest for ye tyme. wher according to ye grace geven me from god, from ye fyrst verse of ye 24 psalme I beat out ye tryal of 3 questions, fyrst shewyng how lawful a thing was travel & meerchandyse, and y^t wee had best ryght to y^e

[1] See p. 83.   [2] See p. 36.

Indyes,[1] next y^t wee myght w^t safe consciens honestly trafique among the infideles making exchange of ware, how ever some think y^t we cary owt necessaries, and bring home superfluyties,[2] lastly y^t ye appoynted tyme of a mans life can not be shortened, althogh he encownter w^t a thousand perils.[3] wch questions debated I exhorted every man to religion and manhood, & shewde how both these must be knyt up in love & so ended. W^ch doen after wee had dyned wel and byd many a harty prayer both for hir Maj^tie and for hir Cowncel and for many of our good frends by name, our Anchors were wayed, and we fell down w^t a tyde to Cawshot,[4] wher wee rode ye next day taking yn such things as weer wanting.

1 May 1582. Our second waying at Cawshotte[5]

On May day when we had taken yn as wee supposed al, our necessyties and gote our whole company aboorde, ye generall, Mr Alderman, Mr Towerson & Mr Castlyn tooke agayn the last mouster of them & left ye fleet thus ordered:

In the Galleon Leicester	Edward fenton generawl
	William Hawkins lieftenant
	Nicholas Parker capten at land
	Richard Madox Minister
	Miles Evans ⎫ merchants
	Matthew Tailboise ⎭
	Christofer Haul master
	abowt fourscore sailers
	24 necessary men beside
	and a dozen of boies

[1] The arguments Madox might use to support this proposition can only be conjectured. John Dee had set out in 1580 the Queen's claims to the North-West, based on King Arthur's conquests (Cotton MS Augustus I. i. 1).

[2] This argument was used in *The Libel of Englysh Policye* written about 1436, and was commonly repeated.

[3] The hour of every man's death was foreknown and decreed by his Creator, a belief which bred a fatalistic attitude.

[4] See p. 83. Fenton says they dropped anchor in Hamble Hole, off the mouth of the river Hamble.

[5] Printed by Wagner, *Drake's Voyage*, p. 452.

In the Edward
- Luke Ward viceadmirawl
- John Walker minister
- Randol Shawe ⎱ merchants
- Peter Jefrei ⎰
- Thomas Pearsie master
- abowt 54 for sailers
- 16 necesarie men beside
- and 8 boies

In the frawnces
- John Drake Capten
- Wylam Markam M^r
- 14 saylers. 2 boys

In the Elisabeth
- Thomas Skevington Capten
- Rafe Crane M^r
- 12 saylers 3 boys

When this muster[1] was taken we wayed again in ye name of god, & after we had fawlen a leage toward ye wyght Mr Alderman Barns & his company took ther leave, whom w^t teares we commended to god bequething both them & al other our owners, hir maieity and our selves to ye protection of ye almyghtie & so according to ye posey of ower ship: *Under the conduct of Christ wee forowed the seaze.* And when ye next day we had shot of the nyeldes, a southwest wynd aryzing put us in agayne to ye wyght wher we contynued plying of & one, sometymes at yarmowth & sometymes at ye Cows for the space of twenty days, yn wch seazon for ye better ordering of ye whole viage both in good exercyse & in advised keeping of company, the generall delyvered to eche vessel severall instructions the coppy wherof hearafter followeth.

A Copie of our Articles [*2 May 1582*][2]

Certen Articles, set down by Edward Fenton Esquire Captayn generall appoynted by Hir ma^{ty} for the discovery of

---

[1] The numbers in this roll are 41 above the prescribed 200, while the so-called 'travellers', including Wilkes, Gilman, Cotton, Symbarb, and 'M. Dore', are not mentioned. For a more complete muster see p. 157.
[2] See p. 58. Fenton sent these (his own) Instructions to the three other ships on May 2.

China & Cataia by ye southward to be observed by ye whole fleet & cumpany under his conduct & government

1 Fyrst for as much as in no action can be looked for any good event or successe wher god is not syncerely & dayly honored, you shall therfore cause to be sayd twyse dayly aboord y^r shipp the usual service appoynted by hir m^{ty} in the Church of England.

2 Item y^t you & all those under y^r charge geve due reverence to suche as be appoynted ministers of gods holy word w^tin this fleete upon payn to be punyshed for doing the contrary according to the qualyty of the offence.

3 Item y^t you suffer noe swearing, dycing or cards playing, or other vayn talk w^tin y^r ship upon payn y^t any one offending in any of those crymes, being by curtesy warned of those faults and wil not leave them off shall be punyshed sharply for ye same.

4 Item y^t yf any one of what cawling or condicion he shal be, shal conspire or goe about by violence or otherwise, to take away ye life of ye generall, his lieftenent viceadmirall or any other appoynted in auctoritie under hym wherby that viage may be overthrown or hindred, he or they so offending & being detected or convinced therby by sufficient proofe, shall receave punyshment by death for ye same[1]

5 Item you shal folloe the admyriall as well by daye as by night, and geve so carefull & diligent attendance of hym as in noe wyse you loose his company,[2] and y^t after he shal show forth his lyght in ye poope by nyght all men to to foloe hym and no man be so bold as to go before him, w^towt his lycence or appoyntment, upon payn of pynyshment for the same

6 Item that every morning by 7 or 8 of the clock you shall not fayl yf ye wether serve you to speak w^t the admirall, and in the evening about 7 of the clock to do the lyke to understand his further pleasure

7 Item you shal not ether by day or nyght so nygh as you can

---

[1] Nothing is here said of the safeguards laid down in the Instructions, p. 52 above.

[2] The hazards of the sea made this injunction impossible to observe. That regard must be had to the weather is recognized in Items 7 and 8, which demand a twice-daily hail and a maximum distance of an English mile between the ships.

be further off from the admyrall than the distance of one englyshe myle or so near as you may be w^t y^r safetynes.

8 Item y^t if ye admiral shal happen in ye nyght to put owt towe lyghts than you shal speedyly repayr unto hym & speak w^t hym.

9 Item y^t yf any myschance shal happen unto you by day, you shal presently shoot off one peece and yf by nyght you shal doe the lyke putting also fawth 2 lyghts

10 Item no man shal geve chase to sayl or sayles w^{t}out appoyntment of ye Admiral, upon payn to be sharply punyshed for doying the contrarye

11 Item y^t yf any man come up to hayl his feloes in ye nyght & knoe hym not, shal geve hym this watchword 'yf god be w^t us', the other being of our fleet shall answer 'who shal be against us': to ye end y^t any straunge shipping happening into o^r companyes, warning may be presently gevin to ye admirall, ether by hym or the next being of better sayll

12 Item y^t yf by storme or evil wether we shold be seperated, as god forbyd, then you shal dyrect y^r cowrse for ye islands of ye Canaries to ye southwest of ye ysland cauled Gomara, wher you shall lye off and one ye space of 7 dayes, and yf in y^t tyme we happen not to meete, then you shal direct your cowrse from ther to ye yles of Cape de verde & to remayn & stay ther abowt ye ylands of Bonavista or Maie

13 Item ye better to knoe on an other afare of, after we shal happen to have been so seperated, you shal upon ye discrying one of an other, so far as yt can be wel discerned, stryke and hoyste the mayn topsayl twyse together very speedyly.

14 Item y^t yf any shal descrye land by day y^t he presently geve warning by shooting of a peece of ordynance & putting owt of his flag: yf by nyght by ye lyke warning & putting farth of 2 lyghts, & stryking of all his sayls he hath abrood.

15 Item y^t yf wee shal happen to be trobled w^t any thik fogs or mysts, & therby have cause to ly at hull, ye admyral shal geve warning by a peece and showing of 2 lyghts one above an other and at his setting of sayl shall doe the lyke, being not cleere.

16 Item yf ther shall happen to be any mutynous or

disordered person w^tin y^r charge, you shall keepe hym in safety til he may be browght aboord ye admirall to receave such condygne punyshment as belongeth to so great an offendowr

17 Item y^t upon putting furth of an ensygne yn ye wast of the admirall & shoting of a peece, ye resydue of ye fleet shal repayre presently to hym & understand ye generalls plesure

18 Item y^t yf wee shal happen to encounter or meet w^t any enemyes, y^t so nyghe as you can you attend ye admirall in such sort as you may rather defend y^r selves than be offended of ye enemyes

All thes articles & what others shall be found necessary for the benyfyte of this service, I requyre in hir ma^tyes name, and as you will answer ye contrary at y^r perills, faythfully & truly to observe the same. Dated afore yarmouth aboord the Galleon Leicester, the ij of May 1582

Edward Fenton

xxi Maie 1582. Oure ferst settinge in to the sea.[1]

Munday the 21th of maye the wynd somewhat harting yn to ye northeast, we put owt luckyly (as I trust) into ye sea, and stopping certain tydes, by thursday folowing, wch was the ascension day we wer gote almost to ye sterte,[2] wch when we cold not wether (ye gale bloying stiff at ye west) we turned to Dartmowth & rode in ye range, wch place not being comodious as the wether fel owt, cawsed us on Saturday folowying to turne up to Torbay, wher we rode 5 days after.[3] hear Mr Whode, one of our pilots began muche to mislyke w^t all ye tackle of our ship, espetially w^t ye want of cables, wherupon, as I think, he was sent by o^r General to Sir Frances Drake for some furnyture, but well I knoe he came w^t Cables & ropes to us in a fysher boat from Plymmowth, & wyne that Sir Francis bestoed on us. he brought also a letter to Mr Hawkins, in some discowrtesy taking yt, y^t wee wold staye hear, and myght as well have been at Plymmowth, of wch fawlt to excuse hym self Captayn Hawkins purposed to ryde

[1] See p. 86.
[2] Start Point. It was May 24 (see p. 87).
[3] Until May 31 (p. 87).

to Plymmowth, but the Generall was loth he shold, yet notw^{t}standing he was very desyrous. And now no sooner was he gone away, on thursdy ye last of may, but ye wynd comyng ye northwest we set sayl in o^r cowrse, and by fryday morning had gote past the Stert. Theare when dyvers dyd request y^t wee myght have edged nye unto plymmowth to take in the leiftenent & other that were a shore, ye generall wold not graunt yt; because, sayd he, they see ye wynd & more meete yt is they make some shifte to come unto mee than I to hynder my cowrse for them. mr whode, one of our pylotes, being an open-mowthed feloe, began hearat chafingly to swear, and cawlyng to ye Frauncys, willed hir to stand yn for m^r Hawkins; but ye generall forbad yt, whereby grew great gratching & choler, but anon ye wynde meeting us at west southerly enforced us of necessyty to plymmowth wher we rode in the sownd.

hear Mr Hawkins cam aboord, and requested o^r generall to go ashore, but he refused.[1] than returned he back w^t the Plymmowth men, taking yt unkindly y^t the generall shold not of curtesy do ether Sir Frances or hymself y^t estimation, as to geve hym credyt before his own people, and yn my conjecture yt wold have been a great cause of love and contentment, wher contraryly things fel out w^t bytternes and gratching. For one ye moroes mornyng ye wynd fomyng fayr, the m^r [2] requested twyse y^t he myght send ye pinnase a shore for ye cumpany y^t was ther, but when yt cold not be grawnted, yet seeyng the importunes of ye matter, sent yt notw^{t}standing. Anon ther was shot of a warning peece and after the generall comanded to way anchor, but when ye saylors fyrst had lyngered & after flatly denayed, the general in choler

---

[1] Hawkins had ridden across from Torbay to Plymouth. It was in the forenoon of Friday that Thomas Hood tried to have the *Francis* sent into Plymouth Harbour to bring him back. At 3 p.m. (p. 88) the wind changed and Fenton was forced to anchor in the Sound, when Hawkins came aboard and invited the General to pay a courtesy visit to Drake, which he refused to do. The two chaplains supped ashore that night, and at 4 a.m. on June 2 the wind came fair, when the General tried to leave without the large party of Drake's men (and presumably other Plymouth men) now ashore. Madox's more uninhibited account of the matter is to be found on pp. 163–5.

[2] Hall behaved tactfully throughout.

demaunded the cause, answer was made y^t yn as muche as ech man went upon his venter, they wold not runne headlong into an unknoen coast w^towt those pylots that were appoynted by ye councel, adding moreover that M^r whood fownd hym self so much aggreeved, y^t he wold not returne agayne tyl he knew how he shold be used, the general bad them wayh up anchors, or he wold hang up hym y^t refused.[1] The m^r than pacifyed ye mariners w^t gentil words, requesting them to way & to spread a topsayl in ye wynd, y^t ye absent myght make ye more hast, & promysed to lynger for ther takyng yn. so did they, but when we had lyngered abowt an howr w^t a flyttering sayl, and cold not see them come we spread more canvase & away wente cheere. The viceadmirall cam after and so dyd ye Elizabeth, but nether cold we see the pinnayse or the Frances. Abowt noone Capten Ward came aboord the galleon, requesting o^r generall to cast abowt for ye rest of our cumpany the generall answered y^t they owght to have geven better attendance. Captain Ward replying sayd y^t fel not now so muche in consyderation what they shold have done, (for y^t was manifest) but the thing beyng alredy past what was best for us to doe, adding y^t wynde we myght have commodius hearafter, but men shold we fynde noe more being once hence departed. to this the generall rejoyned y^t he wold go into fawmowth and ther take up a new supply of saylers to furnysh our complement, but when yt was declared y^t ther they wer not to be had, & y^t ye generall saw all men very lothe to goe w^towt the cumpany, he was content to stand back, so y^t abowt 2 hours after the frances came w^t ye leiftenant, ye pilotes and ye rest, having left behynd them one henry kyrkman whom they accused of yl behaviour towards them.[2] Our generall cawled them & as many of his assystants as were aboord into his cabyn, and soberly admonyshed them of ther fawlts, axyng Mr whood wherin he fownd hymself aggreeved y^t he shold speak such words as he had doen to y^e

[1] Hall again saved the situation. He was accustomed to the violence of Frobisher (Document 1), and already had some experience of Fenton's unbridled temper. The crew depended for their wages upon the financial success of the voyage, i.e. upon 'spoil'.

[2] Hawkins complained that he lost face by the defection of his servant (p. 277).

disquyeting of ye whole cumpany. he answered agayn y^t he thowght great scorn not to be cawled to cownsel about waying ye anchors at all tymes, but when Mr Hall had excused hymself thereof declaring y^t hytherto y^t thing had needed no delyberation, for every man saw & knew what was to be doen on this coast, but heerafter he shold be cawled yf yt wold please hym. The generall seeing some weaknes thowght better to knyt up things yn love, than now to begyn w^t punyshment, and therefore exhorting us al to frendly agreement, pardoning & promysing to forget this fawlt, w^t shaking of handes they wear all dismist. I pray god grawnt us harty love among our selves & a reverent regard of duty towards our owners.

junij 2° 1582. The Processe of our viage from England,[1]

On Saturday nyght being the second of june, we last set eye on the Lyzard of Ingland: wherfore on Whyt-sunday, not w^towt teares in our prayers, we comended the safety of hir majesty & ye councel, the muscovy merchants, & all our frends, to almyghty god, desyring that after ye honest dispatch of o^r busyness, we myght at o^r returne fynd them in safety. W^ch god grawnt. And so w^t a good north wynd we held our course (as I suppose by ye direction of furdinando) sowth-west & sowth, purposyng to passe between the yland of Launcerote and barbary, the cause wherof (being much out of our way) I can not guesse (althoe we wer born in hand that they went to fetch an east wynd) but y^t some of ye leaders were carid w^t hope to meete with a Carvel of sugar & canarie wynes: for descrying on saturday folowing a hulk at ye sea, wonder y^t was to see on what an edge every mans teeth in maner wer set on, seeking by all means possyble a cause and quarel to hir, pretending fyrst y^t she was a french man of war, and many other reckoninges, but ye general wold not consent to offer them any wrong, and on ye moroe being trynyty

---

[1] The ocean voyage had now begun. Madox was right in questioning the course run. A sailing ship should make as much westing as possible to avoid being embayed in the Bay of Biscay, and pass to the west of the Canaries, not between those islands and the mainland as Ferdinando proposed (B. T. Somerville, *Ocean Passages for the World* (1950), p. 48).

sonday when both I in ye gallion & Mr Walker in ye Edward, had spoken in o^r sermons ageynst this pretence, & shewed openly ye purpose of o^r viage, & exhorted them to performe ye same w^t an honest care of upryght dealing, many fel to a private gratchyng hearat, and those of whose conscience before, we had good hope dyd not styck to affyrme openly y^t wee wer bound in duty to spoyl all papists, as enemyes to god & our soverayn, of what cuntrey so ever they were. wch begynning brought us into some fear what yssue this eger desyre of them myght bring w^t yt. when we were thwart ye straytes Mr Owtreads ship cauled ye brydget wch hytherto had kept us cumpany now departed from us southwest toward Tenaryfe, we holding due sowth, by hir wee sent letters to Ingland as our last farewell.[1]

On Sunday ye 17 of june in ye mornyng wee had syght of ye canaries, and fynding ourselves to ye west of launcerota and almost past yt, so y^t our fyrst purpose cold take no effect, we bended now more to ye west leaving both yt and Forteventura on ye larboord, came shooting between grawnd Canary & Tenaryfe, by ye 20th of June we had passed ye Tropique of Cancer, sayling stil at pleasure before ye wynde, but now began to be many speeches among us, some fynding fault w^t ye Elsabeth, of whom they desyred to be ryd, some greevowsly accusyng Richard Grafton y^t had dealt yl w^t us for all kynd of provision, espetially green billet, & fusty meale, some complaynyng for lack of water, by reason y^t o^r ships being fyrst pestered w^t muche lumber, cold take yn but smale quantyty therof at Ingland. wherfore the tyme being fayre, & somewhat caulme ye general cawled on Mydsomer day his assystants together, to take advyce of such things as shold be needful.[2]

Junij 24th 1582. The first consultatione heald in the Galleone Leicester on midsomer day, at 2 degrees of longitude & 18 of northern latitude.

Being athwart Cape Blanco w^tin 18 degrees of the line of equalyty, yn as muche as the generall had appoynted the

---

[1] Documents 40, 41, 42.   [2] Document 43.

yslands of bona Vista or Mayo, to be places of our meeting yf any misfortune should sever us, and in as muche as many were desyrous ther to refresh them selves and to be furnyshed w^t water, the sea beyng peaseable & lyttle wynde, he assembled aboord the Galleon those whom yt pleased ye cowncel to appoynte for assystants unto hym in this action & when we wer come together he shewed us wrytten in a paper 2 questions to be consydered of in this maner.[1]

24 junii, 1582 matters to be consydered of as followeth, viz:

Latitude 18. 1. To see what cowrse wee shal hold from ye yslands of Cape de Verde & what tyme wee shal remayn ther for o^r watering.

2. To see ye barques provided of all things necessary, as well w^t victuals as w^t cardes & platts.[2]

When he had red these questions and proceded into some discourse of his owne opinion in the case, at last he put us to consyder whether yt were best water at thes ylandes or noe, and yf wee thowght so requysyte, than to wch ysland wee shold goe, & so gave me the paper to wryte every mans reason & opynion.

These questions as I ymagined being somewhatt intricate, because on thing was set down & an other thing was proposed, & ye question also y^t was proposed stoode on 2 poyntes, I wylled them fyrst to answer what they thowght of ye watring at these yslands and yf hearof they dyd agree, then myght be thowght upon wch yland was fyttest for our servyce.

Hearunto Capt Warde answerethe y^t in as much as he had aboord hym, in the vyceadmirall, very smale store of water and y^t very unwholesome & corrupte, and because the companye myght ye better fresh themselves both by washing of ther clothes & by rumedging of the ship, wch was scarsely yet in any good trym, and because also those victuales wch the barques wanted myght be put into them, he thowght yt needfull espetially at some of thes ylands to water.

---

[1] Document 35, Item 3.
[2] Fenton wished to keep the small ships dependent on the *Galleon* for necessities (p. 68, Item 5).

Captayne Hawkins was also of the same mynde adding moreover y^t wher dout was made by ye generall whether wee shold hear fynd any water or noe, y^t the hyndraunce wold not be great to seeke and yf we fownd any then myght o^r desyre be performed, yf not wee myght the sooner be goene

Thes reasons wer lyked of all the rest particularly, and wee were all desyrous y^t so yt myght be, wherupon the generall adjoyned his consent, althoe he seemed wylling to have goen further.[1]

Than for the place wher, and wch of these ylands, wee referred to the pylots, who told us bona Vista was ye fyttest & moste lykely place, so y^t wee all fully determyned yf pleased god to seeke Bona Vista.

Then touching ye furnyture of the 2 barques, because wee knew not how far god myght by tempest or otherwyse separate them from us, nor how soone, & y^t we cold not leave them in such cases utterly distressed, yt was therefore fully agreed upon by general consent, y^t at bona vista they shold tak yn owte of the shipps victuals for three moneths over and above y^t portion wch they had aboord alredy, and y^t they shold be thorowly provided of all other ther wants what so ever.[2]

This being doen the generall cawled the pylotes, demawnding of them y^t yn as muche as wee were to passe into ye sowtheast sease by ye Cape of good hope, wch was ye best place of rende vow next after this watering, who affyrmed y^t the ryver of plate was ye best and the only place y^t they knewe, upon this informatyon the generawl consenting pronownced y^t yt shold be soe. but Mr Walker not well lyking hearw^t, desyred the generall y^t this matter myght also be proposed to the delyberation of his assystants, partly because he supposed this place to be far out of our way, partly because being come thither wee shold be caried ether by necessyty or by pretences, agaynst our commission to passe throwe ye straytes of Magellanus wherunto he saw many throe desyre of purchase as they cawl yt, much enclyned. The pylotes hearunto constantly avowched y^t of necessyty they

---

[1] The General was overruled, but in fact later got his own way (p. 79).
[2] This was done on June 26 (p. 91).

must come w^{t}in a hundred leagues of this place to fet a wynd to cary us to ye Cape of good hope, and comyng so nye by constraynt yt wold be no hynderawnce at all, the case ryghtly consydered to put yn w^t the ryver, both to refresh our men, and to furnysh oure watring, syth other harboroe than this they knew not til wee shold come to the yle of Java, wch was a long streche. This peremptory speach by those y^t professed knoledge hearin, cut of Mr Walker, and other of us y^t were lothe to have tuched in America because whatever myght be objected was answered w^t wyndes and tydes and currents and reconyngs, wch fel not, as they sayd, into our consyderations. Wherfore to this poynt also wee wholy consented and subscrybed our names as hear followth.[1]

Ed. Fenton, Luke Warde, William Hawkins, Nycholas Parker, Richard Madox, John Walker, Myles Evans, Randolph Shawe, Mathew Taylboys, Peter Jeffreys.

When I had of all this made a breif note in y^t paper wch ye generall had begune, I told them y^t the thing must be presented in a booke at our returne before hir maiesties ho: Cowncel and willed them therfore y^t in respect of the disordered handelyng I myght digest yt in my booke according to there true meaning althogh yt shold some what differ in wordes and y^t than they wold set their handes to the booke, but in any case yt cold not be graunted y^t other coppy shold be taken than ye original, wherfore for the better credyte of this boke, I have annexed at the end therof all those oryginal copyes wch are fyrmed w^t our own handes.

At this present also Captayn Parker in as much as ye general had appoynted hym in stayd of Captayn Carleyl to have the ordering of all at ye shore, requested y^t he myght be alowed to choose hym self a leiftenent and corporalls for the better performance of his service, hearunto was answered by the generall y^t so many officers in such smale cawses wold but make ye common shares in ye ende to fawll short, to wch he replyed y^t rather than y^t objection shold take place he wold

[1] While it was true that the sailing route to the Cape brought a ship near to the north-east shoulder of Brazil, the correct procedure was then to work south until the westerly wind was caught for the Cape. The River Plate lay far to the south-west of this course (Map A, on p. xxvi).

77

owte of his owne share alowe a charges unto his offycers, but ye generall rejoyning told hym that he knew as yet no great land servyce but to fet in a barico of water at a tyme of neede wch myghte be doen w^t out any such ceremoney. As for leiftenent, he wold suffer noe more in the fleet than his owne, and w^t that wee arose, and for this tyme departed.

June 26. 1582 Latitude 16° Of the Islands of Cape de Verde.

On Tuesday morning being the 26th of June wee descryed land in ye west of us wch some sayd was bonavista, some sayd La Sel, but when in the afternoon we had anchored in a fayre bay on the sowtheast syde of yt our pylotes pronownced playnly y^t yt was bona vista, but yet confessed that they were never hear before, nether knew whether we shold therin fynde water or noe. Wherupon the general was in purpose to be goen, but when I perceaved the drift of thes good men to be suche, y^t bringing us to an exigent of water and beverage then must we be constreyned to fil yt in wher ever wee meete w^t yt, and when our fethers were once lymed in pillage, and our handes anoynted w^t spoyle, wee wold not styck to chop up from the fyngers endes to ye hard elboes (wch was the doctryne that they dayly tawght) and when I perceaved y^t ye whole fleete began greatly to gratch and murmure at so sodayn departure, w^{t}owt any tryall, contrary to determination and appoyntment: I advysed ye generaul to send his pynasse ashore, certyfying hym y^t wher ther be such fayre woodey hills, ther was also to be fownd in some parte or other sprynges of fresh water, hearupon Captayn Ward in one pynase and captayn Parker in an other were sent to make serche, w^t store of men and municion among whom I was also crept to see what wold become of the matter. but when wee had rowed abowt a myle, one of our people espied a cupple of goates w^t long beardes, advauncyng themselves on ye syde of a sandy hil, and a lyttle kyd after them, streyt wise ech gave other warnyng to beware, for ther were towe harnesed men on horseback & a dogge folowing them. Than was he cownted the manlyest soldier y^t cold lyft his buckler hyest over his head, and plant his peece in best redynes.

To conclude whether yt were ye dread of thes goates wch I suppose, or the rut of ye shore wch they then aledged or any other meaning wch is hydden from mee, but at ye shore our boates came not, notw^tstanding Captayne Ward sent owt 2 of his men, wch swam·aland and broght us word back of a fayre river, of plenty of goates, of some great cattel, but no evident sygne of people: w^t this tydinges we returned aboord seing by ye way fysh & byrds in great abundance. When the general hard y^t ther was such a rut at ye shore, that he myght not easyly land his boates, he determyned not to stay hear because wee were now before ye sone, and yt wer jeperdy both of tornadoes, of qualmes & of contrary wynds yf ye sone throe our lyngering shold overtake us.[1] This being appoynted, on the morow cam the viceadmiral complaynyng greatly y^t we shold so depart in as much as he stood in some distresse of water, wherfore ye generall goyng aboord hym & fynding y^t true, gave hym a tune of water owt of the Galleon and so in ye name of god as I hope wee proceaded forward on our viage.

Junij 27. 1582. From the iles of Cape de verde to the Coast of guinye.

On thursday ye 27 of June we wayed anchors, having a fayr northren wynde. The master wold have had us kept due sowth,[2] but our pylots wold needly dyrect our course to the sowthsowtheast affyrming y^t of necessyty we must fet an east wynd upon ye coast of guyney, or els cold wee never get throe, for otherwyse great daunger ther was lest on ye sodayn wee myght be embayed on the sholes, wch lye betwyxt the ylse of ascension & Cape de los baxos, on ye coast of bresyl, wch was not past 700 leagues of, or therabowt.[3] These and such lyke reasons constantly & sternly avowched by thes old beaten saylers set me & others new to schole. Ymagening for

---

[1] The sun on June 27 (according to current reckoning) had a declination of 22°47′, which was decreasing, and the ships were in lat. 14° N. They should have kept west of the Cape Verde Islands to avoid these climatic dangers, whereas Bona Vista is one of the most easterly of the group.

[2] Hall might safely have said west of south. To approach the coast of Guinea was fatal if they did not wish to get becalmed.

[3] Madox is here writing ironically, for these shoals of Abrolhos are in the South Atlantic (see Map A, p. xxvi).

certayntye y^t ether Aeolus or Neptune dyd keepe ther martes at appoynted places, wher wee myght purvey and furnysh our selves of such wynds as sholde be necessary for us, but whether this poynt of doctryne be not always fyrme or whether we were unworthy to fynd yt true, I knoe not, but according to the pylots speach ye master was overruled, so w^t ye larboord tack aboord wee hawled to ye sowthsowtheast and on st peters day being ye 29 of June, being w^{t}in 14 degrees of ye lyne wee mett with a south wynd so y^t we were constrayned to runne fyrst upon one boord & after on an other w^t smale advantedge a great while, meeting ye wynd most comonly sowth and sowthwest, so y^t ye northeast wynde whom our pilots heald in an obligation, upon very negligense had broken his Bond, nether cold wee devise in what cowrt best to sue hym, nor w^t what maner of wryt unlesse yt were a Latitat[1] unto Boreas, who thoe he be head borowe & high sherif of the seas yet is he so lynked in kyndred w^t this defendant y^t wee cold hope but for a cold shuyt in so desperate a cause.

Of our people some began to wax syck & some dyed.

July 20. 1582. The first sight of the land of Guinea and a consultation.

Latitudo septentrionalis 6. Uppon fryday the 20th of July after we had for 4 or 5 days together runne upon a south east boord having ye wind at sowth west and by sowth we descryed in the morning a very high land at east north east, beyond ye expectacion of our pylots, wch land they deemed to be ether Capo de Vergas or Capo de palmas.[2] but the generall not meaning to tuche upon yt gave warning and cast to the off-ward wch when ye viceadmiral espied he came aboord us w^t his master & his pylote wyshing y^t wee shold rather stand yn w^t some harborowe for the relief of our companye than to lie bweltyng[3] at the sea w^t owt advauntadge. The generall

---

[1] A writ which supposed the defendant to lie concealed (*O.E.D.*). They were encountering the south-west monsoon which normally blows during the summer months towards the West African coast.

[2] These two capes lie nearly 350 miles apart.

[3] This word is not in *O.E.D.* Its sense is tacking idly to and fro.

therfore both to be advized thearin and also to lern some certenty of ye place, cawled ye master & pilots & some other to shew ther reconyngs & platts, who did somewhat dowt of ye place but supposed y^t we were w^{t}in 4 degrees of ye lyne by accownt of ye ships, for ye sune nor star had not been taken yn 10 days before.[1] The leiftenent & Mr Whood who had coasted this place before & Blaccollar affirmed it to be cape de palmas, but Mr Evans & I wch wold gladly have shewed some lyklyhoodes why we cold not be soe nye ye lyne, were cut of w^t peremptory pronunciations, as thoe thereby we cawled ther knoledge in dowte & so incurred the penalty of presumption. After this question was thus concluded wee grewe in some speach of watering hear. The general was lothe to go aland in any place uppon ye coast of Guynye, fearing as he sayd lest ye contagion of the cuntrey wold rather be the occasion of more sycknes to his people than any recovery of strength. Mr Hawkins told y^t Sir Frances Drake even in this monethe and w^{t}in 2 days of this tyme watered at ye Serra Liona and fownd no annoyance at all. Mr Whood sayd yt was a villanous place for while Sir Francis dyd ther stay to water they set on ye potage pot w^t ryse every meale. Mr Hawkins added moreover y^t his uncle had comended this place unto hym. The generall replyed y^t hear his uncle had lost many men. I was of opinion y^t sometyme when men were so lost as was not expedient for all the world to knoe yt was a very probable report to saye y^t ye contagios murran of the shore had baned them. and wher the Portingals speak evil of yt I rather commend their wyts than beleeve ther words wch seeke to make all other men afrayd to serch owt y^t wherein them selves fynd sweetnes & comodytie, and into this mynde was I browght the rather for y^t I cold never hear grownd of reason why or how yt shold be so unholsome, but only bare wordes wherunto I cold geve but bare credit. Our master perceaving y^t none of ye pilotes knew ye shore aright, was desirous rather to keepe the sea than to fawl in to a road wher both our men & tackle myght be jopardised.[2] M^r ferdinando

---

[1] I.e. there had been no check on dead reckoning.
[2] The dangers of the coast were notorious.

sayd y^t the portingales do water & vitayle hear from January to May but further he knew not.[1] When ye generall saw many desyrous to water and y^t ye south wynd stood so stiff in opinion as ten Nestors[2] cold not have persuaded hym to yield an ynch of his hold, wherby we were out of hope to gayn owght at the sea, the generall demaunded whether yt were better to keepe the east shore or to hawle back agayn northweaste to ye sera liona. Mr Hawkins shewed y^t ye farther we trended eastward the more daunger were wee yn both of embaying and of qualmes, nether did any man ther knoe place of herberowe. But to ye serra liona myght wee goe w^tout losse of way & in a qualme ryde w^thowt hazard or w^t any land breeze put of to our advantedge. Mr Evans desyred y^t wee myght hold on to ye eastward wch was our way, not dowting but by advysed cowrse wee myght w^t this wynd duble ye Cape of good hope.[3] but Blaccoller told hym that in so doing he myght be put into a bay & then lye half a yere w^towt wynd or water, for the current, sayth he, setts to the land and ther is not a breth of ayr sturring. This did ye other pilots constantly affyrme, being lyke to Vergills fame w^ch *Iam [deceptum] ficti pravique tenat qua inducia[e] veri*, and althoe of these matters they knew not much, yet when so ever the cape of good hope came in talk, as thoe ye name of good hope had put them owt of all hope of pillage, wch was the thing they desyred, the pylots ever in Pylates voyce cried crucifie. and thear voyces prevayled for the generall appoynted to go back to serra Liona except ye wynde changed to further us in owr way. And upon this resolution he dismissed ye company, not commytting this as an act in ye register because yt was but a familar debating between hym & ye pilots espetially, althoe other present were bold to utter what they thowght.

July 21° 1582. Of certaine things wch fell owt after this time.

When wee had runne all nyght to the northwest on

---

[1] I.e. before the summer monsoon replaces the north-east trades.
[2] A Homeric hero, famous for his age and wisdom (*O.E.D*).
[3] Evans was wrong, as explained above (p. 77, n. 1), but he was anxious for the voyage to take its prescribed course.

Saturday abowt noone the wynde meet us agayn at ye sowthwest wherupon ye general cawsed to turne our course and put up agayn for the ryver of plate, but now in putting of & on we were on all sydes so embayed w^t ye land y^t ye master had work ynoghe to cleere hymself of yt. Nowe happen unto us dyvers qualmes.[1]

[*Ends*]

Document 37

Sea Journal of Edward Fenton in the Galleon Leicester[2]

Aprill 29° 1582. Emanuell.
Sonndaye the xxixth of Aprill after we had served god and dyned betwixt ij & iij of the Clocke in the after none we sett saile with the winde at n.n.west from Netley roade and cam to Ancour in hamble hoole,[3] the harbour lieth Sowtheast and N.W. next hande.
Monndaye. The xxth daie we staied to dispatch manie things in hamble hoole.

[*May* 1582]

Maie. Tewesdaye the first of Maye abowte ij of the clock in the after none the Commissioners[4] departed and we sett saile

---

[1] The record breaks off abruptly. According to Madox's Private Diary (p. 173) the ship was headed WNW on July 21, but according to Fenton's Journal (p. 94) she only made four leagues in that direction and then took an easterly tack. Madox reckoned any course towards the west as designed for the River Plate. The African coast here trends from north-west to south-east.
[2] Magdalene College, Cambridge, Pepys MS 2133 (second section; unfoliated).
[3] Hamble Hole.
[4] The members of the Muscovy Company (Barnes, Towerson and Castlyn) and Sheriff Oughtred.

83

with the winde at n.n.e and cam to Ancour before yarmouth in the Wight in vij fathoms iij leagues and thence tooke in our longe boates.

vj & vij fathoms on ye W. side of the Needells

Wedensdaie, the ij^{de} of Maye we waighed Ancour earlie in the morninge with the winde at n.e. & by n doubled the Needells abowt viij of the Clock in the morninge, and having brought them n.est of us directed our course S.W. & by S. havinge litle Winde, sente instructions[1] aborde the other Shipps, abowte x of the clock we were to be calmed and the winde comminge southerlie and to the west wardes, were forced to putt in to yarmouth roade againe.

Thursdaie. The iij^{de} daie havinge litle winde in the morninge we staied to see what winde the slake water would bringe us beinge then at southest & by S litle winde, and in the afternone it blew much winde at S.e, upon the floode. that it was thought good to staie till the morninge, being withall verie fowle weather all the night.

ffrydaie. The iiijth daie, verie tempestious weather the winde at S & by e, so that it was sayle worthie if the winde would have served.

Satterdaie. The vth daie in the morninge faire weather but much winde the winde at S & by W., in the afternone were forced to waigh our Ancours & com for the Cowe where we ancored with evill weather.

Sonndaie The vjth daie contynued at the Cowe with ill weather the winde at S.S.e, in the morninge I writt to Sir Edwarde Horsey, and sent the Maiors sonne of Sowthampton home & walked to see the Castle of the Cowe much dekayed.

Mondaie The vijth, faire weather aboade still at the Cowe the winde at S & by e, Mr Brown[2] the precher and others came aborde mee.

Tewesdaie. The viijth daie the winde cam to the e.s.e, about x of the clock in the morninge went to way our Ancours and go to Yarmouth roade but we were be calmed with the winde at S & by W and in the afternoone to ancour shorte of that place.

Wednesday The ixth daie be calmed in the morninge the

---

[1] Document 36, pp. 67–70   [2] From Newport, Isle of Wight.

winde all daie for the most parte at S & by e the Pilotts cam from Plymmouth[1]

Thursdaye   The xth daie the winde cam to the S.S.W. & forced us to waigh and go for the Cowe the bettre to save our grownde tackle, I wrote to Sir Edw: Horsey to borowe xx li to serve the generall account

ffrydaie   The xjth daie it blew muche winde with rain & fogg   *at the Cowe*
at the S.S W. we receaved the Comunion,[2] and stayed the Lordes pleaser, wrote to Mr Alderman Barne &c.

Satterdaye   The xijth daie it blew much winde at S.W & by S,   *at the Cowe*
Sir Edwarde Horsey cam to the shoore side and sent for me & lente me xx li for the use of the shipps. Mr Baynham[3] departed &c.

Sondaye   The xiijth daie Mr Thomas Holmes sente me   *at the Cowe*
hogeshead of Clarrett wine, the winde in the morninge at nW & by W, and in the afternoone at S.S e much winde.

Monndaye   The xiiijth daie verie tempestious weather. the   *at the Cowe*
winde at S W & by W. Mr Smith of Hampton sente a rondlett of sack.

Tewesdaye   The xvth daie the winde at W S W, rec' a lettre   *at the Cowe*
from Sir Eddw. Horsey for the bringinge in of the portingall Shipp within the forte[4] & a hogesheade of wine from Mr Olmes.

Wedensdaye   The xvjth daie in the morninge verie calme. the winde all abowte in the afternoone at S S W in the eveninge rayned with the winde at N W & by W[5]

Thursdaye   The xvijth daie in the morninge litle winde at S W in the afternoone abowt ij of the clock sett saile from the Cowe with the winde as aforesaid but so smale as were

---

[1] Thomas Hood and Thomas Blacoller, two of Drake's men, appointed pilots of the *Galleon* and the *Edward* respectively.

[2] This was the occasion of the first complaint lodged by Captain Skevington of the *Elizabeth* against his master Ralph Crane; see p. 102.

[3] Baynham (an elderly man) retired for reasons of health. He had audited the accounts of Frobisher's voyages. Sir Edward Horsey was Governor of the Isle of Wight.

[4] The ship was 'likely to be stolen away by the knaves in her', wrote Madox (B.M., Cotton MS App. XLVII, ff. 20v–21).

[5] Madox (loc. cit., f. 21) reports that an officer 'came w^t a broad seal to stay Mr Boze (Bowes) tuching some conveance of land made amysse . . . the company in ye Edward were glad to be ryd of so grosse a man & so great a chest'.

forced to ancour abowt viij of the clock in Yarmouth roade.[1]
ffrydaye The xviij[th] by iiij of the clock in the morninge
beinge readie to sett saile & the wind at e.s e it chaunged
sodainlie to the Sowth & S & by W and so remayned till the
afternoone & then at S W & by S, with much winde as were
driven to the Cowe againe for savinge our grownde tackle.

Satterdaye The xix[th] daie, litle winde some times at S and
by e, and some times at S W & by S.

Sondaye The xx[th] daie verie Calme till a xj of the Clock, and
then we had the winde at e & by S wayed & sett saile but were
becalmed before we had past ij leagues with the winde at W.

Monndaye The xxj[th] daie sett saile from Grornerde[2] roade at
viij of the clock in the morninge the winde at N e and were
cleare of the Needells at a xj of the clock havinge brought
them n e. by e edged to the sowthwards, M[r] Bowes[3] cam to
me with lettres & for his things were a shoore & behinde I
was at his desier forced to sett him aborde a boote at the
Needells. abowte iij of the clock in the afternoone were

*the cost lieth
e by n, n.e, &
W.S.W, 4
leagues*

becalmed havinge St albons pointe[4] W. of us, and so
contynued till 5 of the clock at what time havinge no winde
and the floode undre foote cam to Ancour thwarte St Albons,
at midnight we waighed driving with thebb and cam thwarte
Portlande at vj in the morninge and for wante of winde
ancored there to stempe the floode.

5 Leagues

Tewesdaye The xxij[th] daie at vj of the clock cam to Ancour
thwarte Portlande havinge no winde to chase at 12 of the
clock at Middaie sett saile with the winde litle at S and by W
cam to Ancour to stempe the floode at 20 fathom havinge

4 Leagues

brought Portlande e. and by S of us, and at Midnight wayed

[1] Madox (loc. cit., f. 21) reports that on this day John Hawkins gave
them news of the great Spanish fleet sent out for the Moluccas (p. 161).
It was then actually in Rio de Janeiro.

[2] Gurnard Bay, two miles south-west of Cowes Castle.

[3] 'When we wer come to hurst castle, y[e] Elizabeth being behind shot
off a peece and stroke sayle, w[ch] put us in a dowtful mervel, but when we
had stay[d] y[t] was M[r] boze was now come agayn, and desyred y[e] pynnace to
stay for his chest w[ch] was comyng to Yermowth by water, but our generall
wold suffer noe stay wherfore he was set on shore in y[e] Wyghte and when
he was ther he cried unto the bots ging to take pytty on him and to take
hym back w[t]owt his chest but they refused' (Madox, loc. cit., f. 22).

[4] St Albans (or Aldhelms) Head, on the Isle of Purbeck.

our Ancour & sett saile with the winde at W.n W., wente N.
Wedensdaye The xxiij[th] daie cam to Ancour betwyxt v & vj
of the clock in the morninge thwart Apsham[1] and no winde 3
leagues, & at xij of the Clock sett saile with the winde at S &
by W, cam to Ancour thwart the Berrie[2] 6 Leagues, and then
at midnight sett saile with the winde at N W by N, Laye
W S W to Doble the Starte

Thursdaye The xxiiij[th] daie at vj of the clock in the morninge
havinge the floode in hande cam to Ancour thwarte the
Starte, havinge brought the same W.n.W and Dartmouthe
n, n, W from us with the winde at W & by n, at Middaie we
sett saile in hoope to doble the Starte, but the winde blew
much at W S W , and forced us into Dartmouthe Range
where ancored.

ffrydaie The xxv[th] daie it blew verie much winde with greate
stormes at W S W, we staied in Dartmouthe range, sent my
Pynnasse a shoore to be repaired[3]

Satterdaie The xxvj[th] daie we Ancored still in Dartmouthe
range with the winde much at W & by S, & at W S W.

Sonndaye The xxvij[th] daie. abowte iiij of the clocke in the
morninge the winde was at S stormye. We waighed and cam
to Torbaye and there ancored, havinge much Winde & Raine
at S W & by S, sente the purser to Sir ffr. Drake for Cables &c.

Monndaye The xxviij[th] daie. the Winde in the morninge at
S.S e. & moste parte of the Daie at W & by S. & W & by N.

Tewesdaye The xxix[th] daie the winde some times at N W, at
W N W and N W & by W, verie cold & tempestious, still in
Torbaye.[4]

Wedensdaye The xxx[th], the Winde at W N W and N W by
W, blew verie muche Winde, at midnight the purser reatorned
from Plymouth with Cables & other provicions.

Thursdaye The laste of Maie, abowte viij of the clock at the
night the winde cam to the N & n ne We sett saile ymmediatlie

---

[1] Topsham, on the Exe estuary.
[2] Berry Head, Torbay.
[3] 'Sending o[r] men ashore to mend o[r] boat, at nyght blancker & his felo
carpenters wer missing, & while y[e] rest sought for them they wer al taken
by y[e] watch and layd up' (Madox, loc. cit., f. 22).
[4] 'Frye [a quartermaster] was set in the bilboes for lying ashore'
(Madox, loc. cit., f. 23).

from Torbaye and abowte midnight cam thwarte the Starte the winde at N.W. This daie my Lieutena*n*te[1] wente to Plymouthe.

[*June* 1582]

ffrydaie The firste daie of June abowte iiij of the clock in the morni*n*ge we were thwarte Sawcome. litle winde at W n W, and abowte iij of the clock in the afternoone wi*t*h the winde at W S W we putt into Plymouth Sownde[2] where we ancored. Satterdaie The ijde daie. abowte iiij of the clock in the morni*n*ge the winde cam at N N W. We made readie to waigh, sent my Pynnasse a shoore for my Lieutena*n*t and the heade pilott,[3] who reatorninge not unto me, [I] sett saile with my for topsaile abowt eight of the clock, Leaving the ij Barks to row in o*u*r men, and for that they bothe sett saile, and the Elizabeth but followed, bringing in none of my companie, I cast abowte for Plymouth againe abowte one of the clock in the afternoone, and abowte iij mett the ffrau*n*ces and rec. in my companie, and so directed our course S W & by S, having the Lizarde n.n W of us abowte a xj of the clock in the night wi*t*h the winde at n n e 14 leagues. from thence till vj of the clock in the morni*n*ge[4] S W & by S vij Leg'.

3 L from the Lizarde

Sonndaie The iij[d] daie we rann from vj in the morni*n*ge till vj the nexte daie V watches S W & by S and one watche S S W, 25 leagues.[6] In the watche after midnight we mett a Newcastell [ship] wantinge water & victualls &c who we relived wi*t*h bothe.

the winde ene, SW & by W 36 L altitude[5] 47.48

37 L, SWbS

Monndaye The iiij[th] daie we rann from vj of the Clock in the morni*n*ge till vj of the clock the next daie vj watches S W & by S   37 L

---

[1] William Hawkins.
[2] This was necessary because the wind changed, but for the events of this day see pp. 71, 163.
[3] Thomas Hood.
[4] Fenton, who had hitherto observed civil time, beginning the day at midnight, now changes his reckoning, starting the day at 6 a.m.; but he later reverted to the normal sea-reckoning, i.e. noon to noon (p. 92).
[5] The term 'altitude' was still used for latitude north of the equator measured in degrees and minutes.
[6] The day was divided into six watches of four hours each. For the method of reckoning the ship's run, see p. 297.

Tewesdaie The vth daie we sailed from vj of the clock in the morninge untill vj in the morninge the next daie SW by S 30 L. altit. 46.30
SW & by S.
30 L

Tewesdaie The vth daie we sailed from vj of the clock in the morninge untill vj in the morninge the next daie SW by S 30 L.

altit. 46.30
SW & by S.
30 L

Wedensdaye The vjth daie we sailed from vj of the clock in the morninge till vj the next morninge S S W, 35 L,

SSW, 35 L

Thursdaye The vijth daie we sailed from vj of the clock in the morninge till viij at night S S W. 10 L, and from thence till vj of the clock in the morninge the next daie Sowthe 15 L, Tooke ordre for the locking upp of the Stewarde rowme after the Companie served for the preservacion of our victualls; and the Kayes brought into my Cabbon by the quarter masters.

SSW 10 L
S 15 L

ffrydaie The viijth, we sailed from vj of the clock in the morninge till vj in the morninge the next daie S. 35.

S 35 [L]

Satterdaie The ixth We sailed from vj of the clocke in the morninge till vj of in the morninge the nexte daie S 20 l, mett with a hoolk from St Lucar laden with salt, told of us of preparacions of Shipping to meete the West Indias fleete from the same place.

S 20 L.

Sonndaie The xth We sailed from vj of the clocke in the morninge till vj of the clocke in the morninge the next daie S, 9 L.

S 9 L.

Mondaie The xjth We sailed sailed from vj of the clocke in the morninge till vj the nexte daie in the morninge 25 L S.

S 25 L
altitude 38

Tewesdaie The xijth We sailed from vj of the clocke in the morninge till vj the next daie in the morninge S, 36 L.

S 36 L

Wedensdaie The xiijth, We sailed from vj of the Clock in the morninge till vj the next daie in the morninge 35, the Bridgett[1] departed.

S 35 L
the starr in 34

Thursdaie The xiiijth, We sailed from vj of the clock in the morninge till 8 at night S, 21 L, from thence till vj the nexte daie in the morninge S S W, 15 L. sawe a flyinge fishe.

S 21 L.
SSW 15 L.
foggie weather

ffrydaie The xvth We sailed from vj of the clock in the morninge till 4 of the clock the next daie in the morninge S S W 36 L.

36 L SSW
foggie weather

Satterdaie The xvjth daie by 4 of the clock in the morninge

---

[1] Henry Oughtred's ship which had kept them company hitherto. She carried their letters home.

we discovered Launcerott one of the Islandes of the Canaries sailing S S W and the same bearing S S E of us, cast abowte and went E. for ij glasses,[1] but the Lande trendinge so farr to the eastwardes by reason the winde & currunte were not hable to doble the same, but ymmediatlie rann S W & by S. & SW all the daie longe to fetche upp forteventura bering 30 L, Longe. and so to run betwixte him & the Grand Canarie, spending the all the night in that sorte of & on, havinge verie foggie & hazie weather.

being s e &
4 L, from the
Grand canarie.
had neather
variacion nor
declinacion[2]
SSW 17 L

Sondaie The xvij[th] we sailed S W & by W alonge the Grand canarie till vj of the clock in the afternoone. at what time we altered our course and wente S S W, having brought the Grand canarie e.n e of of us 5 L and Tenerif n w & by n, sailed till 8[3] of the clock in the morninge 17 L.

altit' 27.55
SSW 36
Parkins died

Mondaie The xviij[th] we sailed from viij of the clock in the morninge till viij the next daie S S W 36. L, tooke downe our maintopmaste and fished it, old Parkins dyed.

SSW 24 L.

Tewesdaye. The xix[th], We sailed from viij of the clock in the morninge till viij the nexte daie S S W 24 L,

SSW 5 L,
S & by W 30
L. The Starr in
23.25

Wedensdaie The xx[th] We sailed from viij of the clock in the morninge till xij the same daie SSW 5 L, and from thence till viij of the clock the next morninge S & by W. 30 L.

S & by W 28
L Y[e] starr in
21

Thursdaye The xxj[th] daie, We sailed from viij of the clock in the morninge till viij the nexte daie S & [by] W 28 L. Sawe the Crossiers.[4]

S & by W 26
L ye starr in
20. Ric. Salte
dyed.

ffrydaie The xxij[th] daie, we sailed from viij of the clock in the morninge till viij the next daie S and by W, 26 L. This daie the sonn rose at e.n e, & ij degrees to the north wardes, made the daie xiij howers & 20 minitts Longe. being in the Latitude of 21 degr. & 10 minitts. finde by the globe that the sonn at London rose the same daie at halfe a pointe to the N e and sett at within halfe a pointe of the N W.[5]

---

[1] Probably 'half-watch' sand-glasses taking two hours to run.

[2] The compass variation was believed by some theorists to be zero in Grand Canary. By 'declination' Fenton may mean the 'dip' or vertical inclination of the needle as observed by Robert Norman. In neither case was his statement correct.

[3] Fenton now starts to reckon the course from 8 a.m. to 8 a.m.

[4] The Southern Cross (see p. 300).

[5] A pair of library globes appears to have been part of the normal

Satterdaye   The xxiij[th] we sailed from viij of the clock in morninge till viij the next daie S & by W, 32 L.

S & by W 32 L the starr in 19.5 m

Sonndaye   The xxiiij[th], we sailed from viij of the clock in the morninge till viij at night S & by W. 14 L, from thence till v in the morninge SW, 10 L, from thence till viij W SW 4 L. Sate in Councell[1] aggreed for watering at Bonavista, victualling the Barkes for 3 months, and appointing our next wateringe place at Rio del Plata.

SW b. W 34 L SW. 10 L W.SW 4 L

Monndaie   The xxv[th], We sailed from viij of the clock in the morninge till 4 of the clock in the afternoone W S W. 10 L, and from thence till viij in the morninge W, 22 L.

WSW 10 L W 22 L.

Tewesdaye   The xxvj[th] abowte ix of the clock in the morninge we discovered Bonavista, Lying S W & by S. and N e & by n, and abowte one of the clock in the afternoone cam to ancour on the Northe parte therof in 14 fathom faire sande. sent owt presentlie ij bootes to view the land & to serche for fresshe water, but by reason the surge of the Sea went high on the shoare our boots could not Lande, onlie ij men swam to shoore discovered water which was brakish.[2] Putt in three monthes victualls into the ij Barkes.

this Islande is full of Goates & salt petre & supposed to be Litle inhabited.

Wedensdaye.   The xxvij[th], I stopped a leake in the Powder rowme in the Gallion, sent instructions aborde the Shipps, waighed ancour abowt ij of the clock[3] in the afternoone and so contynued alonge the sowth side of the Islande till viij in the night, and then the west pointe of the Lande bearing N & by W of us 4 L, of we sett our course S.S e, till viij of the clock the next daie 16 L.

n & by W 4 L SSe 16 L

Thursdaye   The xxviij[th] ws sailed from viij of the clock in the morninge. till viij the next daie S.S e 34.

SSW 34 L

ffrydaie   The xxix[th], We sailed from viij of the clock in the morninge till vij of the clock in afternone S. Se 2 L. from

altitud, 13.36.

furniture of the Great Cabin. Given the sun's declination (or its position in the ecliptic) and the latitude it was a simple exercise to find the bearing and the hour of sunrise and sunset. There was as yet, however, no English text-book on the 'Use of the Globes', and this demonstration was probably made by Richard Madox.

[1] For the Minutes of this Council see Document 43; see also pp. 75–7.
[2] See pp. 78–9.
[3] Fenton's sudden departure without watering was interpreted as a means of forcing his companions into piracy to relieve their wants; see pp. 169, 200.

thence till midnight 2 L di S S W. and from thence till 4 of the clock in the morninge S S W 5 L. from thence till midaye S & by W 10 L.

Latitude 12. ½
calme weather
the wind all a
bowte

Satterdaye The xxxth. We sailed from twelve of the clock in[1] the morninge till vj in the afternone S W by S. 5 L. from thence till Middaie the next daie e & by S, 7 L.

[*July* 1582]

1 of Julie.
altit' 12. 20.

Sonndaie The firste of Julie. We sailed from twelve of the clock at Middaie till xij the nexte daie S & by e 20 L, kild iij Sharks.

altitude 11

Monndaye The ij^{de} daie, We sailed from middaye till twelve of the clock the next daie 18 L. S & by e.

altit' 10 5

Tewesdaye The iij^d We sailed from Middaye till the next daie at xij the winde at S W & S S W, & gott nothinge.

altit' 9. ½

Wedensdaye The iiijth We sailed from Middaie till midnight S & by e 8 L and from thence we sailed till middaie upon divers partes of the Compasses havinge muche Raine & no winde.

altit' 8. ½

Thursdaie The vth we Laye from Middaie till twelve the next daie S e & by S. 22 L.

ffrydaie. The vjth. We sailed from Middaie till x of the Clock in the morninge the next daie S e & by S. 14 L.

W 14 L.

Satterdaye The vijth. We sailed from 10 of the clock in the morninge the winde at S, till ij of the clock in the afternone the nexte daie W. 14 L.

Sacrie & Kente
dyed.   Se 13 L

Sonndaye The viijth daie, We sailed from ij of the clock in the afternone till twelve of the clock the next daie S e. 13 L.

Se & by e 12
L.

Monndaye. The ixth daie We sailed from Middaye till twelve the next daie S e & by e. 12 L.

W & by n. 12
L, ye starr.[2]
7. 15

Tewesdaye The xth daie We sailed from Middaye till twelve the next daie W & by N. 12 L.

---

[1] Fenton now adopts the normal period of sea reckoning from successive noons. He was meeting contrary winds and making little headway.

[2] It was unusual to take the latitude by the North Star within nine degrees of the equator, for horizon haze makes observation difficult. But they had been without a reading for five days, and had no sight of the noon sun for many days subsequently.

Wedensdaye The xjth daie We sailed from Middaye till viij *put downe some of our ordynance.*
of the clock in the morninge W & by N. 10 L.

W & by N 10 L

Thursdaye.   The xijth daie We sailed from viij in the *E & by S 20 L.*
morninge till middaye on fridaie E & by S 20 L.

ffrydaye.   The xiijth We sailed from Middaye till twelve the *E & by S 12 L.*
next daie E & by S 12 L.

Satterdaye. The xiiijth We sailed from Middaye till iiij of the *W 8 L.*
clock the next morninge W. 8 L. and from thence till xij. 4 L *e.se 4 L.*
e.S E.

Sonndaye. The xvth daye, We litle winde much Rayne & *S.Se. 5 L.*
fogge till xij of the clock the nexte daie wente S S e 5 L.

Monndaye. The xvjth daie. muche Rayne & fogg We sailed *Se. 24 L.*
from Middaye till the next daie at xij of the clock S e. 24 L.

Twesdaye.   The xvijth daie rayne & fogg we sailed from *Se & by e 20 L*
Middaye till twelve the nexte daie S e & by e. 20 L.

Wedensdaye.   The xviijth daie stormye we sailed from *e.Se. 24 L*
Middaye till twelve the next daie e.s e. 24 L.

Thursdaye. The xixth daie. We sailed from Middaie till ix of *e & by S 20 L.*
the clock in the morninge the next daie E & by S 20. L. at *the wind at*
what time We discovered the Cost of Gynnye Lyinge e.S e & *S & by W.*
W N W.

ffrydaie The xxth daie. abowte ix of the clock in the morninge
We discovered the cost of Gynnye the Lande Lyinge e S e,
& W N W. and the winde at S & by W. litle, cast abowt &
Laye N W & by W, sente for the Captens & maisters aborde.
to have their opinions What We Were best to do;[1] Capten
Warde with his Master & Pillott of opinion to goo for Serleon[2]
aswell to water there, as relive our companies being sick. the
residue of my assistanntes in sorte aggreinge therunto: and I
consentinge to the same, so as either the harbour might be

[1] For the discussions held on July 20 see pp. 81–2. The pilots and
masters were seriously out of their reckonings, partly because of the
seasonal change of winds and currents of which they were unaware.

[2] Sierra Leone was one of the earliest landmarks on the West African
coast whose position was established by the Portuguese. It was considered
to be in 8° 20′ N. Drake had watered there in 1580 on his return voyage,
and hence young Hawkins and the two pilots boasted that they knew all
about this coast. Cape Las Palmas was reckoned by seamen as in 4° N,
Cape Vergas as 10° N. The notorious Shoals of St Anne lay off Sherbro'
Island.

obtaignned (which was dowtfull in respect we we were shott to the Eastwarde therof) or our Companies relived for their healthes, consideringe the contagionness of the Coast, subiect to sicknes, Calmes and great Rayne, wherof We had stoore with contynuall foggs, as in x daies before, We Were not hable to take sonne or Starr, and therfore uncertaine with *thus* what parte of the Lande we fell: onlie by our recknings

abowte the Latitude of 4 degrees & di: the Lande showinge in this forme.[1] and, supposed by the pilotts of Sir ffrauncis Drake's to be the river of Seste;[2] havinge a greate race of tide thwart the same; Abowt iiij of the clock in the afternone the Captens & maisters departed to their Shipps, We had much Raine the Winde cam at S W & by W & we Laye. went till xij the next daie S S e 20 L.

our soundings were 65, 90, & 60 fathom black oze N W by W 3 L. Se, by e 16 L.

Satterdaye the xxijth daie we sailed from Middaye havinge much Raine & litle winde till foure of the clock in the afternone. We wente N W & by W 3 L, from thence till twelve the next daie S & by e. 16 L.

The winde for most parte at S S W.

Sonndaye The the xxijth at Middaye We cast abowt Laying it W & by N. sawe lande e & by N of us. sownded & had 55 fathoms black oze & gravell. and so contynued our sowndinge till 4 of the clock and had 90 fathoms stremye grownde & so till viij and then afterwardes we found no grownde at 120 fathoms: wente till xij the next daie 26 L. W N W.

WSW. 24 L the winde at S & by e

Mondaye The xxiijth daie, the Master at Middaye went in the Boote to sownde and founde grownde at 350 fathom by Lettinge fall a smale Ancour or graplinge, and therby discerned the Corrante to sett (as he saide) from the west, which was the cawse as (I suppose) We Were contrarie to our workinge & course forced on the Coaste of Gynnye and our Shipps 60 Leagues before us & our Recknings:[3]

---

[1] See above, p. 81. Among the first lessons of an apprentice to the sea was profile-drawing, since errors in dead reckoning were notorious, and landmarks were relied upon where possible.

[2] The River Cess (or Cestos), in 5° 25′ N; *Rio dos Sestos* in the Portuguese charts.

[3] This discovery of the equatorial counter-current which flows from west to east was disconcerting to the theorist, who considered that ocean

We sailed from Middaye till xij the next daie W S W. 24 L.

Tewesdaye. The xxiiij[th] daie. abowte a xj of the clock in the forenone our mayne topmaste brake vij foote above the mayne mast & brake our mayne topp, We sailed from Middaye till xij the next daie. W S W 26. L.

altit' 5.10.
WSW 26 L.
the wind at S
& by e.

Wedensdaye. The xxv[th] in the afternone we gatt up our maynetopp (god be praised) well amendid makinge readie to have upp our maynetopmast the next daie, sailed from Middaye till xij the nexte daie. S & by W, 20 L.

S & by W 20
L altitude 4.59
winde at S.

Thursdaye The xxvj[th] we sett upp our maintopmast received a lettere from M[r] Walker mencioninge the sicknesse of their Companie, lamentinge our not wateringe, at the Isles of Canaries or Cape de Verde, (havinge now been from Englande not fullie ij monthes) and therefore desiers a Councell with the next daie. I had will to aunswer by mouthe if weather had served, beinge sorie for their necessities, but not willinge to seeke releif in Gynnye, wher it was more liklie it shold have hazarded the healthes of the whole Companies, then recovered the few in daunger.[1] Besides that the weather grew faire and winde served to go for our appointed harbour; sailed from Middaye till xij the next daie 26 L. S W.

alt' 4.3

SW. 26. L.

ffrydaye. The xxvij[th], we sailed from Midday till xij the next daie S.W. 24 L.

Satterdaye The xxviij[th], I wente aborde the Edwarde Bonaventure, where I founde divers of the Companie infected with the scorvie and founde not above vj hoggesheades water aborde theim, as they confessed; Caried M[r] Banestre with me to Looke of the sick, and presicute things to compforte theim withall,[2] sailed from Middaye till xij the next daie W. 16 L.

W 16 L.
the winde
s.b.e

Sonndaye The xxix[th] daie, we sailed from viij of the clock in the morninge till viij at night e S e 8 L and from thence till viij the next morninge W. 8 L.

e S e 8 L
W 8 L

Monndaye The xxx[th] daie, I wente aborde the Elizabeth to examyn a mutynie there hapned, & fyndinge thoffender

The winde at
SSW & S &
by W

currents were due to the *primum mobile* and, like the heavens, moved from east to west. See p. 173.

[1] See pp. 172, 181

[2] This was the occasion when Fenton intercepted and read certain letters; see pp. 173–4.

punished him at the yardes arme. which brake: his offence was the strikinge of the Masters mate, and it was examyned & punnished in the presence of Capten Parker, Mr Madox, and Christopher Hall the Master.[1] We sailed from viij of the clock in the morninge till viij at night W & by n 12 L from thence till xij the nexte daie at W &. by S 12 L.

W & by n 12 L
W & by S 12 L

Tewesdaye The xxxjth daie, we sailed from Middaye till xij the next daie S e & by e 25 L.

Se & by e 25 L
the winde at S.

[*August* 1582]

Weddensday the first of Auguste The first of August the winde contynewing Sowtherlie so as we were not hable to get to the Lyne; and havinge beaten of & on the space of one monthe, and our water scantinge; I called my Assistaunts together,[2] to have their opinions whether it were necessarie to water or kepe the Seas, who in respect of our wante of water, and in regarde of the contraritie of the windes, held it requisitt to water presentlie; and the rather for the preservacion of our beare and compfortinge of our Sicke men: being thus concluded, We called before us the maisters and Pilotts of the fleete tunderstande their opinions what place they helde most fittest for that purpose. Whose aunswers were, that in respect we founde no water or place certein where to have the same in the Isles of Cape de Verde: Sereleona in Gynny was the most nighest and fittest place for the purpose, unto which place we presentlie directed our Course, having from Middaie till vij of the clock at night sailed e.s e, beinge about vij of the clock at night and Laye N.e., and sailed till xij of the clock the next daie. N e. 24 L.

alt. 4.37.

the winde at S
ese 4 L.
N e 24 L.

Thursdaye. The ijd daie, Edwarde Stooks,[3] and David Evans baker dyed. We sailed from Middaye till xij the nexte daie N.e. 24 L.

Altit. 5.40
Ne 24 L.

[1] The cook, Julian Saunders, had fought with the master's mate, and then leapt overboard. For an account of the incident and its sequel, see p. 174.

[2] For the Minutes of this Council see Document 44; and for details, p. 175. Luke Ward's more detailed narrative (*Pr. Nav.*, pp. 647–72) now begins.

[3] The 'plat-maker' or chart draughtsman. These were the fifth and sixth men to die on board the *Galleon*.

ffrydaie The iij^de daie We sailed till vj in the afternoone e.S e *altit. 6.39.*
5 L. and ymmediatlie discovered Lande as we winded abowt
12 or 14 Leagues of beinge a parte of Gynnye. spente the *The winde at S.*
night till 4 in the morninge windinge Ne, & Ne & by e and
founde our selves within 4.L. of the land. beinge a verie high
Lande & full of woode., & (made the night before to be
Sereliona) sownded & founde, 80, f. black ozye sande, and so
trendinge a Longe to the Northwardes within iij L, & ij L
and Least had sowndinge. 45.35.25. & 14 f. fathoms blacke
ozye sande.

Satterdaye The iiij^th daie, bearinge in to the Shoore N.Ne, *altit. 6.43*
within one League, founde the same to be but a baye,[1] and
havinge the winde at Sowth haled of to the sea NW. the *the winde at S.*
Master beinge then a shoore founde freshe water and 13
fathoms hard by the shoore, brought me Gynny beanes &
other triffles, affirminge the Corrante sett SW & by S and
NE & by N into the shoore. We sailed from Middaie till xij
the next daie W & W & by N havinge for sholdinge till viij at
night 35.25. fathoms black sandie oze, and from thence till
Middaye 15.16.17 & xix fathoms black sandie oze &
sometimes reddy sandes.[2]

And all this time we haled a Longe the shore within j L.
havinge sailed 24 L. with the opinion of some to be Sereliona,
which could not be. by all liklehood, by reason our height
would not answere, either our Charts our altitude, by a degree
& odd Mynitts. We tooke the Sonn in the same daies
whereupon I examyned eche mans Charte aborde me &
found them to aggree in height, but some contrarie, in whom *24 L. n.*
I founde more witt, then conninge skill or iudgmente.[3]

[1] 'A fayre baye called C. de monte', wrote Walker; *C. do monte* in the
Portuguese charts. They had passed Cape Mount (in 6° 37′ N), and the
coast now trended NNE to form a wide bay. See the profiles sketched by
Fenton and Madox (pp. 98, 176). The Admiralty chart of Cape Mount
Bay (No. 2478, from a survey of 1904–5) marks a 'Cotton tree
(conspicuous)' in very much the position of the single tree drawn on the
skyline by Fenton (see next page).

[2] Christopher Hall and Luke Ward took soundings continuously in
these dangerous waters, where there were rapid changes of depth.

[3] Each man made his private interpretation of the observations recorded
in the steerage. In latitude 6° 43′ N their position was more than 90 sea
miles south of Sierra Leone. On the following day Ward took out his
'skiffe', and after anchoring it confirmed the east flowing current.

[This coastal profile, drawn by Fenton off Cape Mount on August 3 or 4, is on the last page of his MS Journal.]

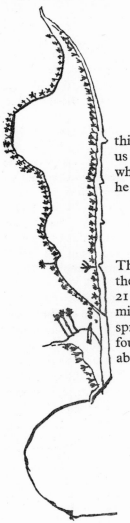

this pointe did bere est and be southe of us when we had 21 fadoms in oze and when we had 17 est southe est and when he did bere southe est we had 13 fadoms

This tre did bere northest when we hadd the foresaid depes the depest which was 21 fadoms we were three quarters of a mile from the shore here we found too springes of freshe water. in this water we found a kanathe and muche fisshe lepinge above water.

Sonndaye. The vth daie abowt Middaie we had some Raine. Which brought the winde upon an instante from the Sowth, to the NNW & divers other points of the Compasses & within ij howers Roinge wee winded S e. We had sowndinge 35 fathoms We sailed presentlie W & by Sowth, kepinge the Lande beinge verie Low Lande & woodie undre our Lee, contynued this course. till 4 of the clock in the morninge. havinge sholdinge some times 35, 25 16. & 17 fathoms black sandie oze. 16 L. and from thence till ix of the clock we bare with the Lande. N.W. with the same sowndinge till abowte a xj of the clock, havinge but xij or ix fathoms white and yellow sand., winding till xij of the clock W & by N our *20. b. W.* sowndinge at that instante beinge ten & ix fathoms white water and white sande, made ij or iij Ilands to the N e of us & so haled the sholdes of St Annes.

Monndaye. The vj^th daie. ran upon the St Annes sholdes till vj of the clock at night in xij. x. ix. viij. vij & vj & di fathoms and Cam to Ancour in ix fathom & di founde the Corrante to sett S.S.W. and N.N e, havinge the iij Ilandes upon the sholdes e & by N from us, and winded W & by N. 5 L, In the *W & by N 5 L.* morninge watche the Barke Elizabeth put to sea by occasion I knowe not, whom I could not see afterwardes.[1]

*altit. 7.14
Heath the
Carpenter
dyed.*

Tewesdaye. The vij^th daie abowte ix of clock in the morninge I cawsed the Barke ffrances to go before & sownde,[2] and if they founde undre vj fathom & di to reatorne or otherwaies to kepe a heade of us. & upon deeper sowndinge to strike their topp saile, which after a mile runinge NW they did and so we waighed our Ancour & sett saile, followinge of them and findinge vij & viij fathoms vj fathom & di. x & xj fathoms, & so to vij againe windinge NNW, We cast abowte. and cam to Ancour in ix fathoms, having Lost sight of theim by [reason] of greate foggs and Raine: shott of ij peices ordinaunce after We cam to Ancour, and ymmediatlie had sight of theim who

*the winde at
SW & by W*

*NW & by W
1 L & di*

---

[1] In fact she had lost an anchor. Ward had been aboard her earlier in the day, but Fenton was always anxious about her Captain's loyalty.

[2] According to Ward, 'M. Hawkins came aboord us, with whom my selfe, our master & pilot had some conference what was best for us to do, and how to seeke a harbour being on a shallow unknowne to us all. In the end we thought good at 9. aclocke to weie, & send the Francis afore, and to get into deeper water if we could' (*Pr. Nav.*, p. 648).

cam to Ancour by us, and not Longe after we had sight of the Barke Elizabeth (the Lorde be praysed) In this time We sailed NW & by W i L & di.

Wedensdaye. The viijth daie. abowte x of the clock in the forenoone we sett saile, directing the Bark ffrances to go halfe a mile before us and to sownde, and by a litle pencill in the mayntopp to give us warninge of her sholdings, viz. eny weave therof standinge for vj fathom. and if she cam undre vj fathom to caste abowt;[1] went v howers, NW 4 L. havinge vij fathoms & di and for most parte 10 and ix & di white sande; and so ran till vij at night for the most parte N, & N & by e havinge in the ende & before we ancored xv fathoms & di at what time we had brought an Ilande caryinge this forme

_ᴖᴧ_ e & by N of us, |then| fynding our selves over the sholdes of St Anne to the Northwardes. Lying to the Northwardes in vij degrees & a terce, large contrarie our chartes. sailed 3 L,: the Eliz. reatorned to us.

N. 7 L.

Thursdaye. The ixth daie. abowte foure of the clock in the morninge we sett saile and for the most parte N e. till Middaie havinge the NW parte of Sereliona upon the heade of us being from the Lande 3 [L] & the Ilandes in this forme

_ₒᴏᴖᴧ___ᴖᴖᴖᴧ___ sowthest & by e and by sowthe, havinge 10 & ix fathoms & di sowndinge and bearing N e. had the ends of the Lande of Sereliona upon the pointe of Ne & by e & Se; cam to Ancour within the firste pointe of Sereliona in vj fathoms & di abowt vj of the clock at night.

altit. 8.8

ffrydaie the xth daie. I wente in the morninge of in my Pynnasse, aswell to view the wateringe place, as speciallie to sownde, for the bringinge in saffe into harbour of our Shipps and, a Longe the Sowtherlie shoore of Sereliona within a quarter of a mile founde, 7, 8, 9. 10, 15—and 16 fathoms, In the afternoone, waighed Ancour and cam into harbour (god be praised) in good saffetie. and Roode in 10 fathom water within fawconett shott of the Wateringe place.[2]

William Burges dyed

Satterdaye The xjth daie, wente to visitt the Companies

---

[1] The *Galleon* drew 17 feet. [2] See Madox's charts (Pls. VII, XII).

aborde iche Shipp and founde manie sick in thedwarde Bonaventure of a swellinge in their knees and mouthes (which is onlie the scorvie): Carried our Caske a shoore and fell to *altit. 8.45.* trym the same and fill water: The Northerlie Lande over against Sereliona as we were & roade in harbour Lyeth next *a northe* hande Northe, and est & by N.: Seraliona lieth W & by *a Northest.* *or verie neare* north and est & by Northe. When you have brought the highest Mountaigne of all Seraliona S & by e of you, you maie comme to Ancour in 10 fathoms good grounde and harde by the Wateringe place. Seraliona is a high Lande. full of woodes & Mountaignes, having manie Wilde bests. as Oliphantes &c and is full of Lymons, Palmitie trees and other straunge herbes. and as it seemeth litle inhabited: betwixte it and the Northerlie lande, which is Lowe Lande & full of sholds is abowte iij Leagues. The mayne River which runneth betwene thies ij Landes, is a goodlie river and seameth to runne farr upp to the S.e.warde.

Sonndaie The xij^th daie, we receaved the Communion and gave god thanks, aswell for his deliveraunce over the Sholds of St Annes, as our saffe arrivall in Seraliona. Muche Raine. the winde at SW.

Monndaye The xiij^th daie, I Called my Assistaunts together[1] aswell to examyn certein wordes tendinge to Mutynie and derogacion of her Majesties aucthoritie (unworthlie Layde upon me) as also against Certein principall officers in my Shipp, made parties by one Ralf Crane, Master of the Barke Elizabeth, who to maintaigne his owne disobedience brought theim in question, as mayntaynours of this faction, as sayinge that if I had punnished him for his disobedience (which before I pardoned) my Master Mate, the Master gonner & his mate. would have throwen the Bilbowes over in contempte of iustice, which by due examynacion they were purged of and he punnished in the Bilboes, but not accordinge to the meritt of the facte[2] he desserved. Washed and made cleane the Shipp.

[1] For the trial of Ralph Crane see Document 45.

[2] 'We by generall consent agreed, that he should be put into the Bilbowes, which was done: but within halfe an howre at mine, and others request, he was upon his submission released. Which done, we dined al

Tewesdaie The xiiijth daie, much Raine in the morninge the winde for the time at NW & by N. I did visitt the whole fleete and followed the dispatch of our water Caske.[1]

Wedensdaye The xvth daie, muche Raine, thownder & Lightninge the winde SW; gott x tonnes of water aborde.

Will Robinsons brother dyed

Thursdaye. The xvjth daie much Raine, Rommaged to bestowe our water & other things in ordre.

ffrydaye The xvijth daie, I wente to fishe. and into a Baye, where growes upon trees infinitt nombers of Oysters upon Trees, verie straunge to behold: which in respect of the straungness and plentie of oysters, I named it Oyster Baye.

Satterdaye The xviijth daie, abowte a xj of the Clock in the forenone we discovered a Canow cominge from theast parte of the River. which showinge a desier of conference. by a flagg of Truce. We admitted therof with the like signe from my Shipp, Wheruppon they cam aborde beinge iij Portingalls havinge traffique in this River for Negroes, Rize and Oliphante teethe; the only traffique (as they informed me) they have in thies partes: And beinge robbed (as they said) of their Carvell iij or iiij monthes before. by certein frenche men, repaired to us for succour of some Barke or Pynnasse, yf we had any we mente to departe withall: The Barke Elizabeth beinge then to be Caste, aswell for certein Broyles betwixt the Capten and a stubborne knave, the Master,[3] as thought insufficiente to be carried or do further service, but to be burned there in harbour: we entred some conference with theim a farr of for the byinge of the Barke. for the which they offred 60 bushells Rize & 400 weight of Oliphante teethe: herupon breathe was taken by us, and other conference entretaigned for the government of the Countrey

Jesper Dowart a merchaunte, & francis frerie Merchant, of St Diago[2] Md. that their traffique is our bridgewater clothes Redd.

with the General, and after dinner, with my boate and skiffe, we went and brought the tree for fishes for our maste into a sandy Baye' (Ward's narrative, *Pr. Nav.*, p. 649).

[1] 'I [Luke Ward] met with M. Hawkins, M. Maddox, M. Walker, M. Lewes & divers others which all supped aland there with sodden Oysters, and a fresh Mullet and Rice Pottage, & came late aboord all hands . . . ' (Ward's narrative, *Pr. Nav.*, p. 649).

[2] For the full story see p. 180. The Portuguese were Jaspar de Wart, a Lisbon merchant, the Venetian-born Francis Freer of Santiago (Cape Verde Islands), and a servant.

[3] Ralph Crane, but see p. 101.

and Rulars: Who enformed me. that one farmr[1] was cheifest
K. and of the greatest power in those partes, and had undre
his subiection and his contributaries two kings of the Northe
side of the River, called, Torria, & Jarima. This farmr, is a
[Sambest?] and dothe warr upon a People Called the Sapps
on the West shore: if he take any Captives of Straungers not
in trade with him, he cutts of their heades, and leaves theim
to be eaten of his People (if they have Likinge): he is constante
and iuste of his worde (as they informed us) but none of the
rest of the K., of the Northe side & Tagovinie is their Cheifest
Towne: The Chiefest Towne the K. of farme hath is called
Carrnorre. stronglie fortified with tymber: his forces be
10,000 persons with Bowes & arrowes, swordes & Targetts
In thende we concluded with theim for 8ᶜ [2] of Rize & 10
Oliphants teethe, Waighinge 500 weight, to deliver the Barke
Eliza: ij Ancours, ij Cables, her Sailes, cordagg, ij buses of
chandels and 20 li of powlder, and this aggreement to be
performed within 4 daies.

Sonndaye The xix[th] daie, much Raine Daie & night with
thonnder and lightninge

Ric: Cove dyed. Wind at SW

Monndaye The xx[th] daie, faire weather, gott in certein
timber for our necessaries, & some water.

the winde at WNW & WSW

Tewesdaye The xxj[th] I wente upp the River a iij L. aswell to
discover the Nature therof, as the sholdings, and founde
12.13.10.7.5.4. fathoms alonge the Se shoore and a place
more convenient to water in then where we did ride. In the
meane time, my Lieutenant & Capten Warde with divers
others beinge a fishinge in Oyster Baye discovered in the
freshe river an Allegatie which the[y] killed with much a do
beinge in lengthe nigh 12 foote: whose skynn I cawsed to be
saved, and his fleshe beinge broyled was like veale, and
savored like Muske to the eaters & smellers therof.[3]

the winde at e in the forenone, & in the after at SW

Wedensdaye The xxij[th] daie, The Portingalls reatorned to us
with the greateste parte of their Rize they were to deliver for
the Barke Eliz: and the Oliphante teeth: which I delivered in

---

[1] Fattema, see p. 108.
[2] 800 bushels.
[3] Walker in his Diary (see p. 203) gives a lively description of the killing
of this alligator.

this sorte, In Rize for the Gallion Leicestre 45 bushells & 300 wei*ght* of Oliphante Teethe. To the Edwarde Bonaventure 30 bushells Rize and 200 wei*ght* of Oliphante Teethe. And to the Barke ffrau*ncis* 5 bushells Rize. [*Margin: Memoranda* that Signior fra*u*ncesco, tolde me that havinge brought the Ilande of Brava WnW off of you, you should fynde sholdinge in 20, 16, & 6 fathoms. to ride in, full upon a freshe river when ys meane water.]

at e   Thursdaye. The xxiijth. I cawsed my boote to be new mended, & made an end of my romagi*n*ge.

winde at SSW   ffrydaie The xxiiijth I ended my wateringe, and gathered Lymons[1]

winde at SSW   Satterdaye The xxvth, I fetched such tymb*er* aborde as my Carpenters had felled for thuse of the shipp.

winde at SSW   Sonndaye The xxvjth, surveyed the furnito*u*r deliv*e*red to my Companie aborde the Gallion.

Monndaye The xxvijth. I stayed for the Comi*n*ge of my rize behinde, & to order & repaire things amisse in my Shipp.

winde at SW   Tewesdaye The xxviijth, I was fayne to unrigg my foretopp and to amende the tressoll trees being brocken: my rize was broughte (saving 3 bushells w*hi*ch they were not hable to p*er*forme. Rec*ei*ved of theim Sold by the merch*au*nts for a brasse pann vjs viijd & xv yardes of hollande at xijd Le y*ar*de, w*i*th an old shirte of Mr Evans,[2] iij q*u*arters of an oze of gould in goodnes of the frenche Crowne, amountinge to a xlijs vjd.

---

[1] For the confidences which Madox received on this day from both Ward and Fenton see p. 180. Everything pointed to a start being made during the next few days.

[2] Luke Ward gives more detail of Evans's transactions (*Pr. Nav.*, pp. 650–1). The merchants were naturally anxious to make trade contacts especially with the native king, but through Captain Parker Fenton kept them from going up-country (see p. 186, n. 2) on the pretence of assuring their safety. According to Madox the merchants asked the Portuguese for only double the value of the goods 'wherew^t ye general was offended & indeed not w^towt cause, for to sel to merchants is no gayn . . . wher o^r venture is 3^s duble our ware, to sel for twyce duble gayne is manifest losse' (Cotton MS App. XLVII, f. 43). Madox also reports that on this day (August 28) 'The general caused to be fyxed fast in a stone at ye watring place a square plate of Copper w^t this inscription and forme: Edwardus Fenton armiger per Elizabetham reginam Angliae classi praepositus ei quae regiones Chinensem et Cathaiam descooperire destinata est. August 26, 1582'. The 'forme' was of a coat of arms with the motto *Rien sans dieu* beneath, and the initials E and F on either side (Pl. IV).

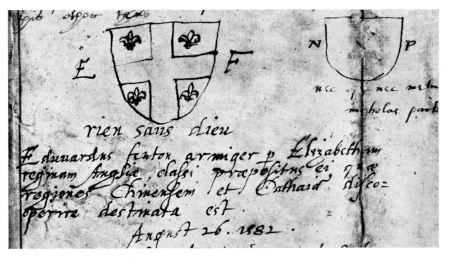

rien sans dieu

Eduardus fenton armiger p Elizabetham
reginam Anglie, classi præpositus ei q ̃ ̃
regiones Chinensem et Cathaiā disco=
operire destinata est.

August 26. 1582.

IV. The copper plate set up by Fenton at Sierra Leone

As copied by Madox; B.M., Cotton MS App. XLVII, f. 43

Madox's entry reads: 'The general caused to be fyxed fast in a stone at y^e watring place a square plate of Copper w^t this inscription & forme.' Nicholas Parker's shield is left blank. (See p. 104, n. 3.)

Wedensdaye The xxix[th] much Raine. labored to ende our *Dom diego de*
tressell trees and gott in our peice of tymber framed to peice *flores with a*
our maintopmast.
wrie mouthe.
generall of the
Bamfora Kinge of Madyrbombe, Sherabola and Sansena, *Spanish fleete*
Kings adioyinge to him at warrs one with an other in the *for the*
beginnynge of the new Moone. *straetes.*[1]

Thursdaye The xxx[th] daie, ended our tressell trees & gott up *at SSW*
our maintopmast.

ffrydaie The laste daie, ended all wateringe & other things *winde at SSW*
and prepared our selves for the Sea. attendinge a good winde.

[September 1582]

Satterdaye The first of September, sett saile with the winde *September*
at Ne. skanted within ij miles Runyng and so cam to Ancour
Sonndaye The ijd daie. sett saile betwixte iiij & fyve in the *the winde a Ne*
morninge with a smale gale at Ne, wente west & W S W till
Middaye. The ij points of the harbour of Seraliona lieth N &
by e & S & by W. And when you have brought the Ilande of

Madrebomba lyinge in this forme ⌒⌒⌒⌒ S & by e
of you, you are cleare of the Rock, having then vij fathoms you
shall come into 15 fathoms, and ymmediatly into 10 & 9 & di.
at iij of the clock in the afternone cam to Ancour being calme.
the wind SSW, 6 L. from the shoore.

Mondaye The iij[d] daie the winde at SSW, bare in againe *Henry Mellars*
with Seraliona, to amende the tressell trees of my Maynetopp, *dyed.*
Ancored 1 L & di shorte of the shoore.[2]

Tewesdaye The iiij[th] daie, we turned in againe for Seraliona,
the winde being at SSW all contrarie, but ancored shorte
3 L havinge no wind to chace us.

Wedensdaye. The vth daie. I cam into Seraliona where I
ancored the winde SSW.

[1] Fenton evidently now had further warning of the Spanish fleet, of
which Don Diego Flores was in general command. On the following day
Ward 'went on lande, and observed the sunne, and made proofe of other
Instruments', i.e. he was preparing to go to sea (*Pr. Nav.*, p. 651).
[2] The defect in the mast appears to have been only an excuse for turning
back. Luke Ward writes that all day the General remained aboard his ship
'which time we discoursed', i.e. argued. On the following day Richard
Madox (p. 181) learned Fenton's plan to return to the Cape Verde Islands
and secure wine by 'purchase'.

Thursdaye. The vj[th], Tooke downe my mayne topp & topp mast, preparinge aswell to fishe my mayne mast, as to repaire and lengthen my mayne topp mast, wantinge vij foote in lengthe. of that he was before he was brocke, and also to make new the tressell trees.[1] fished for an ancour and Cable of thedwarde Bonaventure Lost in cominge to ancour, but could not finde it.

ffrydaye The vij[th] sett upp my Smithes forge & felled Timber for my maynmast.

at SSW   Satterdaye The viij[th] day intrenched abowte my Smithes forge with woode for to defend theim against any sodaine of the Negroes and built an oven.

at SSW   Sonndaye The ix[th] daie, In the afternoone built a howse for Capten Parker on the shoore and Lefte Companies with him for the guarde of the Smithes & Carpenters.

at SSW   Monndaye The xth daie applied the seeking of things for supplie of my wantes.

at SSW & *NW*   Tewesdaye. The xj[th] daie, swiped a freshe for the Edwardes Ancour & Cable but could not finde it. ended the squaringe of a peice a tymber for my fishes.

winde at SSW   Wedensdaye The xij[th] daie, there cam aborde me one Loyes Anrikes[2] a portingall with whom I bargayned to give him iij bushells of salt for v of Rize. He told me of one Massatamba a Negro kinge above Casamaura hable to bringe 5000 horse to the feild and of suche uprightnes in Iustice as no straunger or any other travelling his Countrey & Losinge any thing (beinge found) is presently hanged upp in his Court & so restored: he is served at a Table in other ordre & Civilitie, then any other of those brutishe K: comonly be.

at E, & *SSW*   Thursdaye the xiij[th] daie, brought the fishes and my mayntopmast aborde; Loyes Anrikes departed for the rize he was to deliver me.

at SSW   ffrydaye The xiiij[th] daie, begann to frame the fishes for our maynemast. muche Raine.

---

[1] Such extensive repairs would necessitate a long stay. For Hawkins's comment see p. 278.

[2] Details of the transactions with these Portuguese, who included Lewis Henriques, are given in Ward's narrative (*Pr. Nav.*, p. 652). Meanwhile, on September 11, Fenton had spoken to Madox of his scheme for settling in St Helena (p. 181).

Satterdaye The xvth daie, much Raine, a sworde fishe founde, killed by an Allegathie. *wind at NW*

Sonndaye The xvjth daie, fished in the afternoone tooke sowles & other fishe, gave liveries.[1] *at S e & SSW*

Monndaye The xvijth daie, sett upp one of the sides of our fishes. *winde SSW*

Tewesdaye. The xviijth daie, sett upp the other side of our fishe *at SSW*

Wedensdaye. The xixth daie, finished the Tressell trees. *at N & SSW*

Thursdaye The xxth daie, The Master grew into some speaches with me, havinge founde falt with his slacknesse in followinge our Common busines (sayinge he would be Master wheather I would or no) *at SSW & NW*

ffrydaye The xxjth daie, I called some of thassistaunts together[2] tunderstande their opinions wheather they thought those speaches tollerable or to be used to me, and whether I had aucthoritie to displace him or no: who hearinge my Master not hable to denye the wordes (though sorie for the same) It was aggreed I might displace him, whereupon not seekinge his overthrow, I was content to contynue him in his place, with Condicion that he should before the whole companie at service confesse his falt and to desier my favour, acknowledginge not to hold his place of Mastershipp but by my favour and clemencie, which he performed accordinglie: This fallinge owt grew by neglectinge the serche of my maynmast periched in the parteners[3] &c. *at S.Se & NW*

Satterdaye The xxijth daie. sett upp my mayntopmast & fynished the wullinge of my maynmast. *at e.Se & WSW*

Sonndaye. The xxiijth daie, The Negroo cam from the North shoore to dyve for thedwardes Ancour & Cables Lost.

[1] Walker (p. 205) says that the liveries were of broadcloth of popingaye green. Fenton had three men in his personal service. Ward reports that he had 'divers debatements' on this Sunday with the General, while the two chaplains complained to one another of their most unfortunate position (p. 184).

[2] For Fenton's accusation against Christopher Hall see p. 206. Ward agreed that the General might displace his Master, but entreated him not to do so. In the end Hall asked pardon for having 'overshotte him selfe in undecent speeches' (Ward's narrative, *Pr. Nav.*, p. 653).

[3] The 'parteners' were timbers strengthening the mast at deck-level. Fenton makes no mention of the arrival of a Portuguese caravel with forty fettered slaves, besides women and children, some of whom the English company purchased. See p. 209, and Plate VIII.

at e.Se & SW.
We founde
Lignum vitae
growing there

Monndaye. The xxiiij[th] daie, putt a new forsaile to the yarde, sett tym*ber* to be sawen for provic*i*on, w*hi*ch we founde eaten w*i*th the wormes verie much, so as we were fearfull to bringe it into o*ur* Shipp, and havinge pr*o*vided fyer woode, founde it so full of wormes as we Lefte it.

Markham[1]
dyed at e.Se &
SW

Tewesdaye The xxv[th] daie, finished the rigginge of o*ur* Shipp: Rec. a Coppie of the Invoys of the m*er*cha*u*nts in the Edwarde Bonaventur.

Lawrence
Tripp dyed
aborde
thedwarde

Wedensdaye The xxvj[th] daie, rec. a token from Kinge fattema, viz. a Monkye and a greate toothe of an Oliphant, the winde at eSe & SW

K. Farma hath
wares with the
Lympas; much
gould supposed

Thursdaye. The xxvij[th] daie, I wroote to Kinge fattema a *lett*re of thanks by his serv*a*unts, the coppie Rcm [below] and sente him therw*i*th in lieu of his reme*m*braunce, a yarde & di of broode redd clothe, with 10 powndes of powder, a smock of Russia worke for the Quene. with a ij[d] glasse and to his servaunts ij elves of course narrowe Lynnen clothe—Le peice.

*Memoran*da that the Portingall told me that the Indians use to give of the Barke of a tree called Silacroma to drinke, to suche as be suspected of fellonie, wherw*i*th if he be boched he dieth, or otherwaies doth vomitt it upp againe & so is cleared of the suspic*i*on.

This daie I placed Ric' faireweather *Maste*r in the Barke ffrau*n*ces.[2]

A coppie of a
*lett*re to
King fattema

Kinge fattema, I have receaved thy curteous and princelye token beinge a monkey & an oliphants toothe, for the whiche I geve the right humble and harty thanks. And now fynde that suche reportes as I have hard of thye upright dealleinge towards all Strang*er*s of honest and good behaviour to be answerabell to truthe and good meani*n*ge and the Kinglike Place thowe ma*n*nageth Evenso were yt not that I am*m*e

[1] William Markham, master of the *Francis*, had been master of John Winter's ship on Drake's voyage. Ward reports going ashore to his burial on this day. It was on the same day that he called his own master and chaplain to his cabin and informed them of Fenton's private plans (pp. 206–7), which Madox had summarized in his Diary the night before (p. 183).

[2] A week later (October 4) Fenton wished to appoint Arthur Cotton as the new master's mate of the *Galleon*. But Master Hall recommended one John Davis (whose name is not in the Muster Roll), and lots were cast, when Davis was successful (see p. 185).

Commaunded by the moste vertuous and renownied Queene of England whosse subiect and servant I am, not to depart on lande from the charge her majestie hath committed to me, I would suerly have seen the my selfe, Ledd therunto aswell by the courtesey thow haste shewed me as the desier I have to see thy greatnes and to have ussed some conferrance with the towchinge a further Amytie and traffique to be hade hereafter betwixt the and the Queene my mistres subiects which (in her highnes name) I vowe, shalbe performed towards thee and thyne accordinge to all truthe and fidelitie: praying thee that thies my letters maye suffice with owt further conferrence, to establishe the same, as the thinge I muche desier. In token wherof, and that I will remayne frend to thee and thy frinds, and enemye to thy enemyes, I have sent thee by thy servants thes bearers a pece of redd Clothe with som powther for thy selfe, and a smocke and a glasse for thy Queene thow Lovest best, desieringe thee to accept therof as from him that will bothe love and serve thee. Beinge right sorie my busines and occasion hasteth me awaye before I myght have the with me. And so kissinge thy hands, I wishe the all happie successes in all thye accions accordinge to the greatnes of thy princlie mynd ffrom aborde the Gallion Leicestre the xxvij[th] of September 1582. Thyne in all service and fidelitie

Ed. Fenton.

ffrydaye The xxviij[th] daie, I ended the fishinge of my maynmast in the parteners, and trymmed my boote, much dekayed. *at e.Se & W*

Satterdaye The xxix[th] daie, provided water & brought other things in ordre. *chauncelour[1] dyed at e.Se & W*

---

[1] Nicholas Chancellor, son of the famous Richard, had been in the service of the Muscovy Company as a clerk since adolescence. Madox says his death was the result of shock, when he found himself separated from his party in the West African forest (Cotton MS Titus B. VIII, f. 185). Ward relates that on this day: 'After dinner M. Walker and I went aboord the Admiral and grew in argument concerning our going roome to the Iyles of Cape Verde or whether it were better to proceede forwards with the provision we now have. At this conference was the General, Captaine Hawkins, Captaine Parker, M. Maddox, M. Walker & I. After sundry debatements we concluded to proceede . . . I imparted to the M., the pilot, M. Shaw and M. Jeffries what had been determined' (*Pr. Nav.*, p. 654). See also p. 208.

at e.Se &
SW. my self
Capten Warde
Capten Parker
Mr Madox
Mr Walker
Tho: Hoode
Blaccoller
pilotts.

Sonndaye   The Laste daie, Beinge aborde the Edwarde Bonaventure, and I havinge with good consideration entred into the dekaye aswell of our Drink of all sortes, as other victualls: propownded this question to such of the Assistaunts as were presente,[1] what Course, was thought most fitt to hold aswell to accomplishe the voyage, as relieve our victualls (and the winde contrarie to go by Cape Bone Esperance;) it was thought by all their Consents that to performe thaccion and provide for all wantes the Straits of Magelan was the onlie waie, which by thadvise of Tho: Hoode & Blaccoller pilotts, was fullie aggreed upon.

[*October* 1582]

the first of
October

my self.
Capten Warde
Capten Parker
& Capten
Hawkins
Mr Madox
Mr Walker.
Evans had
practized,
at our first
coming into
harbour to go

Monndaye The first of October: Milles Evans[2] being accused of divers vile speaches aswell towardes my self, as in generall againste all thaccion; and beinge called before us, and the accusacion redd unto him confessed the same, & without desieringe of favour or beinge penitente for his fault, made request to be dismissed of his charge, and to be sett aborde the Elizabeth sold to the Portingalls, which (in respect of his stubbardnes and mutinous disposition & other vile practizes) was yelded unto by us as a thinge most necessarie for the

---

[1] Ward's account of the Council Meeting (omitted from the later edition by Hakluyt) is as follows: 'This day during the time our dinner was dressing, the General assembled us before named in Commission into my cabbin where he propounded divers questions and doubts touching our going forwards, all which being answered, it was agreed to proceed for the straights of Magellan; and being in the South Sea, to deale as occasion should be given. In this conference grew many hotte and disdainfull speaches and comparisons between Captaine Hawkins and Captaine Parker, and also the Generall as offended with Captaine Hawkins used speaches to him very displeasant which with much adoe was all in the ende pacified' (*Pr. Nav.*, p. 654).

[2] Miles Evans had from the outset wished for a trade voyage as planned and had evidently made himself unpleasant (p. 185), for Ward reports behaviour 'which seemed so odious and unhonest, that M. Walker, M. Maddox, M. Parker, the Lieutenant and I concluded with the Generall that he might displace him, which thing Evans earnestly often desired, saying he would go into England well enough, as from hence in the Elizabeth with the Portingals, with whom in the afternoone he made freight, and carried his chest, a barrel, & 2 packes aboord, which I, M. Parker, and Lieutenant Hawkins searched by the Generals order' (*Pr. Nav.*, p. 655). See also p. 205.

quiet of all the accion: Rec. in xiij Barrells of Rize in exchaunge for salte

for St Tiago & become a frear at Se & SW

Tewesdaye The ij^de daie, at vij of the clock in the morninge we sett saile from Seraliona with the winde at Ne, but so smale as we cam to Ancour abowte 10 of the clock against the rocke in vij fathoms & a quarter.

at Ne wente WNW 2 L

Wedensdaye The iij^de daie, abowte ij of the clock in the morninge we sett saile and went SW & by W & WSW 6 L and cam to Ancour abowte Middaie beinge becalmed.

winde at Ne wente SW & by W & WSW 6 L

The same daie abowte viij of the clock at night we sett saile with the winde at eNe and went till xij of the clock the next daie 15 L. WSW havinge lost the sight of Seraliona. sownded at 45 fathoms & had no grownde.

at eNe 15 L. WSW.

Thursdaye The iiij^th daie We sailed from Middaye till xj of the clock the next daie 12 L NW the winde at SW & by W litle.

altit. 8.10 12 L. NW

ffrydaye The vth daie, at Middaye becalmed, at 4 of the clock in the afternoone the winde at NW and at W by N and so contynued till xij the next daie, we wente SSW for the most parte. 12 L.

altit. 8.40 SSW 12 L.

Satterdaye The vj^th daie, at Middaye the winde was at e N e, we went SSW till xij the nexte daie but in sorte becalmed. 6 L.

at e.Ne SSW 6 L.

Sonndaye The vij^th daie, at Middaie becalmed, and so contynued till xij of the clock the next daie. we wente as the flood caried us one waie. and thebb thother waie. were in greate extreemitie of heate and dyvers of my companie fell sick.

altit. 8.16

Gregorie the smith dyed.

Monndaye The viij^th daie, at Middaie becalmed and so contynued till vj of the clock the next morninge at what time the winde began to blow NNe & Ne till Middaye little winde, wente SSW 4 L.

at NNe & Ne SSW 4 L

Tewesdaye The ix^th daie, at Middaye litle winde wente SSW till xij the next daie 8 L

altit. 7.40 at Se

Wedensdaye The xth daie, at Middaye litle winde, I wente aborde the Edward to visitt the Companie. and so to the ffrances, wente till viij of the clock in the night 6 L SSW, and till xij of the clock then followinge SW 3 L.

altit' 7.15 Painter dyed SSW 6 L. SW 3 L winde at e.Se & Se

at eNe
SSW 15 L
W 3 L

Thursdaye   The xjth daie, At Middaye becalmed, much Raine in the morninge. at ij of the clock in the afternoon the winde was at eNe, wente till ix the nexte daie SSW 15 L and so till xij W 3 L.

altit. 6.15
winde at SE
by e

ffrydaye   The xijth daie, at Middaye, wente W & by S. and so in effect becalmed all those twentie foure howers.

altit. 6.10
at SSW
SSW 7 L

Satterdaye   The xiijth daie, at Middaye. wente SSW with litle winde till next daie at xij of the clock 7 L

at Ne & SSW
altit. 6.20
Launcelott
Robinson died

Sonndaye   The xiiijth daie; At Middaye becalmed wente SSW and Se till xij the nexte daie 8L

altit. 6.46
winde SSW &
at Ne

Monndaye   The xvth daie At Middaye wente Se litle winde and SSW, till xij of the clock the next daie 9 L.

altit. 6.21
winde at SSW
& e

Tewesdaye   The xvjth daie, At Middaye becalmed wente NW and SSW 6 L till xij the next daie.

winde at e &
Se

Wedensdaye.   The xvijth daie, At Middaye we wente SSW & SW. till xij the next daie 6 L

altit. 6.0
winde at Se &
by e
SSW 21 L.

Thursdaye   The xviijth daie. At Middaye we wente SSW with a reasonable freshe gale till xij of the clock the nexte daie 21 L.

altit' 5–0
winde at Se
& by S
SW 16 L & W
5 L

ffrydaie   The xixth daie, At Middaie we wente SSW with a reasonable freshe gale till iiij of the clock in the morninge SW 16 L and till xij W 5 L.

at Se & by S
& e & by S

Satterdaye   The xxth daie. At Middaye we wente SW litle winde 5 L and SW & by S 8 L till xij the nexte daie.

at Se & by S
& SSe

Sonndaye   The xxjth daie, At Middaye litle winde. wente SW & by S 5 L and WSW 5 L till xij the nexte daie.

at Se & by S
& SSe

Monndaye   The xxijth daie. At Middaye. litle winde. wente till xij the next daie SW & by W 8 L. much Raine.

at e.Ne & Ne
& e & by S &
Se & by e.
SSW 6 L
SW & by S
5 L

Tewesdaye   The xxiijth daie At Middaye much Raine the Edwarde & ffrancis bare SSe of us and we bare with them for iij or 4 glasses S & by e till it was calme & then by the fogg we lost sight of them, wente SSW 6 L & SW & by S 5 L. till xij the nexte daie, The Shipp & barke with us.[1]

---

[1] See p. 186. Fenton had feared they would 'depart'. On October 29 he sent Fairweather and a 'M. Dore' (perhaps the Italian reported in the *Leicester* at St Vincent; see p. 252, n. 1) to fetch a hogshead of pork from the

Wedensdaye The xxiiijth daie. At Middaye we went SSW *at Se & by e*
9 L, till xij the next daie, the winde at Se & by S. *altit. 3.20*

Thursdaye The xxvth daie. At Middaye we wente till xij the *altit. 2.40*
nexte daie W & by S 18 L. stopped a leeck. *at Se & by S*
& S & by e

ffrydaye The xxvjth. At Middaye we wente till xij the nexte *altit. 2.26*
daie SW & by W 25 L. *at S & by e*

Satterdaye The xxvijth; At Middaye we wente till xij the *altit. 1.46*
nexte daie SW & by W 14 L and W SW 10 L. *at Se & by S*

Sonndaye The xxviijth At Middaye, we wente till xij the
nexte daie 18 L SW & by W. Stopped iiij Leakes in her
Bowes.

Monndaye The xxixth daie. At Middaye we wente till xij the *altit. 0.38*
nexte daie SW & by W 18 L. SW 4L *at Se & by S*
& Se

Tewesdaye The xxxth. At Middaye we wente W S W till xij *altit. 0.11*
the next daie W S W 15 L *at Se*

Wedensdaye The xxxjth At Middaye we wente till xij the *at Se & Se*
next daie WSW 15L. *& by S*

[November 1582]

Thursdaye 1. of November The first of November. Called *altit. 0.15*
the Cap*t*ens maisters and Pilotts aborde[1] me and finding
my self 15 minitts to the Southwarde of the Lyne and within *The weather*
160 L. westwardes of the Cost of Brasill with the winde at Se, *verie temperatt*
as September
demaunded of theim their opinions whether it were better to *in Englande*
Caste abowte & stande to the Ne or to beare with the Coast
of Brasill still; who in gen*e*ral after manie disputacions *wente till xij*
therof; held it best to beare with that Cost for releif &c, if *the nexte daie*
SW & by W
happelie before o*u*r fall therw*i*th we founde not the winde to *23 L*
enlarge so far furth as we might lye o*u*r Course for Rio de
Plata or the Straight of Magalan.

Edward. This was no doubt when Fairweather imparted the information
that the General had given orders to fire on his two consorts when they
appeared to be leaving him. The evening before (October 28), when Ward
approached the *Galleon* to give the customary hail, he had been told that
'if the wind scanted one point more they meant to cast about, which we
thought not best for certain causes' (*Pr. Nav.*, p. 656).
[1] For Madox's report of this conference see p. 187. He alone records
Ferdinando's suggestion to make for the Gulf of Mexico. Brazil was, of
course, south-west of them, not north-east as Hakluyt writes, but all
disagreed as to the amount of westing they had made when working their
way across the Doldrums.

A note of suche sorts of victualls[1] as should Rem*ain* this daie aborde me by ordre aswell of that was Layde into the Shipp as that was then spente. viz.

supposed to be but xiiij butts	Beare	tons	12	Stockfishe	4000
	Porke	hogesheads	24	Buttre firkins	45
	Breade		11000	Peas Barrells	23
	Beif	hog*sheads*	5	Otmeale Bar*rells*	27
	Wyne. Canarie tons		7	Rize Bushells	100
	Mamsey	tons	2	Oyle litle firkins	5
	Vinegar	hog*sheads*	9	honye Barrells	10–1700 gallons
	Syder	hog*sheads*	vj	Meale Bar*rells*	99

altit. 0.31
Se & by e &
Se

ffrydaye The ij^d daie, At Middaye we wente till xij the nexte daie wente SW & by W 18 L

altit. 1.7
winde eSe

Satterdaye The iij^d daie, At Middaye we wente till xij the nexte daie SW 25 L

altit. 2.7
winde eSe

Sonndaye The iiij^th daie, At Middaye we wente till xij the nexte daie SW & by S 27 L

altit. 3.24
winde eSe & e
& by S

Monndaye The vth daie, At Middaye we wente till xij the nexte daie SSW, 26 L

altit. 4.46
winde e, & e
& by S

Tewesdaye The vj^th daie, At Middaye we wente till xij the nexte daie SSW 26 L.

altit. 6.10
winde e & by S
& eSe

Wedensdaye The vij^th daie, At Middaye we wente S & by W 9 L & SSW 15 L till xij the nexte daie.

altit. 7.15
winde e, & e
& by S

Thursdaye The viij^th daie, At Middaye we wente till xij the nexte daie SSW 25 L

altit. 8.29
winde e, & e
& by S

ffrydaye The ix^th daie, At Middaye we wente till xij the next daie SSW 24 L The sonn sett at WSW.

altit. 9.40
winde at e &
by S

Satterdaye The xth daie. At Middaye we wente till xij the nexte daie SSW 21 L

altit. 10.36

Sonndaye The xj^th daie. At Middaye we wente S & by W

[1] Fenton now makes a monthly assessment of provisions, which may be compared with the allowances set out in Document 34. The figures are, however, not consistent. The beer, for instance, was reduced by $3\frac{1}{2}$ tons during November, but the remaining $8\frac{1}{2}$ tons had gone during December. The gentlemen apparently drank rather more than a tun of wine a month, and certainly some of them drank to excess.

till xij the next daie 21 L, I was aborde thedwarde to see Mr Walker beinge sicke: Put on my Petticoate.[1] *winde e, & e & by S*

Monndaye The xijth daie, At Middaye we wente till xij the nexte daie S 22 L. *altit. 11.41 winde at e, & e & by N*

Tewesdaye The xiijth daie. At Middaye. we wente till xij the nexte daie S & by e 22 L. I wente aborde Thedwarde to see Mr Walker being verie sicke.[2] *altit. 12.53 winde e.*

Wedensdaye The xiiijth daie, At Middaye. we wente till xij the nexte daie S & by e 24 L. *altit. 14.15 winde e.Ne*

Thursdaye The xvth daie, I wente aborde thedwarde Bonaventure, aswell to see Mr Walker beinge, as to enquire of some disorder and discorde reported to me to bee there, w*h*ich upon enquirie I founde most untrue,[3] At Middaye we wente till xij the nexte daie S & by e 26. *winde at e.Ne & Ne & by e*

ffrydaye The xvjth daie, At Middaye we wente till xij the nexte daie 42 L S. The sonne sett at WSW and rose at eSe. *altit. 17.0 winde at e.Ne & Ne*

Satterdaye The xvijth daie, At Middaye we wente S 3L, & SW & by S 20 L. till xij the next daie. *altit. 19.20 winde Ne.*

Sonndaye The xviijth daie, At Middaye we wente SW & by S, 31 L. till xij the nexte daie. the sonne sett betwixte the WSW & S & by W. *altit. 21.44 winde Ne*

Monndaye The xixth daie, At Middaye, we wente SW & by S 30L till xij the next daie. *altit. 22.15 wind Ne & eSe*

Tewesdaye The xxth daie, At Middaye we wente till xij of the clock the next daie SW & by S 25 L. *altit. 23.15 winde Ne & N*

Wedensdaye The xxjth daie, At Middaye we wente till xij the next daie SW & by S 32 L. *altit. 24.14 winde Ne & N*

Thursdaye The xxijth daie, At Middaye we wente till viij at night SW 7 L, & from thence till xij the next daie W & by N 8 L *altit. 25.24 winde N, a good gale. & SSW.*

ffrydaie The xxiijth daie, At Middaie we wente till xij the nexte daie SW 20 L. *altit' 25.53 winde e.Se & Ne*

[1] A small coat worn beneath the doublet (*O.E.D.*).
[2] There is no explanation of this in the Diaries. See p. 188.
[3] By the 17th of the month Walker was believed to be on the point of death, and the officers and gentlemen of the *Galleon* came to take their leave of him. The daily visits continued, and Ward reports 'speaches', i.e. angry words, between himself and Banister, who brought the sick man a potion.

winde Ne. fogg & Rayne

Satterdaye The xxiiij[th] daie, At Middaye we wente till xij the next daie 20 L. SW.

winde Se, e,Se, & eNe. fogg & Raine,

Sonndaye The xxv[th] daie, At Middaye we wente till xij the next daie SW 25 L. Was aborde the Edwarde Bonaventure, aswell to see M[r] Walker[1] as to examyn their stoore of water, who had iij tonns by opinion, and no more.

winde e,Ne, & Ne

Monndaye The xxvj[th] daie, At Middaye we wente till xij the next daie SW 20 L. In rommaging for water founde 16 tonns, wherof 14 tons were runn owt, & so I but ij tonns lefte in all the shipp.

altit. 26.45 winde NNe & NW & NW & by W.

Tewesdaye The xxvij[th] daie, At Middaye we went till xij the next daie SW 20 L and yet the winde cam abowte to the NW.

winde at WSW & Ne

Wedensdaye The xxviij[th] daie, At Middaye we wente till xij the next daie S & by W 13 L. we mistrusted a Curraunt from the S.[2]

altit. 27.46 winde Ne & N & by e & S & by W, much Winde & fogg

Thursdaye The xxix[th] daie. At Middaye we wente till iiij of the clock the next daie in the morninge 20 L WSW. and from thence till xij of the clocke WNW 6 L, much winde & fogg.

winde SW

ffrydaye The xxx[th] daie, At Middaye much winde & fogg we wente till vj of the clock the next daie in the morninge 16 L NW & by W.

[December 1582]

Satterdaye The first of December at vj of the clock in the morninge. we discovered the Cost of Brasill[3] verie high Lande 8 L of bearinge in with the Lande NW & by W: the storme contynued, & was verie cold weather: iiij howers after sownded and had 5 L from the Shoore 38 fathom and ij howers after 30 fathom all black ozey sande within one mile

[1] On this day there was also a general perusal of the masters' and pilots charts and reckonings (see p. 189), and on November 26 Ward reports 'The Admiral haled us & told us he would put into the River de Plata'.

[2] They were edging in towards the land but the winds became irregular, and on November 30 set in from the SW so that they were obliged to take a northerly course, and according to Ward it was 'so cold that we were glad to put on winter apparel'.

[3] They were just south of Catalina Island, in latitude nearly 28° S. Ward (who was an excellent seaman) describes in detail how soundings were taken and harbour safely entered (*Pr. Nav.*, p. 659). See Map B.

& di of the shoore had 15 fathoms and ymmediatlie 12 fathoms of like grounde. halinge the Coast to the Northwards, The Lande towardes the shoore in some partes Low lande & Champion with white sande but for the most parte woode and highe land, & a bold Coast to fall with, having vj or vij Islandes to the Sea ward or sea bord; abowte iij or 4 of the clock in the afternoone we cam to Ancour in a Baye where we had 9 fathom oze grounde mixed with Shelles, and ymmediatlie putt our Bootes to Shoore to seeke Cheiflie for freshe water (beinge our onlie wante) and to view the Countrey, which we founde verie thick of smale woodes & a kinde of Brambell, so as our people had much a do to passe, neither was there any liklehood of habitacion (saving that they founde a howse, built (as we suppose) by some Christians distressed, or that framed theim selves to inhabitt there for a time.)

We founde good stoore of freshe water, stoore of ballast (which we had want of) Sage, parsley & other stoore of herbes, younge white herons and gulles, and so reatorned to our Shippes.

[*margin: this day.* primo December SW winde. Put an new maynsail to the yard. The Remainder of the victualls[1] supposed in the Shipp viz: Bread 1100. Beare tons 8½. wyne all sorts tons 7½. Aquavita barrels 7. Porke barrels 21. Beif barrels 4 Stockfishe 4700 Butter firkins 44. Oyle barrels 7. Meale Barrels 100. Otmeale Barrels 27. Peas Barrels 26. honye Barrels greate & smale 17. Rize Barrels 100. Vineger hogsheads 7. Muskadine Runletts 11. Shoott at great black wild boore.]

Sonndaye The ij^de daie. After we had served The Lorde, I wente aborde thedwarde to See Mr Walker, and fell sodainlie sick:[2] Sente Capten Warde, Capten Parker & my Lieutenante to the Shoore to prepare our wateringe Place in good order and to searche what other releif they cold finde, Who view alonge the Sea side, founde great stoore of fishe; Capten

altit. 28.10
no winde till
night at NNe.

---

[1] See p. 114.
[2] Walker was beginning to recover, and the next day left his bed (see p. 210).

Warde sendinge for his Nett, drew a draught & caught therat 500 Mulletts & great Basses as we supposed, and so reatorned aborde. giving god right humble and hartie thanks, I named this Baye, The Baye of good compforte, in respect of soundrie reliefs wee founde there. it highes v foote water or therabowtes.[1]

winde Calme

Monnday The iij[de] daie, I washed my Shipp & gott in some Ballays & stoore of hoopes amongest other fishe gott some smelts large & good.

winde NNe
altit. 27.55

Tewesdaye The iiij[th] daie gott in some Ballaze & water. Gott the roote of a ferne cont*aining* 21 foote in Lengthe, and [as bigg as the calf of reasonable mans legg, *deleted*] 19 ynches at the roote, 16 ynches in the midst and xij at the top. the ferne growing owt of the same.

winde NNe &
Ne & by N.
much winde.
altit. 28.20

Wedensdaye. The vth daie, Labored still, abowte o*u*r water & ballaze: found wild olif tres wilde date tres being the palmata & wild suger Canes.

winde NNe &
at S.

Thursdaye The vj[th] daie, we discovered a smale saile[2] to the Northward going to the Southwards and sente Cap*t*en Warde and Cap*t*en Parker w*i*th the Barke ffrancis & my Pynnasse, who the same daie reatorned w*i*th her, having xxj persons in her wherof vij were frears goinge (as they saide) for the Riv*er* of Plate there to inhabitt, as their confessions will appeare more at large &c.[3]

winde Se

ffrydaye The vij[th] daie, We finished o*u*r wateringe in effect. supplied the Barke ffranc*i*s with iij monthes victualls, romaged the Spanishe Barke: had some conferrence towching o*u*r goinge through the Straights of Magalan,[4] seing we

---

[1] The range of the tide. Cf. Madox's chart of the bay (Pl. XIII).
[2] See pp. 190, 210.   [3] See Documents 47, 48.
[4] See pp. 191, 213. Hakluyt later omitted the following passage from Ward's narrative, as it had appeared in 1589: 'Further it was determined that Captaine Hawkins, Master Talboys, Master Jeffries, Master Hoode, Master Blacoller and two sailors of each shippe should romage the prize, about the appointment of whome grew unkinde, and hot speeches, between the Generall, and Master Parker, against me, concerning authoritie, and government, and also captaine Hawkins finding himself injured, was plaine with them both! so that we were beyond the termes of commissioners and fell to plaine brawling, and bragging: the circumstances I omit, as too long, and unfit to be written. Time being thus spent, the Generall called for wine, and ended all contentions, and so we dined there with him. [Continued on next page.]

understoode of the Spanishe fleet beinge there (of whom though nothing affraide) yet to see how most convenientlie we might water and woode there, and not discovered of theim or at Least to passe by theim to the westermost parte of the Straight, there aswell to supplie our wantes as to forefoote all such messengers as happelie they might sende into the Sowth sea to give intelligence of our cominge thither.

Satterdaye The viij[th] daie, Dispatched the Spanyards to their Barke,[1] and tooke some triffling things of theim, to supplie our necessities: finished our wateringe, and Conferred[2] of some things towching my viceadmirall &c. *winde N & Ne*

Sonndaye The ix[th] daie I dyned aborde my viceadmirall, and founde a certein sweete woode supposed to be Sassafrasse, good to cure dropseys and to drinke ynwardlie &c. In the River de Plata there growth a leafe like the Leaf of an Artichock, wherof they make Cordagg for Shippinge which they call garavalaf, & also it serveth for ocam, and they trymm their pynasses with waxe in staed of pitch.[3] *winde S & calme.*

Monndaye The xth daie, Beinge readie to sett saile the winde was at SSW with foogg & Raine. *winde SSW*

Tewesdaye The xj[th] daie, Calme in the morninge, in the afternone abowte iij or iiij of the clock the winde was at Ne by N. *winde Ne & by N*

Wedensdaye The xij[th] daie, We sett saile by vj of the clock in *winde NNe*

'After dinner they searched the barke and found in her divers trifles, which are noted in a paper by themselves. I went a fishing and came aboord, from whence the Generall fetched me, and went aboord to the old Frier in the barke [*Francis*]; after we had talked with him we came aboord, and there supped in the Edward with me the Generall, M. Maddox, Captaine Parker, and Master Hall: we debated of divers causes before, and after supper, and so departed, with promise to dine with the General the next day' (*Pr. Nav.*, p. 661).

[1] See p. 192.

[2] See p. 213, Ward writes: 'After I returned aboord and having divided the necessaries to each ship his part, we entered into consultations, when Master Walker propounded certain questions to the General of unkindness by me conceived against him, which moved him to some cholericke termes with me, which I answered: and in the ende, all matters almost being agreed betweene us, then began the contention with Captain Hawkins, which contention was tedious and not fully ended before supper, and began again after supper: so that about 10 of the clock after supper we came aboorde' (*Pr. Nav.*, p. 661).

[3] Fenton makes no mention of the letter addressed to 'Frobisher or Acres' which he gave this day to the Friars (see p. 192).

& N & by e.
departed from
the B. of good
compforte
foggie weather
wind SW

the morni*n*ge The Edwarde havinge brooke her Catt in fyshinge her Anco*u*r the same runn owt ende for ende, wherby we were forced to spend the morni*n*ge to recover the same, in the afternone directing our course S & by W till iiij of the Clock the next daie in the morni*n*ge 16 L, from thence till Middaie WNW 8 L.

winde S & by
W 60 of my
men sodagnlie
sick with a
paine in their
heads &c.
winde at NNe

Thursdaye The xiijth daie, At Middaye, beinge w*i*thin one L, of the Shoore and havinge 20 & 18 fathoms sowndinge of ozey sande, the Lande beinge a Lowe Lande and Lyinge Ne & SW, we caste abowte, and wente ESE & E & by N till x of the clock at night 4 L & SW & by W till xij the nexte daie 14 L.

winde NNe &
S & b[y] e, &
Se & b[y] e.

ffrydaye The xiiijth daie, At Middaye we wente till 13 howers S & by W 14 L, and WSW, 5 howers 2 L, and SSW, 2 howers i L and the residue becalmed.

altit' 30–1
winde S &
SW & by S &
at E & Se &
b[y] S

Satterdaye The xvth daie, At Middaye we wente till Midnight SW 12 L, and from thence till xij of the clock S. 7 L: some howers were spente in calmes Raine, thonnder & lightni*n*ge.

altit. 31.0
winde e.Se
& e, & N &
NW

Sonndaye The xvjth daie, were At Middaye w*i*thin vj L of ye shoore, 12 & 14 fathoms sholdinge. We wente till 10 of the clock in the night S & b e 8 L, and till xij the nexte daie S 13 L. Manie fyers made on the shoore.

altit' 32.7
winde W & by
S, & SW & by
S, & S & by W
altit. 32.25
winde at e &
b[y] s & Se &
SSe.

Monndaye The xvijth daie. At Middaye we wente till ij of the clock in the morni*n*ge E & by S. 6 L and from thence till viij of the clock Ne. 2 L. from thence till xij of the clock SSW 2 L. Began our Bevorage.[1] Tewesdaye The xvijth daie, At Middaye we wente till iiij of the clock NE 1 L, thence till ij of ye clock in the morni*n*ge SSW 8 L. thence till xij [of] the clock SW & by n. 6 L.

A note[2] of suche instructions as wer gathered by the examination of thosse Spaniards whom we tooke at the baye of good comfort uppon the coaste of Braeselle. The cheifs wherof was John de Neyra an ould fryer, the next ffranc*i*s de Vera an Younge gentellman.[3]

---

[1] The meaning is not clear.
[2] The whole of the following 'note' is scored out.
[3] Don Francisco de Torre Vedra, nephew to Don Juan, Governor of the River Plate.

1. Impri*mis* that for the fortifyinge and inhabityinge of magellanns streyts and the conquest of chila was great pr*e*paration in spayn the beginninge of Sommer an*n*o 1581 so that abowt the enterence of september followinge the fleete loosed from St Lucar but wer w*i*th yll wether twysse or thrice put in agayne not with owt great Losse

2. The 9 of december followinge an*n*o 1581 they set saylle laste and cam to St yago 16.[1]

Wedensdaye. The xixth daie, At Middaye we wente till viij of the clock at night SW 6 L. & till iiij in the morni*n*ge SW & b W 6 L, from [thence] to xij of the clock NNW 4 L.

winde SSW & S & b[y] e & W & b S

Thursdaye The xxth daie, We had conferrence[2] towchinge o*u*r goinge by the Straight of Magalan, wh*i*ch upon debatinge was altered &c, and shaped o*u*r Course for St Vincents in Brasill. At Middaye we went till vj at night e 3 L. and so NNe 4 L. the residue becalmed.

altit. 33.15 winde S & SSW

ffrydaie The xxjth daie At Middaye becalmed & so till iij of the clock in the afternone, from thence till vij of the clock at what time we cast to offard NW & by W 2 L, from thence till xij the next daie NW 5 L.

winde Ne & Ne & b N & NNe & N

Abowte 10 of the clock in the night we lost the Barque ffr*ancis*[3] in verie faire weather & litle winde & bearinge but o*u*r mayne & fore saile. But viij howers before I made the Cap*te*n acquainted w*i*th o*u*r Course for St Vincente

Satterdaye The xxijth daie, At Middaie we wente till v of the clock in the afternone NW & by W 4 L from thence till v in the morni*n*ge 8 L ESe, from [thence] till a xj of the clock W & by S. 4 L. and so till xij of the clock NNe L.

winde Ne & b[y] N & Ne & NNe, & N & W & by N

Sonndaye The xxiijth daie, At Middaye litle winde w*i*th a greate fogg. wente till xij the nexte daie NNe 20 L.

winde SSW

Monndaye The xxiiijth daie, At Middaye we wente till ij of the clock in the morni*n*ge NNe 14 L. from thence till vj of

wind E & e & b S. & NNe & SSW

---

[1] See Document 50. The English ships still 'stood in next Land S.W. all day and night', wrote Ward.

[2] After a warning the night before (see p. 216), the fateful conference was called, for which see Documents 51-6, and p. 217. It was fully recorded by Luke Ward (Document 57).

[3] The ships were becalmed for nearly 24 hours, and John Drake left company at 10 o'clock on the evening of December 21. See pp. 194, 218. The most southerly latitude recorded was 33° 15'.

the clock NW & b W 1 L. di and so till xij of the clock Se 2 L.

altit. 30.50
winde e.Se
SSW & e &
b N, & Ne &
NW & b N.

Tewesdaye The xxvth daie.[1] At Middaye we wente till iiij of the clock in the afternone, NNe 3 L. from thence till N. 3 L. from thence till 4 in the morninge NNW. 6 L. and from thence till xij the nexte daie S & b[y] e 6 L.

altit. 30.15
winde Ne &
b[y] e & NW
& b N.
much winde.

Wedensdaye The xxvjth daie. At Middaye we sownded beinge 3 L from the shoore & had xiij fathoms sandie oze, and caste abowte, the lande bearinge of us NW & b W. Wente till a xj a clock at night SSe 7 L and thence till xij the next daie Se & b[y] e 9 L.

winde N & b[y]
e & Ne & b N
& N & b W

Thursdaye The xxvijth daie. At Middaye much winde. went till vj of the clock in the morninge the next daie eSe 9 L. and so till xij. W. 2 L.

winde NNE &
N & b[y] e

ffrydaie The xxviijth daie. At Middaye We wente till xij the nexte daie WNW. 18 L. much winde.

winde N &
b[y] e & N, &
e & b S.

Satterdaye The xxixth daie. At Middaye we wente till vj of the clock WNW 3 L. from thence till x of the clock E. 1 L, thence till one of the clock in the morninge NNe. 1 L, thence till 6. 1 L½ and so till xij of the clock calme.

winde eNe &
Ne & b[y] e
altit. 31.10

Sonndaye The xxxth daie my viceadmirall cam aborde.[2] At Middaye we wente till xij the nexte daie NW 8 L½ & Se & b S. 6 L. Sownded at vij of the clock at night & had 28 fathom black oze vij L from the shoore.

winde NNe &
N & NNW

Monndaye The xxxjth daie At Middaye we wente till xij the nexte daie, NW & b W. 5 L, eSe, 6 L, & e & b N. 3 L. & Ne. 5 L. Abowte vj of the clock in the afternone sownded & had 12 fathoms sande & Shells within sight of Lande. 3 L & so cast abowte to thoffard.

[January 1583]

the firste of
Januarie.
altit. 31.28.

Tewesdaye The firste daie, Remayned by estimation the sorts of victualls followinge, viz, Beare nil. Breade 10300,

---

[1] Only Madox (pp. 195–8) records the anxieties and discussions of the last ten days of December.

[2] Ward reports: 'The 30. day being Sunday, after Sermon, dinner, and observation of the Sunne at noone, we hoysed out our skiffe: the Master, M. Walker and I went aboord the Admiral where we had a banket of sweete meates: after that ended, the General and I fell into familiar conference several by ourselves of the state of our voyage, & debated long in the same good sort: then being neere 4. of the clocke we took our leaves, & came aboord . . . ' (*Pr. Nav.*, p. 664).

Meale Barrells 100, wyne of all sorts tonns 6½, Aquavita *winde NW &*
gallons 80. Porke hogesheads 16½, Beif ho: 4. Stockfishe 2400, *SSe.*
Butter firkins 41. Oyle sweete Barrells 5½. Peas B. 14, Otmeale
B. 25½. Rize Bushells 90. Honie B. 7, & vinegar ho: 7. wente
till xj the next daie NNe 16.L. the other hower becalmed.

Wedensdaye. The ij^d daie. At Middaye we wente till till xij *winde SSe &*
the next daie NN e. 9 L, Ne b[y] e. 1 L. & N. 2 L. & N & b W. *S & Se b[y] e*
2 L.

Thursdaye. The iij^d daie. At Middaye we wente till xij the *winde eSe &*
next daie NNe. L. N & b[y] e 1½ L, N. 3 L. N & b W. 2 L. *e b N & eNe,*
NW 1 L & eSe 1 L½. *& NNe.*

ffrydaie. The iiij^th daie. At Middaye wente till xij the next *altit. 29.13.*
daie N & b[y] e. 3 L, SSe 3 L, Se & b S. 4 L, Se. 2 L, & NNW *winde Ne & b*
2 L. at v of the clock in the afternone. being within L of the *N. & e & Ne*
shoore, cast abowte having in depth 18 fathoms redd sande. *& b N. & Ne.*

Satterdaye. The vth daie. At Middaie wente till v of the clock *winde e & b N*
in the afternone NNW. 2 L. and then caste abowte. beinge *& Ne & b N*
within iiij L of the shoore havinge 20 fathoms sowndinge ozey *& Ne*
sande, and so till xij the nexte daie we wente SSe 5 L, and Se, *much winde.*
7 L.

Sonndaye The vj^th daie. At Middaye we wente till xij the *winde Ne b N*
next daie Se & b S. 4 L. & Se. 9 L. & Se & b[y] e 4 L. much *& NNe. much*
winde. *winde.*

Monndaye The vij^th daie At Middaye we wente till xij the *alt. 30.30.*
next daie Se, 8 L. and Se b S. 15 L. much winde. *winde NNe &*
N & b[y] e.

Tewesdaye. The viij^th daie. At Middaye we wente till v of *altit. 31.43*
the clock in the afternone Se. 3 L. then castinge abowte went *winde N b[y]*
till ij of the clock in the morninge W & b N. 9 L. verie *e*
tempestious and so till xij of the clock W & b S. 6 L. *& N. &*
NNW.

Wedensdaye. The ix^th daie. At Middaye we wente till xij the *altit. 31.56*
next daie N. 5 L & N & b e 20 L. & NNe 4 L. *winde SW & b*
W & SSe, &
eSe

Thursdaye. The xth daie. At Middaye we wente till xij the *winde SSe*
next daie NNe. 38 L.

ffrydaye The xj^th Daie. At Middaye we wente till xij the *alt. 28.30*
next daie N. 32 L. and N & b[y] e. 6 L. *winde SSe &*
eSe & e b S.

Satterdaye. The xij^th daie. At Middaye we Sounded and had *altit. 26.11*

winde Se &
b[y] e & eSe.
& N & NNe.

50 fathoms black sandie oze beinge by reckinge 28. L. from the shoore, Wente till 6 of the clock in the afternone. N. 8 L. sownded & had 34 fathoms black sandie oze, and NW vj howers 8 L sownded & had 29 fathoms white sande with shells, and e & b N. 4 L. Discovered lande xij L of, sownded & had 33 fathoms, black sandie oze and W till Middaye. 6 L. had 15 fathoms ij L from the shoore white sande with some shells.

altit. 25.37
winde NNW
& S & b W.

Sonndaye. The xiij[th] daie. At Middaye we cast abowte being within ij L of the shoore. the lande trending Ne & b N, & SW & b S. wente till xij of the clock the next daie e & b N. 6 L. NNe 12 L Ne & b N 3 L, and N & b W. 5 L. wente to see my viceadmirall.[1]

altit. 24.29
winde S & b
W. & Se. &
eSe, & E.

Monndaye The xiiij[th] daie. At Middaye and all the morninge before we had xij, xj and 10 fathoms sholdinge. white sande, trending a longe the land j L & di of NE & b[y] e & eNe, wente till viij of the clock at night Se 3 L. & Se & b[y] e 1 L,

I suppose, as
the winde
bloweth so the
Currant setteth
on this Coast,
or SW & b W,
& Ne & b[y] e

then we cam to ancour, the winde beinge at Se & eSe till ix the nexte daie, at what time we sett saile. and wente till xij of the clock S. 1 L½. In waighinge our Ancour we brake our Cable a foote from the ancour and also our Boyeroop, and so Loste our ancour.

altit. 24.40
winde E. & e
& b N. & Ne
& b[y] e.

Tewesdaye The xv[th] daie At Middaye we wente till xij the next daie S. 3 L & N. 3 L. & SSe 9 L. beinge abowte 8 L. from the shoore. At vij of the Clock at night we loste sight of Thedwarde.[2]

winde eNe &
e & b S.

Wedensdaye The xvj[th] daie. At Middaye we wente till ij of the clock S litle or nothinge beinge calme, N 3 L. S, 5 L and NNW. 2 L.

winde Ne b[y]
e, & E.

Thursdaye The xvij[th] daie, At Middaye we wente till vj at

---

[1] Within the last two days Fenton must have passed the Spanish fleet lying at Santa Catarina. Don Diego Flores left for the Strait on January 13, while three ships remained behind which subsequently (January 24) appeared at S. Vicente. Ward reports: 'About 3 a clock this afternoone I hoysed out my skiffe and sent her with the Master and Pylot aboord the Admiral, to conferre with them there, who shewing them that I was not well at ease caused the General, M. Maddox, & Captain Parker to come aboord and visit me, where they supped: and having had some conference with him [Fenton] about our dealings at S. Vincent etc. he departed and the skiffe brought the Master & Pylot aboord againe who supped aboord the Gallion' (*Pr. Nav.*, p. 664).

[2] No explanation is given. Fenton must have spent an anxious three days.

night SSe, 4 L. and so till ix of the clock the next daie. N 4 L. and N & b[y] e. 5 L, from thence till xij becalmed.

ffrydaie. The xviij[th] daie, Sente my Pynnasse in the morninge *winde E & Ne.* to an Ilande called Burnte Ilande.[1] aswell to Sownde abowte the same, as to see the same, who reatorned to me againe bothe with freshe water and fowle, and founde good grownde to ride rownde abowte the same in xij fathom: And havinge brought an other litle Ilande ij L½ of from yt, Lying NW & b W and Se & be e, yt have 17 fathoms sowndinge black sandie oze: we wente till xij of the clock at night eNe. 6 L. at what time thedwarde Bonaventure cam to us againe, and so to xij the next daie N & b[y] e. 3 L. & Se & be e. 3 L.

Satterdaye. The xix[th] daie, beinge but calme weather, sente *altit' 24–24* to the Ilande for water, and at Middaie rec*eived* in the same *winde SSe* havinge the winde at SSe, sett saile for St Vincents NNe & *my vice* N & b[y] e, beinge as we supposed 12 L of till vij of the clock *admirall cam* at night 5 L. at what time I sente my Pynnasse to discover the *abord me.[2]* harbo*ur*, and then wente till midnight eNe & Ne & b[y] e 4 L. and so cam to Anco*ur*, even with the mouth of the harbo*ur* of St Vincents.

Sonndaye The xx[th] daie. abowt vij of the clock we waighed *& Monndaye* and sett saile, Lying of & on with litle winde to attend o*ur* *winde WSW* pynnasse who reatorned to us abowt ix of the clock in the morni*n*ge having discovered the harbo*ur*, and there followed *Assosa, L. of* o*ur* pynnasse iij Cannos carryinge in theim xix & xxvj *St Vincents, &* p*er*sons in a peice one of them, Portingalls and Indians w*hich* *slaine with the* rowed being naked, w*ith* theim I had conferrence &c wrote a *K. in* Lett*er*e[4] to the Governo*ur* called Jeronimo Leitao (the Copie *Barbarie.[3]* beinge extante) by those gent*lemen* that cam to me to examyn of whence I was and so cam to Anco*ur* in the harbo*ur* about ij or iij of the clock in vj fathom & di of water, havinge past a barr wherupon you have iiij fathom & bettere. In the afternone

---

[1] Queimada Grande, one of three small but lofty islands which Ward surveyed and charted carefully by means of his compass from a summit viewpoint. It lies between 20 and 30 miles south-west of Santos Bay.

[2] Ward took his chaplain, master and pilot aboard the *Galleon* to explain his absence and exchange news.

[3] 'Assosa': Pero Lopes de Sousa, killed at Alcazar in 1578 and succeeded by his son as donatory of S. Vicente.

[4] Document 59.

there cam abord me one Josef Adorno[1] a Jenawain borne and a Portingall whose name was [Paulo Debriss *crossed out*] Stephano Riposo assistaunts to the Capten whom I entretaigned with courtosie, and delivered the cawse of coming thither, which as a merchante and for trade onlie, to which ende I had written to the Capten before, and also to one Jo: Whithall[2] an englishman there: those Letteres as they told me was not commed to the Captens handes; notwithstandinge I should [have] aunswere the next daie, and so they departed.[3]

altit. 24.2.

Monndaye The xxith daie. I expected the Captens aunswer, which in the afternone I receavid from him by the mouthes of the ij gentlemen before named accompanied with one [Esteva Riposo *deleted*] Paulo Bedeves, a fleminge borne, with iij or iiij lynes in writinge, which I have kept: his aunswere by theim was this, that as of late they had submitted theim selves to the obaysaunce of the K. of Spaine, so had they receaved speciall charge from the K. by Don flores admirall of the fleete general for the Straight of Magalan to fortefie, that if happelie there should come into their harbour either englishe or frenche shippinge, but (especiallie) our Nation, they should neither have trade with us nor yelde us in any respect releif becawse aswell of thoffence committed by Sir ffr: Drake in the Sowth sea as that their was a new fleete of shippinge prepared by us for the Sowth sea, the which they iudged to be this.[4] Into the which we replied givinge theim manie reasons the contrarie, deliveringe theim not onlie a note of our sorts of

[1] The Genoese, 'Joffo Dore', father-in-law of the English merchant John Whithall, who had initiated the sugar trade with London in 1578.

[2] The *Minion* had been sent out, with a handsome gift to Whithall, in 1580–1 (*Pr. Nav.*, pp. 642–3). Adorno and Estevão Raposo owned *engenhos* (sugar plantations and refineries). Debriss or Bedeves perhaps = van de Vries. The Flemish Schets family had estates in the colony (see p. 252, n. 1).

[3] After a long day's work, Ward reports 'Then went we to supper [on board the *Galleon*], and after I got me aboord [his own ship] being weary, but before I went to bedde came divers complaints unto me of the evil speeches and practices used by Thomas Russell, which I partly examined before M. Walker, the Master & M. Jeffries, and finding cause of correction, I committed him to the bilbowes until further leasure to examine the cause: so placing a careful watch with charge to have care of the same, we passed y^t night very wel . . . ' (*Pr. Nav.*, pp. 665–6).

[4] See Document 28.

merchandize, butt offringe theim a sight of the things it self: In this discourse manie things passed betwixte us, but no graunte of trade obtaigned but onlie some releif of victualls they were contente to helpe us withall: Onlie if the fleete had been reatorned for Spain, then they would have delt with us, but now in no wise they could do it, waighinge that the spanishe fleete was to reatorne by them and to have their cheif supplie of victualls from theim &c notwithstanding they took with theim our note of merchandize and some other requests from us to the Capten and so departed with promisses to reatorne us aunswere. They brought me aborde a Beif, a porke with some fruites as Lemons, oranges, Gordes, Quinces, Pynnes &c.[1]

Tewesdaye The xxij[th] daie, I sent the merchaunts with a presente of vj yardes of clothe to the Capten and ix yards for the iij severall persons which were with me the daie before: But they were stayed by the waie by Paulo Bedeves, whose aunswer to theim was, that for asmuch as the Capten and his Councell had not yet mett nor determyned in what sorte to aunswere our demaundes, which should be performed with all speede possible. he willed theim for the presente to reatorne aborde againe, till they had mett and concluded what course they would hold with us, wherof we should be advertized so speedelie as they could effect the same. Manye of the poore Indians repaired aborde me with fruits, to whom I gave triffles and used with all courtesie.

Wedensdaye The xxiij[th] daie,[2] I wente and walked on shoore

[1] Two of Ward's men died and were buried this day. He reports: 'At nine a clocke after service, I sent to bury Robert Rese (Ross), one of the Master's mates, which died this morning: and also after dinner I conferred with the Master & Pilot about the choyse of another Mate for them, but concluded that father Kyd [see p. 159] should be assistant in the watch, but no Master's mate more. Also in the presence of the Master, M. Walker, the Pilot, M. Jeffries, M. Shawe and Tobias the Masters mate, was Thomas Russell examined, and his accusers, which examinations were written by M. Walker, and rest to be further considered of hereafter.' Ward reported this matter to Fenton the next day (Pr. Nav., p. 666).

[2] Ward reports that after dinner he had some private conference with the General and Captain Parker, the two chaplains being present (Pr. Nav., p. 666). Not only the merchants, but Lieutenant Hawkins, were all excluded from this discussion. Hawkins was not resigned to the abandonment of the South Sea project, and on the previous day 'after the olde custome', as Ward puts it, there had been 'foule speeches' between

to view some place where I might most aptlie sett upp my Smithes forges and an oven to Bake our breade in & to repaire our Casks; abowte midnight cam to the shoore side one John Whithall an englishman and was fetched aborde by thedwardes Pynnasse and so brought unto me aborde in the morninge.

Thursdaye The xxiiijth daie, erlie in the morninge Capten Warde brought John Whithall aborde me with whom I and he had conferrence, who seamed to be commed unto us by stealth and to advertize us the Captens doings and further to advize us what in his opinion was best for us to do, wherin he showed us that those delaies in not aunsweringe our demaundes, proceeded of the fearefullnes of the Capten that we were rather men of warr, then merchaunts, and withall had planted iij or iiij Peices for the defence of the Towne, notwithstandinge he tolde me that his assistaunts were of a contrarie of opinion in that they had seen by us, and therefore he thought it verie requisitt we should passe to the Towne of Sancto[1] with our Shippes in Peaceable manner, a meane bothe to cutt of the feare they had of good meaninge, and also procure our dispatche of trade which other waies would be lingred: beinge resolved that in this doinge all things should be well effected, and their showes of warres would prove but shadowes in thende.

Abowte ix of the clock in the morninge cam to me from the Capten Joseph Aldorno and Stephano Riposo declaringe to me that their was order taken for preparinge of us victualls of divers sorts (But no resolucion for trade) which victualls should be brought unto us upon Satterdaie followinge, wherof as we did admitt, so did we urge theim by manie perswacions to receave our trade as before we had delt therin with theim, and to the good meaninge we had to deale as honest merchaunts with theim, wherin we founde theim verie willinge to admitt therof: Onlie the feare they were in of

him and Fenton. For the General had demanded that all should sign their assent to coming to St Vincent (Document 58). Whether he still entertained his plan to seize the Portuguese settlement remains obscure. The colonists were convinced that he did (Documents 59A, 81).

[1] The modern Santos (see Map B, p. xlv, and Pl. V).

V. São Vicente and Santos, *c.* 1570

*MS chart in a Portuguese rutter of Brazil, in the Bibliote ca
da Ajuda, Lisbon (MS 51-IV-38, f. 20)*

Ascribed by Dr A. Cortesão to Luis Teixeira. Probably copied
c. 1586 from an earlier rutter.

revenge by the Spanishe fleete, when they should reatorne with drew their affections and desiers therin But concluded that upon Satterdaie followinge, the Capten and I should meete and have conferrence together upon the shoore with iiij persons a peice, and as we should aggree so to proceede accordingly and they departed with iche of theim a cloke clothe and one for Paulo Bedeves, which they receavid thankefullie.[1]

Abowte iiij of the clock in the afternone there cam into harbour iij greate Bisken shipps[2] of the fleete appointed for the straight of Magalan as the nexte daie I understonde by one of their owne companie, havinge in theim to the nomber of 700 & odd persons. at their comminge we were in quiet ordre repairinge manie things dekaied abowte our shipps, as for the presente I havinge my foretopp downe makinge new tressell trees to the same, and the Edwarde B. her maynetopp, wherupon they viewinge our estates, and havinge as by former conferrence with those of St Vincents a determynacion rather to fight with us, then to suffer us to rest in quiet there, as not Longe after it appeared, for that abowte ix of the Clock in the night they all waighed, and being butt litle winde, would have tawed the vice admirall thawrte my hawse[3] without answeringe me what they were when I hailed him (if I had not by gods good providence prevented the same,) and so have entred his men aborde me havinge within him 222 persons soldiours & marriners, a mattre which I was not for myne owne saffetie to suffre but to defende accordinglie & the rather for that thadmirall & reare admirall followed the same Course, wherupon there grew (unwillinglie) on my parte a sharpe conflicte betwixte him & me all that night, till such time as (god) gave me victorie against him by sinkinge

[1] Full detail of these transactions is to be found in Luke Ward's narrative (*Pr. Nav.*, p. 667). See also Document 59A.

[2] The correct description of the ships (which Don Diego Flores had declared unseaworthy) was as follows: *San Juan Bautista*, Captain Alonso de las Alas; *Santa Maria de Begoña*, Captain Rodrigo de Rada; and *Concepcion*, Captain Gregorio de las Alas (Markham, *Voyages of Sarmiento*, pp. 219–20). But new names appear in Documents 59A and 81.

[3] The three ships ranked as admiral, vice-admiral and rear-admiral. Sea-fights were still normally carried on by a boarding party of soldiers, but the *Galleon* and the *Edward* were of the new heavily gunned type.

him in the place, thedwarde as she might helpinge the same, and the next daie the other ij fought with us till the afternone in a verie cruell sorte, but in the ende (god of his mercie) delivered us from theim without loss of above v men presentlie slaine & 30 sore hurte, the hurte of our tackle & other things and Losse of a cable and ancour, and one of thedwardes.

ffrydaie The xxv^th daie. in the afternone we were (god be thanked) cleare of theim and not in daunger of shott: in the eveninge they waighed and went in to Sancto, thadmirall[1] (as I take it) scant hable to swymm above the water for the manie hurtes she received by us, She was a Shipp of 500 tonnes being viceadmirall before to Don Flores, in her there was 20 peices of brasse viz. demicolveringe, saker and Minion, the Captens name Rodrigo Darradas, havinge in him 230 men The viceadmirall whom I sonke called our Ladie, of the burthen of 300 tonnes with 16 peices of brasse and iiij of iron, viz. demicolveringe, saker & Minion, the Captens name being slaine in the feight was called Quivas [John Darradas *deleted*] and in him 222 men The rearadmirall of the Burden of 500 tonnes called the Conception with 20 peices of brasse of the

---

[1] For further accounts of the fighting see pp. 269, 281, and Ward's narrative (*Pr. Nav.*, p. 667). Pedro Sarmiento, on his return with the Spanish fleet from the Strait of Magellan reported as follows (Markham, *Voyages of Sarmiento*, p. 268): 'Arrived in this port of San Vicente, we found the three ships in it, which had been left at Santa Catalina to proceed to Rio Janeiro; the *Begoña* being at the bottom, with half her masts above water. We were informed that when our three ships arrived, they found two English ships inside the port, being two of the three which had robbed the friar, as already stated . . . Our ships, on entering, found that the English were on shore getting water. Our ships anchored at a distance from the English. The enemy, who at first had given themselves up for lost, seeing that we kept at a distance, went on board and got ready their cannons for the battle, that our people might not come upon them, for at first their ships were almost without hands. Afterwards the *Begoña*, whose Captain was Rodrigo de Rada, desiring to board, came up until she was alongside fighting with the English, while our other two ships did not move. The English in their ship, working their pieces of artillery, killed some of the crew of the *Begoña*, and with the lower deck guns they sank her and sent her to the bottom, the crew escaping to the shore in boats. The boatswain who was an Aragonese went to the English and remained with them . . . Next morning the two English and the two remaining Spanish ships began to cannonade each other, and it was believed the English Admiral received some injury. For the English finally left this port, and went to sea in the direction of the burnt island [Queimada Grande] which is 8 leagues distant to the SSW. On another day only one was sighted [i.e. the *Galleon*]'.

like bore as aforesaid and in her 220 men, the Cap*t*ens name John de Verra.[1]

Satterdaye The xxvj[th] we roade there still, aswell to repaire o*u*r hurtes in the Shipp, and to take in some water, as to waigh iij of their Anco*u*rs they Lefte for haste behinde theim when they cam to feight w*i*th us, two wherof we waighed and the thirde Anco*u*r Lost by an evill Boyroope. In the afternone I went aborde thedwarde, aswell to compforte such as were hurte, as to give thanks to all the residue for their valyant behavio*u*r in this conflict: And abowte x of the clock in the night we waighed havinge verie litle winde at N, & NNW. so as at one of the clock we cam to anco*u*r againe till it was iiij of the clock in the morninge, went S & b W. & S & b[y] e, w*i*th so litle winde as we were scante hable to cleare the lande till xij the nexte daie beinge forced to toogh[2] o*u*r Shipp w*i*th our boote & Pynnasse the winde beinge at E.

Sonndaye The xxvij[th] daie. At Middaye we wente S & b[y] e. 5 L. and N & b[y] e 4 L. and so beate upp & downe till vj of the clock in the morni*n*ge w*i*th much winde at what time we cam to Anco*u*r undre the Burnte Ilande, beinge not hable to get to St Sabastiens Ilande[3] where we mente to have watered and wooded o*u*r selves, by the contraritie of winde, the same Lyinge E from St Vincents. *winde at E cleare of St Vincents*

George, a Grecian borne, whom I saved w*i*th my boote after the viceadmirall was sonke, tolde me that att their comi*n*ge from Spaine the fleete was 22 sailes of shipping, wherof vj was cast awaie on the Coaste and xvj cam to the River of Janaru on the Coast of Brasill where they wintred in theim there was 3200 persons: of theim there was appointed for Chile 600 soldio*u*rs undre the Conduct of Don Allonso Maior and 300 soldio*u*rs with 100 howseholders appointed to fortefie & inhabitt the Straights of Magallan undre the Leadinge Don Pedro Sarmiento: In the River of Janaru they

---

[1] See above, p. 129, n. 2.
[2] Tow. The *Galleon* appears to have carried on deck a skiff, a ship's boat and a long boat or pinnace.
[3] St Sebastian Island lay about 70 miles east and slightly north of St Vincent (now Santos) Bay. Lofty and well forested, it was the landmark for approach from Europe.

lost one Litle Barke, and builded an other there for her, so as
they departed from thence with xvj sailes, thadmirall beinge
a shipp of a 1000 tonns, for the straight of Magalan, but before
there cominge into 38 degrees, ij of theim sonke in the Seas &
a iij^d perished on the Coast, and being in 48 degrees to the
Sowth wardes were forced with a slawe at SSW back againe
into 28 degrees to the Ilande of St Kathrin, & in that Lost ij
more Shipps, so as then they were but a xj in nomber wherof
iij was sente back to seeke us & take us or sinke us,[1] and
thadmirall with the residue proceeded for the Straights
myndinge to Leave one at the be of Plate to Lande the the
600 men appointed for Chile and so to pass theim over Lande
that waie.[2]

winde at E

Monndaye   The xxviijth daie, beinge commed to Ancour
undre the Burnt Ilande, I sente my companie to search for
water there, who brought some from thence, with woode for
an Ancour stocke. abowte 5 of the clock in the afternone the

*Edwarde
Bonaventure
departed*

Edwarde Bonaventure waighed & sett saile, bearinge upp and
downe by us, to take upp her boote & Pynnasse which (I
supposed) were waighinge of their Ancour they Lefte behinde
theim, & so departed presentlie to the sea.[3] blew a good gale
of winde.

wind at eNe

Tewesdaye The xxixth daie. I gott in ij tonns of water, beinge

[1] This does not appear to have been correct, although more than one of
King Philip's advisers begged him to send all English ships to the bottom
(Document 28). According to Pedro Sarmiento (op. cit., p. 256), 'This
was done by Diego Flores because, without these ships, there were none
to take the settlers and friars, nor the stores and provisions', i.e. in order
to wreck the purpose of the voyage, which was to plant a colony.

[2] It had been intended to take the '500 choice soldiers' to Chile through
the Strait (p. 237), but their General lost heart.

[3] No doubt the high wind made it prudent for the *Edward* to head out
to sea, but the shortage of water and provisions, and the interruption of
the repairs they were carrying out while at St Vincent, must have
influenced the decision to make for home. In little more than a week
Walker was dead, and within a month Mr Wilkes, too, had gone.
Meanwhile they were reduced to the extremity of using sea-water in the
cook's galley. Ward reports (*Pr. Nav.*, p. 668): 'The 12. day [of February]
having considered the lacke of water, the company were contented to have
the pease boyled, with three jacks of freshe water and two jacks of salte
water, for the prolonging the same.' A fortnight later he writes: 'The 27
day I allowed a certaine portion of wine to our men, to wit, halfe a canne
of wine to every six men every night at eight of the clock, at the setting of
the watche, to strengthe their weaknesse' (*Pr. Nav.*, p. 669).

all the springe would deliver & hewed tymb*er* for pr*o*vicion of necessaries abowt the Shipp: blew much winde.

Wedensdaye   The xxx^th daie. I stopped a Leake on the Larbord bowe betwixt winde & water or rather undre water. gott in some water and repaired other things dekayed in the Shipp.

winde at ENe.
faire weather

Thursdaye   The last daie, abowt iiij of the clock in the morni*n*ge we waighed not hable to ride any Longer undre the Ilande, and not Longe after it becam calme and so contynued untill xij of the clock: Then we caste abowte & wente Ne 3 L. and from thence till xij the next daie SSe. 10 L.

winde at N &
eSe & eNe
& Ne

[*February* 1583]

ffrydaie   The firste of ffebruarie. There Rem*ained* in victualls by estimation thies p*a*rcells followinge; viz. Breade 4000, Meale 100 Barrells, wyne tons 3 & di, and 9 Ru*n*letts, Aquavitae 4 litle Barrells: Porke hogesheads 11 and ij daies meate: Beif 4 hogesheads: Stockfishe 3000 Cooples; Buttre 30 firkins. Honye Barrells 7. Oyle Barrells 4½ Rize Bushells 90: Otmeale Barrells 24. Peas good & badd Barrells 23: vinegre hog*sheads* 7. At Middaye we wente till xij the next daie Se & b S. 10 L.

primo
februarie.

winde Ne & b
e. & NNe.

Jasper
Worman a
*sailo*ur *dyed*
of the flux

Satterdaye.   The ij^de daie. At Middaye we caste abowte and bare WSW for St Kathelins or the Baye of good Compforte,[1] to water having but vij ton*n*s a borde. & the winde at NNe, went till viij at night 4 L. WSW. and so till xij the nexte daie NNe litle winde 7 L.

winde NNe
altit. 25.55
winde Se

Sonndaye   The iij^de daie At Middaye becalmed and so contynued till viij of the clock at night from thence till vj in the morni*n*ge Se & b S, 7 L. and from thence till middaye WSW. 5 L.

winde at NNe
& Ne.

Monndaye.   The iiij^th daie. At Middaye we wente till xij the nexte daie WSW 32 L. wente alongest the Lande trending N & S.

altit' 26-10
winde at Ne &
NNe. Evan
*Gam*mage *dyed*

Tewesdaye.   The vth daie. Ric. Clarks arme being cutt of [2] he

altit' 26-50

---

[1] Fenton made for the only harbour he knew. He had no beer, very little beef and scanty water.
[2] Presumably amputated by the physician, John Banister.

winde NNe &
N. & Ne &
NW

dyed. At Middaye we wente till half hower to iiij of the clock WSW. 3 L & di. and from thence till xij the next daie SSe 2 L, Se 3 L. & eSe 4 L. & SSW. 2 L.

altit' 27-9.

Wedensdaye. The vj^th daie. At Middaye we wente till iij of the clock in the afternone 2 L. Ese and being then within v L

winde NW &
S. & S & b W.
some Raine.

of the shoore. the winde coming at S & b W. & we within 12 L of St Katherens where we ment to waterd bare upp and went eNe 28 L, till xij the next daie, in hoope that the winde would contynue, that we might either double the sholdes or gett Ca: frio for our watringe place.[1]

winde at SSW
& at Se & Se
& b[y] e, &
eSe. Raine
with fogg

Thursdaye. The vij^th daie. At Middaye we wente till midnight eNe 15 L. and so till xij the next daie Ne & b[y] e. 4 L. & Ne, 4 L, & Ne & b N 3 L.

winde at Se &
SSe much
Raine &
thowndre.

ffrydaie. The viij^th daie. At Middaye we wente xij howers Ne 16 L, eNe 2 L, & e, 1 L. & eSe 1 L & Ne & b N. 2 L. In thies watches we had calmes.

winde at N &
Ne

Satterdaie. The ix^th daie. At Middaye calme wente till xij the nexte daie E. 2 L. & Se. 9 L. and eSe 4 L.

altit. 26.10
winde at Ne,
NW & N, &
NNW.

Sonndaye. The xth daie. At Middaye we wente till xij the nexte daie Se 7 L. and E & b S. 7 L.

winde NNW
& S. much
winde. Bar:
godcharde dyed.

Monndaye. The xj^th daie. At Middaye we wente till xij the nexte daie E 2 L & Ne. 6 L. & Ne & b N. 8 L. & NNe 7 L.

altit. 25.20
winde S. much
winde. & at
Se.

Tewesdaye. The xij^th daie. At Middaye we wente till xij the nexte daie Ne & b N. 28 L.

winde at E &
Se.

Wedensdaye. The xiij^th daie. At Middaye we wente till xij the nexte daie xij L. Ne & b N.

altit. 23.38
Nic: Butler
dyed
winde S & Se

Thursdaye. The xiiij^th daie. At Middaye we wente till xij the next daie Ne & b N. 12 L.

winde S & Se
& SSe

ffrydaie. The xv^th daie. At Middaye litle winde we wente till xij the next daie 17 L. viz: 4 L Ne & b N. & NNe 13 L.

altit. 22.49
winde S & SSe
& WSW

Satterdaye. The xvj^th daie. At Middaye we wente till xij the nexte daie NNe. 21 L.

---

[1] They had turned back northwards. Cape Frio is in 22° 50′ S lat.

Sonndaye. The xvijth daie. At Middaye we wente till xij of the clock the nexte daie havinge litle winde NNe 15 L.

altit. 21.22.
winde WSW & SW

Monndaye. The xviijth daie. At Middaye we wente till xij the next daie N & b W 7 L and E & b N 6 L.

altit. 20.20
winde WSW & E & N

Tewesdaye The xixth daie. At Middaye we wente till xij the next daie E. 6 L. & Se & b e. 4 L. and NW & b W. 6 L.

altit. 20.5
winde N & b W & N & NW.

Wedensdaye. The xxth daie. At Middaye we wente till xij the next daie E. 5 L. & eSe 3 L. & WNW. 5 L. & W. 5 L.

altit. 19.58
winde N & b W, & N, & Ne

Thursdaye. The xxjth daie. At Middaie, we wente till vj of the clock the nexte daie in the morninge at W 8 L & WNW. 12 L.

altit. 19.38
winde at N & Ne

fridaie The xxijth. At vj of the clock in the morninge we discovered high Lande 9 L of and Sownded and had 36 fathoms rockie grownde with some litle Currall and so runninge in west & SW & NW & by W till middaye. had 26 fathoms 23 & 20 all like grownde within 3 L of the shoore, & to the northwestwards lowe lande and at iiij of the clock in the afternone I cam to ancour in the mouthe of the harbour of Santo Spirito[1] some shorte of the barr, having 6 fathoms & bettre of Ozey grownde. A Cannow cam of from the Towne but refused to come aborde me, albeit I hailed with a white clothe, but wente on shoore, and did the lik to me, wherupon I sente owt my Pynnasse and had conferrence with theim in frendlie sorte, declaringe I was a merchaunte of Eng: come to trade with theim, and so they departed reatorninge againe to me to the same place with a lettre from the providour, cravinge an aunswer, which I sente by them presentlie.[2]

altit. 20.6
winde NNe

Satterdaie. The xxiijth daie, I received lettres from the providour which be exstant, without any aunswere of resolucion by reason the Governours absence: and in the afternone, puttinge my self alonge the *shoore* in my pynnasse to seeke water, the Providour cam from the Towne to the water side, (& also the Governour but in the crowdes) after some Parley, I received into my   ij ostages and

---

[1] In a fortnight they had run only 7°, and at Spirito Santo (close to modern Vitória) Fenton renewed his efforts to trade his merchandise.

[2] No records of these exchanges of letters remain.

wente to the shoore and had conferrence with the Providour towchinge trade with theim, givinge him a lettre for the Governour & a note of my merchaundize, which he liked verie well & also iij yardes of fine black for him self which he received verie thankefullie. in like manner I sente to the Governour for a presente 3 yardes skarlett and yardes of Murrey clothe. I had graunte of him to sownd & bringe in my Shipp if I thought it convenient & water enough to ride in, whereof he advized me to be circumspect becawse of the barr, and libertie to woode, water and fishe with my Nett and departed in great frindshipp. [*Margin:* winde at Ne it hieth vj foote water, the harbour Lieth next hande SW & b W. & Ne & b[y] e, & is open to the Sea from the Ne & b[y] e to the Se & b[y] e, riding without the barr. A sonke rock lying Se & b[y] e a Litle from the S parte of the harbour. Massau the Negro dyed.

winde at Ne & NNe

Sonndaye. The xxiiij^th daie. In the morninge verie earely I received a lettre from the Providour with iij Turkye Cocks & some sweete Lymes with a freshe Cheze and abowte xij of the Clock, I received also a Lettre from the Governour Vasco farnando Cowtiniho with ij younge beifs & ij turkie Cocks: Sownded the harbour to thende to have ancored within the Barr, but founde but ij fathoms & di of water, & therfore forced to ride where I did. I appointed Capten Parker to make also certein wells for provicion of water which he performed.

winde at N & Ne

Monndaye. The xxv^th daie. In the morninge I receaved a lettre from the providour with a Beif & other trifflinge fruites with a greate Parratt from the Governour: who advized me that the Governour & Countrey people would conclude as this daie what course they would hold me: I sent him drinkinge Glasses according to his desier with a peice of whit hamshire Cursey for their unhollie fathers & twoo riche purses of myne owne for the Governours wife and the providours with di 1000 of Needells & in the afternone I fell verie sick of a burninge fever, notwithstanding I to shoore & had conferrence with the providour, but could not conclude of any Ende.

Tewesday The xxvj^th daie, I was verie sick & Lett bloud

received a lettre from the Governour which I aunswered ymmediatly.

Wedensdaye The xxvij[th]. The governour wrote to me, which lettre S. fardinando[2] aunswered beinge not hable to do it my self; and a merchaunt by stealth sent aborde a chest of suger in truck for other warres. *my father Madox dyed*[1]

Thursdaye. The xxviij[th] daie. The Governour wrote to me an other lettre with offre of beif for provicion but not trade, and water to be taken in saffetie. Stopped a Leake.

[March 1583]

ffrydaye. The first of Marche. towardes night the providour wrote me a lettre of an aggreement for trade, wishinge I would come to that ende to talke with him & the holie fathers, but being neither hable to go nor write by reason my weaknes, I sente S. fardinando to satisfie theim & knowe their further pleasures, who appointed sonndaye following in the afternone for that purpose. *the first of Marche.*

Satterdaye The ij[de] daie, there cam aborde a merchaunte to fetche things for victualls & sagoe he had sold us.

Sonndaye The iij[de] daie I wrote a lettre to the governour wherin I gave S. fardinando aucthoritie to conclude the traffique, who mett with the providour who had the like aucthoritie from the Governour to confirme the same, as appeareth by their writings remaining with me. There cam from the governour to visitt me iij or iiij gentlemen. In this treatie I founde greate presumption of traison which I dissembled till I had victualls & water[3] *altit. 20.6*

Monndaye. The iiij[th] daie, my water was in effect finished & my shipp in some ordre & readines to sett saile if neede *winde at S.*

---

[1] The only notification of his death, save for the oblique reference in Thomas Martin's introduction to his published sermon 'that shorte, sweete, and comfortable sermon, which that godly, learned, and vertuous young man John [*sic*] Madox, M. of Arte and Fellow of All Soules in Oxforde, in your hearing, preached here in this Chapel of Melcombe . . . hee, now having reaped the fruites of his faith, is made coheire with his and our Christ, in the Kingdom of our good God'.

[2] The Portuguese pilot. Lieutenant Hawkins complained (p. 283) that he was excluded from all these negotiations.

[3] There was probably deliberate delaying action by the Portuguese. The entire Spanish fleet had turned back from the mouth of the Strait in February and was approaching.

required And as in the afternone I was sinying the conclusion of trade betwixt the governour & me, a smale Barke arrived from St Vincents, who brought (as I iudge) intelligence of our former proceedings there.[1]

Wind S & SSW. I began to amend of my sicknes the Lorde be praised. muche Raine.

Tewesdaye   The vth daie abowt six of the clock in the morninge we sett saile from Sancto Spirito & wente till Middaye 6 L E. from thence till vj in the morninge the next daie E & b N, 8 L & thence till xij of the clock 2 L ENe.

much Raine winde at SSe & Se, & eNe

Wedensdaye.   The vj[th] daie. At Middaye we wente till iij of the clock in the morninge ENe, 8 L. and so till xij of the clock being litle winde. SSe. 3 L.

winde at NNe & e, & e & b S.

Thursdaye.   The vij[th] daie. much Raine. sownded at ix of ye clock & had 43 fathoms rockie grounde. At Middaye we [wente] till xij the next daie SSW.[2] 12 L. much Raine.

winde at e & Ne & eSe & e

ffrydaie   The viij[th] daie. Raine. At Middaye we wente till xij the next daie SW. 2 L. & NNe. 7 L and S & b W. 3 L.

wind at E & e & b S.

Satterdaye.   The ix[th] daie much Raine At Middaye we went SSW 5 L & S. 5 L. till xij the next daie.

wind at eNe & Ne

Sonndaye   The xth daie much Raine At Middaye we wente SSW 5 L & S 5 L. till xij the next daie.

wind Ne & b[y] e & N, & E

Monndaye   The xj[th] daie some Raine, putt a new mayne topsaile to the yarde. At Middaye we wente till xij the nexte daie S & b[y] e 12 L. & Se, 14 L.

altit. 23.2 winde at NNe, & N.

Tewesdaye   The xij[th] daie. At Middaye we wente till xij the nexte daie Se 8 L. & eSe 8 L.

winde at N altit. 23.12. & NW & b N.

Wedensdaye   The xiij[th] daie. At Middaye we wente till xij the nexte daie E. 8 L. & e & b N 8 L.

altit. 23.14 winde at NW & b N. & N.

Thursdaye   The xiiij[th] daie At Middaye we wente till xij the next daie havinge litle winde Ne & b N 3 L. and E & b N. 6 L.

winde at N & by W. & N. & Ne

ffrydaye   The xv[th] daie, At Middaye wente till xij the next daie having litle winde Se & b[y] e 2 L. & Ese, 2 L. & E. 6 L.

winde at NNW & N

Satterdaye   The xvj[th] daie, At Middaye we wente till xij the next daie E & b S. 8. & E. 8 L.

[1] Fenton could deceive himself no longer, and early the next morning took himself off.

[2] After standing out to sea he went south.

Sonndaye The xvijth daie. At Middaye we wente till xij the next daie havinge litle winde Ne.[1] 3 L & E. 6 L.

altit. 23.48
winde at NNW & N

Monndaye. The xviijth daie. At Middaye we wente till xij the next daie havinge litle winde Ne & by e. 3 L. & N. 2 L.

altit. 23.54
winde at NW & by N & SSW

Tewesdaye. The xixth daie, At Middaie we wente till xij the next daie N. 3 L. & N & by e, 5 L, & NW & by N. 8 L.

winde at S & SSe & Ne & by N

Wedensdaye The xxth daie, At Middaye We wente till xij the next daie NNW 13 L. & NW & by N. 6 L.

altit. 23.2
winde at Ne & by e, & E.

Thursdaye The xxjth daie, At Middaye we wente till xij the next daie NNW, 5 L. & NW & b N 5 L. & NW. 9 L.

altit' 22–0
winde at Ne. & E, & Ne & by N.

ffrydaie. The xxijth daie At Middaye we wente till xij the next daie NW, 2 L. & Se & by e 14 L.

altit. 21.6.
winde at E & by N. & ENE. & NNe.

Satterdaye. The xxiijth daie, At Middaye We wente till xij the next daie, E. 8 L, and ENe 8 L.

winde at N & NNW.

Sonndaye. The xxiiijth daie, At Middaie, we wente till xij the next daie beinge for the most parte calme, Ne & by e. 4 L. & N. 2 L.

winde at N. & NNW. & WSW

Monndaye. The xxvth daye, At Middaie litle winde with Raine, wente till xij the nexte daie N. 6 L.

winde at Se & SSW & W

Tewesdaye The xxvjth daie. At Middaye. litle winde. wente till xij the next daie N, 5 L.

altit. 20.51.
winde at W & b N. & NW & SSW

Wedensdaye The xxvijth daie, At Middaye, litle winde. our leeke encreased muche, so as we had 400 strooks in ij glasses;[2] & serchinge for the same, founde it to be in the larbour pompe as it was supposed, but it fell not owt so. wente till xij the next daie N. 7 L.

altit. 20.23.
winde at W & SSW.

Thursdaye The xxviijth daie, we putt over a Bonnett with okham to serche for our Leake but found it not At Middaie we wente having litle winde till xij the next daie N. 9 L.

winde at NNW. & NNe. & SSe.

ffrydaie. The xxixth. we rommaged in thold to serche for our Leake but could not finde it, albeit we hadde a weeping of

winde at SSe & Se. litle wind

[1] Fenton had made nearly 4° southing and was well out to the east. He now set course northward.

[2] Presumably strokes at the pump. The leak is not mentioned after April 2.

water in the laborde quarter abafte abowt the Biskett rowme. At Middaye we wente till xij the next daie N. 15 L.

altit. 19.25 winde at Se & S, & S & b[y] e.

Satterdaye The xxx^th daie, we rom*m*aged againe afore the mast, to serche for o*u*r Leake, but could not finde it by reason of the Shipps thicknes of tymb*e*r and closse Lyinge of the same. At Middaye till xij the next daie we wente, having much Raine, N. 24 L.

winde at N & by e.

Easter Sonndaye. The last daie, At Middaie litle wind w*i*th Raine went till xij the next daie NNW 2 L. and E. 10. L.

[*April* 1583]

wind at N & by W altit' 17–32 & W & by N

Monndaie primo Aprilis. The first of Aprill, At Middaie we wente till xij the next daie NNe. 4 L. & Ne & by e, 6 L. and E & by N, 4 L. Victualls of all sortes[1] by estimation Rem*a*ining in the Shipp, viz, In Meale Barrells 82. wyne j ton & di. & ix Ru*n*letts muskadell. Porke hog' 7, Stockfishe 2631 Coples at 60 Coples to the 100, Butter firkins 17, oyle smale Barr*ells* 4. Rize Bushells 80. Otmeale Barrells 22. Peas Rotton, 20 Barr*ells*. Aquavitae smale Barr*ells* 4 & vinegre 4 hogesh*eads*.

altit. 16.58 winde at NNW. & NNe & N & by e.

Tewesdaie The ij^de daie. we serched for o*u*r Leake w*hi*ch by all liklehood we iudged to be betwixte the Stem*m* & the scarfe,[2] but could not com*m*e to stopp it w*i*thin borde, for the hugeness of the tymb*e*r in that place, or otherwaies by cuttinge of some principall peice of tymb*e*r might weaken the shipp At Middaye we wente till xij the next daie E. 6 L. & NW 4 L. litle winde.

altit. 16.47. winde at Ne & by N. & eNe.

Wedensdaye The iij^de daie. At Middaye we wente till xij the next daie NW 8 L & NNW. 13 L.

altit. 15.40 winde at eNe, & e, & e & by S.

Thursday the iiij^th daie, At Middaye we wente till xij the next daie NNW. 18 L.

altit. 14.55 winde at e & b N, & eNe, & e & b S.

ffrydaie The vth daie. At Middaye we wente till xij of the clock the next daie, NNW. 10 L. & N. 8 L, & N & b[y] e, 6 L.

---

[1] Cf. pp. 122, 133.
[2] Scarf: a joint by which two timbers are connected longitudinally into a continuous piece (*O.E.D.*).

Satterdaie The vjth daie. At Middaie we wente till xij the next daie NNW. 10 L. & NW. 8 L

altit. 13.33.
winde at Ne. &
Ne & b E.
Sonne sett at
W & b N, &
to ye
Northwards

Sonndaye The vijth daie, At Middaie we wente till xij the next daie N. 12 L. & N & by W 12 L.

altit' 12–41
winde at Ne &
b[y] e. & E. &
ENe. ye starr
12–5.

Monndaie. The viijth daie. At Middaye, We wente till xij the next daie N & by W. 21 L.

winde at eNe

Tewesdaie. The ixth daie. At Middaie we wente till xij the next daie N & by W. 18 L.

altit. 10–30.
winde a E &
b S. & E.
ye starr 10–5

Wedensdaye. The xth daie, At Middaye we wente till xij the next daie N. 20 L.

altit. 9–31.
winde at E. &
E & b S.

Thursdaie The xjth daie. At Middaie we wente till till xij the nexte daie N. 25 L.

altit. 8–18.
winde at E & b
S. & E

ffrydaye The xijth daie. At Middaie we wente till xij the next daie N & by E. 18 L.

altit. 6–47.
winde e & b S.
& eSe

Satterdaye The xiijth daie. At Middaie we wente till xij the next daie N & by E. 24 L.

altit. 5–37.
winde at E & b
S. & eSe

Sonndaie. The xiiijth daie. At Middaie we wente till xij the next daie N. 24 L.

altit. 4–18.
winde at E. &
ESE.

Monndaye The xvth daie. At Middaie we wente till xij the next daie N & b E. 13 L. & NNe. 13 L.

altit. 2–58
winde at SSe
& E. & E & b
S.

Tewesdaie. The xvjth daie. At Middaie we wente till xij the next daie N & b[y] e 13 L. & N & b W. 13 L.

altit. 1–38.
winde at ESe
& E & b S.

Wedensdaie The xvijth daie. At Middaie we wente till xij the next daie N & b[y] e. 13 L. & N & b W. 13 L. putt a new fortopsaile to the yarde.

altit. 0–8.
winde at ESE.

Thursdaie The xviijth daie. At Middaye litle winde we wente till xij the next daie N & b[y] e. 18 L.

altit. 1–11.
winde at ESe.
& SSe, NNe

ffrydaie The xixth daie, At Middaie we wente till xij the nexte daie N & b[y] e. 26 L.

altit. 2–0.
winde at ESe.

winde at ESe
& Ne & b[y] e

Satterdaye The xxth daie, At Middaie we wente till xij the nexte daie 12 L. NW & b N.

altit. 4–0.
winde at Ne &
b N & NNe

Sonndaye The xxjth daie. muche Raine in the morninge. At Middaie we wente till xij the next daie NW 25 L.

winde at NNe

Monndaye. The xxijth daie. At Middaie we wente till xij the next daie NW. 12 L. & NW & b W 12 L.

altit. 6–12
winde at Ne

Tewesdaye. The xxiijth daie. At Middaye we wente till xij the next daie NW & b W. 22 L.

winde at Ne.
b N. & Ne.

Wedensdaye The xxiiijth daie. At Middaie we wente till xij the next daie NW & b W. 13 L. and NW & b W. 16 L.

altit. 8–8.
winde at Ne &
b[y] e. & Ne.

Thursdaye. The xxvth daie, At Middaie we wente till xij the next daie NW & b W. 26 L.

Mr Bannestre tolde me that my lieuten*a*nte said unto him that the voyage was bought & sold by me before we cam owte, for that I had daielie conferrence with the Spanishe Embassadour.[1]

altit. 9.25
winde at eNe

ffrydaie. The xxvjth daie, At Middaie we wente till xij the next daie NW & b N. 26 L.

altit. 10.41.
winde Ne, &
Ne & b[y]e .

Satterdaye. The xxvijth daie, At Middaie we wente till xij the next daie N & b W 32 L.

altit. 12.18
winde at Ne &
b[y] e.

Sonndaye The xxviijth daie, At Middaie we wente till xij the next daie NNW. 17 L. & N & b W. 17 L.

altit. 14.0.
winde at Ne &
b[y] e. & e.

Monndaye. The xxixth daie, At Middaie we wente till xij the next daie NNW. 32 L.

tooke the N. starr[2] in 14 degr*ee*s & the Crosiers in xv degr*ee*s & di.

altit' 15–30
winde at E & b
S & Ne &
b[y] e.

Tewesdaye The xxxth daie, At Middaie we wente till xij the next daie NNW. 36 L.

[*May* 1583]

altit' 16–16
winde Ne &
b[y] e & e Ne

Wedensdaye pr*i*mo Maii. The first of Maie We putt a new forsaile to the y*a*rde. At Middaie we wente till xij the next daie NNW 12 L. Victualls Rem*ai*ning,[3] viz. Meale. Barrells 54,

---

[1] Such an accusation was part of the general 'smear' currency of the day. Since the previous Sunday the *Galleon* had been in the north-east trade wind belt, and was making considerable westing.

[2] See p. 300. He must mean that an observation of the Southern Cross gave him the lat. 15°½ which he records next day.

[3] Cf. pp. 133, 140. The biscuit had come to an end and the meal was now being used to bake bread.

Porke. Barrells 5. Wyne supposed 3 Butts, Butter firkins 5, Honie smale Barrells 13. Oyle smale Barrells 4. Rize Bushells 80. Otmeale Barrells 21, Peas Barrells 20 and Aquavitae Runletts 4.

Thursdaye. The ij^{de} daie, At Middaie we wente till xij the nexte daie NNW 13 L & N & b W 13 L.

alt. 18.0.
winde e Ne & eSe.
Ric. Rannson died.

ffrydaie. The iij^{de} daie, At Middaie we wente till xij the nexte daie NW & b N 21 L.

altit. 19–30.
winde eSe & eNe & Ne.

Satterdaie. The iiijth daie, At Middaie we wente till xij the nexte daie NW & b W. 25 L.

altit. 20–31.
winde e Ne & Ne

Sonndaie. The vth daie. At Middaie we wente till xij the next daie NW & b N 26 L.

altit. 21–16
winde eNe & e.

Memoranda that Cominge from the Sowthwardes & being in 18 degrees to the N of the Lyne we mett with a rock weede much like to the Giniper with beeries on it which comes from the gulph of Mexico, which the Portingalls call Sarragasse. and cominge to the Northwardes the more aboundunnce ye shall daielie meete therof, and it appearith by the course therof that the Currunnte comes from the W, and setteth to the ENe.[1]

Monndaye The vjth daie, At Middaie we wente till xij the next daie NW & b N 12 L. & N & b W. 14 L.

altit' 22–30
winde at e & b[y] n Water Webb[2] dyed.

Tewesdaye The vijth daie, At Middaie we wente till xij the next daie NNW 12 L & N & b W 13 L.

Wedensdaye. The viijth daie, At Middaye we wente till xij the nexte daie N & b w. 26 L.

altit' 25–00.
winde at E. ye starr 25–30

Thursdaye The ixth daie, At Middaie we wente till xij the nexte daie NNW. 25 L.

altit' 26–20
winde E & b N.

ffrydaie The xth daie. At Middaie we wente till xij the next daie NNW. 21 L.

altit' 27–34
winde at E & Se

Satterdaie The xjth daie, At Middaie litle winde. We wente till xij the next daie N & b[y] e 10 L.

altit' 28–47.
winde at Se.

Sonndaye The xijth daie, At Middaie litle winde. Wente till xij the next daie N. 8 L.

altit' 29–20
winde at Se

[1] They skirted the Sargasso Sea in the west Atlantic, and encountered the edge of the Gulf Stream. [2] The purser (see p. 157).

winde at Se

Monndaye The xiij[th] daie. At Middaye litle winde. wente till xij the next daie 10 L. N.

altit' 30–20
winde at Se &
eSe

Tewesdaie. The xiiij[th] daie, At Middaie litle winde. wente till xij the next daie N. 18 L.

altit' 31–23
winde eSe.S.
varied.

Wedensdaie. The xv[th] daie, At Middaie we wente till xij the next daie. N. 14 L. & N & b W 14 L.

altit' 32–54
winde eSe &
Se

Thursdaye The xvj[th] daie. At Middaie we wente till xij the next daie N. 18 L.

altit' 33–45.
winde at Se &
SW
James Wyman
dyed

ffrydaie The xvij[th] daie, At Middaie litle winde. wente till xij the next daie N 16 L & N & b W 16 L.

altit' 35–25.
winde at SW
& SW & b S.

Satterdaie The xviij[th] daie, At Middaie we wente till xij the next daie N. 20 L & N & b W. 20 L.

Sonndaie The xix[th] daie, At Middaie we wente till xij the next daie N & b W 32 L & Ne 4 L.

Altered my course from going to Newfoundlande[1] by the consente of the whole Companie for Englande havinge then in water v Butts and xij ynches & verie stormie weather.

winde at SW.
altitude as I
gest it 39 &
then for
englande[2]

Monndaye The xx[th] daie, At Middaie we wente till xij the next daie ENe, 28 L.

winde at NNW
& NNe

Tewesdaye. The xxj[th] daie. At Middaye we went till xij the next daie ENe, 21 L, & E. 6 L.

[1] This is the only indication of Fenton's purpose in keeping so far west. The company were in no condition to prey on the shipping on the Grand Bank, as is shown by the number of deaths that occurred during the following three weeks.

[2] They were now in the belt of south-westerly winds, and could expect a quick run home. Meanwhile Ward, three weeks ahead, was in soundings, and on May 27 encountered the first English ship (*Pr. Nav.*, p. 672): 'About 9. a clocke, we shewing our flags, and ensigne, and shooting of a peece, there came two boats aboord us, of whom we bought fish etc. But hearing newes of them of the health of our Queenes majestie, and our country in peace, we gave God thankes.' By the 28th they were just east of the Lizard and on the 29th dropped anchor at Plymouth: Blacoller and Johnson were at once sent ashore for necessary victuals, while the Mayor and sundry gentlemen came aboard to dine. In the afternoon Ward attended the funeral of the two unfortunates, Skevington and the boy Webb, who had died of scurvy during the night. The next day he saw to the ship: 'Betimes this morning I sawe a cable bought, tymber for a Davet, and Anchor stock etc.' His letter to Leicester (Document 60) would have been despatched immediately on arrival.

Wedensdaye. The xxijth daie, At Middaie litle winde wente till xij the nexte daie E. 3 L. & E & b N. 13 L.

winde at NNe & SW. & SSW.

Thursdaye. The xxiijth daie, At Middaie we wente till xij the next daie Ne & b[y] e 24 L.

altit' 3–40 winde SW pears Teeg died

ffrydaie. The xxiiijth daie, At Middaye we wente till xij the next daie Ne b[y] e 37 L.

altit' 40–50. winde at SW & WSW. Evan Jones, Roberte Oking died

Satterdaye The xxvth daie, At Middaie we wente till xij the Next daie Ne & b[y] e. 31 L.

altit' 42–5. winde at WSW. & SW & b S. & NW.

Sonndaye. The xxvjth daie. At Middaie we wente till xij the next daie ENe. 36 L.

altit' 43–0. winde at NW & b W. Roberte White dyed

Monndaye The xxvijth daie, At Middaie we wente till xij the Next daie eNe, 32 L.

altit' 43–39. winde at WSW. & NW. John Waklin dyed.

Tewesdaye The xxviijth daie. At Middaie we wente till iiij of the clock in the morni*n*ge eNe, 20 L. at what time we espied a saile going to the westwardes & so tacked wi*t*h her & havinge but litle winde till Middaye NW & b N. 3 L. & could not speak wi*t*h her.

winde at NW & b W & SSe, & Se.

Wedensdaye The xxixth daie. At Middaye we wente till xij the next daie N. 19 L.

altit' 44–52 winde at Se & b S.

Thursdaye The xxxth daie. At Middaie we had foggie weather wente till xij the next daie N. 4 L. & N & b W. 4 L. & e & b S. 5 L. & eNe 5 L.

winde at E & b S. & e. Petre Derickson dyed & e Ne. & NNW.

ffrydaie The xxxjth daie, At Middaie we wente till xij the nexte daie Ne & b e. 14 L. & eNe. 20 L.

altit' 46–0. winde at NW & b W. & at W. & WSW.

[*June* 1583]

Satterdaie pr*i*mo Junii. The first of June. At Middaye we wente till xij the next daie 36 L. eNe. Victualls Rem*aining* as follow*e*th,[1] viz Meale. Barrells 39. Stockfishe 2081 coples.

altit' 46–50. winde at W & WSW

[1] Compare pp. 140, 142. Apparently neither beef nor pork now

honie 4 firkins & 5 Barrells. Sweete oyle 3 Barrells, Otmeale 20 Barrells. Peas 20 hoggs*heads*. Rize & vinegre 1 hoggsh*ead*.

winde at W. &
SSW. John
Rannsom dyed.

Sonndaye. The ij^{de} daie, At Middaie we wente till xij the nexte daie 20 L. eNe. Stormye.

winde at SSW
& WSW.

Monndaye The iij^{de} daie, At Middaie we wente till xij the nexte daie eNe 18 [*L*]. & e & b N. 18 L.

at SW & b W.
& SW
Rowland
Peterson dyed.

Tewesdaye The iiijth daie, At Middaie we wente till xij the next daie 36 L. E & b N. Stormye.

at SW & b S.
& SW

Wedensdaye The vth daie. At Middaye wente till xij the next daie E & b N. 40 L. Stormye.

SSS [fold]
W [fold]
B Owen died

Thursdaye. The vjth daie. At Middaie stormye wente till xij the next daie E & b N. 30 L. Stormye.

at WSW & S.
altit' 50–19.
Zingo [fold] y^e
Negro dyed.

ffrydaie The vijth daie. At Middaie fine weather wente till xij the next daie E. 24 L. Sownded at v of the clock in the afternone at Tho. hoods request, and had no grounde, notwithstande he supposed him self to be within 60 L of the Lizarde.[1]

winde at W. &
W & b S. &
SSW. Morris
Jones dyed.

Satterdaye. The viijth daie. At Middaie wente till xij the next daie E. 14 L. and E & b S. 14 L.

winde at SSW
& S

Sonndaye The ixth daie. At Middaie we wente till xij the next daie E. 10 L. in this xxiiij howers there was xiiij of them Calme.

winde at Se.
& eNe. & Ne.
& N. Morris
fidler dyed.

Monndaye. The xth daie. Verie Erlie in the morninge we sownded & had 108 fathoms faire white smale sande beinge then upon thentrie of the Banke as Simon Farnando tolde me[2] & at Middaie wente till xij the next daie E. 12 L. & E & b S. 13 L. at viij of the clock in the night and had the like as above.

winde at N &
NNe. muche
winde &
tempestious

Tewesdaye. The xjth daie. At Middaie we wente till xij the next daie E & Se. 24 L. Sounded at vj of the clock at night & had 80 fathoms like the first with some redd specks therin

winde at NNe
& Ne

Wedensdaye. The xijth daie, sownded in the morninge & had the like sholding with some shells. At Middaie verie stormie

remained, and wine is not mentioned. The rotten pease had not been touched.

[1] When they should have been well in soundings.

[2] That is to say, on the Continental Shelf.

we tridd in our mayne coorse & sawe a saile to the west of us *John Jones* till vij at night S. 3½ [L] sownded & had 85 fathoms smale *dyed.* Browne sandes, with litle shells and like shivers of flaxe, and so till iij in the morninge Se. 5 L, and then discried certein holkes with whom we bare till viij of the clock but cold not overtake, SSW, 5 L. then we sownded & had 85 fathoms browne sande with St James shells being upon the Banke & Sillie as we supposed N or N & b[y] e of us, Cast abowte and went for Ireland[1] NW & b N. 5 L.

Thursdaye The xiij^th daie. At Middaie wente till xij the next *altit. 48.48.* daie NNW. 21 L. *winde at Ne. & eNe. & e.*

ffrydaye The xiiij^th daie. At Middaie wente till xij the nexte *altit. 49.52.* daie N. 18 L. & N & b W. 9 L. Sownded at vj of the clock at *winde at e. & eSe. & Se.* night & had 65 fathoms oze.

Satterdaie The xv^th daie. At viij of the clock in the morninge *altit. 51.31.* discovered Lande (god be praised) towardes Yookhall in *winde at Se.* Irelande, havinge then been 103 daies without sight of any Lande, and so wente NNW & NW. with Kinsall, where we cam to Ancour (god be praised) about iij of the clock in the afternone, going N & N & b[y] e into the haven havinge at a Lowe water 9.8½.7. and a quarter lesse, and 5 fathoms and iij and a foote les ozey sande, till you come to N. parte of Barrin Oges Castle, where to thesterlie you maie ride in vj & v fathoms. In your cominge in you muste borowe of thest side. The Tide setts eNe & WSW

Sonndaie The xvj^th daie. wrote to Sir Martin St leiger to see *winde at NW.* if the merchaunts of Corke would buye any our wares, sente *Martin Williams* my Sick men on Shoore & Meale for provicion of Breade. *died.* Sett downe an ordre, that no man should departe on shoore without my Licence, which was contemptiouslie brooken by one Edwarde Robinson[2] who answered me, he woulde aske me Leave butt go and comme he listeth and cared not a farte for the best in the Shipp setting the whole companie in a Mutany upon me.

---

[1] It is possible that Fenton did not wish to appear in England in such bad shape. It was just over a fortnight before he anchored in the Downs and sent off a letter to announce his return (Document 64).

[2] Edward Robinson, one of the quartermasters, had fallen foul of Fenton during the third Frobisher voyage (see p. 4).

winde at NW.   Monndaie. The xvij[th] daie, hired Laborers aswell to fill my water as to keepe the Pompe goinge, which notwithstandinge, one Frye, and one Petre Robinson[1] refused to do any worke, and Robinson beinge strook by me with my coogell offred force against me most disobedientlie & in Mutinous ordre wherby I was in perill of my life. Capten Barkley cam aborde me with divers gentlemen. received letteres from Sir Martin St leiger.

Jo. Ashe died.
Alex. Simonds
died.   Tewesdaye. The xviij[th] daie gott in my water and some woode & beif & beare.

winde at SSW.
much Raine.
Henry Borne
died William
Ducan died.   Wedensdaye The xix[th] daie, the Lorde Corthey cam aborde me with Phineas Adrisco and others. sente S. Ferdinando to presse men at Corke.[2]

winde S. much
Raine.   Thursdaye The xx[th] daie, received a lettere from the Suffraine of Kinsall to have his men I had prest discharged which I aunswered presentlie.

winde at SW.   ffrydaie The xxj[th] daie, Fardinando reatorned from Corke and had prest xiiij sailours.

wind at SSW.
a litle at NW.   Satterdaye The xxij[th] daie. 4 of those prest cam aborde me, thothers reatorned back againe for feare of the rebells.

winde at SSW   Sonndaye The xxiij[th] daie. I fell sicke of an agew.

winde at W.
& NW & b
W.   Monndaye The xxiiij[th] daie. abowte ij of the clock in the afternone we sett saile and wente S till we were cleare of the Rock & then went SSe and Se & b S till xij the nexte daie. 21 L.

winde at NW
& b W. & W.   Tewesdaie The xxv[th] daie. At Middaie we wente till 8 of the clock at night Se & b S 6. L. from thence till vj in the morninge litle or nothinge. sownded and had 63 fathoms smale browne sande with some skallopp shelles & longe white rootes therin wente till 12 of the clock E. & e & b N. 6 L. supposing Sillie to be NNW of us.

winde at W.   Wedensdaye The xxvj[th] daie At Middaie we wente eNe till midnight & then hailed in Ne & b N at 4 of the clock in the

---

[1] Fry was the quartermaster whom Fenton had once set in the bilboes (see below, p. 162), and Peter Robinson was an ordinary seaman. The crew would naturally be incensed at the delay to their return home.
[2] Fenton was still exercising his prerogative, under the Broad Seal, of pressing men into service.

148

morni*n*g discovered Lande being betwene Salcome & the Start, and at Middaie we were thwarte Apsham sailinge eNe.

Thursdaie   The xxvij[th] daie at [vj of the clock in the morning] we had well nigh brought the Wight a sterne of us, *deleted*] viij of the clock at night we *were* thwart Portlande; Hawkins & Tailboyes, beinge dronken Made a Mutynie of me, Com*m*ited Hawkins to the Bilboes[1] &c. *winde at WSW went eNe*

ffrydaie   The xxviij[th] daie at vj of the clock in the morni*n*ge we were thwarte the weight. wente E & b N and were at xij of the clock thwarte Shoram and at viij of the clock at night nigh Baychie. *winde at W & b S. went e & b N. altit. 51.0. wind at SW.*

Satterdaye   The xxix[th] daie in the morni*n*ge at 4 of the clock were thwarte Dungeon Nase[2] where were Certein Englishe Shipps ridinge. wente Ne & b N, and were thwarte Dover by ten of the clock following & wente eNe, and cam into the Downes abowte xij of the clock where we Anco*u*red. it blew verie much winde, sente Cap*t*en Parker on shoore w*i*th *lette*res to the Councell,[3] & one to p*ro*vide a Pilott & vj men with Beare &c. *winde at SW & b W. & SW.*

Sonndaye   The xxx[th] daie. it was verie tempestious so that o*u*r victualls could not come from the Shoore. *winde at SW.*

[*July* 1583]

Monndaye p*r*imo Julii. The first of Julie; at vj of the clock in the morni*n*ge cam o*u*r victualls aborde, sett saile at xij of the clock for goore ende Brought St Margretts Churche upon the height of the Downes open of the middest of the Clifs and wente N & b[y] e. & NNe & had v fathoms, 7, 8, 9 & 10 and some times 12. borowinge on the Goodwin side, we doubled the N. forlande havinge an ebb in hande and no winde cam to Anco*u*r The *Maste*r of the hoopdret cam aborde me. *winde at SSW. & S & b W. & S & be e.*

Tewesdaye   The ij[de] daie. abowte one of the clock in the morni*n*ge waighed & with litle winde came to goore end abowte vj of the clock followinge & ther ancored, attendinge o*u*r Pilott.[4] *winde at S.*

---

[1] For Hawkins's account, see Document 67.
[2] Dungeness.
[3] Documents 64, 65.
[4] I.e. the Thames pilot.

Document 38
Private Diary of Richard Madox[1]

[*January* 1582]

Thursday [January] 11. 1582.

I had Dyck Smotes trotting mare & rode to London . . .

14. [Sunday]

15.

I presented my selfe to my L. of Lester who caused Mr Greene to set me at meat for his own table was ful.[2] I was before Mr Alderman Barnes Master of ye Muscovy Howse, & Sir Francis Drake & others who shewing y^t I was comended to them by my L. demanded what I wold ask. I answered y^t I sowght not gayn but was glad to serve my countre or ther honorable howse or my L. & therfor wold refer myself to them, wch knew better than my self what was fit for me. This answer lyked them, so I was alowed xx^{ll} for my provision, w^t great promyse of bowntiful consyderation. I pray god I may deserve it.

21. Sunday.

. . . I receaved of Mr Aty xx^{ll} & gave hym an acquittanse for yt, being my furnyture for the viage . . .[3]

[*February* 1582]

februarie 13. Tuesday.

Having a letter from my cozin Nicholas y^t our viage was lyke to hold, I prepared myself to be redye[4]

[1] Extracts. B.M., Cotton MS App. XLVII; and Cotton MS Titus B. VIII, ff. 179–221. Abstract in *Cal. S.P., Col., E. Indies, 1513–1616*, no. 221. The Journal begins on 1 January 1582, when Madox is at Wolverhampton, visiting his married sister who has given birth to a child. He then returns to Oxford. Only entries bearing on Edward Fenton's voyage have been transcribed.

[2] It appears that Madox was already known to the Earl, and perhaps owed to him his Dorchester appointment.

[3] Purchases, including books, clothing, bedding and a sea-chest, are later recorded besides 'wax candles 18^d, Conserve of roses 2^s, conserve green ginger 8^s'. Among the books may be noted 'For Plato in Latin 35^s' (presumably the translation of M. Ficino) and 'For an Ephemerides 3^s 6^d'. This was most likely to have been *Ephemerides Joannis Stadii . . . secundum Antwerpiae longitudinem, ab anno 1554 usque ad annum 1606*, published at Cologne in 1581. The first cipher entry: 'Received this month £20. Disbursed of the sum £10' indicates that the diarist's method of private writing was not specially devised for the voyage.

[4] This London cousin has not been identified. Madox had travelled back to Oxford on January 27–8.

I spoke w^t Mr Marten of weymouth and had *14.*
commendations from Dorchester. I wrote bye hym to M^r
Greene.[1] I had approved me by my L. of Lesters letters to y^e
officers a cause for 3 yere, besyde my ordinary days w^t al
profyts resting in ye howse ye mean season, as yf I were
present, my lyverey and coamnes only excepted. Wigmore
& James wer very ernest for my chambers & my study,
beyond ye compase of any desert shewd unto mee.[2] Spent
12d.

I resigned my office in ye Convocation howse to M^r *15. Thursday*
beaumont, being thereunto commended by my L. of
Lecester.[3] [*cipher:* I had of Mr Beaumont there for twenty
marks.] I had also a lycens to preach in all ye world

Mr Torporly and I walked to Ratcliff, Mr Normand showed *19.*
me how the strength of his lodestone was increased.[4] *loadstone*

. . . Mr Furbysher was discharge of ye viage & Mr Fenton *27.*
put in his place.[5]

[*March* 1582]

My brother [Thomas] & syster & I dyned at Mr Hardwycks. *March 1.*
we went down by water to Blackwal to ye Edward Bonaventure
wher we eat & drank & cam home by Ratcliff.

---

[1] This must have been Thomas Martin who published the diarist's
sermon after his death. The Weymouth man brought commendations to
Oxford from Madox's unknown friends at Dorchester, and it is the fact
that he carried this letter to Master Green, a gentleman of Leicester's
household, that suggests a connection between Madox's past employment
and the Earl.

[2] Leicester had written as follows: 'To my loving friends the Warden
and Officers of All Souls in Oxford, after my right harty commendations,
whereas Mr Madox, Felow of your Colledge, is presently to be employed
in publique affayrs into farre parts without this Realme, from whence he
is likelye to return in 2 or 3 years or more, I therefore do hartily pray and
also require you that he may have a cause of 3 years absens from the
Colledge allowed him, and that his absens for the said tyme be no
hynderaunce to his commodytye in the Colledge, but that he may enjoy
all benefytes thereof as yf he were present, and so I bid you hartily
farewell. Your very loving friend Rob. Leicester' (quoted by M. Burrows,
Worthies of All Souls (1874), pp. 91–2).

[3] Beaumont became Deputy Proctor. See Document 79.

[4] Madox had returned to London on February 17, and supped with
young Mr Torporley the next day. Magnetic experiments were now
interesting a number of mathematicians, and culminated in Gilbert's
famous book *De Magnete* (1600).

[5] The only direct information of this change.

4. [*Sunday*] I was at ye cowrt, but my L. was at London, but on Monday I spoke w^t his L. & w^t my L. Howard & w^t Mr Treashuror.[1]

13. . . . I went to ye cowrt w^t Mr Carleyle & supped at Mr Secretaries lodging[2]

14. I dyned w^t Mr Carlil at his brother Hudsons[3] who is governour of Antwerp. He offered me x li to take a boy w^t me.

[*cipher:* But Mr Carleill would not let me.] I supt at youngs key at Clarks howse w^t Mr Banester & Mr Web ye purser.

15. Being w^t Mr Cyprian Lucar[4] he brought me to his neyboure Mr Ashley who maketh plainge cards. This man is of shropshire. He had prepared beads & devises to venter w^t Mr Humfrei Gilberte who is now abowt another viage.[5] He told me y^t he thowght to se when a letter dated at London ye first of May shold be delyvered at China before midsomer folowing *et econtra* for he is vowched upon report as he sayd of ye yndians y^t ther was a saylable passage over america between 43 & 46 degrees throe wch he sayd Sir Frances Drak cam hom fro the Moluccas. I supt at Mr Towerson in Tower Street w^t our general, our leiftenent, Mr Carleil & Mr Ward . . . Mr Towerson[6] hath been 3^s in Gynny in queen Maries daye and gayned well.

20. I dyned at Mr Carleyls w^t M^r general, Mr Parker Mr Carleyle etc. [*cipher:* Here Fenton feareth lest William Hawkins should outmatch him. He proffered fair spices to us promising to sell them a bargain et farther thenceforth.] We went to Alderman Barnes wher we found Hawkins, Ward & of our marchants, & ther we set down a proportion of 90 saylors & 30 other men for ye Gallion, & 60 saylors w^t 20 other for ye Edward, owt of wch ye An Fransis and the frigot at need must be manned.[7]

---

[1] Lord Burghley.   [2] Sir Francis Walsingham.

[3] Christopher Hoddesdon, foremost of the London merchants who purchased sugar from John Whithall (pp. l, 195).

[4] The writer on mathematical surveying and gunnery; a son of the Seville merchant Emanuel Lucar.

[5] There is evidence that Gilbert had intended to sail in 1582, the date attached to the Instructions to Thomas Bavin, the surveyor who was to accompany him. See E. G. R. Taylor, 'Instructions to a colonial surveyor in 1582', *M.M.*, XXXVII (1951), 48–62.

[6] His voyages were printed by Hakluyt in 1589.

[7] See Document 26. The *Anne Francis* had been one of the larger ships

. . . came to the Cowrt w^t my syster.   *25.*

I came to ye Cowrt, my L. told me y^t he woold beg Thomas *26.*
Ely[1] pardon to go w^t us as a fyner, wherof I was glad.

I was at ye Cowrt & coming aboard Mr Screven cam to me. *27 and 28.*
I went with him to London.

[April 1582]

. . . I went to ye cowrt, dyned w^t Mr Screven & Mr Lawley *April 1.*
in my L. Chanselar's lodging . . . I took my leave w^t my L.
of Lester who told me ye queen wold not let ele [Ely] go w^t us
lest we shold fare ye worse for hym, but in tyme er long he
would get him furth, wherof I certified Ely . . . And so I
came back to ye bark wch for lack of mariners (wch wer very
negligent) forfloed a good tyde . . .

. . . ye queen cam by in a barge. ye wynd being slack we *2. Monday*
wayd anchor & went to service . . .[2]   *Initium*
      Itineris

. . . Abowt 6 oclock almost 2 leags from Dover ther cam 4 *16. [Easter*
small barkes in o^r lye, wch o^r companye sayd wer men of war *Monday]*
. . . we weaved into them . . . ye fyrst being taken by o^r
boat had on her dyvers of ye men wch were shipt by Furbisher
for our viage, & after, cause Fenton was general wold not go,[3] *Wee take a*
but fyrst stole a bad vessel & after boording a flemyng *prize*
changed w^t hym & so had paltred up 3 barrels of bysket . . .
They were 9 of ye company and Watson was the capten, ther
was also one willobie a tawl feloe of Dover . . .

. . . Hear o^r bark ye Peter[4] had boorded a man of war who *18.*
said he had don Antonios commysion and had taken a
Frenchman loaded w^t salt, this was a lytle before sunset. Hear
cam by us in his boot Capt Clark a pyrat whom we did not *Clark in his*
then know, and hayling o^r ship drank to us then threw ye cup *bravery*
overbord, but had we knoen hym he shold also have walked
w^t us . . .

in Frobisher's third voyage, and the name here appears to be a slip for the
Bark Francis. For the frigate see pp. 155–6.
  [1] This refiner, apparently then in prison, has not been identified.
  [2] Madox writes a long and detailed account of the voyage down river,
the wait at Harwich and the passage to Dover. Space does not allow of its
inclusion here, but see *J. I. N.*, Jan. 1959.
  [3] See p. 151.   [4] The *Peter* carried stores for the voyage.

19.

We cam w^t al o^r prizes[1] toward Hampton & gave the Castle of Cawshot a bullet . . . here met us Mr Hawl, & along we cam to netley by ye Gallion whom we hayled w^t half a dosen sacres and she us with as many, & after y^t Mr Owtred ye Sherif,   Mr Alderman Barnes, Mr Towerson, ye mayor of hampton w^t others & *nimirum* o^r general & mr parker etc. had visited us we went abord o^r Admiral, ye Gallion Owtred, wch is a very stately ship w^t top & top gallant about 400 tunse & more. She was buylt at Hammel which is fast by, at Mr Owtreads charges abowt 4 yere synce,[2] & hath 2 spaynysh viages w^t smal profit, so y^t I hope her best hap be to come, being reserved for this wch is a greater action. She is made lyke unto ye Revenge but ye Edward was buylt at Rochester 8 years synce & is lyke ye forsyght. ye Gallion was molded by m^r baker & framed by John Ady. her tymber is very strong & she caryeth 42 cast peeces of culvering, sacre & mynion shot.[3] . . . Mr Walker was hear very gallant in a velvet hat.[4] I was told y^t he had preached on Sonday in hampton, & he told me y^t I was register of ye viage & y^t my L. of Leycester had spoken wel of mee & Mr Secretary Walsingham great good who indeed doth not knoe me nether can I tel wher he shold lern any thing of me other wyse than by ye report of M^r mylls & Mr Carleyl wherof nether ye one hath had tyme nor ye other conversation w^t me to knoe me indeed, but Mr Carleil's good nature hath conceved better of me than I can think of myself . . .

21.

I walked northward to wynchester 10 myle. I was told y^t Capten Carleil upon some discurtesy taken wold not goe wch was a great greif unto me.[5]

22. [Sunday]
1. after Easter

. . . I dyned w^t my L. bishop, who for because he was an

---

[1] The 'four small barks' and the *Peter*'s prize (p. 153). The *Edward Bonaventure* being heavily armed, smaller ships could offer no resistance if engaged in piracy or suspected of it.

[2] I.e. about 1578. For the new galleon-built vessels of which the Queen's ships *Foresight* (1570) and *Revenge* (1575) were the prototypes, see J. A. Williamson, *Hawkins of Plymouth* (1949), pp. 249–50; also Pls. II, III above.

[3] Compare this figure with Mendoza's assertions above, p. 37, and those of Fray Juan de Rivadeneyra (Document 49).

[4] Madox gained a more sympathetic attitude towards Walker in the course of this unhappy voyage.

[5] See pp. 42, 64.

Al Sowl colledge man made me great chear . . . Sir Fr. Drake was at hampton & dealing liberawly many ways gave M[r] Banester 50[s] and 50[s] more twyxt me m[r] Walker and m[r] lewes Ootmore, but in y[t] also M[r] Banister made himself a part.[1] Upon [Friday] at night w[ch] I forgot M[r] Hawkyns cam yn w[t] y[e] barque frauncys.

Y[e] mariners wer mustered at M[r] Owtreds wher he made a   *23.* very good & discreet exhortation to them, at nyght I supt ther & lay w[t] M[r] Wil. Barnes. I had good tawlk wth m[r] lewys Otmore[2] & fownd him a good stowt & sensible man, both in his owne profession & otherwyse, althogh other y[t] can do lesse by their arrogant presumption gette among y[e] ignorant an opinion of greater seyl.

We dyned w[t] y[e] generawl. I supt at y[e] Dolphin w[t] y[e]   *24. [Tuesday]* merchants whether rode Sir Humphery gilbert & was offended because they had bowght Luke wards barque,[3] ther y[e] ass & ye mule told us many a tydious tale. I lay at M[r] Dees house w[t] Mr Evans y[e] merchant & bowght a Danske Chest of my host 5[s]. I also entertayned Evan Johns to be my man & gave hym 19[s].[4]

I dyned at M[r] Dees, cam aboord, & after y[t] we had   *25.* appoynted men both for y[e] frances & y[e] Elizabeth we went to m[r] sherif Owtreds supt & lay.

Made my bedstie & set yt up & dyd order my stuf in y[e]   *26.* masters Cabyn w[t] whom I was appoynted to be. We dyned aboord y[e] Edward wher according to y[e] cownsels letter a box sealed w[t] hir ma[ties] privye seal was wrapped in Okam & put into a chest w[t] 3 locks wherof I receaved one key w[ch] is in y[e] til of my lesse chest hanged in a black sylk lace. And an other had Capten Ward., a third m[r] Owtread had to delyver unto M[r] Hawkins w[ch] was not then present.[5]

I was busy all day. Ther cam to me mr harward of Corpus   *28.*

---

[1] See p. 44. Banister was an objectionable fellow, and an ultra-Protestant.

[2] This was the surgeon on board the *Edward*, whom Madox preferred to the Oxford-licensed physician, Banister.

[3] Later sold to him for £40 (see p. 156).

[4] The servant Madox originally engaged had died suddenly in London. Evan Johns was shipped as a tailor and died on the voyage.

[5] See p. 53.

Christi Colledge my L. of Wynchesters chaplayn by whom I sent my L. a bysket. Ther was w^t him the preachers of hampton & other scholers. After came Mr Barloe of Wynchester & saw our cards etc.[1]

29. 2nd Sunday after Easter. The company being together I preached in ye Gallion . . . Ther was o^r general, al o^r captens save Drake, Mr Sherif Owtred, m^r mayor of hampton, Sir Reinolds of o^r Howse w^t others who dyned after under an yawn on ye barbican deck. I . . . sent a fyn bysket to Mrs Hovenden,[2] At 2 a'clock we wayd . . . in waying we broke a cable.

30. They [the Commissioners] came agayne to us and were al day w^t us in reconyng & musteryng . . . Mr Banester who because he hath not scholership to do anything but greedy of a vayn popular estimation to be thowght excellent some thing, cast overbord a curious payr of beads of myne wch Mrs Lucar[3] gave me to exchange at the yndyes because he wold appear very zealous . . . I am abashed to se how he overweenth hym self in comparison of Lewys Otmore who is both for surgery, for personage, for manhod, for wysdom a great deal beyond hym & for modesty w^tout comparison.

[May 1582]

May Day. Mr Alderman barnes, Mr Towerson, Mr Caslyn & ye rest took a muster of al o^r men & fownd them to be more than 200 wch was o^r proportion, but because ye Elizabeth was bowght for burden sake & ye frigot[4] sold for 40 li to Sir Humpfrey gilbert therfor for hir supply & y^t we wer by Mr Hawkins enformed we shold hav vitayl ynogh at ye yndyes we took in *Nota* abowt 30 more but yet this I marked by ye slynking away of some knaves after ther pay y^t yf yt wer possyble, as I knoe not

---

[1] William Barlow, nephew of Roger Barlow the Seville merchant, and author of *The Navigator's Supply* (1597), was already engaged upon experiments with the lodestone.

[2] This lady may have been related to Richard Hoveden, then Warden of All Souls, Oxford. The sending of a 'bysket' by way of farewell remains unexplained.

[3] The mother of Madox's friend Cyprian. Her cousin, Emanuel Watkins, had sailed with Drake.

[4] See pp. 152, 155.

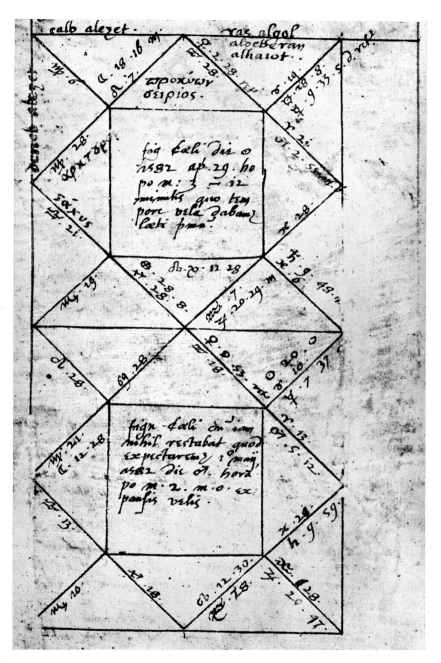

VI. Two horoscopes of Fenton's expedition cast by Madox,
29 April and 1 May 1582

(see explanation overleaf)

Two horoscopes of Fenton's Expedition,
29 April and 1 May 1582

(reproduced overleaf)

B.M., Cotton MS App. XLVII, f. 19

In Madox's day a belief in Judicial Astrology was not incompatible with the clerical profession. The chaplain cast two horoscopes at the commencement of the voyage, for a second weighing of anchors became necessary (p. 66). A third scheme which he drew out on leaving Sierra Leone has not been reproduced.

The conventional diagram indicates the four cardinal points, the south at the top, east to the left. Great circles drawn through these points and the observer's zenith divided the heavens into four quarters, each of which was subdivided into three, giving the 12 'Houses' represented on the diagram by twelve triangles. These are numbered counter-clockwise, the first House, called the Ascendent, being that on the eastern horizon where the heavenly bodies rise. With the help of the Ephemerides the astrologer marked the position of the Sun, Moon and planets on the celestial globe, and then ascertained the signs and degrees of the zodiac at which his twelve dividing circles cut it. Thus in the first (upper) horoscope, the 28th degree of Virgo was on the cusp (as it was called) of the Ascendent. The Sun was in the eighth House, for it was 3 hrs. 22 min. after noon; Venus, in a retrograde phase, was in the ninth House; the Moon in the eleventh. At 2 o'clock, on 1 May, the sun had only reached the 9th house (it was on the cusp of the 10th at noon), while the swift moving Moon was in the Ascendent. What these sky patterns prognosticated, however, Madox does not reveal, unless indeed he hints at it in the phrase 'dum jam nihil restabat quod expectaremus'.

whether yt be or noe, yt were not amysse to hyre men by y^e
week or moneth to ryg a ship not letting them wyt whether
and when al is redy, than to put men in wages for ye viage
. . . The general muster of o^r men in ye 4 gyngs[1] being most
tawl & stowt & al in maner likely men, after y^t we had refused
dyvers hansome feloes y^t made great sute to have gone w^t us
was this:—

[*Muster Roll*][2]

[*The following symbols have been added by the present editor:*

    o *had sailed with Frobisher*
    × *had sailed with Drake*
    + *death recorded on this voyage*]

In the Admyral cawled the Gallion Leycester

o Ed. Fenton Esq
    general
× Wyl Hawkyns leiftenant
  Nicholas Parker Capten at
    land
+ Rich. Madox. minister

Thos. Baynam[3] ⎫
Math. Taybush ⎬ merchants
Myles Evans[4] ⎭

o Christofer Hawl master
  John Banester surgion
  Symon Ferdinando ⎫ pilots
× Thos Whod ⎭
  Rich. Cotton ⎫ travelers
  Ed. gilman ⎭
o Rich. fayrwether masters
    mate

+ Wat. Webbe ⎫ pursers
  Robt. liddyngton ⎭
  Thos. Blancher M^r carpenter
  Ric. carpenter mate
  Nych. Wels ⎫ carpenters
+ John heath ⎭
  Matthew Byrd botswayn
  Thos. Body   his mate
× Symon wood ⎫
× Tho. meeke ⎬ musicians
+ × Rich. clark ⎪
  John Kennard ⎭
  Drum & fife 2
  Christ^r Jackson ⎫
  John Rawlyns ⎬ trumpets
  Ambrose harrison ⎭
  Esdras draper ⎫ stewards
  Tho. Thompson ⎭

---

[1] In each ship mariners were allotted either to the starboard or to the larboard watch.

[2] This Muster Roll in Madox's Diary has been collated where possible with a mutilated copy in Cotton MS Otho E. VIII, ff. 151-5. The thirteen men reported as dying in the *Francis* must have been successively replaced, but the names of those lost in or after the shipwreck of the *Bark* are not known. The name of 'M. Dore' (see p. 112, n. 1) is absent. He was perhaps a London kinsman of José Adorno ('Joffo Dore', p. 126), travelling secretly to St Vincent.

[3] Did not sail.   [4] Sent home from Sierra Leone, 1 October, 1582.

Robert London ⎫ cooks
—   ⎭

o Edw. robinson ⎤
John lynsey   ⎱ quarter
Arthure Cotton ⎰ masters
Wylliam Freye ⎦
John Gates Mr gunner
John Gore [Good] His
                    mate
William Kelly   ⎫
John brandyce   ⎪
+ hugh bowen   ⎪
+ John Paynter   ⎪
+ Robt. Oking   ⎬ gunners
nychol. Edmunds   ⎪
o Henry Kyrkman[1] ⎪
Edw. Chenye   ⎪
Wyl. Dobson   ⎭
Tho. Kydd   ⎫ coopers
+ John Ashe ⎭
+ Lawncelot Robinson ⎫ smiths
+ Rob. whyte   ⎭
+ David Evans ⎫ bakers
John Edwardes ⎭
+ John burden ⎫ taylors
+ Evan Jones ⎭
+ John Rawnson ⎫ showmakers
+ Wyl. Rawnson ⎭
+ Edw. Stokes   plat drawer
Harry bardsey   jueller
Nicholas Banx   poticary
+ James Wyn   barber
+ nichol Butler distiller
        [Sailors]
Charles Caeser
Barth. byston
John Smyth of Hampton
peter Robinson
+ John Joanes
John musgrave

Arth. rosse
Cyprian Boorman
+ Roger parkyns
Rich. bennet
Tege Hues
gyles moone
john Hawl
Henry rising
Denyse Coleman
Thos. Belcham
+ Opeirse tege
William field
+ Zachary stephens
Rob. hessal
John poynton
George gelby
William ynglet
Wyl. Foster
+ Wyl. gamedge
× John grype
+ Peter Deryckson
Barth. myner
+ Jasper Worman
+ morryce fydler
+ John kent
Wat. wood
+ Roland peterson
William persons
John Tegete
Lewys french
John yngleton
John bygford
+ Barth. godchard
+ martyn wylliams
+ Rich. Salt
+ Henry mellers
nichol. Collyns
+ Will. burges
Rob. flynt
Rich. godwyn

[1] Dismissed at Plymouth, 2 June 1582.

158

nathan. crokey
William Ceaser
+ rich. Cove
+ morryce Jones
+ henry Boorn

John Hurlston ⎫
nych. smyth ⎪
math. fysher ⎬ boys
muryce yong ⎪
valentyn holt ⎭

In ye Edward Bonaventure

o Mr. Luke Ward Viceadmiral
+ John Walker minister
  Thomas Persy master
  Samuel symbarb traveller
  Randal Shaw ⎫ merchants
  peter Jeffreys ⎭
  Lewys Otmore surgion
× Tho. blacoller pylot
  Tobyas Parris ⎫ master's
+ Rob. Rosse ⎭ mates
+ o Nycol. Chanselor purser
× John Kyd ⎫
+ Wylliam Duke ⎪ quarter-
  Rob. Mander ⎬ masters
  Wyl. sherwood ⎭
  John Tymberman ⎫
          Mr ⎪
  John Smyth mate ⎪
  John Johnson ⎪
  Rob. seely ⎬ gunners
  Tho. Russel ⎪
  John beard ⎪
  Nychol. edgerton ⎪
  John mansfield ⎭
  Nichol. Allen ⎫
  Wyllyam hues ⎬ carpenters
  Rob. Turner ⎪
  Wylliam charrol ⎭
  rafe lorkyn botswayn
  Wyll. man his mate
  Tege Caroe ⎫
+ John vobes ⎬ trumpets
+ Rob. wood ⎭
  Davy lake ⎫ drum &
  Rob. pemberton ⎭ fyfe

John lyddyn ⎫ stewards
Edmund lytye ⎭
Rich. woode ⎫ cookes
John page ⎭
John reynolds ⎫ coopers
Tho. wylom ⎭
+ Wyllyam wykers ⎫ smethes
John fawx ⎭
John whyt baker
Edw. Davis shomaker
Thom. boyd. jueller
John brian garbeler
Wylliam foster taylor
Antony notte barber
John Johnson distiller
[Sailors]
John pearse
Rob. pearse
John hilliard
Wylliam Dee
John Andrae
+ gryffyn davis
John wylson
John read
John roberts
Tho. swan
John fransis
John Austeyne
Rich. morryce
John greene
mark Towghts
+ lawrence Trip
giles Kyrk
Walter hues
Edmund Driver

+ gregory bool

walter hooker

Wyllyam towrson

+ launcelot Ashe

Evan Wyn

georg brodford ⎱

Rich. percy

+ Rob. Webb ⎬ boys

+ georg robinson

John Collyns ⎰

In yᵉ barque fraunsis

× John Drak capten

+ × Wyll Markham master

+ John godfrey mate

Wylliam Reynoles steward

+ Tho. bennet cooke

+ × John daniel gunner

+ Wylliam hunywel

carpenter

+ Tho. mysendyn surgion

+ Wyll. Darre

+ Thos. bodnam

+ Christ. Champlyn

+ Tho. herdman

Georg. Kyng (or Kiggs)

+ Tho. Chuter

+ Tho. Ogard

Rob. Brian ⎱ boys

+ John whyt ⎰

In ye Elisabeth

+ o Tho. Skevington capten

Rafe Crane master

Randall Fox his mate

+ [William Wilkes merchant]

John Case purser

+ George cox carpenter

Phillip green gunner

Tho. martyn steward

× John blacollar botswayn

Julian sawnders cook

Pawl berry

Rich. shute

Will. wylshire[1]

humph. bradford

× Peter Owyn

James Robson

3.   . . . We set Will. Wyllshire ashore because he was sick and did press a tynker & 2 carpenters to go wᵗ us

4.   Fowle & rough. We tawlked of yngland & Mʳ Cap. Parker concluded yᵗ he wᶜʰ cold endure yᵉ yrysh service & pleaz my L. of Aberg[av]eny myght go for a soldier & a syrvingman in any place of yngland

6. Sunday.   . . . The master & I walked a shore. he told me how frobusher delt wᵗ hym very headyly sure, & how yᵗ frobusher was not yᵉ mariner he was taken to be, as I easyly beleave.[2]

7   . . . Yᵉ sport was yᵗ whylst I stood in a studye being wery

[1] Discharged sick, 3 May 1582.

[2] This no doubt related to the dispute which occurred when Frobisher entered the 'Mistaken Straits', i.e. Hudson's Strait, insisting that he was in what is now called Frobisher Bay. See George Best, *Voyages of Frobisher* (Hakluyt Society, 1867), pp. 241, 296.

of his [Banister's] tawlk & thowght in myself surely this is a very vayn glorious asse, he clapt me on ye sholder and sayd yt is true, man! Mr Parker . . . is a very honest & curteows gentilman, and liberawl mynded, and one y^t thinketh modestly of hymself.

. . . We hard y^t y^e   Mr Owtreads ship[1] wch 8. he sent to ye yles of Pyckery had geven such a fall to a frenchman as made her beshrew her own self, so y^t now she lay wonded at Dartmouth.

reward of picking

We lay stil at yarmowth. M^r whood and M^r blacollar o^r 9. pylotes cam & sayd they wer chased by pyrates

. . . I had reynoldus tables of Tobias to correct, wher in 11. some places they wer false printed.[2]

. . . We hard y^t Capten Lawndrey ye french had taken S^t 15. Mychaels, one of ye Azores in behalf of ye K. of Portingal

Mr Hawkins of Plymmowth ryding to London cam to us. 17. He told y^t ye K. of Spayn had sent 8 ships to ye Moluccas & 5 wer cast away on ye cost of Barbarye[3]

Ther came overnyght 2 sayles whereof one carried ye 20. [*Sunday*] Spaynish imbassador Antonio de Castilio,[4] ye other was ye Bark but they both laded corn to Spain for because they cam proudly in our loofe & wold nether stryke flag nor top, o^r Master went w^t Commyssion to ye Unitye of London wher the Embassador was, to fet away Thomas Claye the carpenter, but Stephen Muns of Lee ther papistical Master cam w^t ye ymbassadors man to have hym released and shewed us ther passport for hymself & al his company but we answered that this belonged to the company of Spayniards & no more. We

---

[1] With Don Antonio's letters of marque.

[2] Probably *Ephemerides trium annorum* [15]*58, 59, 60 ex E. Reinholdi tabellis . . . per J. Feild . . . ad meridianum inclytae civitatis Londinensis supputatae* (London, 1558). Tobias Paris was mate of the *Edward*, and clearly sufficiently educated to undertake astronomical navigation.

[3] After a preliminary disaster in the autumn of 1581 the reconstituted Spanish fleet of 22 ships left Cadiz on 9 December 1581, reached the Cape Verde Islands on 9 January 1582, and Rio de Janeiro on March 24. Here they remained for nearly eight months.

[4] They were lying in Yarmouth Roads (see p. 86), and Antonio de Castillo, formerly the Portuguese Ambassador, was on his way to call on Drake at Plymouth. He had refused to acknowledge Don Antonio as successor to the Portuguese throne. See *Cal. S.P., Foreign, May–December 1582*, no. 56. The *Bark* was the *Francis*.

did also sharply rebuke Muns ye master for his unloyal pryde & because he went abowt to discorage some of o^r men from ye viage. Wee dyned in ye Frances w^t Capten Drake wher we had good chere & good frendly welcom w^towt curiosytye of woords.

24. *Ascension Day.*

We wayd Anchor in hope to have wethered ye Stert, but when we cold not (the wynd being ful west) we turned to Dartmowth & rod in ye range at 15 fathome almost a myle fro shore. Hear we sent our boat to furnysh our watering [*cipher:* The Master told me that had he supposed that the voyage would have turned to pilfering, which now he suspected, he would not have undertaken it.[1]]

At supper we talked of tatlers & counted Hearle y^t betrayed Madder but a knave, as is Nychol, ye Jesuit & [*cipher:* Bodnam in the holy house in Spain no better for he sendeth letters to the Council.[2]]

26.

Mr Hoode cam from Plymmowth & browght me commendations from Sir Fraunces Drake, He browght also some ropes whereof dyvers complayned y^t we did want, but speshall Ferdinando. He told lykewyse a great wonder y^t a horse bite his wyf by ye sholder, and y^t ye Barque hastings was bownd presently for Brazyle.[3]

27. [*Sunday.*]

Robt. Lyddington was sent to Plymmowth for 2 cables.

28.

John Case desyred me to be his frend to ryde hym owt of ye Elisabeth for Capten Skevington was so curious y^t noe man can yndure hym.

29.

. . . Frye[4] was set in the bilboes for lying a shore [*cipher:*

---

[1] The conversation of Thomas Hood and Simon Ferdinando at mess must have opened his eyes; see pp. 171 ff.

[2] The intensive Jesuit mission in England had begun in 1580. Roger Bodenham was an hispaniolized Englishman in contact with the Privy Council, and Mendoza later mentions William Bodenham as a useful contact in a letter to his master dated 4 June 1583 (*Cal. S.P., Span., 1580–6*, no. 339).

[3] This was Drake's ship in which it is suggested that Frobisher and Captain Acres intended to beat Fenton to the Moluccas by going direct to the Strait (see p. 40); but there is no record that they actually sailed, whereas the *Bark Hastings* was certainly in William Hawkins's fleet which left England for Brazil late in 1582 (see p. lv, n. 2). In an *aide memoire* jotted on the document cited (MS Harl. 167, f. 201) Frobisher's name is mentioned, but without explanation.

[4] See p. 158. He was a quartermaster.

It was ill taken: The Master told me Alderman Barnes
thought our General but a foolish, flattering, fretting creeper,
and so I fear he will prove.]

We lay stil in Tor-bay and did nothing. *30.*

Capten Ward was aboard us & had a cobbey.[1] he catcht o[r] *31.*
lord & carried hym home & hanged hym on y[e] shrowds, so
had we good sport. Capten Hawkins went to Plymmothe. I
wrot by hym to Sir Frances. [*cipher:* and would have gone
also but our governor[2] would not permit, because he feared
lest anywise commendation should go to Sir Francis.]

At night the wind feared [veered] to y[e] nornorthwest so
that we set sayle & by morning had got past y[e] Stert.

[*June* 1582]

When some wold willingly have goen to Plymmowth, some, *June 1st.*
as namely M[r] whood, desyred y[t] at least y[e] Frances myght
turne in thither & fet Mr Hawkins but the generawl wold not *A jar begune[3]*
in any case suffer yt, w[ch] made men think y[t] he wold more
gladly have gone w[t]owt hym, than to have had his company,
y[t] M[r] Parker myght have been Leiftenent. Wherupon great
stomach was taken as y[e] effect did declare. but y[e] wynd
fawling to y[e] west southwest cawsed us in despyte to go to
plymmowth, wher we anchored in y[e] Sownd, w[ch] is a very
fayr place. Plymmowth stands in y[e] breech of 2 fayr ryvers
for y[t] hath Cat water on y[e] East syde and Saltash water on y[e]
west, and ech of them yild harbore for 200 great ships to
come forth of y[e] harbore, comodiously w[t] any wynd. M[r]
Walker & I went thither purposely to have walked only, but
M[r] Leiftenent w[ch] was now come from Sir Fraunces Drakes
at Bucland, had us to M[r] Whoodes howse wher we supt, w[t]
M[r] Whyticaws[4] y[t] hath maried M[r] Hawkins syster. & after

---

[1] The verb 'to cob', or give a cobby, in nautical parlance meant 'to strike
on the buttocks'. The crew of a ship were given licence from time to time
to sport and play under a Lord of Misrule. Madox had reported in his
Diary, on 20 May 1582: 'My L. [Foster?] being a little drunk went up to
the main top to fet down a rebel, and 20 at the least after him, where they
gave him a cobbey upon the cap of the main mast' (Cotton MS App.
XLVII, f. 22).
[2] Captain Fenton. [3] See pp. 70–71.
[4] It was from Mr Whitaker that Walker heard the gossips' story of why
Drake executed Doughty. He related it to Madox when they were in

we returned to ye Edward wher we discoursed w^t the Viceadmiral of many mens maners & many matters, [ad]vising how love myght best be mayntayned & good order kept, but wher overweening pevishness is once p[la]nted, & myxed w^t a kynd of creeping dissimulation yt is hard ther to setle ye seeds of any good advice for now beginneth ye hydden poyson so boeth[1] owt. While Mr Hawkins supposed y^t consydering Sir Fraunces Drakes bownty to ye whole company & his endevowr in this viage yt had been a poynt of curtesy to have doen Sir Fr. y^t honour as to have come to Plymmowth, Mr Fenton on ye othersyde, fownd smal musique on this string, but because he supposed y^t what water cam to Mr Hawkins myl was lost from his owne, and besydes also, I know not how, he had as leif go by Sir Frances howse thirsty as cawl & drink. Whether he lacked money or noe I can not tel, & yet Luke Ward told me he borrowed 20 li of Sir Edward Horsey at ye Cowes & 10 li of Sir Frances hear, & had w^t owt any advice of one or other sent a bil of a ℓli to London, wch I ymagin wil be yl welcom, for Alderman Barnes befor hand did besech hym to take heed thereof.

2.   In ye morning the wynd at northwest ye generall wold needs be gon, althoe Sir Frances send us word y^t this morning he wold se us, ye Master desyred y^t he myght send ye pynnayse a shore for ye leiftenent, & ye pilot & others, but ye general wold not agree, yet did ye Master send yt, yn mean season ye general comanding to wey anchors the mariners utterly refused, saying y^t they ventured for the thirds & wold not therfore go w^towt ye pilats. Y^e general hearat storming, ye Master bad them way & after he wold ply for ther comyng, so did they, this whyle I was in ye Edward, wel away went ye Gallion & ye Edward after, & ye Francis was under sayl, but about noone Capten Ward & I went on ye Gallion wher we

Sierra Leone, and as the latter reports it (translation from his Latin): 'Doughty had often been intimate with Francis Drake's wife, and when he was drunk boasted of this to the husband himself. He afterwards realised his mistake and feared vengeance. Hence he sought the ruin of the other by every means, but himself fell into a trap. For he was accused of lèse majesté because he had said that the Privy Councillors could be corrupted by bribes' (Cotton MS App. XLVII, f. 47).

[1] Both, i.e. love and good order (?).

found them in a great murmuring for y^t some thowght ye Frances upon this discurtesy wold stay behind: Then dyd we enter into a close consultation, (for every impudent boy leaned over o^r sholders) whether yt were better hold on o^r cowrse, or turn yn agayn. When ye Master had desyred to go back ye general blamed hym for sending back ye boat & sayd y^t 'what if you lead me back againe to raise a mutynee a ageinst mee.' Thes wordes ye master tooke yl & sayd 'Yf yt be com to this, for my good wil wold I wer a shore agayn.' Some aledged ye want of a great meyny of men, but ye general sayd he wold to famowth & take us a manye as were left. now al the quarel hear hence did spring y^t M^r whood and blaccoller ye 2 pilots sayd they wold not return til they knew how they shold be used. When every man pel mel & spent his mouth w^t as smal discretion for hym self as attendance for the hearer, Capten Ward at last sayd, y^t althoe our lat speed hytherto, & ye fayr wynd presently did wysh hasten & althoe yt had been reason thes men shold have attended us & not wee them, for on thes 3 poynts ye general stood, yet becawse they wer al commended by the cowncel, & because we myght have more wynd but now cold have noe more men, he wyshed us to stand back, So did we, & when we had stood to ye eastward 2 hours ye Frances was comed but throe a quarel risen at Plymouth H. Kyrkman was left behinde, for the leftenent had receved abuses by hym, the General took yt il, and espetially m^r parker, but some thowght us wel quyt of a pyckthank. To councel agayn wher we cauld, & now was every man affrayd of other & those y^t wold have eaten ye backsyde of mowntayns wold not now byte ye fore part of a mole hil. After much adoe we were al frends and so knyt up. [*cipher:* In this discourse I noted the General coloured a base intent with some craft. Mr Hawkins open and glorious but very childish. Mr Parker fine and foolish and lordly conceited. Captain Ward a good round wise fellow. Mr Hood hob glorious.]

We had a fayr wynd and about xi a clock at nyght wer thwart the lysard and by morning as far as Ushant holding our course west sowthwest.

We held on our course sowthsowest & had a fayr north 3. *Whitsondaye* wynd & cold wether, so y^t we ran 30 leags, on [Monday] 40, on [Tuesday] 30, on [Wednesday] 30 and I think on [Thursday] we wer thwart Cape fenester, but far to ye west of yt, for ye pole was 46 degrees[1]

7.　Dyvers of o^r men wer syck & M^r banester had nether skil nor medycine so y^t I wold advise such as shal hearafter appoynt such a viage to prepare good provision of holsom comforts and ordynary salves & let them ly in ye hands of some honest merchant & let the surgion be prepared to use ye salve when need is, & some good clean cooke to mynister ye other cherishings. & so shal x li go farther & do more good than C li in such wyse as owr money is bestoed. All this whyl, I was seasick, and no marvel having changed at once both ayr exercyse & diet, rummatique I was & exceedingly costyve and trobled w^t hartburning wch be appendixes of ye sea, wherfore I cold advise hym y^t is to appoynt such a viag y^t he have of violet flowers, borage flowers, rosemary flowers & such lyke, wch he may gether in Ingland, caphers[2] made, to cumfort hym, & barberis seed & rosemary & thyme to make a lytle broth in an earthen pipkin. Thes things ar lesse costly but far more holsom than al ye suckets and paltry confections.

8.　We held on o^r way, the wether was al this time somewhat myld and somwhat clowdy & a reasonable gale of north wynd

9.　Athwart ye Burlings we had espied a sayle, wch o^r men sayd was a french man of war but al was to have a quarel to his goodes. Mr Capt. parker both because he had mynd to ye booty, & because he wold pleaz ye people wold needs have capten ward to set hym yn wch he dyd, but he was a flemmysh hulk so y^t thereon my words hear & m^r walkers in ye Edward, ye man had no hurt at all.

10. *Trinity Sonday.*　I took occasion at syrvice to speak ageinst ther attempt ye day before, but they were all w^{t}owt pytty set upon ye spoyl. After noone Capten ward & m^r walker cam to us & told how greedy they wer. espetially m^r banester, who for al his creping

Hypocrysy　ypocrysy was more ravenowsly set upon ye pray than any ye most beggerly felon in the ship. and those also wch at ye shore dyd cownterfet most holynes wer now furthest from reason,

---

[1] C. Finisterre is in 42° 51′ N.　　[2] Pickles or conserves.

affyrming y^t we cold not do god better service than to spoyl the spaniard of both lyfe & goodes, but indeed under color of religion al ther shot is at ye mens mony.

ye carpenters boy having stoln a shirt was hoysed to the yerd arme to have been ducked but I begd his pardon & shewd them y^t because we caried felonyous harts therefore god sent us felons among o^{r}selves. As in the xi of Wisdom.   *11. St Barnabyes day.*

We kept our cowrse due sowth stil & passed before ye wynd w^t o^r mayn yerd a crosse al ye way, about 30 legs comonly or more in 24 howrs, and dyvers say they never cam this way w^t so fayr a passage.   *12.*

I wrote letters by Mr Austyn of ye bridget to my syster to [cipher: Mr Atye on all things and Banisters hypocrisy and our bad headpiece] to Mr william barne y^t [cipher: Banister was an hypocrite] and sent verses in commendations of John Banesters works. We were hear at 34 [degrees] & he went sowthwest to cenaries, we held due sowth.   *13.*

By Ferdinandos direction we kept sowthsowest of purpose to have goen between barbary & Launcerote to make purchase[1] of goates or knoe not what els, for al o^r mynd was set on purchase but as god wold on [Saturday] morning we were fawlen to west of yt & so were forsed to leave yt & forteventura on ye larbord & so sayl sowthwest before ye wynd   *14.*

We set yn to the west the graund canarie leaving fortventura on ye larbord, & so passed between yt and Tenariff wch ar both very hygh lands espetially the pyke of Tenarif wch we espied above ye clowds for being hazie we cold not se ye foot of yt. hytherto we had not one hot daye altho we be w^{t}in 5 degrees to the [sun][2] for ye graund canarie wher is made the best sugar lyeth in 28 to ye northe. yt is inhabyted by spaniards. hear is very good marmaled and great store of fyne suckets. luke ward etc. ran yn w^t ye Elisabeth but what he did I knoe not but o^r general was angry. Dyvers told us what plenty of bonettoes and dolphins we shold have al this way but hytherto we smackt no byt of fresh fysh, the lyke they   *17. [Sunday]*

---

[1] I.e. seize by force.
[2] The declination on June 17, according to the calendar then in use, was nearly 23°$\frac{1}{2}$.

told of gurnet and whyting in y^e west but o^r hookes could catch none, & therefor I perceave men must not go to sea w^towt vytals in hope to have flying fyshes to break ther noses agaynst y^e bunt of the sayle.

18. Our mayn topmast was taken down and fyshed for y^t yt had thro lose rocking taken on ech syde a fret. ye general cryed owt of m^r Owtred but ye master sayd ye fawlt was not so great. many of our men wer syck wch we imputed to mr favours bear of hampton for y^t yt was made of brackysh water. yt took them over w^t a sore headach. old Rob. Parkyns of ratclif dyed. we cast hym overboord & gave him a peece abowt 7 a clock at nyght when we wer at 27 degrees. at service in the morning a great yron sledge fawling from ye mayn-top had lyke to have slayn ye botson & 2 more, & yet god be thanked did no hurt.

20. Ther was an eclipse of ye sun in ye mornyng but thro ye foggy haze wch is hear muche, we saw yt not, this morning we passed ye tropick of [Cancer] and soe kept on this course as afore.

21. In ye evening Capten ward cam aboord and m^r walker, They had taken a tortoyse. hear was much resoning whether yt wer better break up the Elisabeth or take hir a long. But albeit ye general & others wold have had hir confiscat[1] yet Luke wards word prevayled for hir lyfe. m^r walker lay w^t me & we ript up much good matter.

24. [Sunday] Midsomer. A councel was cawled in ye Gallion[2] w^t al ye asistants at 18 degrees latitude wherin was concluded by general consent to seek water at ye yle of bonavista & from thence to hold course toward rio di plata, both for ye eaze of o^r men and necissyty of o^r viage. Luke ward in al poynts spoke to ye purpose w^t discretion. so did John Drake and m^r walker, ye rest *utrumque* [otherwise], among al mr Capten parker yn as much as he was to serve at ye land wold needs have leave to appoynt his lieftenent, corporals and syrgeants, or els he wold do nothing, but ye general thowght not meet to have any more leiftenents but his own & so after muche adoe y^t matter was dashed. a coppy of al things I tooke w^t ther hands at yt.

[1] See p. 102. [2] See pp. 74, 91.

I took a purgacion being still syck . . .   *25.*

Fawling west yn 16 degrees north ward we fownd an *26.*
yland wch some sayd was bona vista but others thowght it was
la sal but none cold tell, yt rose on ye sowthwest of us w^t 3
hils in ye land, ye myddest lyke glastonbury tor. Captn
parker & luk ward after we had anchored in ye bay went to
descrye the land, but because ye rut went somewhat hard
ashore therfor they wold not bryng ye boat a shore, and
Capten parker lyke a bold soldier thowght every crib a castle
& every gote an armed soldier. Luke ward sent out 2 w^{ch}
swyming to land descried a fayr river, a number of gotes,
plenty of byrds, but no people & ther was also abundance of
fysh & monstrows great tortuses . . . In fyne when we
returned the general wold not consent to water hear, w^{ch}
thing ye viceadmiral took yl. so dyd o^r Master, but Ferdinando
had caried hym to this y^t ye rather for want of water we myght
robb & both he and M^r whood wch had browght us hyther
w^t promyses of ye greatest cumforts in ye world do now deny
al & say y^t we have delt madly to rune so far owt of o^r way,
I pray god blesse me from such pilates.[1]

In great displeasure on al sydes we wayed to be gone, but *27.*
mr hawkings and furdinando went to descry ye sowthwest of
ye bay, wher they found a fayr freshet & plenty of gotes but
ye general sayd we had water ynogh & therfor wold not stay
wch made ye men much mislyke and so upon

luk ward cam to us to excuse hymself abowt vitayling y^e *28.*
bark for ye general throe ther complaynt had spoken sharply
to hym. Captn Skevington was hear also w^t a great complaynt
agaynst his Master, w^t gawdy words, for every Jack sayth I
am a gentilman & I can tel how to governe & I wil govern, y^t
is scarse worthy to syt & keep flyes from a gawled horse bak.
God send me discreet and wyse governowrs as be gentilmen
indeed and not such crycket-catchers as never cam wher yt
grew. in fyne we made al frends, L. Ward axed my opinion
of M^r walker, I told he myght be trust w^t any thing but w^t a
fayr lasse.

hytherto ye wynd having byn frank unto us and northerly *29. St Peter.*

[1] See pp. xliii, 79.

met us at sowth and and sowtherly at 14 deg. to ye north w^t
muche qualme but yet no rayn as for o^r pilots told us many a
tale wher we must fet o^r wynds & how we shold meet w^t
them as thogh aeolus and neptunus had kept market by y^e
way. but all ther taulk is nothing but w^t vanyty, as for whood
he doth nothing but w^t a bawling mouthe rayl agaynst o^r
ship, ageynst o^r provision, agaynst o^r owners, gape for y^e
spannysh treasures, swalowyng up the men & spoyling them
of ther money alyve, w^t blasphemows bragging ageynst god
& man: ye L. stay ye rage of our syn y^t yt be not repressed w^t
the vigor of his fury, for wyckedness is in our dwelling &
amongst us. so long as ye north wynd blew yt was cooler than
yn Ingland. but now yt is blomy & hot but yet in no great
excesse.

[*July* 1582]

5.6.7.

we wch had hytherto in a maner kept Thom. beggars cowrse
sayling right before the wynd now what between east on y^e
on boord & west on ye other for o^r ship wold ly no nyer, we
got nothing & yet forsooth our cunyng pilates made us
beleive y^t ye wynd was bownd in an obligation to be at east
and east northeast al this tyme of the yer. but m^r hawkins
told y^t they being homward bownd about this tyme of yer
fownd a southwynd at ye Cape of good hope wch browght
them to plymmowth. so y^t ther is no trust.

10.

We beat up & down & did no good. the general told me y^t
ye master was a symple & an obstinate feloe & Thom whood
a wyse, diligent and vertuous man, come w^{t}owt him, quotha.

Al this week we made many boords,[1] some east some west,
we had ye wynd at sowth & much rayn, but ye wether as o^r
English Autumne save y^t ye ayr was more thick and foggy.
and we saw now and then lyke purple bladders swym on y^e
sea, wch our men called carvels[2] tellyng us that they wold
sting sore, when I appoynted the boys y^t wayted to repeat ech
meal a sentence owt of solomons proverbs M^r whood wold
not in any case y^t his boy shold lern any such thing for he
browght him not hyther for y^t purpose, and as for hym self

[1] Tacks. [2] Portuguese men of war.

he wil not geve a fart for al ther cosmography, for he can tel
more than al ye cosmographers in ye world, & wil ryde a horse
w^t any man yn england, and the mayr of plymouth shal not
set a miller to steal his corn, for his wyf eateth as good bred
as the best woman in Devonshire & hath every holyday y^e
best of rosting beaf y^t she can buy for hir money, save y^t horse
bit hir by ye sholder. m^r Banester sayth y^t he healed 200 in
one yer of an ague by hanging abracadabra abowt ther necks,
and wold stanch blood or heal tothake althogh the partyes
wer 10 myle of and y^t my l. of lester told hym at rochester y^t
he wold ye mownseur wer hanged, and y^t ye queen sayd I
thank you good M^r banester, and yf I be able I wil requyte
you. and so she gave hym the advowsons of 2 benefyces w^{ch}
wer sent to hym by Dr Julio but ye Doctor sold them both by
ye way so y^t m^r banester had nothing. but yet m^r stanhop
offered him synce C li for his enterest in ye one, yet he wold
not take yt. having been hitherto very yll and unable to brook
my meat, Symon wood gave me 3 drops of artificial oyl for 3
mornings wch he bowght of M^r buntford a gold fyner at y^e
mayden head in aldersgate street which dryed up my reum &
did me much good, & surely yt is a very excellent balme &
cost a noble an ownce.

. . . being as we suppozed in 5 degrees of ye line or lesse we *20.*
descryed a hygh land abowt 9 leags off at east northeast, w^{ch}
we deemed to be capo de palmas or capo do verga, so y^t luk
ward w^t his Master & pilat seeing us cast offward cam aboord,
& wyshed y^t in as much as we did ly bwelting at ye sea & cold
doe noe good, wee shold stand in w^t some harboroe for y^e
releif of o^r companyes. then was ye councel cawled to se wher
we wer,[1] & now every mans reconyng was behind ye ships
way above 50 leags wherby I did perceave y^t ether they had
not geven y^t allowance to the leeward as the ships list required
or else ther was some current wch set us to ye eastward under
ye wether bow & so I think yt trew, for at nyght we wer in

[1] See pp. 80, 93. In working out the 'course made good' during each
24 hours, the sailor had to use his judgment as to the allowance to be made
for leeway and unknown currents. That there was a strong easterly-flowing
current on this coast had been observed during Towerson's voyage of
1555–6, on which Frobisher had sailed as a young man.

some very rough race at 65 fadom of soft sandy oze lyke bran

& brayd pepper wch I judged to be St Annes shole. Wel, when
the viceadmiral was come aboord w^t his master and blackoller,
o^r general wch had cast to the offard west north west, at y^e
motion of ye viceadmiral & others y^t desyred rather to go on
shore for ye refreshing of o^r men than to lye bwelting on y^e
sea & do no good, for some of us wer dead & many syck,
cauled ye master in cownsel & proposed ye question wher we
wer, shewing his own accownt and others. M^r whood sayd y^e
land we saw was capo de palmas or els he wold fyrst be hanged
and after cut in 1000 peeces. such an insolent spech men
wold not for modesty sack crose, althogh ther wer reason to
ye contrary. then was demanded whether better go forward to
ye east or go back agayn to ye norwest. M^r hawkins w^t good
probable reasons showd y^t ye further we passed eastward y^e
further wer we fro ye river of plate & better therfore to passe
to ye Serliona, for yf we wer ether calmed or fownd ye wynd
in any part of the sowth, we myght harbor ther w^t great
safety, but yf northerlye we myght put of to o^r great

advauntedge. M^r whood sayd yt was a villanows coast, for
when Sir Fr. drake did ther water they set one of ye pottage
pot with ryce every meale. ye general was loth to go thither,
pretending y^t he feared ye health of his men because al had
spoke yl of ye country, but ye very truth was, he feared lest
fynding ther suffyciency for o^r provision, he shold have then
no pretence to passe to the westward. Notwithstanding, M^r
hawkins objecting y^t further we went eastward ye further we
wer from o^r mark & more danger to be calmed, he yelded to
go back to sera leona except ye wynd served. Capt ward as I
perceved undertaking this viage as wel for ye hope of his
experience as of his profyt, & rather more, was desyrous to se
ye shore & on this agreement we departed but presently after,
ye wynd comyng agayn to ye sowthwest wch was before dew
sowth, we brought ye starboord tack aboord and bore agayn
sowthsoth-east w^t dyvers scuds of rayn.

abowt noone ye wynd agayn began to meet at sowthwest so
y^t we way agayn westnorwest & spied land agayn & on 22
[Sunday] 6 past tri^y. being abowt agayn we had land one ech

syde to leeward & fownd our selves so puzzeled y^t no man cold say wher we wer, not having seen sune or stars for 14 days. but of truth we were not so far to ye southward by 3 degrees at ye least toward ye sowth and therefor whether ye current set to ye nornorest by ye reset and yeynmeal of br[azil?]^1 or whether ye streames of rio grande or other rivers y^t fawl myghtyly into ye sea cause some current or whether yt alway do folloe the wynd, sure I am we wer now no nyer than 8 degrees to ye lyne & I [think further] of & now agayn we cast to ye offward to west norwest

ye master went into ye boat & grapeled at 300 fadom & sayd *23.* y^t ye current did set ful eastward, but indeede ye wynd was so byg y^t I knoe not how he shold wel judge . . .^{2}

. . . I went aboord ye Edward with M^r hawkins wher we *26.* had a dolphin, many of them were syck & did complayn ye want of fresh water, so y^t I brynging a letter from Mr Walker to ye general y^t 30 were syck, he tooke y^t eyl & dyd deem yt had byn some practyce of ye viceadmiral, wel god send us wysdom in our governours & honest obediens in ye inferiors, & al hypocrysy let god trye.

the general went aboard ye Edward. I wrote by Mr Banester *28.* to M^r lewes y^t they 2 shold one make muche of an other, desyring rather to reape prayses of others than to attribute unto themselves anything. I wrot also to M^r walker upon the *Literarum* occasion of his letter. I think thus verbatim. In innudae tuae *interceptio* literae magnam bis peperint molestiam, injusta petunt, in . . . cata commemorant, iniqua objiciunt et . . . ae causa quernatur, mitina quaesi posthac scribi 'istace in me caudatur faba', valete tu et dux tuus . . . que amatove vester utriusque R.M: Dixit Galfridus quosdam mussitam me velle partes Domini Fletcheri agere, edisce quaesque et unde hoc

^{1} This mutilated passage is obscure. The word 'yeynmeal' is not in *O.E.D.*, while the reconstruction of the word commencing 'br . . . ' can only be a matter of conjecture. Since it was generally agreed by scholars that the waters of the ocean were moved from east to west by the *primum mobile*, an easterly current was anomalous, but might be due to the reflection back of the waters from the coast of Brazil.

^{2} The boat was held steady by the grapnel, when the log could be cast and its rate of movement measured, but the log might be driven by the wind as well as by the current. Richard Hawkins in his *Observations* (ed. Williamson (1933), pp. 37, 38) discusses the difficulties of this coast.

dimanabit et quid sibi velint hoc dicto, non enim satis assequor.[1] These letters and others ye general did open as I suppose by the provoquement of Mr Banester, in whose head ther is some gelosy, for wel assured I am y^t ther hath not passed me anything whereby ye generl hymself shold hold me in any suspicion, whoze credyt I have hytherto everyway sowght both at land & sea to uphold. what Mr Cotton had wrytten I knoe not, but tuching ye lyke case ther wer sad words betwyxt hym & ye general.[2] I pray god setyle his love among us els he y^t seeketh revenge may quickly ether upon pryvy & false accusations or some other conceyt, distresse hymself of his best frend, & so overthro both hys own safety & ye whole action as yn y^t tale of ye oke & ye bryer is set down.[3]

29. [Sunday]

After clowdy wether in manner al this month and cool winds, now it calmeth and waxeth hot, ye wind at SSW. . . . Captain Skevington supt w^t us & on ye sodayn was a great cry in ye Elisabeth & yt was told y^t one had leapt overboord.

30.

Y^e general went thither to examyn the matter & had me w^t hym to geve them exhortacions. Capt. Skevington by ye way

Farters in the Elisabeth

complayned to me grievously y^t Mr Wilkes wold farte before hym etc. When we came thither we found y^t Julian Saunders, a foolysh felloe, had fowght w^t ye masters mate & after leap overboord because y^ey would not suffer to come unto us, yt was determined y^t he shold be hoysed to ye yerd arme & so let fawl, M^r hawl sayd ye yerd wold break, wel, hoysed he was & in ye swyng ye yerd snapt quyte of in ye myddle, & al cam into ye sea, notw^tstanding after he cam yn agayn, upon his submission he was pardoned.

---

[1] This letter is mutilated and difficult to decipher, but in effect Madox has complained of the injury done by those who had read Walker's letter. The quotation 'I shall suffer for that' is from Terence. Of particular interest is the postscript: 'Jeffrey said that some were whispering that I wished to act the part of Master Fletcher. Find out whence this comes and what they mean by it, for I don't follow.' Chaplain Fletcher had been punished ignominiously by Drake, most probably for condemning as sinful his raids off Peru (Wagner, *Drake's Voyage*, p. 282).

[2] I.e. the case of an intercepted letter. For Walker's relation see p. 201, and for Fenton's Journal p. 95.

[3] This tale was told in the recently published *Shepheard's Kalendar* (1579) by Edmund Spenser.

. . . Mr Taylboise being a lytle overgone (as oft he is) fownd much falt w^t this punyshment of the man. Y^e general overhearing cawled hym. What taulk they had I kno not, but Mr Cotton was bydden geve place[1] to ye commissioners, so was Mr Banester, whether of them tooke ye matter worse I knoe not for yt stung them both to ye hart, but Mr Cotton somewhat & not much better dissembled yt, complayning greatly y^t ye general had his letter & he cold not get yt. So Banester sate beloe & Mr Cotton cam not to supper.

Ther was hard reasoning betwyxt ye general & Mr Cotton, *31.* what was ye effect I knoe not, but now is he set at ye boordes end by ye general w^t great honor. He told me y^t was by reason of a letter of my L. Lumley. now is Mr Banester in *Cotton &* worse taking & sayth he shal dye, & he canot leave syghing & *Banester* *bitter enemies* many foolysh & intemperat words why god shold thus abase hym & for wch his synnes. I was w^t him, and althoe he for ye fasting yet he hath plenty of coole bear & aquavitte, & I fownd chese parings & bacon stored in his wyndoe.

[*August* 1582]

Mr Banester took on so heavyly y^t ye merchants lest he *1. Lammas Day* should fawl into desperation wer desyrous agayn to prefer hym, & al was but ye shiftyng of one peg. so y^t now he is content saving y^t he much repineth at my L. of Lester, y^t he was not made of ye counsel. After dynner, I knoe not upon what motion in ye woerld, ye general fyrst ymparting his mynde to us, and then w^t owr lyking cawled a cowncel,[2] Wherunto when al were come, he propounded that syth our bear spent faster than o^r way wether yt were not good to go seeke water & yf to seek yt than wher. W^t general consent of al save my self yt was concluded Yea and the Serleona appoynted so y^t at night being from yt as I deem about 100 leags we set o^r cowrse northeast w^t quarter wynd towards yt in gods name.

M^r walker told me y^t wher in my former latin intercepted

[1] The gentlemen were placed in order of precedence round Fenton's table at mess. After being degraded Richard Cotton was promoted the following day to the seat of honour next the General. Madox says that he had produced a letter from Lord Lumley, the patron to whom Fenton had dedicated his first book (see p. xxxii).

[2] See p. 96.

letter I had wrytten Domini Fletcheri, y^t was construed that I thowght I was used lyke a fletcher, wherat I laffed, but when ye ryght sense of al was delyvered than they were sory etc¹ . . .

3. At supper we espied a ripling of ye water as we trended eastnortheast; & anon on ye lyeboord we saw a very hygh land wh^{ch} M^r hawkins pronounce absolutely to be Sierra Liona y^t is to say the mowntayn of Lyons, but he was flatly w^tstood by pilot [Hood] and ferede:² and mr parker sayd he wold reason w^t ye best mariner in Ingland & prove y^t cold not be y^t, because the Serraliona lay in 8 and a terce but we were now in 6 and a terce. Notw^tstanding he did not perceave ye current wch setteth full northeast, for we ar fawln as far this way in 2 days as we ran ye other way in 5 days. Great hold [of?] hye wordes ther were, I think we saw y^t abowt a ken [?] of.³ 4th morning being abowt 3 leages of we had grownd 60 fathom & now ech man granted y^t to be y^e same. Y^e sownding was black hose, y^e land very high & y^t on this wyse y^t appeared.

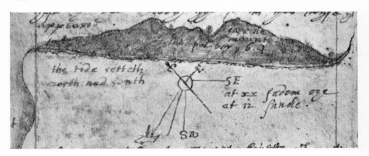

About noone y^e master went yn y^e pynnase & found first 30 fadom oze in sowndyng, & so sholyng to 15 w^tin a culveryn levole a shore & goyng a land he gathered guynia beanes & fetches [etc.] . . . & espied a fayr ynlet of water & a goodly fresh spryng fast by ye shore, but coming back they had but cold thanks, for nether dare some men ventur them selves

---

¹ See p. 174, n. 1.
² Ferdinando.
³ Ken (or kenning), a marine measure of about 20 miles.

nor can not abyde y^t other shal be thowght able to do more than they.

When we had runne westerly al nyght & stil saw the green lee shore w^t one fayre tree & est a humock of trees as is set down thar we fel to recon [what] ye land is, m^r hawkyns & m^r hood to excuse & clere one fawlt ran into a number, [the] one *tam ficti pravique tenax quas* (?) *nucia veri*, the other yf he take an opinion once, aledge what reazon you can, *non magis ille movetur quo si qura silex aut* (?) *stet marperesia cautes,* and yet ye least wager was ether C li or a goodmans head.

5.

[*8. Sunday after Trinity*]

6 [Monday] Because we saw an open, ye Frances & Elisabeth ran yn northwarde to yt, who brought us word y^t yt were ye 3 yland in the mowth of Madrebamba wch al three we might perceeve distinctly, wel wooded, being 4 or 5 leags fro them. M^r whood yet wold not grant yt shold be so, but rather 3 ylands in ye sholding of sierra leona.[1] Hytherto we had deep blew water, but being abowt noon athwart ye westernmost we had fyrste green & then whyte & muddy water at 15 fadom & so sholing westward, at nyght being come to 7 fadom wee shrank back & anchored at 9 fadom wher we perceaved a horsing eb y^t set to east north east, but ye flood not so vehement, yt is ful seay when ye moon is an howr past her meridian.

St Annes Sholes

The Elisabeth was gone from us I kno not how but we sent ye Frances afore who gave us a token of deep water, so y^t w^t an eb abowt 10 a clock we folowed & were anon in 5 fadom & a half but quyckly ran to 10 & vi agayn keeping north west, the sownding was muddy sand, as a myxture of whyte, red & swarfye. now we confessed y^t ye shore we were yn, & wch at ye very fyrst we had seen as ye rippling of ye water did wytnes was Cape de Mownte[2] . . .

7.

We wayed & ran northwest 4 or 5 leags & at nyght had syght of land to ye north and saw ye Elisabeth agayn, wch had lost an anchor & a cable. at night we anchored at ye northwest

8.

[1] There are three islets (the Turtle Is.) off Cape St Anne, and three more, the Ilhas Bravas (now the Banana Is.), to the north of Sierra Leone.
[2] Cape Mount was the high land which, on August 3, Hawkins had pronounced to be Sierra Leone, but it lies more than a hundred miles away towards the south-east. See the profiles by Fenton and Madox (pp. 98, 176).

edge of ye sholes at 15 fadom, the shol lye in rydges in maner east & west like falowed grownd.[1]

9. We wayed at mydnyght & wth in 2 houres were in blew water running north & by west. At day we descryed ye ylands & main of Serra Leone being very high land but as like Cape Mownte as the Middle Temple is like Mamsbury steeple, for thus yt lay,[2] &, the lord, surely o^r pilats had marked spytefully ye form of yt before. But as god will Mr Hood was very syck, for he had a crick in his neck, At nyght wher all the nyght before we had found 15, 14, 12 & 10 fadoms now have we at the poynte of the road at low water 5 and a half. So on the sudden Hood & Mr Hawkyns cried to anchor, & because each thing was not done at a trice they were war and found[3] at ye masters working . . .

10. We ran into ye harboro & had 9 or 10 fadom fast by ye shore.

11. We went to take ye sone ashore and the declination being 12 g.

The latitude of Serraleona 18 mynutes I took ye sone on a perfet instrument at 3 degrees 26 mynutes from ye zenith, so y^t I pronounced ye place to be 9 degrees lacking 8 mynutes. [8° 52'][4]

12. [*Sunday*] We had a communion. After Mr Walker & I wer sent by ye general to make peace between Skevington & Crane, ye fyrst a fyzzling taleberer & a pykethank, ye other a hasty foolysh felloe of his tung, w^t much adoe we had them to shake hands. but in the mean L. Ward had further netled ye peace, for Skevington had carried quarels to them both. [*transl:* I have ascertained for certain that our leader has promised many of the company that he will not return home until he has rewarded them with riches:[5] he has given them clothing, but

---

[1] I.e. like the 'strips' in an open field.

[2] See Pls. VII, XII.   [3] 'Found fault'.

[4] The sun was in the zenith at noon in lat. 12g. 18m. according to the Almanac, from which it could be computed for the time of observation, since the figure diminished nearly 20′ in twenty-four hours. At Sierra Leone Madox found a zenith distance of 3g. 26m. Hence the latitude was 12g. 18m. minus 3g. 26m., or 8g. 52m. Fenton in his Journal makes it 8g. 45m. It is not clear just where the observation was taken, but it was close to modern Freetown which is in 8g. 20m., i.e. the 'eight degrees a terce' of the Portuguese pilot books.

[5] Madox now began to get some idea of Fenton's private plans, which differed from those of Hawkins and Hood, both of whom wanted to make westwards for Magellan Strait.

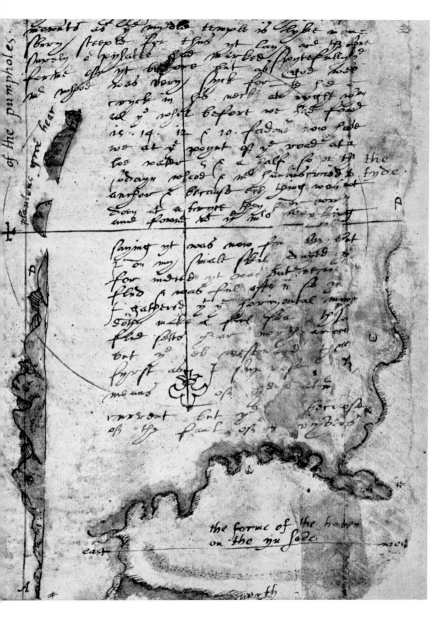

VII. Rough chart and profile of Sierra Leone in Madox's Diary,
9 August 1582

B.M., Cotton MS App. XLVII, f. 34

South is to the top. 'Thus yt lay', wrote Madox, and he made these sketches
to illustrate his criticism of the pilots (p. 178). The position of the anchorage
(in Kru Bay) is indicated by a drawing of a ship, and the relation of profile
(on the left) to shore-line by letters A–D. Cf. Map B, p. xlv.

not at his own expense, but because by these means he hopes to rule the sailors and sea-masters . . .]

Y^e cowncel was cawled & ye case herd of Skevingtons _13._ accusation, so y^t by witnes was proved foolysh words of Cranes and he was set in ye bilboes but quickly came owt agayn[1] . . .

. . . In ye nyght cominly it thundreth & rayneth but y^e _14._ after noone is fayr, hote & drye but yet clowdy. I speak this as wee found and as I suppose yt is when ye sone is nygh ye zenith. but to affyrme yt is so alway because we fynd yt so 4 or 5 days together is scarce to be admitted, and yet most places of late are thus described, and y^t made magellan to caul y^t mare pacifico wher Sir Fr. Drake had after a hundred & 20 dayes together a southwest tempest, and y^t road porto myelice wher this did harboroe w^t most ease and comodytye.[2] [_cipher:_ The general was angry because I was so far and so long ashore. But the cravenish cowardice of captain Parker!]

. . . We went ashore to take ye variation but ye rayn did _15._ hynder us.

[_cipher:_ The general gave me 2 shirts.] _sed timeo Danaos et_ [_Note_ _dona ferentes._ _carefully_]

Peter Owen told Cap^n Skevington that so long as he went fyzzling to ye generall w^t tales to pyck hym a thank so long they shold never be yn quyet. Hearon was demaunded what was a fyzeler & why privy taleberers wer called fyzelers, to this was answered y^t as he wch fyzeleth doth stink worse then a playn farter & doth also lead many into suspition because yt is not knowen whence ye fyst cometh so etc.

Ed. Robinsons brother wch cam fro the Edward y^t mr _16._ banester myght care for hym, dyeth, so that if Mr Banister had half y^t knowledge y^t hymself vawnteth of, and y^t I knoe he wanteth yet as Chauser sayth Wher nature cesseth once to work, Farewel physique, bear ye coarse to church.[3]

---

[1] By Ward's doing. See p. 101, n. 2.
[2] Madox alone among the company had a logically trained mind.
[3] 'And certeinly, ther nature wol not wircke,
Far-wel, phisyk! go ber the man to chirche!'
Chaucer, _The Knightes Tale_, ll. 2759–60.

19. [Sunday] ymediately after dynner we espied at the east point a canow wch some sayd was 20, & much adoe great terror. Capt parker styred abowt to put men fro ye shore and greatly complained ye rashness of men, etc. Well, they showed a flag of truce & we ye like gladly, for those y^t can say Hey corragio, as god shal help me, this ship is able to beat ye Kyng of Spayns fleet, now one sylly canoo doth make them creepe into a mowshole, when al was com yn yt was 3 sylly portingales in a lytle swynes troe, ye one a sage old man in a capuchio of black moccado . . . His name was Francis Freer, born at Venice . . .

20. [*transl:* I try to keep the peace, but in vain. For while formerly he [Cotton] used to bring his slanders and complaints against our two leaders to me, now that he is restored to their favour he carries himself more arrogantly still, and cares nothing, or very little, for anyone's friendship, unless it is someone able to give him something for his greedy stomach.]

24. St Bartholomews day The general and I and Capten Parker dyned at ye Edward. After dynner ye general went aboord but we walked to ye lemmon trees. [*transl:* Ward told me that after this the general would not admit to the Council any but those who agreed with him. As his own example showed the man could rule splendidly over the timid and meek, and over the harmless and gentle, but when he met with some bold spirit who would not carry out wrongs and follies, he showed himself in his true colours as petty and mean.

At supper Master Taylbois, stuffed with food, burst out at Cotton, his charges not actually false, but foolish and pointless. Then Cotton took Parker for his defender, a man whom he is accustomed to pick to pieces in private, and against whom he carries out a secret war.

After supper Fenton called me to him and ordered me to look into the behaviour of those who were qualified to be his councillors. He said that there were certain ignoble, rude, stupid men who were gratified by the honourable title of counsellor, and he desired that these should not come to the Council nor be admitted to deliberations. For just as the Queen, out of all those qualified, called only upon those she

trusted, and excluded the rest, so also he could and would do.]
God send us al wel to doe.

. . . above 50 men y^t wer before geven over to death ar 25.
now become lusty & strong for ye lymmons have scowred ther
mowths, fastened ther teath & purifyed ther blod. Y^e fresh
water baths have suppled ther joynts, healed ther wounds &
abated the swelling, & ye foode of ye oysters hath cort them
up in heart lustyly, so, as long before I told them, the land
was nothing so unholesome as y^t was heald, but no persuasion
yn any thing can prevayle til need come to play ye orator, w^ch
rather useth Carters lodgique than Wilson's rhetorique.[1]

[*September* 1582]

[*transl:* At night the general called me apart and told me he 4.
had seen enough of the insolence and arrogance of the
merchants on account of which he was henceforth not going
to inform them of anything except what he is obliged to
according to law. And since there was no small deficiency of [*A certain
necessary victuals, especially of beverages through the defects   proposal*]
of the casks, he said he would sail back with Francisco Freer
and Camillo[2] to the Cape Verde Islands, where he could
furnish himself better with wine. For he had heard, he said,
that there was a bitter struggle going on between the King
and the Bishop; and according to the side he took he would
have the opportunity of attacking the other . . .]
[*transl:* We dined and supped in the Edward where Ward 10.
(Milo) would not allow Walker to take a little dish of mustard
to the Francis. This is hard! It must be marked up not with
chalk but with charcoal; by the gods, this is to govern
children! We did not intend to put ourselves to slavery when
we so willingly undertook to serve our country, leaving
behind us our fatherland, our relatives and friends, for whose
sake we have crossed the great ocean, but . . .] [*here follows
a prayer*]
[*transl:* The general told me about the island of St Helena, 11.

---

[1] Sir Thomas Wilson's Art of *Rhetorique* was one of the popular text-
books of the day; 'Carters lodgique' has not been identified, and the phrase
may echo some proverbial saw.
[2] Two of the Portuguese merchants.

lying between the equator and the tropic. He said it was a very fertile country and almost completely uninhabited, a place moreover easy and convenient to fortify, and having constructed defences, to plant a colony . . . and there we could await the return of the Portuguese fleet, which, laden with spices, touches there to water in the month of May. It is a wonderful thing how ardently desirous we are for glory and for getting rich, and yet how we run away from real danger and labor, but, now that we fear and dread honesty, I am being driven forward into more serious dangers and more bitter evils. Thou, O, Lord . . .] [*here follows a prayer*]

13.

[*transl:* Hall told me that Frobisher received £1,600 for providing victuals and other necessaries termed useful for the ship, but this provisioning cost less than £500, the rest he kept for himself. He declared that in the same way others engaged in this business were able to provide for themselves . . . In adventures of discovery seldom any man bringeth public good to his own life, more seldom with his own gain, but never if he be careful either of life or gain.]

1582 Septemb.
14. [*Sun in Libra*]

When I perceaved y^t dyvers made notes of our viage & I had nothing but what remayneth in memory[1] to tel when I come home, I purposed hensforwards to keep   breef remembrance of those things that shal happen of any moment & when lesure serveth me to wryte rather in greek or laten for ye exercise of my stile than otherwyse. Therefore of thos things y^t ar passed to this day is: I cam from blackwal in ye Edward Bonaventure ye 2 of April & from hampton in ye gallion on Sonday ye 29 of April & on Whytsonday ye third of june we wer owt of syght of England & so came to ye canaries & after to bonavista, & lastly to serra liona wher we now ar. ther ar many lemons, red peper y^t groweth in trees, graynes growyng in grownd, aples lyke great lylly rootes,

---

[1] This is the opening of Madox's second Journal (Cotton MS Titus B. VIII, ff. 179–221), which he began when he realized that what he wrote was not safe from prying eyes. The earlier one, which ends a few days after this date, was presumably hidden away. The diarist now writes mainly in Latin, or even in cipher, which an ignorant person might mistake for Greek.

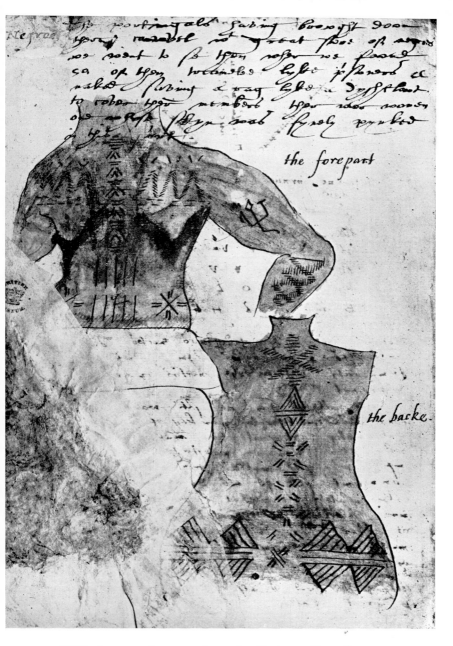

VIII. A tattooed woman, drawn by Madox at Sierra Leone

B.M., Cotton MS Titus B. VIII, f. 181v.

The style of scarification, with linear and keloid patterns, closely resembles that found today in Portuguese Guinea; cf. H. A. Bernatzik, *Äthiopien des Westens. Forschungsreisen in Portugiesisch-Guinea* (Vienna, 1933) II, pls. 239, 241, 245. Some motives, notably the conventionalized scorpion on the left arm, show affinity with Nigerian work in the Benue valley, as illustrated by P. Bohannan, 'Beauty and scarification amongst the Tiv', *Man*, LVI (1956), 117–21, and figs. 4(b), 8(b), 5. See p. 209 below.

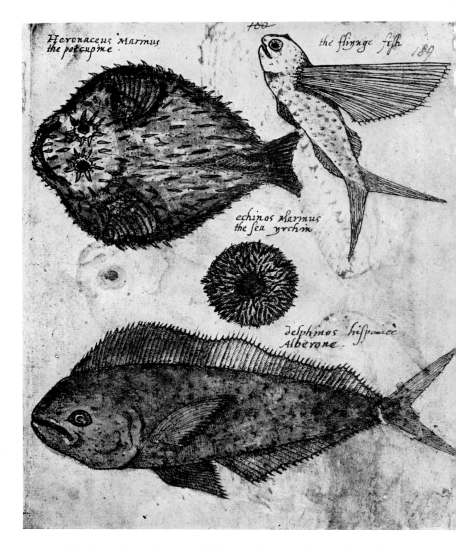

IX. Drawings of tropical fishes made by Madox at Sierra Leone

B.M., Cotton MS Titus B. VIII, f. 189.

Top left, (probably) rabbit fish, *Chilomycterus atinga* (Linn.); top right, flying fish (genus and species unidentifiable); centre, sea-urchin (also undeterminable); bottom, dolphin or dorado, *Coryphaena hippurus* (Linn.). Madox's drawings of fishes may be compared with those made by John White in the Caribbean, 1585–7.

vespertilio marina

X. A tropical fish drawn by Madox at Sierra Leone

B.M., Cotton MS Titus B. VIII, f. 189v.

The fish is *Psettus sebae* Cuv.

XI. Drawings of trees made by Madox at Sierra Leone

B.M., Cotton MS App. XLVII, f. 36

Left, bamboo palm, probably *Raphia vinifera*; right, mangrove, *Rhizophora sp.*,
which he terms 'the oyster tree'.

many dyvirs fyne shelfysh, many other fysh, olyphants, munkeys, dear, buffes and porcupines. For 5 of our men having leave to walk on sunday stragled so far y^t they stayd owt al nyght & were put in ye bilboes for yt when they returned home & y^t worthily because they disobeyed ye general & capten parker . . . the serra liona standeth in 8 d. 2 terces, Hear be many villainous . . . vermyn lyke wyngles gnats wch do marvellously troble us & make spoyl of bred.

I was still ill w^t ye colic.   *15.*

[*cipher:* He[1] means to counterfeit the King of Portugal's sail *24.* and flag, and so to take all as they come to serve him. He [*Mark this*] would very gladly be a King or enter on some great enterprise, but he is a very dissembling hypocrite, not caring for anything but his own vain wealth and reckoning. He doth not trust any as friend on the ship, nor any him. A good reckoning, if our great monsieur had not been desirous rather to rob than to perform his voyage, we might by this time have been at the Moluccas. But he would not water at Cape de Verde. He will give place to no persuasion but necessity, he seeketh both here to reign and to gain a kingdom. He said he had martial law and would hang Draper at the mast. He saith the queen was his love. He would go through the South Sea to be like Francis Drake.]

[*transl:* . . . In the same Aulus Gellius[2] mention is made of an elegant and amusing comedy in which the leading part is played by Clodius, the second by Titus Annius Milo, the third Glaucus, who plays a part in the stead of Clodius. Fourth, Pyrgopolynices, a soldier. Fifth, Quintus Martius, an augur. Sixth Publius Cornicola . . . there was also Colax, a sort of parasite, who hated everything and everyone,

---

[1] Here Madox summarizes Fenton's wild and heedless talk of his plans and claims.

[2] The *dramatis personae* of this supposed comedy provide the nicknames that Madox now uses for his companions, but in fact no description of it occurs in the *Noctes Atticae*. Fenton is Clodius, Ward is Milo, Hawkins is Glaucus, Parker is Pyrgopolynices, Ferdinando is Cornicola or Verres, Hall is Palinurus, the helmsman in Vergil, and so on. On a later page he ascribes some of these names to a story in Livy. See Document 80 ('The nicknames').

another was Palinurus who was rather heedless . . . Now Clodius trusted nobody except Pyrgopolynices, and was jealous even of him, lest he should steal his glory. He was clever . . . choleric, greedy, ambitious . . . cowardly and suspicious. Glaucus on the other hand, foolish and indiscreet, was very boastful yet frank, and after his own fashion upright. But he could not endure Clodius. Milo, who was a great talker, and clever enough, bold and a hard worker besides, yet inexorably rapacious, served humbly. Pyrgopolynices ruled most arrogantly: but although a little swollen headed by military success, he had candour. He was very dull-witted, yet nevertheless thought himself better than the rest of the world, and was ambitious besides.]

Cotton

[*cipher:* Cotton showeth his arse to Water Webb as he was washing, witness Tailboys and others.]

26.

[*transl:* I took a walk with Walker towards the east. He repeated to me what disgrace we should bring upon ourselves, what a stain upon the church, what painful grief upon our friends, if we went back to the Islands[1] and tried to supply our wants by loading ourselves with spoils taken from honest and innocent people. I replied that it could not be otherwise, we should be greatly blamed for wrongdoing, for if a man sets the egg wickedness, what wonder if he hatches out the chick punishment? But we have given him secret and open warning, we have admonished him frequently, we have spoken in the name of Jehovah, we have threatened him with punishment if he does this wrong. To which he [Walker] replied: His blood, and that of all those whome he condemns to sin, be on his own head, we are free from all wrongdoing in God's sight. As I hope we are, and whatever remains in us, let us resist by prayer.]

27.

[*transl:* The General sent to King Fatima by the Portuguese an ell and a half of cloth . . .]

30. [Sunday, 16. after Trinity]

[Council &

Cap^{en} Ward sent for the generall . . . ther dyned wee and agreed to go thorow y^e strayts. y^e general, Ward, hawkins, parker, walker & I, the rest wer not cawled.

[1] The Cape Verde Is. The two parsons have now realized their helpless involvement in wrong-doing. See p. 207.

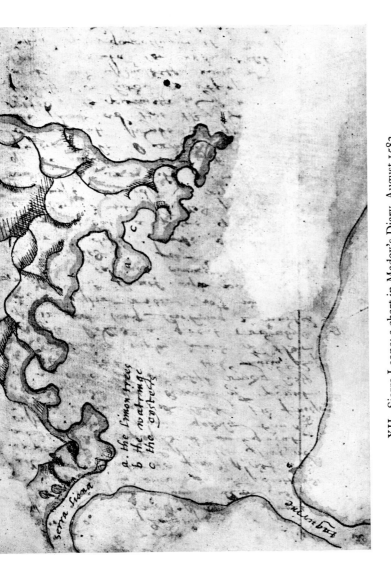

XII. Sierra Leone: a chart in Madox's Diary, August 1582

B.M., Cotton MS App. XLVII, f. 39v

South is to the top. This chart, which shows more detail than Madox's earlier sketch (Pl. VII), is the product of his further surveys and observations. At the point marked 'b' (the watering place) Captain Fenton fixed a commemorative copper plate, on a site in Kru Bay where Freetown stands today. (See p. 104, n. 2, and Pl. IV.)

[*cipher:* Master Hood called said that Sir Francis Drake's *proposal to attempt the* victual in Java cost the value of four thousand pound. Being *strait[1]*] thereof rebuked by Hawkins he said it was much, and that [*The General bad me tear* the people esteemed nought but the best silk and fine linen. *[up] the note of these hot* The General demanded whether there were water enough *comparisons and follies with* through the Straits. He answered four fathom at least. In *Parker and* Moluccas they saw no great ships nor think there is harbour *Hawkins*] for any, nor that we should there fetch spices enough. Hawkins notwithstanding affirmeth all. The General saith that fast by the Strait Moluccas he is informed that there is 80 fathom and rocky and therefore no riding for us. But he spoke doubting to go thither. Hood, because they would rob in the South Sea. Hawkins all at a venture.]

[*October* 1582]

We despatched our busyness to be goen for ye strayts. Mr *1.* Evans had articled for quarelsom words put up agaynst him by Mr Barsey[2] wherupon he was examyned, & so sent back *Evans sent* by Francisco as a man unwoorthy of ye roome. *home*

. . . report was yt Mr Evans wold be a fryar wch thynge yf *2.* yt prove true I wil never trust man after ether for fayth or religion til I have eat at least a peck of salt in his company, but sure ye general used hym wt curtesy, althoe in serching his chest ther was a letter found, for he gave hym wyne, pork, bisket and pease ynogh for a moneth.

ye General chose Arthur Cotton and the Mr John Davis to be *4.* Mrs mate in Rich. Fayrwethers roome, who cast lots but the lot fel to John Davis wch had the place.

[*cipher:* Talking of the giants at Cape St Julian, Parker had a *13.* great desire to encounter with them, but he swore as God *Giants*

¹ See p. 110. Of members of the Council only Ward, Parker and the two chaplains are mentioned as being present. The resolution was taken on the advice of Drake's two pilots, Hood and Blacoller. Madox, however, makes clear that Hawkins also took part in the discussion, although the merchants were excluded.

² Barsey or Bardsey appears on the Muster Roll (p. 158) as the jeweller. He apparently informed upon Evans (p. 110) who was called before the General to answer for his words. Luke Ward relates in his narrative that on August 28 'Mr Evans began to barter away certain of the ships commodities with the Negros, without acquainting the General or any other untill hee had done, whereof grewe more wordes then profite' (*Pr. Nav.*, pp. 650–1).

challenge me I will do the best I can to save their lives, as I believe, for he would sure run away if any danger were.]

15.

[Note these]

Hot still & no wind.[1]

[cipher: The General told at dinner that he dreamt Mr Captain Ward had taken in Mr Evans, and that he was ready to view fair in it, and was sore troubled, being very angry. He told me that 20 tun of beer was wanting by Frobisher's means . . . Hawkins told that the General forbade him to give cloth away which was his own, and for this cause by Parker's master (?) did he give levars (?) which I know to be true.][2]

18.

I made a spher for Mr Parker but did not fynysh yt.

24.

[transl: . . . From under the shadow of our alarms we rejoiced to rejoin our two consort ships which had been sailing at a great distance away, and of whose good faith some doubted, for they had not spoken us for fourteen days. We congratulated one another . . . We had reached, as I believe, 200 leagues from the eastern shore [of Brazil], three degrees and some minutes to the north of the equinoctial line.]

[November 1582]

November 1.
All Souls.

[transl: We have crossed the equator, halfway between Guinea and Brazil, or rather nearer the latter. Drake came to us accompanied by his master and pilot in order to discuss our course. We believed ourselves nearer the Brazilian coast than he did. It was agreed to go in further towards it, and if by any chance we became separated to seek the north shore of

---

[1] They were in the doldrums.

[2] Great dissatisfaction was caused by Fenton's devices to keep the merchants from getting knowledge of the country and people. Madox had written on September 3: 'At dinner we had reasoning [argument] and while M. Parker would commend his own care in keeping his men unscattered & safe, the thing was so ridiculous because there is at all no manner danger, and so odious because none can be suffered to search, that words began to be multiplied. Mr Evans affirming that the Portugals could have brought the King [Fattema] to him, Mr Parker saying it was offered to the General, and indeed it was offered to both but was not accepted, and we looked for great thanks to do the Portugal that courtesy to give him leave so to do, & for more thanks to do the King that honour to let him come into our presence, that he came not at all. Mr Cotton here again retching at Mr Evans was bidden hold his peace, but he meddleth too much' (Cotton MS App. XLVII, f. 44; see also pp. 208–9).

the Plate, and wait there 15 days, and thence go on to
Magellan Strait and there await events.]

[*cipher:* Fernando saith that whatever comes from the South [*A Council*
Sea passeth through the Bay of Mexico, and therefore as good *taken*]
steal it here as there. He said that many a time, being at the
Commandment [Communion?], one hath cried 'a sail!', so
they have left all and followed theft.[1] There were at our
Council the General, Ward, Hawkins, Parker, Madox,
Fernando, Cotton, Hall, Hood, Blacoller, Fairweather,
Drake, Percy. But Talboys was not called either to dinner or
Council. Amongst these was no order of asking or answering,
but all conversed which made me silent. Ward would go
forward. His reasons were the benefit of the shore, the hope
of sails, the supposal to see Brazil in 8 degrees and certainty
thereof, except we saw land at 2 degrees. Master Percy saith
there is no current anywhere, but a tide by the shore. Hood
will stand to the wind and current, for like how he findeth it
once, either the one or the other, and so it is to him for
ever . . .]

[*transl:* When you see the waves sparkle or emit as it were
shining lights, it is a sign of southerly winds, so the Master
told me.]

[*cipher:* When Fernando said: 'General, I told you we were
slipped to the westward', the General, as not hearing at first,
would have passed it. But the fellow following it still, 'Tush',
saith the General, 'I found it myself', thereby noting that he
cannot abide to be seen learn anything of anybody, but has a
proud mind, and for all this we were not, for Fernando [*All my self*]
sailed a month on dry land.]

Dies mihi natalis . . . [*transl:* We heard that Walker was ill *11.*
of a fever, so after breakfast the General kindly and generously
put together some sweetmeats, and went with me to visit and
condole with him.]

[*cipher:* He [Walker] told me that Fairweather said the
General bade him shoot at the Edward. And Blacoller did
hearten them to part, and if he had not well handled the
matter they had been gone, for the Captain was proudly bent,

---

[1] Ferdinando had been arrested for piracy in 1578.

thinking to steer best when he was from under an overseer.]¹

12. [*transl:*] Vice-admiral Ward asked many questions about the rule of the stars, and said that William Borough² was one who filled his hive with other men's honey . . . The vice-admiral asked if I were keeping any journal of the voyage, and argued that it could safely be hidden with him, for before we got back all such would be carefully examined. I denied absolutely, saying that I was so unwell at first that I could not, and afterwards I had neglected to do so. He said the Privy Council would expect it of me. I replied then I would put one together from Hall's daily record. Thus I got rid of a self-satisfied, gaping fellow. For who would of his own free will, put himself under an obligation to a short-tempered and proud man, unless he enjoyed the exchange of liberty for unworthy slavery?]

14. [*transl:* . . . Now with shifted sails we change course from SSW, lest we should fall on the sea-danger of the Shoals of Abrolhos, between the continental coast and Ascension Island, 18 degrees from the equator. We are sailing now in just over 14 degrees. May God preserve us!]³

15. [*transl:* After breakfast Hood made the serious allegation that we had caused discord and fighting in the vice-admiral because of the assertion that we should not return home. I protested that I had nothing to do with it and knew nothing about it. We went over there to make enquiry and found no such thing, but all fancies and falsehoods due to the suspicions of Hawkins, and the exaggeration of trifles!]

22. [*transl:* I drew up certain theorems and proofs by which our General could more clearly and the better understand the motion of the heavens and planets, the use of the globe and sphere, the declination of the sun and stars, as to which he is now uncertain if not actually mistaken. I have also drawn out diagrams by which he can see with his own eyes the course of a ship, especially when, owing to contrary winds, it must tack and traverse . . .]

23. [*cipher:* At supper Hawkins and Hood told that Sir Francis

¹ See pp. xlviii, 112, 209.
² See p. xl.
³ See p. 115. Fenton gives their course as S and by E.

188

Drake was in their debt, and that he had used them very ill: [Of Sir
and that he went to his cabin at 8 a clock, and wind or rain, Francis Drake]
never stirred thence. On that the General told Hawkins the
last of September that Sir Francis said Ned Gillam was a
better mariner then he. The General told me also that Sir
Francis said to a nobleman that we should never come home
again, but I trust in God we shall prove him a false prophet
in that.]

[*transl:* Went to the vice-admiral [the *Edward*] to console my 25. [*Sunday*]
brother, whom we found rather better . . . Hood insisted
that it must be decided whether to make for the shore,
because of the decay of the casks, which are growing weaker,
so that they leak and nearly all our store of water is becoming
exhausted. The vice-admiral [Ward] did not think we should
approach the shore, owing to the fog and the absence of [*A doubtful
wind . . . But to business. They got out their charts, and discussion*]
descriptions, even their sketches, so that from all the various
prospects it could be more easily decided exactly where we
now are. It fell out that a delineation of the Strait of Magellan
was shown which that golden knight of ours[1] had made who
just once passed through it. Whereupon the question arose
as to by what art or industry had he so drawn it as to express
the islands to the life, or how he could be so certain, when he
spent only 17 days, and for eight days with much passing to
& fro had been struggling to round a single cape. His [cipher: *Sir
companions said that they had seen certain gaps in the land Francis
Drake's cards
deeply penetrated by the sea, and that they had imagined that false*]
thus it was.

I indeed am persuaded that Drake either borrowed some
map from the Portuguese or Spaniards, and to their details
added his own, or made it up . . .]

[*cipher:* I cannot keep a daily register of things [as at] first.
Luke Ward told me that all notes should be formal merely,
and therefore willed that he might keep my books. Robert
Lidington told me his Master gave him warning thereof. The
calling for and search of Evans' box approved this true
words . . .

[1] As to Drake's chart, see pp. 38–40.

Fourthly the Master[1] is saucy to read all my writings, but one may say he loved me well and made much of me. To this I answer that he used so to do even to them whom behind their backs he much dispraiseth to me, and therefore had I great reason to suspect the like, especially by he (?) intercepted my letters, which he had not done had he trusted me. But he must answer all this homecoming. But he that durst put the merchants forth the Council and keep all in else (?) himself, and threaten martial law, and devise to rob the Portingals, and to dwell in St Helena and not return, nor careth he for answers, but he hath not so done. A good cause, for being crost in his reckoning, he could not, and thenceforth did never openly attempt it; for Mr Walker and I devised how to prevent his mischief. What moreover my reckoning found among those who set Evans home was cause himself desired it, because we might stand in more fear to do ill when one was turned back to complain:[2] because the General swore openly that both of them would not go together, and said he was the worse that day he saw him. Ward, so soon as Evans was gone out of the cabin, said he did not such like, and sought to have a passport, And now he shall not if he would.]

[*Evans' departing Caitiffly spoken*]

[*transl:* Ward came to us for breakfast and after breakfast reasons were offered by all by which we are shown to have reached between 27 and 28 degrees towards the south, a hundred leagues more or less from Rio de Janeiro. Hood moreover swore by all that was holy that the port of Plymouth was not better known and more familiar to him than Magellan Strait, nor could ships ride there less safely . . .]

[*December* 1582]

1.

The Brazil coast. I am of opinion that we are in about 30 degrees south latitude . . .

6.

[*transl:* At dawn Drake came to us and pointed out a ship slipping by. Good God! what an ovation, what a commotion, what an uproar! Who? What? Why? . . . Ward and Parker,

---

[1] The opening of this cipher passage is obscure, but it is clear from what follows that 'the Master' was Fenton.

[2] Whether Evans ever reported to Leicester is not known.

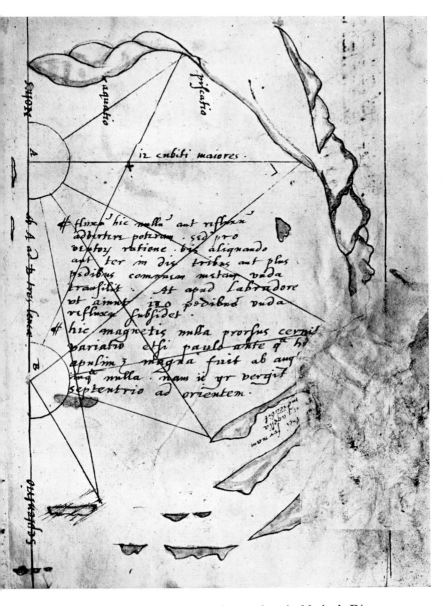

XIII. The Bay of Good Comfort: a chart in Madox's Diary

(see note overleaf)

XIII. The Bay of Good Comfort: a chart in Madox's Diary

(overleaf)

B.M., Cotton MS Titus B. VIII, f. 211

Madox understood the principles of charting from the sea. The ship's boat was held at point A, where a forward bearing was taken on the middle islet of the 'Sow and hir Pigs', at bottom left (cf. Pl. XIV), and a back bearing on a coastal landmark (apparently Punto do Ouvidor, 28° 05′ S). Five further compass bearings were then taken on prominent landmarks. The boat was now rowed towards the forward bearing mark for an estimated distance of three leagues and held stationary at point B. The back bearing was checked and the new bearings of the same five landmarks taken. The points of intersection of the pairs of rays drawn to each landmark fix the five positions, which serve as a framework for a sketch-map. In this case the landmarks would have proved extraordinarily difficult to identify from the fresh angle, nor could islands and promontories be distinguished from one another at sea-level (cf. Pl. XIV). Madox's dissatisfaction is indicated by his cancellation of an island. The chart is drawn with south to the top.

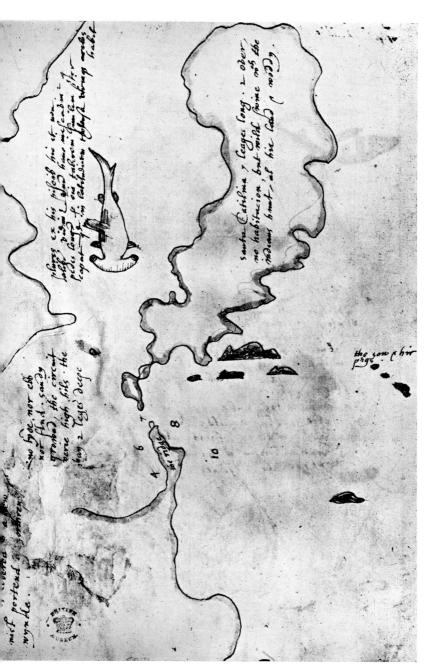

XIV. Santa Catarina Island: a chart in Madox's Diary

(see note overleaf)

XIV. Santa Catarina Island: a chart in Madox's Diary

(*overleaf*)

B.M., Cotton MS Titus B. VIII, f. 211v

The chart is oriented with west to the top, north to the right. Soundings taken round 'the ridge' are in fathoms. 'The Sow and hir Pigs' (modern name Trez Irmãos) provided the forward bearing mark in Madox's charting operation illustrated on the preceding page of his Diary (see Pl. XIII). The two charts are on approximately the same scale, and overlap. The fish, at top right, of which (Madox writes) 'I saw many here, and nowhere else', is a Hammerhead Shark. Cf. Map B, p. xlv.

when putting a prize-crew on the little ships, contend for supremacy . . . the prize is brought in . . .]

[*transl:* A council is called . . . There came before us a young gentleman named Johannes Torre de Verda, born in Cordova . . . On this information[1] a debate was held regarding these captives whether to send them away with their ship, or to take them with us, or to set them aland and take their boat . . . If we carried them off (it was argued) our journey would be hindered, for they could bring us bad weather so that we could not sail quickly, thus our own sailors would soon come into danger, for their victuals would be consumed, their candles and wood. Considering with what unwillingness and almost under compulsion they had supplied provisions for our companions in the little Francis, what would they do for these strangers? For Drake,[2] who has taken all his calculations from the dead purser, pretends that many of the things which they had received have been taken away and scattered, to lie hidden amongst us, and he says other things of the same sort. Well, Hawkins, now cruel, now pitiful, stands now for them, now against them, childishly unreasonable. Fenton says craftily (and I believe not from hypocrisy) that it seems to him that their liberation would do us no harm, for if they go away quietly others will not be forewarned against us, whereas if they are robbed others will be excited to caution, while they themselves would spread the matter abroad as much as possible to get their revenge. Taylboys and Jeffreys agreed, as did Parker. Shaw was not called, and took no part in the debate . . . It was therefore decided that they should be sent away in peace. Nevertheless it was agreed to satisfy in some part the greed and rapacity of the sailors; there dined on the Edward all the members of Council except Hawkins, and a wonderful

7.
[*A noisy discussion*]

[*Drake, forsooth, denies the provision of the pinnace*]

[1] By the old Friar (see pp. 212-3).

[2] This passage is obscure. Fenton in his Journal (p. 118) says that on this day, December 7, he supplied the *Francis* with three months' provisions, but John Drake suggests that provisions were filched from him. The Latin passage so far as it is legible runs: 'Nam Hypogemon [Drake] qui rationes omnes demortuo senescallo sufferatus est, fingit jam plura tradita esse qu illi receperunt disseminatoque est illorum obsonia apud nos latere, ceteraque ejusmodi.' And in the margin Madox adds: 'Hypogemon nempe viaticum negat ancillae.'

treaty of friendship was built up—but fallacious and fragile].
[*cipher:* Seek more the 21 of December.]

8.

[*transl:* They took from them a net, sugars, an axe, ginger for planting, iron bands for strengthening the casks, certain sweetmeats, nails, bells, all to the value of £10. But we gave them back their books and ornaments. Fenton kept back some books and a number of trifles for himself, for he always looks after himself first. And he observed the customary feast in the Galleon, where Ward was present, who had said that he would take his departure unless such doings were stopped, and that Parker ought to be killed, and other abominable things.[1] A man at first violent but soon fearful, he apologized and when asked if he was going to behave himself properly, promised that he will. The two sware to mutual friendship without any deception, and he swears that never before had they been greater friends. Which is impossible. He speaks as though they ever had been friends! And my view is that they never have nor never will be friends.]

9. *Sunday*

[*transl:* We took with us Richard Carter, who lives in Asuncion. The Edward carried off a Portuguese, the former involuntarily, the latter by his own wish. His wife made a formal appearance in the Edward, but she was not admitted. She wept . . . believing herself deserted. The old friar[2] and Francisco were pleasantly received here and were given what they had earnestly sought, letters in Latin to Frobisher or Acres,[3] telling them not to touch these people, but to follow us to the Cape of Good Hope. This however was done as a blind so that they should not suspect our going by the Strait.]

17.
[*Note carefully*]

[*cipher:* There is to be noted that Hood and Ferdinando be always sick when they come to the shore. Nando hath counselled to go back again and rob St Vincent's, and so him. The Master telleth me the General is very fearful to go through the Straits, because of the Spaniards, and casteth

---

[1] For the fuller story see Walker's Diary, p.214.
[2] Dinner that day was aboard the *Edward*, when Friar Juan de Rivadeneyra and Don Francisco de Torre Vedra were present, as related by Luke Ward.
[3] This is the only indication that Captain Richard Acres, who had fought in Ireland, was expected to have accompanied Frobisher on his proposed voyage to the Moluccas by the Strait (see p. 45, n. 2).

many doubts, And where to rob poor men was no conscience, now to hurt such as are able to hurt us again is a grudge to conscience. Soothly a just judgment of God to make our cowards manifest! And now see what it is to deal colourably, for had he meant honesty a first, these doubts now had not needed. But Ferdinando, a ravenous thief, hath brought the matter to this pass.]

[*transl:* All in the fleet were summoned.[1] The danger from 20. the Spanish fleet was strongly and vigorously placed before the pilots, masters, captains and gentlemen. We asked the sailors what ought to be done. All cried our for passing the Strait except our own master, who thought we must get supplies first, and Percy who urged rather to attempt the Cape of Good Hope, and Ferdinando who stands out as the head and origin of all evil. Jeffrey and Shaw think that going by the Cape we shall avoid all danger and keep within the law. Taylboys swears he would rather perish by the sword in the Strait than die of hunger in the archipelago. Walker also thinks it should be advised, if it can be done safely within the law, because of the shortage of wine, of which there is no hope by the Cape. I ask time to think it over. So do Hawkins, Ward & the General. Parker says it is necessary to go by the Strait, but giving no reasons therefor. Hawkins soon brings his opinion in writing, to the effect that of necessity we must go through, as otherwise there is no possible way of making up our provisions, and in this matter his written words are vehement. I cooly consider that, our needs having been supplied, we should expressly seek the Cape, but if this cannot be so, then the Strait. If neither, then after honestly selling our goods, to return home. And I made this plain to him because I had already perceived that he was aiming at a Kingdom, and this not merely by suspicion but by actual evidence, in the first place by some words which carelessly escaped him, and by some actions which suggested how his purpose was to be effected.[2]]

Hawkins said [*cipher:* The General told me he hoped to do

[1] For this important conference see Documents 51–7.
[2] Fenton eventually approved the third alternative suggested by Madox (Document 56).

some notable thing, which I guess is either to spoil St Vincents and there to be King, or to pass to St Helens & there attend the Portugal fleet from the Moluccas, or to lurk about the West Indies till the King's treasure come from Panama.] [*transl:* At dusk the sails being shifted we turned back northward. There were bitter complaints among the crew, for they now believed themselves cheated. About 33° S.]

21. [*transl:* Parker argued very earnestly that he had forgotten himself and not weighed his words. He asked to correct them. Clodius (Fenton) agreed. But he wants to treat them as part of what he actually said at the Council. 'I proffer, I write, I propose', he read out. But (says Fenton) let me have your original, I want that, by your leave, to use as an outline, both go together. Puffing out his cheeks, Parker immediately angrily left our cabin. Hardly had he gone when he was called back, and returned. Now indeed, my good fellow, can anyone call you brave? Luckily Drake came to dinner and brought a ray-fish with him.]

[*cipher:* After dinner in great grief Parker bewailed to me his estate and how by table talk he had been led to this action which now, he was out of doubt, would never be performed. He muttered how much the general hath been beholden to him and his friends and how strangely he was now used, saying that he would rather desire to live here than return into England with such infamy as we were like. I pitied the man indeed. He is very jealous of his reputation, but hath not in him to maintain it.]

[*transl:* Opening the Ephemerides he showed me that without doubt this matter had first come into question on the 7th of September, when hitherto it had been in dispute whether it was preferable to make for the Strait[1] . . . and Drake and Hood swore that they could open the way by force and steal the more from the midst of the enemy . . . It must be noted that in this debate Fernando took no part and so is [*The Bark lost*] not mentioned in the Minutes . . . A night of bright stars, a moderately steady NNE wind blowing, quiet and fine.

---

[1] There is no evidence of any discussion on this date. The decision to make for the Strait was taken on September 30 (see p. 110).

About ten o'clock the Bark was seen for the last time. Pray God keep her safe.]

[*transl:* There is not a little stir aboard, although confined to 22. secret whispering.[1] Hood, too, carries himself angrily and [*Consternation*] with an evil mind, for he suspects that it was done not without the advice of Hawkins, for between him and the Captain of the Bark there was a long discussion the other day. This seems the more probable because Drake was often threatened, when he asked for provisions, that he would be dismissed and another put in his place. Others believed that either a broken mast, or a faulty compass, or a leak, or some other damage or hindrance was in case . . . there was hope however to see him, damaged, in St Vincent harbour.]

[*transl:* Parker is almost out of his mind. Hawkins, too, 23. [*Sunday*] coming to me secretly, asked what would happen to us next? I do not know. Well (he said) either we seize the town of St Vincent, where he is to be made King, or we make for the island of St Helena, and when the Portuguese fleet arrives, laden with spices from the Indies, we fleece them as they come, alternatively some among us intend that we betake ourselves craftily against the Spanish fleet in the Gulf of [*What Mexico, which brings great quantities of gold and silver, as Hawkins much as you will To do such things is criminal and damnable, suspects, not without reason*] nor will I ever consent. Here (I said) take care of yourself, only whisper such words. He added that all the sugars now in Brazil are firmly promised to certain London merchants to whom we were doing an injury if we should purchase them for ourselves.[2] There was now ay left for us the refore but to go home in disgrace, for the only safe, easy and suitable way, through the Strait, was closed to us by cowardice and fear. And no hope remained of passing the Cape of Good Hope. A hope, indeed, for impossibilities! What then? (I said) for we are forbidden by our bond to pass the Strait, except under urgent necessity, and to weigh the matter well first. Everything Drake did, he answered, was done with vigour and considered purpose, and he was led to determine to pillage the shores of Peru, if we reached the Pacific, because he desired the booty

[1] I.e. about the vanished *Bark*.   [2] An agreement is implied (pp. l, 126).

and the glory for himself alone. And indeed, what he relates is probable, and that is why, as I believe, our Drake[1] has such a desire to get there, so as not to be inferior to Sir Francis in anything, and indeed to outdo him in many ways, as he once confessed to me . . . Hawkins said further that he had asked Ferdinando whether Fenton had ever spoken to him about St Helena. He swore by the gods that he had never heard any mention of it, But I know with absolute certainty and it is clear as day that he was the first originator of the idea. Yesterday evening Parker brought me his opinion as formed at our last Council, written in his own hand, and asked me to accept it, which I did. For I see the man is much concerned lest there should be any hidden jealousies between himself and Fenton. He has little intelligence or wisdom, but is nevertheless eager for praise, and rather timid . . .]

25. [Christmas Day]

[*transl:* . . . Hawkins, indeed, was splendidly attired for the solemn festival, which when Fenton noticed, not to be behind him, he too put on something elegant. But Parker had never been so untidily dressed (like Bardsey, a silly paltry fellow, and the most insolent wretch alive). He attacks Talboys with loud abuse when it happens that he is unwilling to obey his orders, for his excessive confidence in Fenton makes him overbearing & intolerable.]

26. St Stephens

[*transl:* When it was clear to everybody that our merchants were not willing to work for nothing, Ferdinando, who for good reason had hitherto pretended to be ill, now came out openly. He said that there was now no hope for us unless (in order to be recompensed) we went a begging alms. He was a pauper in an alien air, and he had got to give his servant 10 marks and a shirt. Fenton congratulated him on his good spirits: Trust me, we shall be well off, for there is profit to come of this venture! Not so, he replied, for they will not trade with anyone who has not a Portuguese permit. But you, said the General, have such a permit. Certainly, he replied, but now they have submitted themselves to the King of Spain, and so I am as objectionable to them by law as I can

---

[1] The text has 'Hegemon' (Hood) but the context demands 'Hypogemon' (Drake).

possibly be. How is that, I asked. Because, said he, I am at war with the King of Spain. What, said I, are you not a subject of our Queen? That is so (he replied). And we are at peace with Spain, I said. But I, he said, have a free pardon from five Privy Councillors for carrying on war with Spain. Which I do not believe, I said, for if it is true it is not possible for anyone to live honestly in this ship which has a permit for illicit war. And I, said he, do not doubt to see you too become a willing thief . . . That is unnecessary, I said. And indeed conditions [have arisen owing to which] Fenton is being induced to have recourse to honest trade which once he greatly disliked. [This was why] he had sent Evans home, and got rid of the Bark [Elizabeth]. For he suspected that between him [Skevington] and Drake [it was planned] secretly to turn back for home. He judged that if once we gave ourselves up to piracy, any place we desired to live in would have to be shunned. For to come home rich with booty is neither safe nor respectable. Did we wish to come home after carrying out robberies, that was a capital offence, for which all would be blamed alike. The actual perpetrators, who should be arrested, are quite other than I myself, yet I shall fell the smart most severely if I go back, while to remain away is an even harder choice. For I know no one who would willingly die an exile from his country. Nor can I remain alone. The business of provisions makes any proposal to continue the journey impossible. There is nothing left but to help ourselves as much as possible by honest trade, if we are not to be reduced to within only half a step of our last farthing.]

[*transl:* Today the General gave me a handkerchief as a little present. Really! how greedy and false he is, for he hides his bottle of wine secretly and never takes it out unless he sees me to have begun my prayers, then he boldly brings it forth, and sucks up the wine without any more admixture than plenty of sugar. Podalyrius[1] does the same, who like Hypocritas models himself upon Jennarius, and does not come to the common table. He then indulges his own

29.

---

[1] These three nicknames presumably designate Banister, Cotton and Taylbois respectively. Podalirius was the son of Aesculapius. (See p. 320.)

inclinations to the utmost, and feasts happily in his own cabin, where he consumes more wine than any ten men . . . As the day became calm we discussed Drake, and Ferdinando said something about the Bark which was meant to indicate we know not what. He also said that if we did not find her in Port St Vincent, he would then openly proclaim what he had heard from the General. He told someone that there was a lot of unnecessary fuss. He [Drake] had more provisions than we supposed, we should take into account the three months supply which had been insisted upon at the first. And Hawkins, calling me aside, said that he considered there was no doubt about their safety, for their Captain would find many places were he could have victuals, 'for if he makes for those openings beyond the Strait, and thence crosses the ocean, he will find a continual supply, so I think there is no doubt but that he will return with great honour, for yesterday evening at about 10 o'clock he should have drawn level with the south latitude of the Strait'.]

[*December*] *31.* [*transl:* The wind blowing northnoreast we took our course northwest . . . The day overcast and cold.]

[*Diary ends*][1]

Document 39
Private Diary of John Walker[2]

[*June* 1582]

. . . on the last of May, and in the afternoone about iiij a clocke we sett sayle and cam into plymouthe Sounde the fyrst

[1] On December 29 Madox added a note to what he had written on October 19, when he had been bled in the left arm: 'but my arm hath byn stif ther ever syth'—an ominous report.

[2] Extracts. B.M., Cotton MS Otho E. VIII, ff. 202–23, 160–4. Abstracts in *Cal. S.P., Col., E. Indies, 1513–1616,* nos. 202, 214.

of June in the afternoon & there rode. Aboute vi of the clocke Mr Madox and I wente ashore and supped with capteyne Hawkyns, captayne Drake, Mr Whytacres at Mr Whoodes house, pylote in the Gallyon, but after supper we came aboorde.[1]

The 2: we sett sayle about vi of the clocke in the morninge & sayled alonge the coste of England and that nyghte passed the lyzard w^t a good wynde. [*Note in another ink:* Captayne Hawkyns lose his boy.][2]

The 3 beinge whyt sunday I preached of concorde and the coming of the holy ghost, and the same day was sea-sycke & so contynued untyll the vith day, all whyche tyme we had the wynde at north & by east for the most parte & so untyll the ixth

the 9 at 10 of the clocke in the morninge we mett wth a shippe of [late] upon the Spanyshe seas of whom we learned newes that the king of spayne had prepared (at there coming from St Lucar) ix shippes to go to the yndies and ii to the strayghtes of brazyl & that in one of these 2 go 30 monkes . . .

At this tyme we were 38 degrees from the equynoctial.

Upon the 20 in the morning we entered (as I take it) the tropycke of cancer & at noone had the sun for o^r zenith

The 22. Allmost at nyghte the vyceadmirall and I in o^r skiffe wente aboorde the gallyon & because it was nyghte & the wynde blew I was feareful to enter the skiffe & so stayed all nyghte in the gallyon

the 23 I lykewyse contynued there

the 24 M^r vyceadmyrall wth the M^r, merchants, & pylote came aboorde the gallyon where conclusyon was had of wateringe at bona vista an yland of C. verde, & lykewyse of o^r course to ryo de plate, there lykewyse to water & refresh o^{r}selves. after supper I came aboorde The edwarde whereof I was verye gladd for I lyked not the badd entering into a shippe the wynde blowinge

26 . . . in the afternoone Mr Captayne warde wente wth a [skiff] to enter the lande[3] to seeke for freshe water, but when

---

[1] I.e. returned to their respective ships.
[2] Henry Kirkman (see p. 72, n. 2).
[3] See pp. 78, 91, 169.

they came to shore the sea wente so hyghe that they were not able, only ii of o[r] men, vide Russell & marks swamme a lande where was store of goates but no freshe water, for they were not passe half in the lande:

The nexte daye in the morninge beinge the 27 we were to have watered & have proved further (for doubtless ther was a plenty) but the Generall wolde not staye but in the afternoon set sayl & awaye they wente. notw[t]standinge the ii barks drew neere the shore and founde a convenyente landynge place, for one gyng went upon lande. ther departing wantinge water was agaynst C. Wardes mynd.

[*July* 1582]

the 2 . . . This tyme there was some abuses amongst sundry of the companyes w[ch] did not a lyttle greeve o[r] captayne consydering the greate care he contynually had to keepe them in peace . . .

the 3. The Captaynes greyfe was such & so moreafter by reason of the premysses that he grewe towards sicknesse, but at length by goddes helpe he recovered, castinge his care upon chryste. This day I delivered lessons unto youth (?) of the want they should sustayne lackinge a guyde etc.

21. We lay alonge the coste but went not w[th] the shore, yett o[r] vyceadmirall used all meanes possyble to have his men refreshed, but the generall w[th]stoode etc.

26. M[r] Maddox, C. Hawkyns, C. Drake came aboorde us where we were merry w[th] a dolphyn. our vyce-admyral had kylled y[t] morninge. About 4 of the clocke M[r] Maddox in o[r] boate was sett aboorde the gallyon. C. Hawkyns went aboorde the bark Francys w[th] C. Drake. I sente a letter by M[r] ma[ddox] to the generall, wherin I sorrowed the greate sycknesse happened amongste o[r] companye (for then had we 30 men infected wth some sycknesse,) and lykewyse the wante of water, complaynyng of our not watering in the ylands of Cape Verde, etc.[1] . . .

[28. the general] reproved [Ward with] these wordes viz: I [alone] wyll rule & I know what is go[od I wyll be] obeyed &

---

[1] See pp. 95, 173.

wyll commande every man in the [company the] lest and the best, wth many suche w[ords]. Our captain M[r] Ward [to these] great speeches reanswered nothing more [than in] the manner defendinge the good husbandrie was [to seek] water., but in truthe the cause he so hardilye dealt [was] for a jelosye he concejved agaynste me, by reason of [a letter] M[r] Maddox sente me that daye by M[r] Ba:[1] whyche letter he intercepted & redde (but the same beinge in latyn he could not understand it, for y[t] he understoode not latyn perfectlye) and ymagyned some secret practyces betwyxte us two, after this many reproaches on his syde bytterly passed, we ceassed to talke, I desyring a more pryvate place to speake in, for he spoke openly to all [within] hearing. the generall wente down wth o[r] Cap. into the C[abin], and I to salute M[r] Ba: who told me of a letter M[r] Madox [sent] me but intercepted by the Generall. We passed the tyme for i or ii howres in veywinge o[r] sicke people & in some other [conference] but my wordes were they never so reasonable, were unpleasing to the Generall. styll he standinge upon his aucthorytye as though I wente about to injuyng the same. At lengthe he & o[r] vice-admyral syttinge above in the poope I demanded openly for a letter M[r] Madox sente me w[ch] I understode he had. He dynyed not the letter, but sayde he had to talke wth me about it. The vycead departed and he entered speeche in manner chargynge me wth M[r] Maddox letters. I excused myself as ignorante of any matter betwyxte us that myghte concern hym and the lyke I thoughte I myghte safely say of M[r] Maddox. but he wolde accepte no escuse but raged me still w[th] the letter. I requested I see the same, who graunted I should see it but not have it. When I had readd it and perceived the matter in the[2] . . .

. . . other shipping, yf we tooke a part wherw[t]all o[r] men brought from those ships [to make] restitution when we came home to England [could] he do it lawfully or no: I said he might [not, for evil may] not be done that good may insue. Upon this [we reasoned for a] tyme but in the end I persuaded from it [rather not] to take anything w[ch] is not o[r] own, other

[1] See p. 173.   [2] A long hiatus in the text.

make ye lyke motions. But I liked of no one proposition b[eing] one & all repugnant agaynste the worde of god. In fine we ended in frendshyppe savinge that in those questions of [spoiling] other mens goods, for thereunto wold I not nether (by gods grace) consent unto. And in truthe I spoke my opynyon very freely. But I perceyved he was prepared to goe into the S.Seas but thereunto wylle not I agree. About 6 of the clock receiving friendly vale, they went aboorde, but his coming was to no end of bettering our condytyon. more then this, one Mr Cottoun, a gent. wrote unto me (wth whom I had very small famylyaritye) the generall lykewyse intercepted his letter, but that letter after he had shewed me the same & I readde it, he kept it but wolde not delyvir it for some words conteyned there; wch were that he was sorye there was no better agreement amongste us: but (in truthe) what his meaninge was therein I understode not. Before the generall and I ceassed talking: I requested hym very earnestly to deal wth Ferdynando the pylote to deale wth more contynence in his conversation & wth more modestye in his speaches for that they were (as I affyrmed) offensive to god, & nothing chrystyanlyke, for y^t he rejoyced in thinges starke naughtey, bragginge in his sundrye pyracyes. The generall dyd assure me of amendement & so we departed . . .

[*August* 1582]

The 4. in the morninge we bore in wth the coast of Guinia supposing the same to have byn serleona but we found it a mayneland and a fayre baye called C. de monte, for the barke Elysabethe wente harde asshore & then ancored, and some of o^r men wente a shore where they found freshe water and a ponde of freshe fyshe and dyvers fruits as pomegranates & sawe lyttle howses but no people, but because the bay was open to the sea we wolde not staye there but made into the sea & sayled alonge the coast and founde it all a maynelande contrary to all o^r plotes and cardes as we ymagined; but it happened otherwyse, for we were farre off Serleona & that was part of Madrobamba.

Aug. 9. [fell in with Sierra Leone.]

The 12 . . . In the afternoon the general sent Mr Madox & the master of the Gallyon to me & requested me to go aboorde the Elysabeth[1] . . .

18 . . . The King of Spayne had sent xx sale of ships who were gone to the Strayt of Magellane & likewyse vi shippes of frenche men who were gone the same way.[2]

20. The vyceadmiral tooke the skiffe & wth him the master and pilot and went to [plot] the coasts and rivers in the harbour. I wente to the Generall wth whom I [passed the] daye sometymes in conference wth him . . .[3]

21. In ye morninge ye vyce admiral & I went aboorde the Gallyon to the general, who wth the master & Mr Madox & C. Parker were gone into the ryver to a dyscovery.[4] We had broken o^r fast wth some freshe fyshe wch C. Hawkyns cawsed to be made ready for us . . . we chanced to espy a great crocodyle in ye water, wher we besett wth our nettes but coulde not take hym. at length after mutch beating up & downe after him we sett o^rselves in order, some wth calyvers, some wth fysh-gygges,[5] other wth speares & other wth swordes & targetes, purposinge to fyght it out wth him, wth whom we had mutch adoe to avoyde the danger, etc. At laste C. Hawkins caste a fish-gygge in into hym under the hynder leg wherat he made at the nearest man and w^tall gaped wth his mouthe wch was monstrous to looke upon. The vyce-admiral beinge ready with his calyver shott into his mouth, wch entered into his throat, whereat he was amased but yett yeilded not: the pylot shott his peese at him, who lefte some peeces of it in the fore-legge, divers strake wth swordes & pykes but could nothinge hurte him, in truthe we had a very warlyke battyle wth hym, but in fyne we conquered hym.

30. After supper C. Drake made a dyscourse of some of Sir Frauncys Drakes voyage & also his extremityes in the voyage: This done they departed to their shippes

31 . . . The portingales stayed supper and beinge nyghte

---

[1] For the court martial of Crane see Document 45.
[2] This information given by the Portuguese was correct.
[3] Fenton revealed some of his secret plans to Walker.
[4] See Pl. XII and p. 103.   [5] Fish-spears (*O.E.D.*).

before we wente to supper we called for candles (the table being covered under a Awnynge upon the sommer decke) but presentlye there happened suche aboundance of contynuall lyghtening w^tout ceasinge that the same mynistred suffycyent lyghte to suppe by, but afterwardes there folowed greate thunder & rayne. This daye one of o^r merchants Mr Jeffrey shott wth a goun at a buffe and stroke her but she escaped.

[*September* 1582]

2 Sunday . . . At noone C Hawkyns came aboorde us to have the merchants pryce certayne clothes he saythe Mr Alderman Barnes & Mr Towerson had prayd shuld be taken into the adventure. o^r merchantes wente aboorde wth hym to the Galyon, but pryced them so hardely that C. Hawkins thought him ill dealte withal and after o^r merchants came aboorde some wordes passed wth the vyceadmiral, but occaytyoned there unto by the badd valueing by of the Gallyons merchants:

11. The viceadmiral wente wth the longe boat to sweepe for o^r cable & ancor but myssed it. I wente aboorde the Galyon where I founde the generall ready to goe ashore to C. Parker, who requested my company, wth whom I and Mr Madox went & then we dyned. after dynner Mr Madox & I wth some other wente after certain buffes wch my man broughte worde he had seene amongste the lymon trees but we founde none . . .

12 . . . I went with the viceadmiral . . . aboorde the Galyon and there dyned, wth whom we [had speech] concerninge the state of the countrey etc. after dynner C. Hawkyns went to shore to C. Parker and I to sleepe: after a whyle the generall called for me wth whom I had [speech] & a large dyscourse of all matters in partycularyty y^t concerne this voyage, as o^r returninge to the ylandes of C. de Verde for o^r gayning of wyne etc. (but I wold not yeelde) wch yf we obtayned not (*inquit*) o^r voyage were utterly overthrowne. The generall & Mr Madox wente wth me to the vycead. to supper, for the portyngales were invyted to suppe aboorde the Ed[ward] wth the vyce ad^l: After supper everyone

departed to there shippes & I to bedd. that nyghte we had 2 tornadoes, o^r skyffe drove awaye: but was found agayne

The 13. o^r men wente ashore to mende o^r foresayle. The Portingales were aboorde us & from us went up into the countrey in o^r skiffe (for they had borowed it) to fetch the ryce. This nyghte the campe broke up on shore for C. Parker by myshappe of a shrubbe received hurte in his legge & the turnadoes wth wynde & rayne so used them that the bellowes were lefte unwatched & the forge unlooked upon

The 14 O^r carpenters & o^r men wente to cutt woodd. At nyghte come aboorde, our saylers murmured for wantinge there suppers & at there small allowances, for wch cause they wolde not sett the watch. The master came into the Cap. cabbyn where he & I were alone & made there complaynte and grudging knowen, who presently wente forthe amongst them and appeased them wth promyse to amende there myslykinges wher upon just cause they myslyked & wth frendlye & wyse perswasyons satysfyed there myndes. I stayed walking upon the hatches untyll 12 of the clock & then went to bedd, where I dreamed straungely of my arryval back in Englande etc.

Sept. 16 [Sunday] I preached *ex luca* 17 . . . after dinner the vyce-ad: & I wente aboorde the generall & there we passed the afternoone & supped. [I] & Mr Maddox complayned to the other *de miserrimis nostris captibus* etc. afterwardes we came aboorde aboute 8 of the clocke. This day the generall gave his men new lyveryes of brodd cloth of popyngay greene.[1]

The 17 in ye afternoone the vycead[1], Ca. parker & bothe the masters wente to sounde the yland in the northern side surliona & so returned before nyght home agayne etc.

The 18 I wente ashore to angle where I mett Cap. Hawkins & Cap. Parker which appoynted to meete me there, where we had merye pastyme wth hooking the lyttle fyshe. Afterwarde we had fyshed we went after the byrds nestes wch were buylded wth greate arte, the same hanginge upon lyttle sprygges over the water, the mowthes or entraunces of the

---

[1] See p. 107, n. 1.

nestes they made hanginge downwardes to defende them from monkeyes and Auntes. At length we came aboorde and I went wth them to supper w^t the generall. After supper the vyceadmiral sente his boate for me.

21. In the morninge the generall sente for the viceadmiral and me, who at o^r cominge made knowen unto us the injury receyved at Mr Haulls handes,[1] wch was (amongste other words betwixt them) that he sayde he woulde be master whether the generall would or no etc. the generall callinge us together into his cabin, who arre the vyce ad^l. the leyftenaunt C. Parker, Mr Maddox & I, sent for the master and layd open his faults: the Master excused hymself as cleere of any juste cryme & spoke somewhat playnly. The generall replyed & sayde durst he speake suche wordes to the Queene. Yf he durste not why dared he presume to speak to hym: after many suche lyke wordes the Master was commaunded to departe: And then I beganne the [sic] intreate the generall to treate the matter wth some clemencye (for the wordes the generall did charge him with were justyfyed by the leyftenaunt) who consented (for he sware he shoulde be dysplaced) upon this condition: that the Master sholde kneele unto hym at dyvyne servyce tyme & confesse his fault & aske pardon. The vyce-admiral replyed that although he had her Majesties commissyon yett he had not her royaltye etc. in fyne we concluded if the Master shoulde confesse the faulte & requeste ye generalls frendshypp, whereunto he willyinglye condyscended, wch at prayer tyme he performed & the vyce-ad^l & I departed to o^r shippe ymmedyatelye. After dyner the vyce ad^l. & I in o^r boate went a shore where we angled in a lyttle ryver & took some lyttle fyshes, wth wch pastyme we rested o^rselves. 2 howres afterwarde we wente thence and passinge into the lawnes & within the woodes we espyed Mr Maddox . . .

25 . . . The vice ad^l: called me & the master to his cabbin [and gave us] the rehearsal of an intente the generall had (for [he told it] when aboorde us that afternoone) to go backe to the ylandes of [cape verde] & there to staye and gyve chase to

---

[1] See p. 107.

everye shippe to the end to furnyshe hym self of a long tyme & vyage. [He told his] further purpose and requyred o^r opynyons: to whom I answered (for in truthe I knewe all the generalls purpose before as he had dealt pryvately wth me but coulde not wynne me) to returne backe were not only an overthrowe of o^r whole vyage but suche and so greate a dyscredyte to the churche of god & my professyon that the enemye myghte have greate cause of tryumphe to heare that 2 professours of the gospell shoulde in so noble actyon become pyrates. and I wyshed rather to dye then any such myscheyfe shoulde happen unto us wth many other wordes to that ende: *idque lacrimis:*[1] the Master in lyke manner was unwylling to retyre backe etc. The vice-ad^l. when he harde my wordes dyd not [dissent] but showed what it was to leave so noble a enterpryse & so go on in o^r voyage and allso verye greately with zeale professed my opynyons sayinge and protestynge that wth the losse of his lyfe he wolde preserve the opynyon the nobylitye of Englande had of him: and goodwylle the merchaunts did beare hym, and was concluded by the helpe of god to get forwarde whether the generall did or no: But fyrste we thought it needefull to perswade hym to go on the voyage because we wolde not do anythinge hastelie etc.

Sept. 26th very early I wente wth Mr Maddox to shore who came . . . we toe bewayled o^r myseryes etc. and concluded to make tryale if we coulde wynne the generall to goe on the voyage.[2]

The 29 being St Mychell's day at after dynner the vyce ad^l. & I: havinge determyned before to deale playnely wth the generall for the goinge forwarde (yf it pleased god) on o^r pretended voyage, when we came aboorde hym, the vycead. began to commen wth hym concerninge the portyngales who had taken our skyffe. At lengthe the vyce ad. upon y^t occasyon called me & Mr Maddox unto hym to aske o^r opynyons what he myghte do in conscyence in respecte of that matter etc. We replied as we thought beste etc. Whereupon I beganne to speake of o^r going to the ylands of C. de verde . . .

[1] See pp. 278–9.   [2] See p. 184.

The vice-ad¹. sente for the master, the pylote & the 2 merchants into his cabbyn to whom he made knoen the generalls devyse and purpose.

Sept. 30 in the morninge oʳ men broughte aboorde a monstrous fyshe after veiwe thereof the generall went into the vice ad¹ˢ. cabbin where were lykewyse there Ca. Haw. Ca. Parker. Mʳ Madox & I: & makinge offer of matter for the voyage beganne to tell us of some extremytyes lyke to happe for wante of foode, wᶜʰ was awnswered by all men etc. Then he alledged the greatnesse of oʳ shyppes, how unfytte they were for dyscoverye & that matter was debated of, and the 2 pylottes Mʳ Whood: & Blacoller were called, & their opynyons asked: we concluded we shoulde fynde water ynoughe etc. then the generall wolde of us what way was most profitt whether throughe magellanes strayghtes or by C. of good [hope] . . . amongste other conference & talke the generall made a greate doute of the passage of oʳ shippes for there greatnesse; & more, affyrmed yᵗ our mechandyze eftsoons wolde not buy us vyctayls. This I harde Mʳ Whoodd affyrme.¹

[October 1582]

The fyrste of October early in the morninge the generall sente for the vycead¹. and me who wente: when we came thyther he called us together, *videlicet* the vice-admiral, Ca. Hawkins, Ca. Parker, Mʳ Madox & me and there made manyfest dyvers injuryes he sustayned at Mʳ Evans handes etc. Mʳ Evans was called for and there denyed nothinge. He was urged wᵗʰall but earnestlye desyred to be dysmyssed and that he rather wolde be in England than heere, & that the Portyngales wolde carrye hym home etc. as appeareth by the Artycles whereunto are oʳ [hands set]. upon wᶜʰ cause we consented he shoulde go: yet notwᵗʰstanding Mʳ Maddox & I labored wᵗʰ him to staye wᵗʰ us, & procured Mʳ Taylboys to entreate his stayinge but prevayled not. At afternoone Mʳ Maddox & I went ashore & there *promissis datis tamquam fratres in christo* [*metimus semper*] *permanere.* We came

---

¹ For the events of September 30, see pp. 110, 184–5.

aboorde & after supper the vycead. came; Ca. Hawkins, Ca. Parker & I wente aboorde the portyngales to buy some of their slaves (for dyvers of o^r men were deadde) where we persuaded Mr Evans to staye wth moste earneste requestes, wherew^th any man myghte well have been moved, but he was obstynate etc. We had 4 negroes, & there we had a boy wch the vyce-ad. exchanged for a boy he had before. This done we came aboorde etc.

Oct. 3 . . . In the afternoone I fell sodenly sycke wth a vehemente vomyting & extreeme purginge: Ca. Hawkins came aboorde. There supped . . . All this nyghte I was very sycke

The 4 in the morning Ca. Hawkins in our skyffe went aboorde . . .

The 5 in the morninge I prayse god, I felte myselfe somewhat recovered but was very weake & feeble . . .

The 6 . . . This day I [was let] blodd in the ryght arme.

Oct. 16 . . . Robert Marks, Parker & John Collyns ye goonners boy were whypped at the capstyn for robbing ye stewards roome of beere, byskett & cheese.

Oct. 23 We lost sight of the Gallion.

Oct. 24 We were in 3 degrees 10 minutes. At night we bore up and hailed each other.

The 29 we went SW and by S. This day the master of the Francis came aboard as from the general for a hogshead of pork who told us the general had given commandment to his gunner to shoot at them for their keeping so much into the weather etc.[1]

The 30 we were under the equinoctial circle. The wind came larger and the first watch we went S and by W

[November 1582]

The 9. about 3 of the clocke in the morninge I fell dangerously sycke [of a] burning calenture: all that day I sweatt & burned extremly so I was lett bloodd . . .

---

[1] This report of Richard Fayrweather is perhaps the basis of what Madox later heard from Walker (p. 187). Fenton was nervous of the desertion of his pinnaces, and 'them' probably meant both the *Francis* and the *Edward*.

The 11. The generall hearinge of my sycknesse came to visit me wth whom came C. Parker, Mr Maddox, Mr Banyster & all the gentlemen in the Galyon: they brought wth them conserves of dyvers sortes & sweete meates in great quantytye: Now I began to grow sycker and more weake. Mr Maddox stayde wth me all nyghte wch was a very sycke nyghte to me.

The 12. I was in greate daunger of deathe but I prayse god I was ready whensoever the lorde had called. I had made my wyll and testament & had dysposed all thinges orderly: the vice-admiral & Mr Madox were my executors.

The 17. I was in suche extremytye that I thought myself paste all recoverye, and so dyd all aboute me: & therefore fyrste I prepared myselfe to dye & after sente for the master, the pylote & there [bade them farewell] . . . they of the Gallion & they of the Francis [in this] extremytye of mine came . . . to take there leave of me . . .

[December 1582]

Dec. 3 . . . all this whyle from the ninth november untyll the 2 of december I never came forth from my bedd, in so mutch that now I am so weake that I can nether sytt nor stande all the fleshe is consumed of my body. I lyke to an anatomye. But I hope to god to recover my strengthe this beinge the third daye I feele myself a lyttle stronger.

The 4 I went forth of the cabbyn and walked upon the hatches but founde myselfe so feeble that I scarse was able to stande.

The 5. I lykwyse growe strong. I prayse god and am able almost to walke.

1582 6 Die Decembre[1]

. . . about 5 of the clocke in ye morning . . . we dyscryd a barke saylinge alonge . . . not farre from the entraunce of ye porte . . . where were o^r shippes at ancor *videlicet* in the porte . . . aboute 28 degrees in lat: to the sowth from ye equynoctyall lyne. Worde of this barke was presently

---

[1] This part of Walker's Diary (Cotton MS Otho E. VIII, ff. 160–4) was written up at a later date, when he felt stronger.

broughte to ye vicead. who [was] then in rysinge from his bed. He wthall speedilye dyspatched hym selfe wth the newes to ye generall: who stayed not longe there but (in his own skyffe wherin he went) came back to the shyppe syde and called for some furnyture of defence as a steele targett etc. away wente to the barke Fransys whyther some were gone out of the Galyon before to make her ready, for she shoulde fetche in this sayde barke. ymmedyatelye she hoysed sayles so that before Ca. Parker coulde be readye to come from the Galyon (for he was appoynted by the generall to go wth the vyce-ad.) they were under sayle, yett he came well ynoughe aboorde them, the wynde was northerly and therefore coulde they not gett forthe of harbour but were towed forthe wth the Edwardes skyffe & the Galyons. The Galyons skyffe was sente wth the Barke to give ayde yf neede were etc. They had sayled more than 4 or 5 leages but they were so nyghe that the[y] shott at her whereupon she struck sayl. Before they came to her [they had] greate wordes to the company [saying] y^t yf they came to any fyghte [or tried to] boorde the barcke whosoever wolde [do so would] have a pyke or other weapon thrust [into him] but hereof was no neede for the Cap^n. Parker and five more wente aboorde the [Spaniard] only Tobias the masters mate in ye Edward fy[red] whereat the captains were dyspleased. [The number] on the barke was 21 persons whereof seven friars & 2 were women with a young child, [all] Spaniards. The chestes were looked into [and the] keyes taken from the owners & what was [there] they quickly had searched. The wynde being [contrary] they were constrayned to come to ancor: about   of the clock the wynde turned & came at   the two barkes, the Francys and ye pryse [set sayll] (for they called the barke a pryse) and came into the harbour about 4 of the clocke. but whyle these thyngs were a doinge there fell a contraversy betwiste the vyce-ad. & Ca. Parker: and hott words [passed], belyke it was for there auctorytye in this de[. . .]. When they were in harbour & at ancor the fryars from the Francis (for thyther they were carryed before) were sente aboorde the Generall whither lykewyse the vycead.

wente but came into ye rode in the pryse. There the fryers delyvered suche thinges as were enquyred of: wch were of the fleete gone for the straytes.[1]

The vycead[1]. came aboorde who I [perceived dis]pleased. I enquyred what were [his griefs. He said] he was not well dealte wthall by [those] of the Gallyon for the generall had geven commandement that all shoulde departe the pryse [except] Ca. Parker and his 2 men & that he shoulde [send] two more to them to watche there at nyghte, whom he sayde shoulde have byn Mr Symbarb & Mr Wylkes. but when he came by the prise & called to Ca. Parker & tolde hym the [order to] the generalls men that those of the Galyon should come aboorde, (for there were dyvirs of the Galyon wth Ca. Parker) but they wolde not. Wherupon he came away & sente none. Other matters in bryefe he tolde me whyche after I learned more at large.

Dec. the 7. The vycead. went aboorde the Galyon who stayed not there longe but Mr Jeffrey was sent for who after was appoynted wth Mr Taylboyse, and was appoynted to go aboorde the pryse & to take an Inventorye of all thinges in her: The Generall at this tyme called the commyssioners to consulte what myghte be done in these causes (I my selfe was not there for I was sycke & then began to recover. I had the callenture & kepte my bed 17 dayes) where there happened a very greate controversye betwyxte the vyce-ad. & Ca. Parker whereupon the[y] grewe to very unsemlye comparysons etc. but was appeased afterward.[2]

. . . it was there determyned & thought [whether] to take the barke from the Spanyards and to sett them on shore in the wyldernesse [or] to carrye them alonge wth us to the Strayhtes of Magellane. but to carry them thyther I [understood] there vytualyes woolde be spente whereof [was] no greate plenty & therefore the general [asked] Mr Maddox wth Mr Jeffrey because he understood the language to perswade the olde fryer rather [to go] a shore in some harbour they knewe then to take [such] a voyage in hande: the olde fryer who was [the] cheyfe father wepte bytterly alledging

---

[1] See pp. 229, 231. [2] See p. 119.

they [would] be eaten of the Indyes etc. and desyred [the] generall by them to be good unto them etc. At Service tyme the Generall came aboorde wth the [viceadmiral] to sup wth hym & to conferre concerninge these matters & to have my opynyon. Mr Maddox & Ca. Parker were lykewyse there; and the General [began] to tell me what benefyte god had sente in our handes as these men, for by them they understood that the Kynge of Spaines fleete was gone to the Strayghtes there to fortyfye & that they were [16] shippes with 3000 persons who wyntered in the ryvir of Januarye & went thence the xxx of october, & that 4 of the shyppes were for Chylye in the S.Seas wth 500 very choyse men, the nomber that shoulde fortyfye the strayghtes was 360. [The name of the General] was Don Flores etc. and he [was chief of] the reste, whereof one of ye reste [was a man] of good accompte called Don Francisco[1] . . . of them etc. and y^t these men were inhabytent at ryvir of Plate, the havinge obtayned leave of the governour of the countrey to go to spayne 2 years synce [to bringe] more fryers, other matters [he[2] tolde] me of lyke cause wch for brevytye I [omit.] This being tolde he showed me ye grete hurte these men myghte do us in o^r voyage [if] we lett them go to the ryvir of Plate [considering that if] we were to vytayle in the S.Seas that they myghte sende over by lande in shorte space to the portes there whereby we might be prevented etc. & ther fore requyred my opynyon therein. I desyred pacyence to speake my mynde wth libertye wch was graunted. Fyrstly I in verye simple manner shewed what was Chrystyan charytye & the effectes thereof & after that w^t was a good conscyence & the effecte etc. whereupon after a verye longe dyscourse I concluded y^t we nether myghte wth charytye or conscyence ether take the barke or anythinge from them or hassarde their bodyes upon shore whereby ether the indyans or wylde beastes shoulde devoure, & so we shoulde be gyltye of the sheadynge of y^er bloode [which god would not] leave unavenged upon us etc & [I shewed that] the hurte they myght do us [was none] for that they were

---

[1] This was Don Francisco de Torre Vedra. 'He' was Fray Juan de Rivadeneyra, Fenton's informant.   [2] Fenton.

ygnorant of [our intentions]. The Generall & the reste havinge [heard me] used some speaches to & fro but verye [soon] all concluded to lett them have their barke & to go on there voyage. by this tyme supper was ready beinge 9 of the clocke [and we supt] and were mery & thanked god for his be [. . .]. at after supper I verye earnestly [asked] the Generall & the reste presente to give [me leave] to saye somewhat more wch was graunted [and I] presently and abrupte begann to showe what [boun]tyfull love was & of concorde I sayde the [same] and alledged reasons & examples to approve [the bene]fyte of them bothe etc. and of the contrary [the evil] as mutche, spending in both half an hour. The reason that moved me thereunto was [that] I ether suspected or knewe betwyxte the Generall & Ca. Parker on one parte & the vycead. on the other was but *mediocris amitia vino dissimulate.* In fyne I expounded myselfe & shewed my own opynyon, requestynge them to joyne together in a [conclusion] & perfection of agreement thet shoulde not be wth out greate [*sic*] any peece dyssolved: . . . in the ende . . . I did knyte up so perfect [a friendship as] was indyssoluble: but it happed [that] hereupon they went home & I to [bed for] my heade dyd ache & I was sycke [The next] day in the morning earlye I lyinge in [my] bed the vyce ad. came to me and burst out in these wordes y^t for his parte he was not yett [conclud]ed in ye frendshippe & y^t he had recyved [dis]curteseyes at the Generalls handes and that unlesse [these] & other matters were reformed he wolde not [conc]lude to the frendshippe but wolde turne [heade] to tayle and wolde goe from hym yf his [com]pany wolde go wth hym, I replyed that his [com]pany wolde not leave the generall w^thout juste cause, then (sayde he) I wylbe sett on shore & shyfte for my selfe etc. I tolde hym I was hartely dismayd to heare this and wylled [him to let me] understande his gryefes and that I doubted not but [I could] redresse y^em etc. he tolde me sayinge the Generall thinkes to tye me to that obedyence y^t when I come into a harbour I shall not go ashore w^thout askeinge his leave & I see no suche reason, & other matters wch I wyll tell when tyme serves, etc. I tolde him how mutche I myslyked of dyssentyon & because the occasyon geven to leave companye myghte be occasyon of the overthrowe of o^r voyage I wolde shewe the Generall what he sayd etc. & that I doubted not but upon this extremite . . . to make a more perfecte frien[dship than] would have been etc: which he a[greed. He] & I were bydde to dynner to the Galyon [where I] was desirous to goe because I . . . & there I shoulde talk wth them [that] the day before sent me a platter. When we wente aboorde, ymedyate the company entered into councill & the matter was againe for the spanyards & fryars what should [be done] wth them. for new perswasions had a[vail]ed: many reasons were tossed to & fro, the lieutenant woolde have had them sett on shore but I stode to my olde matter & in end with the good consent of the Generall & [vycead.] it was concluded as before, and they sygnyfyd so mutche to the olde fryer. Don Francisco who dyned there wth us rejoysed thereat etc. The vyce ad. & the lieutenant went wth them aboorde the barke & they had some sugar & sweete meates wch the fryers bestowed upon them *no: vo:*[1] whereof they had good store & we wanted. In the meane season I sygnyfyed unto the Generall the dyscontented mynde of the vyce ad. in all thinges as is before. the Generall amased hereat for he thoughte he woolde deny the goinge from him, but I sayde I wolde justifye it, and that I knewe he wolde not deny any thinge.

. . . about 5 of the clock cam aboorde [the sugar and] sweete meates: at after supper the Generall [and the Commi]ssioners urged the vycad: wth w^{ch} [he was aggriev]ed: & because I reported it the Generall asked me to speake it agayne: I beganne to [open] the matter in everye poynte in effecte as before: the vyce ad. denyed nothinge. Then the generall requyred of whether he thoughte himselfe to good to by vycead. when her Matie had appoynted hym Generall etc. who awnswered [he did not] but used further wordes shewinge his greyfe. [Hereupon] many thinges & wordes passed and all myldlye answered & well objected: in the ende [I] desyred as I had broched this matters & now that it was

---

[1] *Nolens volens.*

come to this poynte & dysposed of he wolde geve me leave to speake in the matter: wch being graunted I earnestly requested the generall to forgett what had byn sayde & done etc. & the lyke to the vycead. etc. & that now they wolde geve me leave as goddes mynyster to make them frendes, after mutche adoe it was graunted & all concluded frendes wth a chrystyan promyse the performaunce whereof I charged them under goddes name fullfill: wch they vowed and so god continue it: after this about 10 of the clock the vyce ad. & I went aboorde having invyted them[1] to meete the Gents. ['to dinner' *deleted*] . . .

The 9. the General, the Leyftenant, [Cap. Parker, M^r] Maddox: Don Francisco & the fryers [dined aboard] us. the Generall tooke into his one of [their ma]ryners to be his pylote upon this coaste [and the] vycead. tooke another etc.[2] & so when the [wynd] served us to leave the rode wch was . . . [we] lefte the barke & men there & wente our way . . .

The 12 in the morning we sett sayle out of the Baye of good [Comforte] called by the Portyngals porte do don deygo[3] for there was he and his shippinge caste away. It standethe in 28 degres to the S. of the equynoctiall lyne . . .

The 15 . . . the people . . . are of greater stature than any Englisheman for they be of 7 or 8 foot hyghe (for so the Spanyarde y^t ys in o^r shippe dyd tell us) . . .

The 20. The Generall havinge called us the nyghte before [the vice ad^1.] the merchants, the master & pylott & I wente aboorde the Admyral where we dyned and after dynner the Generall made known unto us the cause of his assemblynge of us:[4] wch was sett down in 2 questyons, the fyrste was that he was advised of a Spanish fleete gone to the Strayghtes of Magellane who were in [15] ships and were gone oute of the Ryver of January the xxxth [of October] wth 3000 men wth women & chyldren in them, whereof 360 were [to fortifye] the strayghtes by ward of bullwarke, upon w^chcause he [sought] by what meanes we beste myght escape their

---

[1] To meet the Spaniards (see p. 119).
[2] Richard Carter (Document 49) and Juan Pinto (see p. 192).
[3] Dom Rodrigo.
[4] For the Council of December 20, see Documents 51–7.

daunger & passe the strayghtes or whether it were necessary
to go that way. These 2 questyons was yf we went that way
what course were beste to be kepte, whereupon the master &
pylotes were called, who coulde assure us of no safetye to
passe & escape there force but they doubted not there strength
etc. when they had sayde what they coulde & woulde they
departed. Then dyd the generall demand our opynyons. The
merchants, Mr Shaw & Mr Jeffrey woolde have . . . I
thought . . . whom to annoy we wolde be lothe, and to
[fear] I thoughte great folly, & that suche a voyage [could]
not be performed wthout some daunger, For, sayde I, *quis
[si deus] nobiscum quis contra nos.* Capt. Parker: he in effecte
[said the] lyke, & so did the lyeftenaunte but in other termes:
The [vyce ad^l]: he shewed the greate daungers of the passage
& alledged other reasons to approve the same, and therefore
concluded that it were better to seeke relyfe upon the coast of
America or Brasil, a convenyent place to trymme up our
decayed caske etc. which coulde not be done in the strayghtes
where we determyned to do it & after this done should
procede as shoulde seme good to the generall and his
assystants. The generall requyred a tyme to yeelde his
opynyon, who at after supper gave up his mynde in wrytinge
to this effecte that he wolde not adventure his shippes & men
upon suche a known daunger, & had many sounde reasons to
establyshe that he spoke, & in fyne concluded that he wolde
not go throughe the strayghtes but wolde furnyshe hym selfe
of necessaryes upon this coaste & thereupon put us to choyse
whether we wolde venter into the River of Plate 50 leages up
the ryver whyther we were promysed to be safely broughte by
one Carter whom we had then on boorde us [where we]
coulde have vittayles of all sortes sufficyent . . . [it] was
past 9 of the clocke & then the vyce ad. & the reste came
aboorde & ymmedyately we caste [about] whereat o^r men
greatly murmured fearinge for the voyage. This day Mr Hall
sayde there vyctayles was [wanting nor] he wolde never
consent to goe to the Strayghtes nor no man else: for [the
Spaniard should] not take hym by the throte for vytayles.
The 21 being S. Thomas day at after dyvyne servyce the vyce

ad. made known the cause of there goinge backe who at laste [were] satysfyed. This day it was all day calme . . . At the begynninge of this nyghte we lost syghte of the barke ffraunces whom we suppose to be [gone] back to the Strayghtes of Magellan.

[*January* 1583]

Jan 20 . . . certain boats came from St. Vincent.

The 29 in the morninge we havinge loste the Ad. the vycead. resolved the questyon & callinge the assystaunce & the chyfe of the shyppe to hym: whether we myghte fetche the ad: where we suspected hym to ryde & what were beste to be done. the master, pylott & masters mate affyrmed that it was impossyble to reatch the ylande & what to do they knewe not for the safetye of oʳ lyves more then to beare of into the sea, whereunto we all condescended, the vycead. confyrming it: in hope to meate our Ad. at sea we bore off S e & sometymes S & by [e]

The 30 we went as before[1]

[*Diary ends*]

Document 40
Miles Evans to Leicester
13 *June* 1582[2]

Honorabell & my syngular good lorde my [letter] maye be geven yʳ L. to understand that the [ships] departed plymoth wᵗʰ a very good wynde, god be praysed, hyld wᵗ us so fayre

---

[1] Almost at once he fell ill again and died.
[2] B.M., Cotton MS Otho E. VIII, f. 146. Abstract in *Cal. S.P., Col., E. Indies*, *1513–1616*, no. 208. This is the first of the batch of letters sent home in Oughtred's ship the *Bridget* which left the fleet in the Canaries in mid-June 1582 (see p. 89, n. 1).

that we have towed owr bote hyther. [I believe] that owr generall wyll goo throwe the streytes of Magalan [for he had] some talk wth me abowt going that waye for he and the pilotes sayd that the pasage that way sertayne, and contrarywyse makes the cape of Esperanza dowtefull wher upon I made awnswer that I wulde folowe [our instructions] in all Respectes.[1] yt maye plese yor hono^r to unterstande that [our general] and all the captaynes wth the Reste of the companye are in [good health] wth owr shypes in good order who I praye god prosper and send [us] sucses in owr vyage. and not havinge ells to advertis yor hono^r of [at this] time I sese, prayinge god preserve yor Lpp in good helthe and [give your] hono^r good suckeses in all yor take in hand wth moche encrease of honor to gods plesur: the see in the latetoude of 35 degrees north est of S. vyncene 50 leges the 13 of june 1582

yor Honores assured servant
to his power   Myles Evans

[*Direction:*] To the Ryght honorable and his Syngular good Lorde and master the Earlle of Lessetaur, etc. this in Corte.

Document 41

John Walker to Leicester
14 June 1582[2]

. . . otherwyse we had byn by [this time already half way to] Asia: all the men in the whole fleete god [be thanked are in] healthe: only in the Galyon viii or ix are sycke of [a] feever

---

[1] Fenton's real intentions at this date must be a matter of speculation. It was then William Hawkins's wish to go directly to the Moluccas after passing the Strait.

[2] B.M., Cotton MS Otho E. VIII, f. 148. Abstract in *Cal. S.P., Col., E. Indies, 1513-1616*, no. 209. The letters which Madox wrote are not known.

but all lyke to recover. I doubte not but y^r [L. has] harde of the greate inconvenyence whyche was lyke [to have happe]ned at Plymouthe by reason that the generall upon [some hap] sett sayle and leafte Mr Captayne Hawkyns & the two [Pilots] and divers other on shore & wolde not staye for them [but on] the perswasion of Captayne Warde and some one or two [others he] caste aboute after we had sayled fyve leages and mett [them] at the Landes Ende in the frauncys, whyche matter [was like] to have bredde a greate myscheyfe but y^t we appeased it [even] in the begynninge. But now (god be praysed) there is amonge us as great a concorde & frendly unytye as may be amonge any people, & all thinges goe well wth us: and no doubte but god wyll blesse us; for o^r people are wonderfully reformed bothe in rule of lyfe & religyon towardes god. In the Edwarde Bonaventure we have daylye morninge and eveninge prayers besyde other specyall prayers at other tymes of the daye Everye Sunday I preache and after dinner we have conference in the scryptures wherewth [all] the maryners who never harde sermon in their lyves are marvelouslye delyghted. Captayne Warde governethe his charge wth greate wisdome & pollecye, who doubtlesse is so suffyciente a man every waye that he is well worthye to governe any greate charge. I wolde to god y^r L. dyd knowe hym as he deservethe. I beseche yor L. to contynue yor honourable goodnesse towardes me wch shalbe a suffycient recompense of my voyage: the Lorde god preserve yor L. in moste happye estate with the dayly increase of honor.

The 14 of June 1582: in the latytude of 35 degrees.

yor honorable L. humble servant
& chaplayne
John Walker

[*Direction:*] To the Ryghte honorable the Erle of Leycester my verye good L. & master at the Courte geve these.

Document 42
John Banister to Leicester
15 June 1582[1]

. . . my good Lorde I yor poor [servant pray the] good god to graunte unto you [his] care & blessinge both now & evermore . . . [gen]erallie but wryte unto yor honor of o^r estate [now reaching the] Canaries. god be thancked, we have all o^r heathes I myselfe was never soe well on ye land as I have bene since. god hath blessed us with a wyse generall & one y^t liveth in . . . [w^t an able] mayster & carefull pilotes & zealous & paynfull preachers & y^e . . . wth a prosperous wynde soe y^t we live together in christian love & brotherhood. good god graunte it longe to continew amongst us. Thus much I am [bold] to certifie you of o^r estate, now I am in most humble manner to beseech [you to be] good unto my poor wyffe & familie who have noe other succor under god but [yor L.] if they shoulde be injured and oppressed any wayes, but above all things my L. looke unto yor owne health & safegarde, truste not too much to these dissemblers of y^t papisticall sorte I meane, whose promisses, othes & vowes are nothinge, for [they are] altogether enclyned to rapyne & sheddinge of ye innocente blode & ye profession [of the devil] his gospell, but yor honor god be thancked is wyse & hath tryed oute their wicked, [treacher]ous enterpryses, & as I have always wished [soe] doe I hartilie pray y^t they maye [be driven] not only out of Englande but from ye courte & such as o^r good & gratious pr[ince] norished a longe tyme unknowne, god turne their hartes & graunt unto her majestie a longe and most prosperous raigne, or noe longer wishe I to live. Good my Lorde [forgive] me y^t I am alwayes thus bold wth yor honor, for truly it greeveth me at ye harte to see &

[1] B.M., Cotton MS Otho E. VIII, f. 147. Abstract in *Cal. S.P., Col., E. Indies, 1513–1616*, no. 210.

heare how they make ye courte a cloke to cover their wicked & dissemblinge practyses untill they may spie out a tyme to putt them in execution. Thus besechynge o^r good god to graunte unto y^{or} honor longe health y^t you may be still an instrumente to sett forth his glory & further ye continuall encrease of godly preachers y^t ye gospell may florish in Englande to goddes glory & o^r everlastinge comforte I cease. from my cabbin the xv of June.

Y^{or} honors humble obediente servante during lyffe

Jhon Banester

[*Direction:*] To the righte honorable his singular good Lorde and master the erle of Leycester at ye Courte give these.

Document 43
Minutes of the Council of
24 June 1582[1]

24° Junii 1582
Lat. 18

Matters to be considered of as followeth viz:

1. To see what course we shall hold from the Islandes of Cape de Verde. & what time we shall remaine ther for o^r watiringe

*Tuching y^e
second question*

2. To see the Barques provided of all things necessarie as well wth victualls as cartes and plattes

To ye second part of ye fyrst question. Cap. Ward. thinketh yt necessary to tuch at ye ylands of Cape de Verd, because both he hath aboard hym smal store of water, & y^t very unholsome also, & for ye more cumfort of ye companye both to wash ther clothes, & ye better to remedge & trym ye ships, & put vytayles in ye barks wch they want.

Hawkins, thinketh as doth ye viceadmiral & for ye same causes & ymageneth y^t we may soon see whether ther be

---

[1] B.M., Cotton MS Otho E. VIII, f. 159. Abstract in *Cal. S.P., Col., E. Indies, 1513–1616*, no. 211.

water ther or noe, & yf not may soon be gone w^{t}owt hynderance of the viage.

Parker, ys altogether of ye former mynde & led therunto by ye same causes.

Madox. so is also Mr Madox

Walker. Mr Walker for ye former reasons thinketh also necessary so to be.

Evans. thinketh yt also needful

Cotton lyketh very wel of ther purpose

Taylbushe lyketh hearof also wel

Jefferyse is lykewyse of the same mynd.

Tuching ye furnyture of ye 2 barkes [it was] also agreed by general consent [that they] shal be provided [with all things] necessary for 3 moneths.

Also ye generall cawled ye pilates and demanded of them wher was ye best place next to water, who did all think best ye rio di plato, & therupon he lyking hearof did also appoynt yt so to be. and consydering that of necessytie, we must passe wthyn a hundered leages of this place to fet ye wynd for ye Cape of buon speranza[1] and y^t we wer not to ventar so far w^{t}owt some refreshing wch we wer enformed no other place wolde yeld, therefore al the rest whose names subscribed hereunto consented

	Edward Fenton
Nicholas Parker	Luke Warde[2]
	William Hawkyns
	Richard Madox
	John Walker
	Myles Evans
	Randall Shaw
	Mathew Tailbois
	Peter Jefferey

[1] This argument shows a general ignorance of the route (see Map A p. xxvi).

[2] Neither of these two signatories would allow precedence to the other.

Document 44

Minutes of the Council of
1 August 1582[1]

1582.

Upon Lammas Day (beeyng the fyrst of August) beyng abowt 4 degrees to yᵉ northe of yᵉ lyne, and by estimation 100 leages according to my own reconyng[2] from Cape de verga & nornorwest yᵉ ylands of Cape de verd, the general in consyderation yᵗ ther myght want water to our fleet yf the wynd contynued long at yᵉ sowth, as yt had been in maner this moneth, or lest yt shold fal qualme as yt myght do, & so distresse us of beverage assembled yᵉ company of assystants wᵗʰyn the Galion Leycester, & proposed to be consydered of thes 2 questions:

Imprimis whether yt be better to turne to yᵉ most commodious place of land & ther to adventure for water, or to proceed & lynger at yᵉ sea in hope of rayne.

Next yf yt be thowght meet to seek water, toward what place we shal bend ourselfes for yᵉ performance of oʳ desyre, wᵗ quyckest dispach and least daunger.

Hearof yt was thus reasoned.

Pro primo.

1. Jeffreys thinketh we shuld rather now seek yt, then hearafter, lest yᵉ wynd qualmyng, when well we canot do yt, or lest by beating long until yᵉ wynd fawleth fayr oʳ water may deceav.

Mʳ Shaw layth down 3 consyderations, yᵗ is the consideration of yᵉ wynd, yᵉ lyklyhood of yᵉ qualme, yᵉ [avoiding offence] of portugales, upon yᵉ grownd of all wᶜʰ (he thinketh) yᵗ presently we shold seek water.

Mʳ Taybush upon his smal experience in thes causes reason by yᵉ opinion of other men, yᵗ we . . .

---

[1] B.M., Cotton MS Otho E. VIII, f. 158. Abstract in *Cal. S.P., Col., E. Indies, 1513–1616*, no. 212. See p. 96.
[2] Madox is writing.

Mr Evans is of ye same opinion w^t ye former

Mr Walker is altogether of ye same opinion

Mr Madox thinketh y^t yf ye wynd hold at . . . pleasure turne roome to land, yf w^towt jopardy we may come . . . watering.

Captain Ward thynketh yt very expedient partly for spare of store of beare, wch yf yt wer abayed wold goe further, partly because ye sycknes wch procedeth of heat among the men, by ye refreshing of fayr water, wold be muche eased & appeased.

The general in consyderation of al thes reasons before aleged whereunto he also agreeth, doth conclude in the fyrst question y^t we shal by any means seek a good watering place wth as much speed as is possible.

Touching ye second question ye masters & pylots wer cawled to geve verdyct of ye best place, who did on this sort delyvir ther opynions. When ye masters and pylots had thowght ye sur leon best to water yn, althogh some dowted of the wether in y^t place, yet knew they not any such rode or assurance of water elsewhere. The assistants, axed their opinions, did thus delyvir ther myndes.

Mr Peter Jeferey reserveth hymself hearyn to ye opynion viz. Surleone. In lyke manner Mr Shaw, Mr Taylbush, Mr Evans, John Walker both because we have concluded [to] seek water and ar assertained by ye pylots yt to be ye next place, and best assurance of good rode & fayr water, lyketh Sur Leona. So doth Mr Madox. So doth Capten Parker, desyring god to give us health; & so Mr Capten Hawkins, not knowyng any better, or nearer, or in maner any other place.

Capten Ward lyketh also of ye sur leona [as] wel for ye nyghnes of ye place [as for] avoyding of offence y^t might grow by goying to ye ysles of Cape Verde [which] by commission we are adjoyned [not to do] . . .

Document 45
The Trial of Ralph Crane
13 August 1582[1]

Upon an information geven to yᵉ general of some disorder in rafe Crane mʳ of yᵉ Elisabeth the assistants were cawld, before whom thus it were handled.

Captain Skevington being examyned sayth yᵗ rafe Crane sytting at yᵉ messe sayd (but he knows not when) 1. yᵗ whyl fenton was fenton he would not come to yᵉ sea wᵗ hym agayn. 2. Also he sayth yᵗ yf yᵉ general had set hym in yᵉ bilboes, they shold have been thrown overboard by John Gates & by John Good,[2] I mean yᵉ bilboes.

Hereunto Rafe Crane doth thus answer yt being threatened wᵗ yᵉ bilboes he oftn sayd yᵗ yf he had been set yn, perhaps he myght have been the last yᵗ shold have byn set yn, for perchance yᵉ bilboes myght have been throne overbord, other thynges he denyeth.

Further being axed why he shold not obey his Capten sayth yᵗ wher the capten had him attend of the viceadmiral, yᵉ general had gevn him charge before to come twyse a day to hym and otherwyse he was willing.[3] further more he chargeth Mʳ Skevington did say yᵗ yᵉ commissioners had apoynted him luke ward Capten and yᵗ yf Mʳ frobisher had been general his place shold have been better, and yᵗ he cauled Mʳ Wylkes his lieutenant

Upon his oth John Case[4] examyned in yᵉ first denyeth utterly,

---

[1] B.M., Cotton MS Titus B. VIII, f. 280. Abstract in *Cal. S.P., Col., E. Indies, 1513–1616*, no. 213.

[2] Two of the gunners in the *Galleon*; see Muster Roll (p. 158).

[3] There was evidently a difference of opinion as to whether the *Elizabeth* was to serve as pinnace to the *Edward* or was directly attached to the *Admiral*.

[4] The purser of the *Elizabeth*. Madox reports that Case had approached him while they were still in the English Channel to get him transferred 'for Cap. Skevington was so curious that no man could endure him' (Cotton MS App. XLVII, f. 22v).

ye second he confesseth, adding to John Gates & M^r good, Ric. fayrwether, and being demanded whether ye Capten or M^r to have geven moste occasion of offence he sayth y^t ye childyshe dealing of ye capten gave other cause to fayle.

Laurence Trip[1] to ye first denyeth to ye second he confesseth upon his oth but nameth not by whom it shuld be.

Mr Wylkes[2] on his oth to ye first denyeth, to ye second he confesseth, not naming any man particularly but in general ye gunners & quarterm^{rs}.

Thomas Marten[3] on his oth sayth to ye fyrst y^t rafe Crane shold say he wold never come to se agayne, w^t such a general & yf they were both on land agayn he wold not put of his cap to hym. To ye second he confesseth *ut supra* for Case.

On his oth Peter Owen[4] to ye fyrst answereth y^t he hard hym say he wold never come to sea agayn w^t Mr Fenton & to ye second he confesseth, but not naming any but indeterminately ye gunners

[Tuching these cases ye general w^t his assistants thus consulted, *deleted*]

Touching thes cases ye general thought good to caul [Crane agayn, *deleted*] those y^t were accused.

First Rch. Fayrewether denyeth yt utterly, y^t he never ment such thing. So doth John Gates and so doth John Good.

Now rafe Crane also cawled agayn denyeth also ever to have had any such conference w^t any of them

This doen ye general axed ye opinion of ye assistants whether this is worthy of punishment.

The leiftenant sayth he thinketh yt punyshable but greater punyshment he can not have then hear openly to be proved a lyer. Capt ward thinketh this vaunt tendeth to disorder, ye punyshment he reserveth to ye general

Captn Parker is of ye same opinion w^t Captain ward. Mr Madox thynketh ye man ought to be punyshed for example sake but ye maner how he he wold have by discussion to be considered of.

[1] A seaman in the *Edward*.
[2] See p. 13, n. 4.
[3] Steward of the *Elizabeth*.
[4] Seaman on the *Elizabeth*. One of Drake's men. See p. 179.

Mr Walker thynketh ye fawlt great, and therefore to deserve in respect of ye mallyce of ye mans mynd to be sharply punyshed.

Mr Evans is of Mr Madox mynd, y^t is to say, the punyshment to be advisable   considered in respect of ye place wch ye defendant bore.

Mr Shaw wold not this to escape pynyshment for harkening other men, but ye maner how he reserveth to ye General.

Mr Taylbush is of ye same mynd and so is Mr Jefreys

The general thinking this matter to proceed of great mallyce & tended to a common mutynye and an overthrowe of ye whole action pronounceth y^t he shold go in ye bilboes, ye rather also because some honest men were brought into slaunder.[1]

[*Signed:*] Edward Fenton, Luke Warde, William Hawkyns, Nycholas Parker, Rich. Madox, John Walker, Myles Evans, Randall Shawe, Mathew Tailbois Peter Jeffreye

[*Endorsed:*] Cranes desorders examined and punished. August 13 1582.

Document 46
The Friars' Bark
6–9 December 1582[2]

The 6. daye in the morning, before 6 of the clocke, wee sawe a saile which went towards the southwards, the Admirall not having knowledge thereof: I went aboord, and certified him, who appointed me to goe and bring her in, and to take

---

[1] Presumably the two gunners. See pp. 101, n. 2, and 179.
[2] Luke Ward's narrative, *Pr. Nav.*, pp. 660–1. This formal account of the events following the sighting of the small Spanish bark may be compared with the stories told by Fenton, Madox and Walker (pp. 118, 190, 210).

Captaine Parker, and some of the Gallions men into the Frauncis, and the Admiralls skiffe with us: so wee gave her chase, and tooke her sixe leagues to the Lewards of the place we rode in. Then not being able to fetch the roade againe, we ankered in the sea. I, intending to come away in the Pinnesse, and leave the Francis, and the prize together, being readie to depart, the winde blewe at South, a stoute gale, and raine, so that about sixe of the clocke, we ankered in the roade, where our ships ride in.

After we had taken them, and that Captaine Parker, and I, were aboord, we had much talke with them, before they came to the shippes, and being ankered there, the chiefe men were carried aboord the Generall, which was a Gentleman, named Don Francisco de [Torre] Vera, Nephew to the Gouvernour of the River de Plate, named Don John de Torre Vera.

We found an Englishman, named Richard Carter, borne in Limehouse, who had bene out of England foure and twentie yeeres, and hath bene neere twelve yeeres dwelling in the River of Plate, at a Towne named Ascension, three hundreth leagues up the River, whither they were now determined to goe, and inhabite, having two women, and two yong children, seven Friers, the rest boyes, and saylers, to the number of 21 persons.

The olde Frier [Fray Juan de Rivadeneyra] was had in great reverence among the rest: insomuch as they called him the Holie Father, He was abiding in no place, but as Visitor, he went visiting from Monasterie to monasterie.

The substance of all the speeches was, that the Spanish Fleete was before the Streights of Magellan, as they thought, for they were departed sixe weekes past from the river of Genero, where they had beene seven moneths to refresh and winter. And that these were not of that companie, but came out of Spaine, the 26 of May, 1582, in a Barke of foure score tunne, and foure score persons of purpose, for the River of Plate: The Friers beeing eighteene in number, could not agree, and their Barke was a ground at Spirito santo, like to be lost: therefore the olde Frier boughte this small barke of 46.

tunne, at a port, named Spirito Santo in Brasile, and so devided themselves, and comming from thence, lost companie at sea, but they thought they were before at the River of Plate. After his speeches, I went, and appointed (by the Generals order) men to remaine aboord the prize, with Captaine Parker, and brought one of the Portingals sayles away with me,[1] and came aboord, when I founde that our men had filled water all day.

The 7. day in the morning, the Generall sent for me, where he shewed me, and Master Maddox, certaine articles, which the Friers, and marriners Spaniards were examined of,[2] which tended altogether to the knowledge of the Spanish fleetes intent, and of the meanes whereby wee might be discovered by the way of River de Plate, by land to Peru. In this time came the rest, after whose comming was debated, whether it were best to take the boate, and people with us, or not, which was not determined, but referred till further examination.

Then was determined to passe by the streights, notwithstanding the Spaniards were there, but not to set up forge, nor to build pinnesse, but water, and so thorough[3] . . .

The 8. day afore noone, Master Walker and I, went aboord the Admiral to dinner, where was determined to discharge the Spanish barke, named Our Ladie of pitie, and all the men, except Richard Carter, the English man, and John Pynto, a Portugal, which dwelled at the River de Plate . . .

The 9. day being Sunday, in the morning, I sent master Shawe and master Geffries aboord the Admirall, to peruse the Spaniards letters: wherein they found the estate of the Fleete, which was in the streights of Magellane, as by the note thereof appeareth . . .

[1] To remove an essential piece of equipment was an age-old way of detaining a ship of which we may read in Herodotus (*History*, bk. III, ch. 136). The ship was a 'Portugal', although the company were Spaniards.

[2] See Documents 47–50; and pp. 113, 191.

[3] This decision was reversed on December 20 (pp. 121, 217).

Document 47
Interrogation of the Friars[1]

[1. Item] To understande their [nations], qualities and habitations

2. Item to learne when they came [hither] and from what place. In what [ship] her burden & name. The number of persons were in her and where she is now [gone] and for what places she goeth.

3. Item To understande how long they have been in the coast of Brasill and [in] what harbours and what the goodnes of those harbours be, & what releif there [is] founde there

4. Item to learne what was the cawse that they devyded themselves from their shipp & companie and whether they be goinge

5. Item to understande what sholding or depth there is in the river of Plate, what be the names of the townes the Spanyards possess there, what nomber of people in eche Towne, of what force they bie of, and what is their trade & goodnes of soile

6. Item to understande the distaunce from those places from Chili or any other partes of Peru and how longe the river of Plate hath been inhabited by the Spanyardes.

7. Item to learne when the fleete gonne for the Straight of Magelan departed from Janevera,[2] the nomber of their shipps, their burdens, the Capten names, the nomber of mariners

   [What part of the] straight they mean to [fortify]

[8.] Item to understand whether any [other the K. of Spain's] shippinge be appointed to go [into the South] Sea or that they attende any [fresh] supplie owt of Spaine.

[9.] Item to learn whether any of them has been to the

---

[1] B.M., Cotton MS Otho E. VIII, f. 174. See Documents 46, 48; and p. 212.   [2] Rio de Janeiro.

Straight of Magalan or the Sowthe Sea & in what Places.

Document 48

Answers to Interrogations[1]

. . . he is gone w^t ye fleete [as a] man was desyrous to go to ye ryver of plate

[3.] 28 of March y^{er} cam to the ryver of Jan[uary] ye whole fleet. wher they stayed til y^e [end] of November, & being vitualed for 18 months ther [provision] foysted so they bought flesh & meal y^t cost 9000 ducates, ye mele made of rootes At S. Vincents wch is 30 or 40 leages from ye mouth of January ther flesh was beast & bacon [of which] ther is store beast 300 li befor ye fleet . . . 12 riols a hog & 4 ducats. Other harbors being no mariner he knoeth not, but in that place may ryde al ye ships in ye world.

4. This bark cam fro spirito sancto in Brasil to ye R. of January. Al thes say he[2] came from Spayn 26 of May last in purpose to ye River of plate & coasting guyny they came to ye spirito santo wher ther ship was cast away at ye 3 Kyngs. Y^e friar bowght this ship of a portingal ther for wyn & oyl wch he saved in his other ship. 8 days fro January to st. vincent where they stayd til munday senyght last, to beg beaf & pork & meal & se yf ye bark wold com after whych they left a mending wher ther are al Portingals. 2 leagues up no entrance for a great ship above 250 ton

5. He knoeth not.[3] But goeth to passe fro ye ryvir to peru.

---

[1] B.M., Cotton MS Otho E. VIII, f. 175–6.
[2] The 'old friar' was Commissary for the Plate Province, and was resident in Lima.
[3] The hydrography of the River Plate. See p. 231.

wch is river of good ayres[1] 60 leags fro ye mouth a
late dis-peopled now renewed. Thense to Santa Fe 90.
Thence to ascention 150. Thence to guayro & to spirito
santo. Fro st fe to Potosi 300 leages. no going by land to
Cusco. The cuntrey is ful of horses in al ye river of plat
y^t 20,000 men may traivel over on horse back. Cloth of
coton. The rest he knoes not.

[6]   fro st. fe to Cordova 50 leags. Thens to st john de
frontera in Chile 50. Thens to cokimbo, a haven 50.
now st fe is 250 up in ye mouth of ye river so al is now
200 leagues ·

From potosi to St Fe 300 legs & 30. from potosi to lyma
400 legs

From potosy to stecho or tallavera 150. to st yago de la
stera 50 leg. to Cordoba 80 leags to st fe 50 leags.

From lima to guanaca 80 to Cusco 70 to ye new town 70,
to plate 70, to potosy 18.

From ye mouth to potosi 480 thens to lima 400 summa 880.

7. The first of november.[2] 15 ships for one was [sunk] y^e
general diego floryse de valdese . . . in ye galeasse of
biscay of . . . ye viceadmiral is ribera in a great ship.
[In the Arriola] a great ship is capten Palomares . . .
wch cam out of spayn & 300 dead. abowt y^e . . . ther
wer al countreys mariners. how many [they were] he
knoeth not. They went to possesse y^e [Straits] and to
fortyfy abowt ye mydle in ye narowest part wher it is
but half a leag long over & on ether syde to set 200 persons

don alonso de soto major is general of some of the
ships for chila whether he wil tak 600 soldyers presently
in 4 ships. Some ships must [return] back agayn to
Spayn. They carrid 15000 to provyd vitayls & cam to st
yago & st vincent. The soldiers for Chila cam willingly,
ye rest perforce

8. Three other ships were prepared to have com w^t them
but ye King sent them to terceras

9. Only ye old friar hath been dweller in lyma 9 years

---

[1] Buenos Aires.
[2] The departure of the Spanish fleet from Rio (p. 231).

Document 49

Relations of Juan Perez [Richard Carter] and Fray Juan de Rivadeneyra[1]

(i) Juan Perez

I left this Capitania of Espiritu Santo for the Rio de la Plata, in company with the Father-Commissary of the Franciscan friars [Fray Juan] at the end of October of 1582, and on the way stopped at the Rio de Janeiro where we found the royal fleet of his Majesty about ready to sail, which he had sent out to make settlements in the Strait . . . and as we were going out to sea the fleet took its course and we went along close to shore on the way to the Capitania de San Vicente, where we remained fifteen days. After we left this port, we went running along the coast to the Island of Santa Catalina, some eighty leagues from San Vicente in order to stop there and take water. This we did, and after we left there, and while in front of the port of Don Rodrigo, about three degrees further on, an English *zabra* [the *Frances*] of fifty tons burden, well equipped and with twenty-odd men came out to us. They captured us and took us alongside two English ships which were in that port at anchor, and were on their way to the Strait of Magellan. They were very well equipped, not only with artillery but with men and everything else. The *capitana* [*Galleon*] was of about 400 tons burden carrying fifty pieces of artillery, mostly of large size, and had seven very good cables, among which was one of 150 fathoms in length and of 2,500 strands. She carried instruments and engines for throwing fire, artillery, forty tons of powder, and 180 men, among whom not ten were thirty years of age.

---

[1] Extracts, translation. Seville, Archivo General de Indias, 2.5.2/21; translation in H. R. Wagner, *Sir Francis Drake's Voyage around the World* (1926), pp. 398–402, from which these passages are, by permission, reprinted. Fenton must have liberated Richard Carter (for whom he had no further use) on arriving at Spirito Santo (p. 135).

Among them were five pilots and forty men who could take the altitude of the sun.[1] The *almiranta* [*Edward*] was of 300 tons, and as far as artillery munitions of war, crew, and rigging were concerned, corresponded to the *capitana*. The pilot who was in the *capitana*[2] told me that she belonged to an English gentleman named [*illegible*] and that she had been in Cadiz when Diego Flores took refuge there during a storm . . .

These ships were made ready in England after Diego Flores had left with his fleet, with the licence of the Queen of England and her Council, in order to go to the South Sea by the Strait of Magellan, and from thence to the Moluccas, for which purpose these ships had along with them 20,000 *crusados* worth of goods to trade with the natives . . . As soon as they left a story was circulated that Diego Flores could not reach the Strait of Magellan, but that he would have to pass the winter on the way, either at the Rio de Janeiro or at the Bay of San Julian where Magellan wintered with his fleet. It was said that they could pass through the Strait while Flores was wintering . . . More, what I understood from them was that they would not go to the Moluccas until first they had taken some prizes in the South Sea as they had done the first time . . . they took from us the wine we carried and the conserves we had made in San Vicente, as well as two or three boxes of nails which they needed to put together a launch which was carried aboard the ship to be set up in the South Sea, so that they could use her for going along close to land. From this port they sailed . . . with the purpose of going to see if settlements had yet been made in the Strait of Magellan, and to see if they could pass through. While in the latitude of Rio de la Plata, there was a general meeting of all, and the captains of the other ships went to the meeting in order to come to some resolution. They agreed, inasmuch as Diego Flores was now ahead of them as they had been informed, that the *capitana* should

---

[1] Without accepting these actual figures, it is clear that very many of those aboard the *Galleon* were practising themselves in astronomical navigation.

[2] Thomas Hood, who had little regard for the truth.

return to San Vicente along the coast in order to break up the voyage, and there exchange their goods for sugar. To this decision the Captain of the *zabra* [John Drake] was not willing to consent, and as soon as it was night he tacked in the direction of the Strait. The other two ships continued their course to San Vicente, where they arrived very easily by means of a Portuguese *derrotero* for the coast which they had with them.[1]

(ii) *Fray Juan de Rivadeneyra*

Therefore they have made a fleet according to what I was told of two galleons and *pataches*, as well fitted out as those which I saw.[2] These are better equipped, larger and better than those of the Spanish fleet which his Majesty sent to the Strait of Magellan. On each of the two galleons which the English Lutherans have, are eighty guns of cast-iron. The galleons are very strong and the *capitana* very new. There are also a *patache* and two launches with 350 English Lutherans on board. There are also 6,000 ducats in merchandize and many Lutheran Bibles and other books in Romance, as well as two clergymen of their perverse and damnable sect, a great quantity of warlike stores, a super-abundance of pitch and tackle, and a sufficient quantity of food and wine for two years . . . The crew are well-equipped and well-dressed, the captains with their chains and medals and gold buttons, all very anxious to encounter the General, Diego Flores de Valdez . . . and when they have defeated him they will attack the forts in the Strait, which they said is a league and a half wide in the narrowest part. They say that the Governor of the Strait, Pedro Sarmiento, will be there alone, since the Governor of Chile, Don Alonzo de Sotomayor, with his 900 Spaniards, will have left for Chile, and they will find Sarmiento and his men so weak, naked, starving and freezing,

[1] Document 75 shows the type of rutter carried.

[2] Fray Juan was told of Frobisher's ships which were intended to make directly for Brazil and the Strait. He therefore begged for a safe conduct as Madox relates (p. 192). He greatly exaggerates the strength of his captors, but his description of their fine clothes agrees with what Madox records (p. 196) about young Hawkins's splendid attire on Christmas Day, imitated by Fenton.

that they will carry them away in their ships . . . They said it was a country in 54° of latitude, colder than Flanders, and without the provision that Flanders had of good houses, stoves, clothing and lining. . . . March 19, 1583. To the Governor of Tucuman.

Document 50
A Council on the Friars' News
7 December 1582[1]

[*Endorsed:* Rob. Leicester. Seynor pedro.]

(*i*)   Pedro Sermento general of ye straits to ye viceroi of peru don martin henriques. fro Spain 9 decemb 1581. to cape verd Ja. 9. to ye river of Janniver Mar. 25. ther wyntered 7 months & day. Wher we spoyled o^r goods & helth for yt is a land of gret infirmyty *et multi mortui.* We departed hence w^t 16 ships for ye streyts ye 30 of Octob. Ther goeth w^t us don Allonso de sotto major, governor of Chillo, w^t 500 choise men and municion.

I need vitalyes, powder & municion, for our proportion herein is in terceyra *neque dehuc spes.* I will send the K. letters from ye Streyts. *Festina. in tu sole spes.*

(*ii*)   A letter wrytten by the generall of ye forces for the straites named Pedro Sarmiento, to ye Viseroy of Perow, donne Martin Henrykes Viseroy of Perow

---

[1] B.M., Cotton MS Otho E. VIII, ff. 199, 156. This document includes (*i, ii*) summary and translation of Pedro Sarmiento's letter to the Viceroy of Peru, (*iii*) the questions put to the Council, (*iv*) decoding of rough cipher notes made by Madox round the margin. Sarmiento makes clear that the hoped for fresh supplies for the Spanish fleet had been diverted to Terceira, a point in favour of Hawkins and others who wished to pass through the Strait no matter if it were occupied. The section marked (*iv*) indicates that the occasion of making the notes was the debate of December 7, as to which both Madox and Walker give some details in their Diaries. For Fenton's account see p. 118.

1. We must be supplied & holpen at y^r hands as a thing y^t concerns ye churche & ye glory of god

2. We came forth of Spaine ye 9 of Dec. 81 & came to Capo Verde ye 9 of Ja. next. & came to ye river of Jeneiro ye 25 of March wher we wintered 7 monthes & days. wher we spoyled o^r goods & helths. For y^t yt is a land of great infirmytye, wher we had many dyed. We departed hence wth o^r 16 ships for ye Straits ye 30 of october

3. There goeth wth us Don Allonso de Sotto major, governor of Chello wch hath wth him 500 men, good & choyse and good munition.

4. I particularly shall have great nede of [victuals] & powder & beastes as his ma^{tie} doth com[mand] and for great hast y^t I had I cold not [send] y^r Excellence ye Kinges letters but shall send them from ye Straits by a [trusty] messenger. wch I think hardly . . . for other gret affairs y^t I shall . . . trubled here . . . the ships y^t his ma^{itie} should send . . .

(*iii*)   To consyder whether yt be reqsyt to cary this bark with us or noe.[1]

To consider wher the Spaynysh fleet nowe is. Blacoller sayth y^t in one place ye Streyt is but a leag broad twyxt ye 2 lands so fyre twyxt 2 poynts or headlands, who sayth ye narrowest place is at ye goyn owt wher be mountayns, y^t no ordynance can be planted.

(*iv*)   [*cipher:* Ward said use them well for others would . . . but privily he said it was no matter if . . . Hawkins inconstant every way. Parker, Madox, Walker, say will spend victuals. must be unrigged. cannot feed. will lose men. take sugar, hoops, sucket, nails, tools, botes(?)][2]

[1] See p. 212 and p. 263. Peter Jeffery acted as translator and interpreter.
[2] See p. 192.

Document 51

Questions Propounded by the General
20 December 1582[1]

Dec. 20

First that whereas we be uppon [purpose] of the Straight of Magalan, and [now by] good intelligence are enformed of a fleet [of 15] Sailes of Spanishe Shipping and 3000 [men which] past the xxx of October last from [the River] of Januarie for that place (whereof 260 [are] appointed to fortifye and inhabitt them) [we seek] whether they beinge possesst of the said place wth their said forces, we maie with any lykelihood of o^r safeties attempt o^r former purpose wthout the overthrowe of our selfes & o^r voyage.

Secondlie findinge o^r selves fitt to proceede there-in, what course we shall hold most meatest, to avoyde their forces and to worke o^r best saffeties, aswell in regard of there forces, the strengthe of the place unknown to us and the smalnes of o^r companies to answere the same.

Document 52

Opinions of the Assistants
20 December 1582[2]

. . . as much of o^r . . .

. . . long contynue only w^t . . . for ye passing throe ye Strait . . . none of them y^t be o^r pylotts can [tell] us of any

[1] B.M., Cotton MS Otho E. VIII, f. 193. Abstract in *Cal. S.P., Col., E. Indies, 1513–1616*, no. 215. These were the formal questions put to the fateful Council of December 20; see also Document 57. The decision of December 7 (p. 118) was reversed. See also pp. 191–2.

[2] B.M., Cotton MS Otho E. VIII, ff. 183–4. Abstract in *Cal. S.P., Col., E. Indies, 1513–1616*, no. 220.

other way to passe . . . remained which by report we do need . . . there . . . y^t we must either passe [through the strait] to trye ther force or else return [back w^t o^r] viage to the Moluccas unperformed; for [to fear their] forces before we see them and [on the] Spaniards reports wer folly for [it is known that] such voyage as this can not be passed [without] danger.

Si deus nobiscum quis contra nos.

I request a short tyme to delyvir my mynd in wryting.[1]

William Hawkins

Capten Parker thinketh y^t now yt is to late to talk of goyng by ye Cape of Good Hope in respect of ye wynd wch doth yete hinder as hytherto hath doen or els needed not this [matter] to have come in question.

Now for ye other extremytie ether to passe or return back, wch he thinketh must needs be one of ye 2. he desyreth rather to [pass] theron than other wyse, except we may be better supplied of this syde of Brasil, & so muche ye rayther for certaynty of vitayls wch he hopeth to get in ye south sea but can not lern any place on this syde wher we may be refreshed yet.

Mr Lieftenent desyreth he Nicholas Parker may set down his mynd in wryting.[2]

The Vyceadmiral is of opinion y^t we ar in noe way in case to passe by Capo de bona speranza nether yet wel able w^t this smal store y^t we hav left to passe ye strayts, consydering w^{t}al how strong an enemy is in ye strayt before us, as we ar assured. wher o^r gretest hope of water & other refreshing was. whom to offend we ar forbydden and whom to encownter he is very loth & consydering ye harm y^t they may do us, & benyfyte can we reap none at ther handes, but great lykelyhood of ye overthroe of o^r whole state, waying what small force we have in respect of thers. & y^t . . . we shall come in place wher to . . . decay is lyke to be greater & . . . of lesser power than now yt is wherefore to conclude his [opinion] is y^t yt behoveth us to seek some place [upon] this coast to supply our necessyties.

[1] See Document 53.   [2] See Document 55.

He is ye rather led both by report he heard in Ingland and, information of some Inglysh[man] we met w^t hear y^t ye coast of Brasyl [is] inhabyted w^t portingales, among whom we may hope to fynd curtesy ynogh, and trafficking with reward of gain and to be supplyed of o^r wants [in return for] such triflyng merchandyce as is lykely to decay on our handes, and purpose yn this being once perfectly [performed] to proced on o^r viage after, in such [sort] as shall be thowght best than, to ye general and his assistants.

Luke Ward
John Walker.

Captain Drake thinketh we may [pass the Strait with a] good wynd altho not w^{t}out danger.

Mr Ferdinando sayth he was never [there and] can not tel how the retches lye.

Mr Fayrwether thinketh we must neede [venture] yt except we had a place hear to [buy] victayles yn

Mr Hawl thinketh yt not expedient because [it] wil be a long way before we shal come [to any] place of vitayling

Mr Percy thinketh y^t we must of force venture thro because we have not vitayls to go by the bona speranza unlesse we cold vitayle hear.

Peter Jefreys thinketh y^t in as muche as we are to passe this way only for vitayls and ar altogether uncertayn to fynd vitayles when we come thither, yt wer better to go by ye Cape of Good Hope ye rather to avoyd [the Spanish fleet.][1]

Herewith Mr Lieftenent replying sayth we ar as certayn to get vitayls hear in ye south sea as at home in England.

Mr Shaw is of ye opinion wt Mr Jefreye for y^t he supposeth he hath hard y^t we ar to ronne 800 leages[2] after we come thro the Strayts before we fynde any watering place.

Mr Taylbush supposeth yt better to ventur upon ther bodyes than by goyng by Speranza to put o^r selves in greater hazard by want of necessaries.

by me   Randall Shaw
by me   Mathew Tailbois

---

[1] See p. 263.   [2] Presumably to the Moluccas.

[*Direction:*] To the Right Honorable The Lord Treasurer,
The Earle of Leicester, and Sir
ffraunces Walsingham, Knight, & to
either of them gyve these.
at the Courte

Document 53
Opinion of William Hawkins[1]

. . . wyne & other necesarys, we are in [need to make] the
adventur thorow the Straights of magalan, in hope [of gaining]
our monye wheras goinge by cape bonnespei [there is none].
agayne for brasill ther is no hope for money [since] the country
geves it not.

Also for that our voyage is so honorable and not to [be
made] but by passynge the Straytes, for that it is now our
[best way] to the molucos I thinke it most meat y^t wth gods
helpe and [without] feare to proseede, not knowinge anye
suffycyent objection [thereto] to be alledged.

Also for goinge by cape bone spe or backe agayne home I
thinke by occasyon of leakage we are nether way able to
proceed.

Wm. Hawkins.

[1] B.M., Cotton MS Otho E. VIII, f. 194. Abstract in *Cal. S.P., Col.,
E. Indies, 1513–1616,* no. 216.

Document 54

Opinion of Richard Madox[1]

. . . [for] ye avoyding of all da[nger] . . . ether in offence to our . . . the Spanyards, & so displeasing her [majesty I thi]nk ye safest way were to trym [our ships and] furnysh o^r watering w^t what supply were [there at the] next[2] harboroe and so to commyt o^r selves to [hope] of a good wynde to bona speranza.

Thes causes hearunto moving me bee these—1° our articles of instruction wherby we are enjoyned and forbyddyn this way, but upon good consyderation. I suppose ye commyssioners were ye more careful, for they had no smal suspicion, whither, and to what end the Spaynysh fleet was gone.

Next because I suppose wee may in maner as soone [find] refreshing eastward as westward wch is thus shewn

At ye begynyng when ye ryver of plate was appoynted our first rendevou, yt was ye rather agreed upon because o^r pilats dyd informe us y^t of necessyty we must come w^tin 100 leags of yt to fet a wynd,[3] seying o^r refreshing hear shold be no prejudyce to o^r passage y^t way, wch yf at y^t tyme were true yt is also not unlykely to be true styll. Agayn our m^r thinketh y^t consydering ye wending & troblesome way yt will be yet 3 moneths before we can come to any place of refreshing in ye south sea & y^t w^t a good wynd. Now in this space I trust a good wynde may cary us to some happy place eastwards wher we may be releeved. further I can not gather by any probabylyty but y^t we shal need more variety of wyndes by ye strayts than ye other way.

Now yf the weaknes of thes reasons condem this opinion *Secundus*

[1] B.M., Cotton MS Otho E. VIII, f. 195. Abstract in *Cal. S.P., Col., E. Indies, 1513–1616*, no. 218.
[2] 'The nearest harbour', i.e. on the hither side of the Strait.
[3] See p. 77.

to be vayn then do I think good to adventure ye second choise yf wee may be assured y^t her Ma^ty wil not take yt yl in respect of offence done to her brothers subjects and ye rather for these encoragements.

1. Fyrst ye daunger we dread cometh ether by ye straytnes of ye place, or ye number of our w^tstanders, or bothe. now yf ther total power be planted on ether syde the shore, wch at ye least as I think is a leag over, than have we a myle in ye middest at ye least to travers & play w^t owt daunger of any ther greatest shot.

But yf ther power be in ships only then doth the place help us consydering y^t in such a strayt we cannot mach¹ passt one to one or 2 to 2 a tyme, now . . . be none at all . . . place for to rest ther other . . . place wherin to fortyfye . . . To these 2 former choyses, in as much as [the whole] cumpany must adventure w^t us both thinges [?] my opynion is y^t ether ye best sort or [some] myght be browght to lyke your determyn[acion as a] thing to think expedient in this case altho in [truth] very inconvenient. I am hearby led: fyrst because I hear alredy ther great gratching for y^t [they have] not ther store in al poyntes answerable to ther expectation allbe thanks be to god ther hytherto been no want of any felt among us, nore noe careful mean neglected by [w^ch] ye store myght be increased. yet do they secrytly [murmur] and say that they shall starve in the end and y^t they [shall] return home beggars. wch speeches being moved w^tall enforceth me to fear least god, herew^t provoked to wrath lay y^t plage on o^r heades wch wer causeles at fyrst, so y^t than ye generall shold not be able to endure [their] intolerable murmurings, wch wil not styk to exclaim y^t he had browght them to such mysery from which he [cannot] releeve them.²

Tertio   Lastly yf ye proportion of o^r remayning b[eer] and vitayle, being scant and decayed and o^r meat in jeperdy of spoyl wch is supposed, and [other] daungers greater yf yt hap amysse, than they [can] hope yf ye best of lykelyhood fawl owt, in

¹ There could be no general engagement in these narrow passages, where there was no room to manoeuvre.

² Madox, as chaplain, was in a good position to learn the temper of the ship's company.

[our] reconyngs. we must trust thos y^t kno what is sp[oyled] & what remayneth & what state ye merchandize do[th] stand. than must we in my conjecture seek by advice wher we may best vent those commodytes that we have, and return home w^t an honest account of as lytle losse as may be ether of stock or tyme, in as much as we ar cut of from y^t hope wch in ye begynning and purpose of o^r viage was of us al conceaved.[1]

1582 Decemb. 20th. Rich. Madox.

Document 55
Opinion of Nicholas Parker[2]

. . . contrie wynds and uncommon . . . course hether for the streights in hope this waie to passe [without] other henderaunce. And now finding a second lett by the K. of Spaines fleet to be gone [thither] w^t forces of men & shipping muche exceedinge ours, there to anoye [us] maie Nevertheless I waying oure hard case, in consumynge of tyme & spending of victuales, not to be holpen on this side, to proced herafter in any place to . . . [we are] put to retourne to oure countrye w^{t}out doinge any lawdable matter to oure perpetual [dishonour] do houlde my opinion in this sorte. where God is served and pleased, he will geve victorye to smal numbers againste multitudes as in many exampeles maie be gathered and in [particular] Otho, one of the Germane Emperours, wch was environed on everie side, not w^{t}oute great [danger] of sundrie nations, at one instante, as the Frenche, Bohemes, Franckes, hungarians, [yet] y^t god delivered hem, so no doute will he defend us from this like danger and more [over] not diserved in hem, other reasons lede me, that we maie proced w^{t}oute suche perills objected. firste that Lieut. Hawkins &

---

[1] This last course was finally adopted by Fenton.
[2] B.M., Cotton MS Otho E. VIII, f. 196. See p. 194.

the pilotts that had passed that waie before [with] Sir Frances Drake, vouched that the narrowest parte of the straightes was above one English mile & a haulfe broade, and the lande on ether side so highte & rockie that it was impossible to gett upp any ordenance to yt, to hurte us. besides the lardge reporte of there strenght nede not so muche amaze us, as we ought rather to be encuragede wth the opportunitie of time, wch hereafter will not be had the like, if there be any intention to passe that waie for furtheraunce of o^r voiadge, being likewise assured of the discomfeted estate amongst them, thorowght wante of victuales, wine, powder, and apparell,[1] whereby many have alreadie perished, & moste likelie to encrease, livinge in place where nether of these greate wantes can be supplied this winter, wch the coldnes of the climate, so far different from theres, & these nations not able to abide yt longe, as generallie hathe ben judged of us,[2] wth the former wantes. againe no other course to me knowen or hard of on this side the streights, that might so muche repaier oure broken estate, and further the voiadge as this (wch if I maie understand) shalbe as willinge to yelde our consent for performing (?) the same, as these simple reasons have enduced me before.

Nicholas Parker.

Document 56
Opinion of Edward Fenton[3]

[My] opinion was albeit [some thought to] passe by the [Straight] of Ma[gallan was] th'onlie waie (supposed) to

---

[1] See p. 237. Parker had studied Sarmiento's letter (Document 50).
[2] This point was also made in the anonymous pamphlet advising the English colonization of the Strait. See Taylor, *Hakluyts*, p. 142.
[3] B.M., Cotton MS Otho E. VIII, ff. 190–1. Abstract in *Cal. S.P., Col., E. Indies, 1513–1616*, no. 219.

supply [our wants] and performe o^r voyage yet meny [and]
infinite dangers we are like to fall into under taking the same,
wth the sa[me] likelehood to find such supplie of victuals is
ymagined (and o^r necessaries required to be holpen wth)
having so greate enemyes to encownter wth us, and the forces
of the Kinge of Spaines remayninge by allikelehood in the
same place and readie to oppose against us where they shall
happen to meete us. Besides o^r instruction from their hono^{rs}
espresslie forbiddeth the same (onlesse by necessitie we be
forced therunto) against whom as all others in league wth her
ma^{tie} we are (by vyolante meanes) forbidden to deale: Butt
deale by honest merchantes in place where we should happen
to come. And therfore hold it better certeintie for . . . we
maie supplie o^r wants . . . o^r reputacions, then so easilie
. . . to undertake the same: and then (. . . of god) as we
find o^r selves inhabil [to] passe on o^r Jorney by Cape Bona
[Speranza]: And therfore myne opinion is to goo . . . for
(Rio de Plata) or St Vincents [on the] Coast of Brasill before
we set anye further Course: wch ij places thoroughly sifted (I
suppose) will deliver us (w^{t}out danger) thinges necessarie to
accomplish o^r voyage. and to repaire o^r caske and surveye o^r
merchandize (thought to be in muche dekaie) by reason the
openesse of the Gallion Leicester in manie places.[1] W^{ch}
thinges (by allikelehood) could not be done in the Streaight
of Magalan; though o^r necessities (chieflie) . . . myself
to . . .

Edward Fenton

Considered by the whole Assistants . . . for St Vincentes,
rather than for the [River of] Plata, wch the Pilottes nor
maisters [have] no likinge of by reason the shalownesse [of
the] River there: and a place thought more [fit] to supplie o^r
wants etc.

[1] The leak in the *Galleon* troubled Fenton when he finally left Brazil
(pp. 139–40), but the whole tone of the document is evasive. There is no
suggestion that the purpose of the voyage is to be abandoned.

Document 57

The Council of 20 December 1582:
Luke Ward's Report[1]

The 20 day, about 10. a clocke aforenoone, we went aboord the Admirall; viz. Master Walker, the Master, the Pylot, the two Marchants, and my selfe, being directed so to do by the General: upon our comming the Generall was going to dinner where we also dyned with him: having dyned, the General called us his Assistants into his cabben, and there delivered to us in writing two demands, to bee by us considered upon, and he to have our opinions therein.

The effects of the demands were these.

1. Whether it was best for us to adventure our selves to passe the Streights of Magelan or not, considering the force of the enemy, which we knew to be there before us: and also that our determination was there to set up our pinnesse, make yron hoopes, carrene our ships, and do all our necessary businesses for the full accomplishment of our voyage.

2. Demand was, if that course were not thought best, which way were meetest for us to take.

To the first we were of opinion, that it were good to heare the opinions of Captaine Hawkins, Captaine Drake, and the 2. pylots, which had passed the streights and knew the harbors, and likest places to be fortified, & inhabited or not, who were called, and the 3. Masters with them: their opinions were as divers as their names, & asmuch differed, as before this time they weare wont usually to do: only they all agreed in this one point, y^t it was impossible for us to passe ye streights without seeing, and incountring with the ships although the fortification of the lande did not annoy us, which being long and throuly debated, and their opinions with the

---

[1] Luke Ward's narrative, *Pr. Nav.*, p. 662.

3. Masters demanded, which accorded not scant any one with other, they were dismissed.[1]

Then the General received the opinions of us his Assistants, beginning with the yoongest in auethority first, which when he had harde them all over, & being set downe in writing under our hands, he tooke deliberation till after supper to give his determination.

When we had all supped then he sent for us downe into his cabben, and delivered in writing his determination, (which was) to victuall, and furnish our selves on this coast, before he proceeded any further, and named 2. places River de Plate, or S. Vincent to be chosen.

For the better deciphering of River de Plate, & the commoditis thereof, was called before us, Richard Carter, which doth dwel there, who could not assure us of any wine except we could stay foure moneths for it, but other victuals plenty: the river is shoale & dangerous, ye road 7. leagues from any towne, or place of commoditie: which considered with the trecherie that might from thence be used, into the streights by sea, & into Peru by land, we all concluded to go to S. Vincent, which place is inhabited by Portingals, and where in honest sort we might conveniently have all our busines done.

With this resolution we tooke our leaves about 8. a clocke at night, & being come aboord, presently bare up, and went roome, having all the day before beate up the winde larboord tacked East-southest til at night: after it was a litle winde all night, we went North next hande.

The 21. day after service, I declared unto my company, the intent of our returne to the Port of S. Vincent, wherewith they were wel satisfied being before doubtfull that we should not proceede, but returne without performance of our voyage.[2] . . .

---

[1] No suggestion was made of rounding the archipelago of Tierra del Fuego. It is doubtful whether any of the four men who had passed the Strait could grasp the significance of Drake's discovery of the absence of Terra Australis even had they been informed of it. And Madox (p. 189) had thrown doubt on Sir Francis's chart.

[2] They were told that the return was for revictualling and refitting the ships, but there had been murmuring (see p. 217).

The 22 day in the morning we missed the Francis, which by all presumption went roome in the beginning of the night.

Document 58
Agreement for St Vincent
20 *December* 1582[1]

. . . passed y^t way, either [through the Strait or] goe by ye cape of good [hope without] supply to furnysh both our [barks]. wherefore he made offer of 2 places [wherein] to releeve us w^t such things as for y^e [rest of] the voiage were wantyng, viz: the ryver of Plate and St Vincents, but because both of the said pilotes were loth to hazard our shipping far up ye River of Plata as of necessytye we must if we took y^t place, and y^t we had good [hope] to fynd them frendly at St Vincents, therfore [it] was agreed of all the assystants w^t what [speed] wee might to go thither.

Edward Fenton
Luke Warde   Nicholas Parker
William Hawkyns
Rich. Madox
John Walker
Randall Shaw
Mathew Tailbois
Peter Jefferey

[*cipher:* Tuesday, Aquarius 22]

---

[1] B.M., Cotton MS Otho E. VIII. f. 189. The agreement was made late on December 20, but according to Ward (*Pr. Nav.*, p. 666) Fenton secured all their signatures to it on January 22 (see p. 127, n. 2). This explains the footnote to the document, where the symbols for Tuesday and Aquarius are followed by the figure 22. January 22 was a Tuesday and the sun was then in Aquarius.

Document 59
Letter to the Governor of St Vincent
20 January 1582/3[1]

(i) [Draft]

[the cause of] my comyng hyther unto you [is in] respect of
ye favor my [countrymen] have heartofor rec^d of y^r L. [in
purpose] to have some trad w^t you in such [sort as] belongeth
to just & honest merchants [with] such merchandyse as I have
brought [hither] for y^t purpose & wil in al . . . onesty trad
yt w^t y^r   for . . . whereof I hartely pray you to
ad[mit and] to vouchsafe me y^r favor therin to bring in my
ships unto you. [I] kyse y^r L. hands & rest at y^r devot . . .
praying god to guyd you in al y^r actions from aboard my ship
ye 20 of January 158[2/3]

Yr. l. in al curtesy to comand

Ed. Fenton.

(ii) [Fair copy]

. . . an   English   man,   sailor . . . you   may   make
interpretation . . . y^t the cawse of my commyng hither
. . . of yor L. is cheifly to have trade w^t yow in such sort as
belongeth to honest merchants for such merchandize as I
have brought for that porposse and will in such sort justly
trade wth yor L. for the same. Wherefor I hartily pray yow to
admyt and to vouchsaf [me y^r] faver therin and a pilot to
bringe in my shipp unto yow. Do kyse yor L. handes and
rest . . . devotion, praying to god to guyd yow in all y^r
actions from abord my shipp the 20 of January 1582

yr L. in all curtesy to command   Ed. Fenton

[1] B.M., Cotton MS Otho E. VIII, ff. 192–3. Abstract in *Cal. S.P., Col.,
E. Indies, 1513–1616*, no. 222. Fenton now makes no suggestion that he is
merely seeking provisions (p. 247). The Governor was Jeronimo Leitão
(p. 125).

Document 59A
Inquiry at St Vincent
8-9 February 1582/3[1]

[Andres de Eguino stated] ... at the time that I, doubling the headland, discovered the said port, a little before the setting of the sun, I saw there two English corsair galleons of great strength who had occupied the [port] and terrorized the inhabitants with their threats ... If I had delayed a few more days the enemy would have set up artillery at some fortified point and dared to defend the port against a large fleet and taken possession of the land ... and although it is true that in the battle I lost one of the ships, the S. Maria de Begoña ... even so much has been gained and your Majesty has been well served in our driving the enemy from this port ... since from this base he could have controlled the whole Brazilian coast ...

[1] *Probança echa do pedimento del contador Andres de Eguino ante el Governador de la Capitania de S. Vicente ... sobre el suceso que tobo con el ingles que allo in este Puerto.* Extract, translated. Seville, Archivo General de Indias 2.5.2/21; modern transcript in Biblioteca Nacional, Rio de Janeiro (microfilm supplied by Mr Keith Short). Eguino, in command of the three ships which attacked Fenton, asked the Governor of S. Vicente for a formal inquiry. Fourteen leading questions were put to six prominent citizens, to which all assented. These questions (printed in Document 81) provide the Spanish version of the incident as sent to King Philip. The answers reveal incidentally that the colony was quite unprotected, and although the panic was exaggerated, observers were impressed by the two banks of guns on the Galleons. The only evidence of intended violence was derived from hints thrown out by Simon Ferdinando and from a conversation overheard between the Italian on the *Leicester* (M. Dore?) and José Adorno (p. 112). The witnesses were Braz Cubas, *alcaide mor* of Santos; Simão Machado, Governor of Santo Amaro (see Pl. V); João Baptista Malio, overseer of a sugar plantation belonging to the Flemish family of Schets; and three other Royal officials of the colony.

Part III

THE AFTERMATH
(Documents 60–73)

Document 60

Luke Ward to Leicester on his Return
[29 May 1583][1]

Right honorable maie it please y^r ho^r: to be advertized of my aryvall here this daie, wth the Edwarde Bonaventure: after many contrarieties since o^r departure out of England: For beinge proceeded into 33 digrees to the South wardes: uppon entelligence from a Spanishe gent. and certen freers wch wee mett in those parts, Sailinge towardes Ryver de Platte, in a smale barke: wch came from the Spanishe fleete gon before us towardes the straightes of Magelan, under Conducte of Don floris de valdies; o^r generall assembled his assistaunce unto him, propoundinge some questions unto us, and havinge receyved everye of o^r severall opynions subscrybed under o^r handes; accordinge to y^r ho: Instructions; he determyned to reterne to Saint Vincentes An town and harbor of Brassell, enhabited by Portingalles, wch lieth 24 digrees to the South wardes of the Equinnoctiall: as the meetest place to supplie o^{r}selves of many thinges wch we wanted. Ther we aryved the 20 daie of January followinge, and began to put o^r shippes in order, havinge the promyse from the governer ther, by severall messingers to be supplied; and w^{t}in two daies himself would come to confer w^t o^r generall:

The 24 of January at afternoon unloked for of us, we descryed Three Spanishe shippes, wch came bearinge in about the pointe, ankred w^{t}in fawcon shott of us, presentlie we made o^{r}selves [ready] to defende, expectinge some

---

[1] B.M., Cotton MS Otho E. VIII, f. 185. Abstract in *Cal. S.P., Col., E. Indies, 1513–1616,* no. 223. Ward comes straight to the point and announces the reason of his return, that is to say the encounter with the Spaniards, and his enforced separation from the General.

message from them, but they at [about] tenn of the clock when the flud served them, lett slip ther [cables] and came dryving in meaninge to have borded and taken [us] w^tout any great losse. But contrary to ther accompte [we answered] them in such sorte that next morning their vizeadmiral was sunke hard by us, nevertheles thother two ships [fought until] next afternone: and then being clear from [them we mended our] Torne Shippes and made [sail for Burnt Island].

Ther we arryved the 26 of January when we ankered in an uneasy Roade all daie. Towards evenynge we attempted to weigh o^r anker and gett in nerer to o^r Admyrall wh^ch Ryd better then we did. But w^t the force of the winde and the Sea-gate o^r cable broke and we faine to sett saile, to kepe up, sendinge of o^r boote to weyh o^r Anker, wch they did, and w^t great pirrell at eyht the clock at night, we recovered o^r boote and men, being then farr put to leewards from th'ile, that we could not feche againe, althoughe we kepte up w^t a stout saile all night, in hoope to recon yt, w^tall the winde encreassinge and to o^r disadvantage, we were faine next daie to stand ot to sea or ells to peryshe on the leeshore.

Thus we lost o^r Admyrall ryding still all alone, the Frances lost o^r company the 22 daie of dicember, yett we kept up alonge hooping to meete o^r admyrall In the end after many daies expectacon in vaine, by the [counsel] of those wch in so hard a case I ought to take advice [of], it was determyned to returne to this o^r countrie, being unprovided of many speciall nessysarys. In [our] seekinge to watter on the north parte of Brassel, we fell amonge the most warlike, and Traitorus canybals, w^t some Frenchmen; that are in all that cost, when we had smale relef: and so constrayned to provide . . . [but one] ton of watter: since wch tyme god hath mercyf[ully furnished] us w^t raine watter, and prosprous winde [whereby we have] byn able to bringe home the Shipp. In [order to refresh my] weake company, I remayne to provide some [necessary] victuales; wch done, god willinge I will . . . es w^t her: In the mean . . .

[Luke Ward]

[*Endorsed:*] 1583 Fenton viag.

Document 61

Report of Master Percy
[June 1583][1]

June 1582. The 2 day of June we departed from the Sound of Plymothe leaveng the Fraunces behynd us, captayn Hawkens, bothe owr Pylotes and 40 of owr best men.[2]

1582
Fenton Voyage

The wind nor norwest

The 16 day we fell withe Lancerot.

The 17 day we pased betwen the Grand Canary & teneref haveing the syght of bothe

The 26 day we came to the yland of boonwest[3] and came to an anker at 2 of clock in the after none myndeng ther to fyll water

The 27 day abowt 3 of cloke after none owr ambrall weed[4] and went to sey we foloeng them withe owt fylleng any water at all

The 20 of July we fayll withe the cost of gynney haveng syght of Cap de Palmes

The 10 day of Awgust we cam to Soralyon and tared ther all the rest of the monthe

The first of september we went to sey agayne and the 5 daye we cam in agayne land and tareed ther tyll the 2 of october and then we went agayne to the sey

The ferst of Desember we fell withe the cost of brasell between 28 and 29 degrees and harbred in 27 degres and 50 menets

The 12 day of desember we departed from the Bay of Comfort praise god.

---

[1] B.M., Cotton MS Otho E. VIII, f. 150. This ill-spelt fragment is a reminder that the ordinary English ship-master, trained by apprenticeship, was still rarely capable of profiting by the new navigational techniques pressed by William Borough and others.
[2] The dozen or so of Drake's men, the crew of the *Francis*, and presumably other Plymouth men.
[3] Bona Vista.
[4] 'Our Admiral weighed'.

The 20 day of desember beeng in 33 degres 30 menets or ther abowt owr generall called us abord & demanded owr openenes for passeing the straytes but when he had hard owere manes[1] openeon he and owr captayn with the consent of 2 or 3 mor sayd playnly that he wold not goo for the straytes

The 20 daye of Janewary we cam to Sent wencent wer comeng backward 31 dayes

The 25 day in the after none wee were put [into] the harbroo and rod ther at the mowthe of [the river] tyll the 27 day and then we weed and [set] to go ther and that nyght we dobled the . . .

Mownday being the [2]8 day haweng . . . thet morning we spllet our maynsayle . . . of we could not wether the eyland [and recover our] ambrall. but wer fayn to anker [and to put] our new saylles to the yard and . . . [we] broake our cabell so that . . . boat and owrself . . . day and nyght . . . the wind at est so that we stod to the sowtheword and at nyght by so sowthe est [S S E] tyll med nyght and then the wind cam to the est northe est so we went est by sowthe est so by next day we cowld not fetch of the eyland, by thes menes we lost company of the gallyone.[2]

Document 62

Evidence of Master Percy
[June 1583][3]

. . . [we] departed from Plymouth [with the Galleon and] the Elizabeth: the F[rances we left behind be]cause ther men

[1] Possibly 'men's', in the sense of the masters and pilots who were called in (p. 193).

[2] The main purpose of the enquiry was to learn why the *Edward* had left the *Galleon*.

[3] B.M., Cotton MS Otho E. VIII, f. 200. Abstract in *Cal. S.P., Col.*,

were a shore but [found her again] and kept company altogether in continual [view] to the Isle of Canaries. And so wthout [delay to the] Isles of Cabo Verde, and there anchored, at the [island of] Buena Vista, thincking to have watered there, but [the general] departing the next daye, they folowed him to [de]grees on this syde thequinoctiall and fell on [the coast] of Guinea, abowt Cabo di palmas, and there [were] beating of and on about 14 dayes. Here the [master] and others were desirous to knowe of the Captain what [reason] to make to this Cost, being not the course for this voyage. And his aunswere was that Sr. Fr. Drake had taken the [self-same] course and so would they.[1]

Percye being demanded why him selfe being one of the Commission in the Instructions would agree to a course so contrarye to the Instructions sayeth: that he understood he was appointed by the C[ouncil] to be of the Commission,[2] but that neither the Generall nor the Captaine ever called him to any Counsaile.

After this they put backe to 8 d. 35 m. northwards to porte Serra Leon, on the same coste of Guinea. There they filled water & trymmed there caske, the cause of their returning backe was because the pilott knewe this Porte; and none else knowe any other on that coste: & to fill water was neadfull. They taryed here abowt 7 weekes to fill water and to amend the admiralls mastes that were spoyled and broken. Here was a determination by the Generall and his Counsaile to goe back to the Isles de Cabo Verde, and there taking in wynes, to goe to Sta Helena to inhabite and to take the Portingall fleet, coming from thest Indias, and to send home the Edw. Bonaventure wth the spoyle. But this determination brake the next daye: so they went on forwardes on their voyage, till they came to the Baye of [Good Comfort].

. . . left the boote . . . the Baye. He knowing noe . . .

Then was the Elizabeth sold for ryce and olphants teeth. ye cause of wch was to bringe the men nearer togither many being deade

---

E. *Indies, 1513–1616*, no. 232. This appears to be a clerk's report of interrogations put to Master Percy.

[1] The mariners evidently knew something of the danger of approaching the African coast (see p. 79).

[2] The masters and pilots were not members of the Council (see pp. 51, 76, 187), but were to be called in for consultation on navigational matters.

12 men were taken out . . . [They sailed] alonge the coste southwarde to 33 d. [south the line] where the Generall, calling the Cap., the [minister], the Master, the marchants, & pilott aboarde: asked them [their opinions] for going backe to St. Vincent, there to sett [up the forge] etc. and to make thinges necessarye, eyther for pr[oceeding] or retourne. The marchants, masters & pylotts [disliking] the goyng backe, were put out of the generalls [cabin] and after a litle consultation by the generall [and the rest] the generall punlished his resolution for retourne [to St] Vincent. The generall flatly resolved he [would not] passe the Streights, because he thought they were fortyfyed: and the cause why he so thought was, that here in england they were advertised of a fleet gone out of Spayne: and because, they of the Portugals [bark] told them the same. And by Cabo de buena Speranza they could not go, being November and the [wynde] contrarye. So they retourned to St Vincent, whyther wthin 2 or 3 dayes came the Spanyardes [in 3] shippes of warre, one of 600 tonne, the 2d of 500, the 3d of [400] abowt 5 of clocke in the eveninge, and anchoring wthin shott passed wth 2 or 3 shott of eche syde, till at 11 of clocke, in the night, the tyde serving, they slipped anchore and drave upon our Admirall thincking to bourde her. Whereupon began & continewed till between 4 & 5 in the after noone the next daye: the Spanish vice admirall was suncke abowt one of clocke in ye night wthin 2 houres after the fight beganne. the englishe went away first and of the englishe the galleon an houre before the Edward.[1] When the English were out of shott, the Spanyards gate also higher up into the haven, The cause why the englishe left the fight, having the advauntage, he thincketh to be because (as it is reported) the men of the galeon were droncke wth a hogshead of wyne they had drancke, in the heat of the fyght. Heare they ran to an Island . . .

. . . chartyng, they made homeward . . . southward, on the coste of Brasile in the . . . where they had 5 men

[Upon] this resolution the Barcke Fraunces departed by night

---

[1] Percy's straightforward account of events can be accepted, although not necessarily the gossip which follows regarding the *Galleon*'s departure from the fight.

slayne by the [Indians when] getting a tonne of water, abowt
the . . . [they had] 4 or 5 tonne of rayne water, wth w^{ch}
they [came to] Plimouthe
[*Endorsed:*] Mr Percy. master of the Bonaventur

Document 63
Narrative of Peter Jeffery
20 June 1583[1]

The gallion Lester.
The Edward bonaventure
The bark Frances
The Elizabeth.
From Hamton water we departed the first of maye 1582. &
came the same daye to houarst Castell whear & at ye Cowes we
remayned tyll the 21th of maye. the 24th of maye we came to
Dartmoth range, whear we staide & at Torbaye tyll the last of
maye the first of June we came in to ye baye of plymothe and
went thence ye second daye, leaving be hind us, the barck
Frances wth Mr Hawkins, o^r pilots and dyvers others, tyll we
came as far as lorn(?) whear we cast about for her, & having
ronn a smale way backewards, we sawe the frances comyng
towards us, & when she came to us we went on o^r course, &
put off the coast y^t night, to the sea on o^r viage, the wind very
good.
The 13th of June departed the briget from us w^t o^r letters
The 16th of June we came to ye Islands of Cannarie.
The 24th of June y^t was agreed to water at the Ilands of
Cabo verde. The 26th daye we came to on of thes Islands

<hr>

[1] B.M., Cotton MS Otho E. VIII, ff. 186–7. Abstract in *Cal. S.P., Col.,
E. Indies, 1513–1616*, no. 224. Jeffery, the youngest of the merchants,
expected the voyage to proceed as planned, and accepted neither Fenton's
nor Hawkins's schemes to divert it.

called buena vista whear o^r boates went aland to sek for water but found non. The next daye we wear agred on to go to ye westward of y^t place to another baye, whether the frances was sent be fore us. wheer they went aland, & fownd both beastes, goats & water, but as we wear goinge thither the Generall bare off & went to see, wch forsed us to follo wthout watring.

The 20th of Julye we fell wth ye coast of gynne in 4 degres be north ye lyne, by an esterly course y^t we going & ye corrant y^t desserved us and set us theron.

The second of Augost, y^t was agred on, to go backe to ye shore near 8 degrees be north ye line, thear to water, & releive our sycke, whear those y^t wear dissesed recovered their helthe.

The 9 of Augost we came in to the sarlyona whear we [stayed] tyl ye first of sept^r, then putting of to ye see, & being not 7 leges of but ye generall retourned in againe, by reson he found his mayne mast not able to serve wthout fishing, where we remayned tyll ye third of october. in this place ye general mene to leve the barcke called ye Elizabeth, wthout consent of [Council or] us ye marchants, & wold not suffer us to go up the country nor other wise to se what might be had in y^t place.[1] [When] she was all unrigd there came downe seartaine portugals from the Ilands of cabo virdes and bought her of ye generall for [80 mews] of Rise and 15 oliphantes tethe, Thear was also [an intent of the general] to make for ye Ilands of capoverdes thear to take [the Portugal ships] into o^r hands, & then to go for ye Iland [of St Helena] south ye line, & thear to inhabit etc.

On the third of october we departed from [Sierra Leone] . . . as it was reported, for we . . .

The first of December we fell wth ye coste of brasyle in 28 degres be south the lyne, called Don Rodrygo, whear we waterd, & departed thence for ye straits ye 12th of December. At this place passed by us a smale Barke, wth fryers and other, for river de plata. W^{ch} barcke was brought in by ye frances y^t

---

[1] This prohibition during the long stay in West Africa naturally irked the merchants, who saw immense possibilities of later trade. Only Ferdinando with his negro was allowed to take a trip up country. For Madox's comment see p. 186, n. 2.

was sent out for her, wch fryers told us of 15 sayle of spanysh ships, y^t departed amonth before out of rio jenero near under ye south tropicke, wth 3000 men. Whereof 4 ships with 5 C choyse sodjers shold pase ye straits for chyle & of ye rest 8 C to inhabite in 4 forts to be made in ye Straits, 2 at the entrance & 2 at the going forth etc.[1] Notwthstanding all this no motion by any y^t I cold hear y^t fered them.

The 20th of December o^r generall called o^r captain, Mr Walker, Captain Drake, o^r master & pilat & us ye merchants of ye Edward to come aborde him, demanding of us & the rest what weye we might best voyd the Spanerds forse etc . . . & after much debating theron, the generall & others alledginge, dyvers doubts & casualtyes y^t myght hapen yf the spaneards wear in ye straits or had fortyfied etc. & no other way [but] by the straits do o^r pilats knowe etc. I was ther forsed to speke [first my] opinion being yongest.[2] To wch I answered I merveled y^t [we] came, hither to go this weye wch we were forbiden, & wthout [consent] of us the merchants, etc. therfore my opynyon was to [go by] ye cape, yf wind & weather servid, onlese we might be sure [to find] vitualls in the South See. wch o^r generall so gretly wanted by report, this or to ye like speche was my opynyon as I said & so was all the rest, some for ye Cape & some for y^e [Strait] except o^r captain & ye generall as I remember, whos opynyon [was] plainly to retorne etc. for ye generall said for ye cape [we could] not go for want of dyvers nessesaries, etc. & for ye strait he wold not go, tyll he had refreshed his wants, and [he] bad us chuse, whither we wold go to river de Plate then the best place was by ye masters & pilots thought to be [St Vincent] . . .

The 20th of Janerie we cam to St Visent being nearest [28 degrees] be south ye line, from where came sertaine canoas [into the] baye to us of portingalls y^t dwelt thear. who required [answer] from o^r Generall, to ther governor to kno wherefore we [came. His] letter as I hard was requesting

---

[1] Jeffery is here at fault. The forts were to be placed at the second Narrows, well within the Strait.
[2] See p. 249. Madox registered his opinion succinctly (p. 241).

trade or traficke & not vitualls or nessessaries,[1] & so was his request, by fernando ye portingale, by word [of mouth] to others y^t came from ye Governor ye same daye, & after we came into ye harbore, but ye next daye after [the Portugals] came againe & told o^r generall y^t they cold not trade [with us] for y^t they had submytted them selfes to the [K. of Spain who] had bound them not to traficke wth any . . . as present to the Governor being 3 yeards of scarlet & 3 yards of a fine mourry colour & 9 yards of fine black cloth for ye 3 men y^t came to us from ye governor, but as we wear near ye towne, wch laye 3 myles up the river from o^r ships theer cam a canow against us, willing us to retorne & assone as theyr governor had determyned what to do, they wold bring us Answer thereof, but we had non sent us tyll ye Spaniards came in to us.

The 23 day at night cam abord us one Withaul some time Mr Dors mane, Genoys, who was maryid thear in y^t place & came to se whether he knew us to be merchant men etc. wch the Portingales douted of, who shewed to us that they fortifyed ther towne for fear of us for dyvers occasions y^t they saw in us not to be lyke others etc.

But the 24 day before night came 3 gret shipes of ye Kinge of Spains ships, sent for ye Straits, & ankered w^tin shot of us wthout ye bar, who scouring their ordynance & making them selves redye to deale wth us & we in like case to defend, then at 9 of the clocke in ye night or thearabouts came driving in to us wth the tyde, ye viceadmirall mynding to bord us, and the other 2 ye Gallion, but be cause the gallion let slyp & came nearer us, ye vise-admirall boarded ye gallion to whome we bestoed, & to the other 2 that rid styll ahed of us, such shot as we wear able, al ye night & next day tyll dinner. At wch tyme we wear forsed to depart from them, in wch fight we sanke ther viseadmirall & 3 botes foule of ded men wear brought aland out of ye 2 shyps remaynenge as the Indian told o^r generall y^t came abord of him into ye rood. Wth the loss of 5 of o^r men & xi hurt, & in ye Gallion 1 slaine & 19 hert. As to ye report made to y^r honors of ye gallion going out

[1] See Document 59.

from us, & o^r captaine being abord them wth our skiffe above an owr, & leving us fighting wth them, yt is trewe.[1]

The 27 daye of Jan we departed out of the baye of St Visente after we had taken to ye Gallyon a tonn of water, asked of us. mynded to go to an Iland to ye northwards of this part, called Saint Sabastian whear yt was appoynted we shold confer together, what now wear best to do, but the wind being so contrary y^t we wear put to ye southwards of St Visente & forsed to take an evell r[oad] at a small Iland 7 leges to ye southwards thereof. ye 28 day by means of the splitting of o^r mayne sayle from ye yeard, but when [we] had brought o^r new sails to yeard, & purchasing to get [from the] rod & nerer ye gallion, o^r cabell brake, wch forsed us to [stay] & plying to & fro under ye Iland from noon to night, by ye corant we were [set] so far to leewards on ye lye shore, y^t whear ye next daye we [would] have recovered the Iland againe, but by means of the [wind] was so contrary & a lye shore, & not abell to recover . . . of, wear forsed to keipe of & on at se hoping [the generall] wold follo us for we cold not come to him, But after sertain days, being put fare to y^e . . . wth contrary wether, & had lost o^r [hope] to meet with him for that ther wear no other . . .

 . . . [had the wind served] us to the coast of guinny homewards, we ment to prove what traficke we might thear have had, but the winds wear not so good for us to recover our place in ye cost of Afryca, to water or refreshe o^{r}selfes, but were forsed with the cost of Brasyl in 6 degres be south ye lyne to seke fresh water, whear we lost 5 of o^r men & xii hurt by the Indyans,[2]

The xii of March 1582 being forsed thear to ye sea, relying on the providence of Almighty god from whom out of the hevens, was all the water we had tyll we came to Plymoth, being ye 29th of maye last, & although yt was lothsome & not good for man's bodye, as aperyd by us, y^t when we came to Plymoth of

The fleet returned & came to Don Rodrigo in 4 days after we departed thence. There they met wth the friars & learned of our being there. Being within 34 degrees be south the line the 20th of December the Francis left our company.

---

[1] It is clear that this incident aroused great resentment in the *Edward*. Luke Ward reports that he went in his skiff to the *Galleon* to make enquiry when she turned away from the fight (*Pr. Nav.*, p. 668).

[2] At the island of Fernando Loronha, according to Luke Ward, who relates the tragic visit at length.

60 persons or thearabouts not 6 sound or helthfooll, yet we wear glad thereof.

Thus acording to y^r honors demands as my symple memory wold serve, have set downe, in brevytye, the efecte of all things y^t paste in this o^r sorroefall travell etc. this 20 of June 1583.[1]

Your h. most hombell at Command

Peter Jeffery

[*Endorsed:*] The 20 of June 1583 [P. Jeffrey] marchant touching Fentons viage.

Document 64

Fenton to Burghley and Leicester on his Return, 29 June 1583[2]

Right honorable, my dutie most humblie used. I am right sorie to advertize yor. L. of the badly proce(e)dinge and successes of o^r voyage, wch albeit hath been followed by us wth that care and dilligence that apperteyned; yet suche hath been (by godes appointmente) the contrarinesse of windes (growinge by o^r late settinge from Englande) as we could not proceeede by Cape Bona Spei accordinge to o^r instruction, beinge the first of December last before we gayned the Coast of Brasill, in 28 degrees to the Sowthewardes of the lyne, where we were forced to water, naminge the place the Baye of good comforte, in respect of the releif of the freshe water and fishe we founde there (a greate comfort to us all)

[1] This dates the enquiry as taking place while the *Galleon* was in port in Ireland.

[2] P.R.O., S.P. 12/161, art. 16; and B.M., Cotton MS Otho E. VIII, f. 162. Abstract in *Cal. S.P., Col., E. Indies, 1513–1616*, nos. 225–6. This diplomatic letter provided the official explanation of the failure of the voyage. The late start lost them the wind for the Cape; the Spaniards were in the Strait of Magellan; the Spaniards took the offensive at S. Vicente, and then made their stay at Spirito Santo inadvisable.

And notw^{t}standinge there moved some speaches there for passinge by the straight of Magelan being owt of hoope to passe by the Cape of good hope (aswell in regarde of the contrarines of the windes, as by reason o^r victuall was then much dekayed and spente) the only waie (supposed) bothe to supplie o^r wantes and accomplishe o^r voyage whereunto, as I gave care for the presente: So upon bettre deliberacion & debatinge the Course wth my self, I founde it a matter worthie of further consideracion, before I easylie or unadvisedlie undertooke the same (and the rather havinge certen intelligence by certen Spanishe frears wee tooke in a smale Barke passing for the River of Plata,) of the kinge of Spaines fleete departed from the River of Januario on the coast of Brasill the first of November past for the Strait of Magalan, being in number 15 sailes of Shipps, and in them three thowsande persons of all sortes undre the conduct of Don Diego Flores admirall of the same fleete, wth provicion to fortifie the same Place, and to leave certein companies to inhabitt and defende the same, undre the charge and government of Don Pedro Sarmiento, wherefore we being in 33 degrees and bettre to the Sowthwardes and the 20th daie of December, I called my assistants eftsones together, demaundinge of them whether they thought it a course to be followed by us, aswell in regarde of the K: forces gone before us to guarde and fortefie the same (as beinge so thought meete) was the Place where of necessitie we must water and repaire o^r wantes, w^{ch} (by all liklehood) could not be done: but by endaungeringe the whole; Besides y^r hon^{rs} instructions straightlie forbiddinge me the same, unlesse by necessitie we were forced thereunto: herin every man's opinion was delivered, wherin I founde such contrarieties, that albeit some was willinge to undretake the same (rather lookinge into the gain ymagined would be gott into the sowthe sea) than well waighinge the presente or future perills wch might growe thereby unto us, yet my self wth some others, better digestinge (as we supposed) the great dangers that might ensue thereby unto us, held it a greater suertie for the preservacon of the whole, rather to undertake some other course and seeke some other place, where wth lesser perill and better hoope of relief, we might in honest sorte repaire o^r wantes and so afterwardes frame o^r course accordinglie. wherin for the preave I offered them two choices, the one to goo for the River of Plata, where (was supposed) we should finde victualls of divers sortes: the other was St Vincentes, on the coast of Brasill, where in respect of the daielie frequentacon of merchantes wth trade for that Place, there was also great hoope we should finde supplie of all thinges necessarie for us, wherby we might the rather passe on o^r jorney by the Cape of good hoope, or at least vente o^r merchandize in honest trade there, and so reape some such conveniente gaine therby, as might (in so greate an extremitie) make y^r L. and others rather gayners then loosers by the same: to wch Place all thassistants consented to goo, rather then to the River of Plata, whereof the maisters and pilottes had no likinge, by reason the shalownesse of the River there: And so directinge o^r course to St Vincents, my self wth the Edwarde Bonaventure arrived there (god be praised) in good saffetie the xxth of januarie followinge (the Barke Fraunces beinge departed from me the xxith of December before) w^t out acquaintinge me wth the same. And ymmediately upon my arrivall there, wrote a letter to the Cap^{en} in Englishe, by reason I learned of one of our Nation (called John Whithall) in creaditt wth him, who might interprett the same, and sente it by a Cannoo wch cam from the Towne to us. signefyinge to him that I was a merchante of Englande camed (of purpose) wth soundrie sortes of merchandize to trade wth them, wherupon he sente owt certen of creaditt to view o^r o^r Shippinge, who beholdinge the same, judged us at the first, rather to be men of warr than merchantes, yet after some further conference used wth them and doinge them all the courtosie we could, showinge them wthall a note of o^r merchandize, wthout givinge them occasion of offence: in thende they delivered me a letter from the Cap^{en}: wherein he referred me for aunswer of myne (not understandinge the same being in Englishe) to the bearers: who declared unto me, that as they were now becomed

Subjectes to the K. of Spaine, So had they expressly commandement from him (upon loosse of life and livinges) that yf happelie either the frenche or any of o^r Nation should arrive there (but especiallie us) they should not onlie do their best to staie us, But denie us all maner of releif and fav^r (in respect of the spoiles and roberies comitted by Sr Frances Drake in the Sowthsea) Herin we used manie persuasions as well to excuse him, as to gaine their fav^r and frendshipps for the supplie of o^r presente wantes and trade wth them. Wherin aswell those reasons we gave them to deswade the contrarie as the greate courtoisies we showed them, wrought in thende such an ympression in their myndes as they both consented to supplie us wth victualls, and undre handie furthwith to trade wth us for such Sugers as they had, and that the seconde daie followinge, the Cap^{en} and I should meete to have further conference.

Within iiij howrs after we had ended this consultacion and conclusion (beinge the iiijth daie of o^r aboade there) arrived iij greate Spanishe shipps of the complemente appointed for the Straight of Magalan ancoringe somewhat shorte of us abowte iiij or v of the clock in the afternoone, and in them 700 and odd persons Soldiers and mariners (as afterwardes we well understoode): So as upon the view of them, we hastened wthall expedicion to putt o^{r}selves in ordre (havinge then iche of us one of Toppe downe, to be amended). wch before viii of the clock in the night was eftsones repaired & rigged and readie to answere any occasion whatsoever: Abowte ix of the clock in the night for more hast they lett slipp their Cables in the hawse, and towed towardes us having litle or no winde, being readie to laye me aboarde, wthowt halinge or speakinge to me, not wthstandinge I called soundrie times to them, bothe to understande of whence they were, and what they mente to come in the nyght in such sorte to us. and receaving no aunswere of them, but liklehood to be presentlie entred was forced (in [absence] of further conference or courtosie) to presente them the Bullett, or else to suffre my self to be taken & spoiled: The feight grew whott on bothe sides and the Admirall and viceadmirall readie to borde me divers times.

But in thende god of his greate goodnes and mercie gave me some advauntage of them by sinkinge the viceadmirall (beinge a Shipp in countenance equall to myne and full of hable men) whereby the feight calmed betwixt us till the morninge, at what time it was eftsones renewed on bothe sides, and contynued till the afternoon.

In both wch conflicts, (god be praised) we lost not above fyve men, and not XX^tie hurte. But of the Spanyardes slain, hurt & drowned a great number as I was informed. Wherin as I am first, and chieflie to give the hon^r and glorie to god, for his greate mercie & goodnes so favourablie bestowed upon me, So am I muche to recommende to yor L. the vallo^r and courages of my companie amongst whom I maie not forgett this gentleman & bearer Cap^en Parker, who aswell in this conflict as in all other occasions wch might further the voyage, hath showed himself no lesse valliante then dutifull, wise & discreete, in all this action, most humblie besechinge yor L. to yeld him y^r good favo^r and countenance for the same, as a gent. worthie to be ymbraced for his vertues, & well hable to serve her Matie & his countrey bothe by Sea and lande.

Thus yor L. maie see in what good towardnes we were, to have done good to all adventuring in this voyage (notw^tstanding o^r former pretence took not place accordinge to o^r desiers) had not the K. forces in suche sorte overthrowen o^r honest proceedinges: who now purposelie sent to feight wth us or take us, where they should happen to meete us or finde us: otherwaies I dare well assure yor L. (as this gentleman well declare unto yor, to whom I beseech yor give creditt) that we had brought home wth us in honourable trade above 40 or 50,000 li wch hindraunce and great wronge (in my poore opinion) your L. and others are not to put uppe, Butt to have yor recompence at the K. of Spaines handes, who in a pretence so just and honourable and trade so honest, hath to yor greate wronge and hindraunce so overthrowen the same. Besides the utter undoinge of a great number of her Maties poore Subjectes, adventuring and travailinge in this voyage: To whom as there is nothinge due (butt upon courtoisie) yet aswell in regarde of their great paines taken therein as their great poverties growinge thereby Am to be a most humble Suto^r to yor L. and other thadventurers, that not^{wth}standinge all yor hono^{rs} greate losses like to growe thereby, yet it maie like yor to take some such compassion of theire poore estates, as there maie be some such litle porcion advaunced, as maie stande wth yor honorable liberalities and good likinge to bestowe to their releif and succor of their poore & presente necessities.

Towchinge some trade wch I have discovered, and maie growe yerelie beneficiall to or Countrey (beinge wiselie governed and followed) I reserve amongst other thinges to ymparte to yor L. at my repaire to yor.[1]

The departing of the Edwarde Bonaventure from me, within iiij dayes after the feight and of myne entertaynment afterwardes at S^{to} Spirito and what hoope of trade I was like to have there (if I durst have been bold to have staied) this gent. can deliver unto yor. L.

And I eftsones beseech yor L. that there maie be some spedie order & course taken for appointinge some suche of wisdom and creditt, as will to receave the Shipp and goodes of me (whereby charges maie be lessened) as to examyn of some desorderlie speaches and great desobedience used of late towardes me (and beinge proved) will tooch me verie neerelie in reputacion & creditt: or otherwaies will deserve in thoffender verie sharpp punishmente, to thexample of all others attemptinge the like againste their governors in contempt of her Matie and Commission and the overthrowe of all good accions & suche as shalbe appointed to execute & governe the same.[2]

Do praye to thalmightie to guyde & blease yor good L. in all yor honorable accons.

from aborde the Gallion Leicestre endinge in the Downes the xxixth of June 1583

yor L. most humblie to commaunde

duringe Life

Edwarde Fenton.

[1] This presumably refers to West African trade, since the trade Fenton hoped to establish in Brazil is hinted at in the following paragraph.
[2] The reference is to William Hawkins (see p. 149).

[*Direction:*] To the right honourable verie good lorde, L. Burleigh, Lord and Treasorer of Englande

[*Endorsed* in Lord Burghley's hand:] 29 June. Edward Fenton. Downs.

[*Postscript:*][1] I maie not forgett to recommende most humblie to yor L. good favour Mr Walker yor L. chaplaine (if he be retorned), who hath shewed him self a verie vertuous and dutifull gentleman towardes me in all his aboade wth me. And no lesse have I found Mr Bannester (most sufficiente in his arte) and verie zealous in the worde of god. Mr Cotton recommended by yor L. to me,[2] hath shewed him self every waie an honest & valiant gentleman, who was sore hurte in the fight butt (thankes be to god) well recovered. I most humblie besech your good L. to yeld them yor favorable countenance when they happen to come to present their humble duties to yor L.   29th June 1583

Edw. fenton
fro the Downes.

[*Direction of copy with postscript:*]

To the right honourable my very good Lord Thearl of Leicester one of the [members] of her Maties most honorable Privie Councill.

Document 65
John Banister to Leicester
[*29 June* 1583][3]

[I trouble] y^r honnor wth these few lynes partly [to send my duty] unto yor L. and partly to fortifye your [expectation

---

[1] This postscript (Cotton MS Otho E. VIII, f. 162) is attached to the copy of the letter which was addressed to the Earl of Leicester.

[2] Both Walker and Banister were placed in the voyage by the Earl, and this postscript indicates that Richard Cotton (who was said to be fleeing from his creditors) obtained his traveller's berth at Leicester's request.

[3] B.M., Cotton MS Otho E. VIII, f. 197. Abstract in *Cal. S.P., Col.*,

of me. God has] afflicted and layd his crosse uppon us in very [truth for] o^r just ponyshment dewe for o^r disobedience and [disregard of] his devine maresei. And trewly my L. ther [was no day] we passed but o^r bodies dyd feele an aulteracion . . . and from stranght to wekenes: yea, and to many [loss of] lyffe and except his myghti hand and owtstretched [arm], [notwith]standing o^r synnes, had staied us ere we had fawllene and [perished] thus: and his mercey hath preserved this my weak & [sinful body] from the swallowinge gulphes of the sea and devowering Jars [of our] journyes. And furthermore hath reysed unto me in my extremity frends as dyd comfort & releve this my silley and weak carkase. [Among them] our General Mr Edward Fenton whose godly government & care . . . hath byne great to discharge wth a safe contience this his heavy & trubblesom charge, that yt hath almost brought of his langyishin bodey and [feeble] lymes to the grave the Lord comfort him. And Mr Parker who hath [dealt] both fryndly and curtisly with me, god make me thankfull therefor.

And now my Lord I will certifye yor honnor of such persons as god hath called to his mercy. owt of the gallion Leycestur, and howe manie deseased of every syknes. And first after we passed or owne clymate and drawing wthin fower degres of the tropicke lyne of Canser wch was abowt the seaventen of June at wch tyme dyvers of o^r men fell sudenly syke and such as had thinne & drye bodies were infectede with whott burnyng & pestifures fevers, but the other sortt wch had grose and thike bodies wer molested wth the skyrvey. Of the firste infection dyed eight and of the skyrvey two And three of a surfett All the rest throwe gods providence lettinge blude & purginge wer all recovered for that tyme. But when we came to the coast of Brasell abowt the twenty of november to a harbor wch o^r generall called the

E. *Indies, 1513–1616,* no. 229. It appears from this medical report that a good deal of illness resulted from immoderate feeding on arrival upon land. Purging and blood-letting were the physician's normal remedies. Owing to the mutilation of the volume, MS Otho E. VIII, it is not possible to say whether Banister made any reference to the illness and death of Richard Madox.

bay of good comfort, wch place standeth in 28 degrees of the sowthewards of the lynne nere unto the tropick of capricornes: The same daye that we departed from that harbor allmost all o^r men fell sycke wth great payne in their heades, stomokes, backes, shortnes of brethe & heavenes of their wholle bodies: wch syckness I gather came partly by the chaingeinge of the clymat & partly throwe there owne disorder of insatiable feding on freshe fyshe, muche drinking could water & lying in the ayer on the hatches in the night season. but god be thanked after purging and letting of blud not one that perished of that syknes, yet when we came to St Vinsentes in the same coast abowt the twenty of january o° 1583, wch place standeth in 24 degres the sowthwards of the lynne [near under] the tropick lynne of capricornes, ther dyd o^r men fall syke of a great lossenes of their bodies and by reson of descharge & bytinge humor ther was made excoriations of the bowells cawsinge torments in their belles and flux of blud still flowing wth excrement. Of which syknes there dyed fyve. And when . . .

. . . stomakes, belles . . . in the mowth great paynes, skyrttes thereof wch we in our . . . we hav the benefyt of Imbrethinge and . . . [the] chiefest greffe that they complayned of the . . . [I will] certify your honnor more at large herafter if yt [please yor honnor] of this syckenes there dyed nyneteen parsons for . . . sorte dyd requier bothe for meat & medeson coud not [take it they] was so weke. When we wer besett wth o^r enemyes [we had twenty-five] men hurt wherof one presently dyed & two other which had grevious woundes & other acsidentes deseased, lykewyse some almost . . . recovered. We had thre negrowers who [departed] this present liffe and a boye that was drownd but the ser[. . .] is unknowne. So that the wholle nomber that the lord took from us was forty-fyve. When we cam to the coast of [Ireland] to a harbor called Kynsall wher as o^r gennerall wth [care] & dilligence dyd provyde for his weak companey both wyne & bere, fresh fyshe & fleshe wch for the weak was relefe & comfort to their hongerey and febell bodies & such as were desierous to go to the shore for their health wear permytted.

But wth this alteration of freshe vitalls, ther wer almost every[man] subject to some infyrmytie. Some wth suden swellings and payne of ther brestes that they could scant breathe, some to . . . &, some to lossenes of their bodies and some wth swellings in their coddes & privat parttes that it is allmost un[fit to be] spoken. but such meanes as art could devisse both by . . . bathes hath been put in view. Thus hath o[r] good god [taught] us wth dyvers afflyctions to humbell orselves & make us obedient to his will. All w[ch] sykenesses my good L. with their . . . yngs & prognostications shall, I trust, if yt pleasse the lord of his mercy to geve me leave, I will sett down at large wth remedies for relef & sucker of maney thowsents that shall perform thesse waterey pilgremages. Thus my good L. have I troubled yor honnor wth this longe & abrupte letter, beseeching yor L.shippe to pardon my rudnes, I cesse. besechinge or good god even for his mercy sak to graunt to you & all yors the sweete encreasse of his sprituall peasse & blessynge bothe now and evermore. From the gallion Lezetur

Your honnors humble & obedient servant to commaund
during life

Jhon Banester.

Document 66

Fenton to Leicester
[*July* (?) 1583][1]

[*Direction:*] To the right honorable his verie good L. thearle of Leicester one of the l[ords] of her Ma[ties] most honorable privie Counsaill.

[1] B.M., Cotton MS Otho E. VIII, f. 149. Abstract in *Cal. S.P., Col., E. Indies, 1513–1616*, no. 230. This brief letter seems to have been written by Fenton from his place of confinement pending an enquiry into the failure of the voyage. See p. 287.

. . . L. to aunswer [the charges of which] . . . you are informed of against [me] for as much as I ernestly desier [to have] my purgation therein. I most humbly [beseech] yor good L. (as well in regard the [state] of my weaknes not hable farr to [travel] by reason of a great swellinge and [acheing] both in my Stomack and legges) to appoint some such to heare those cawses unto whom I maie resort wth that healthe & strengthe I have, and wth that [favor] that the place of meetinge for the same [may be] not farr remoote from my lodginge. till [it] shall please god to grant me better habilitye of bodie to travaill further therin: And that in those meetinges and conferrences, it maie please yor L. to commaunde the attendance of the pilottes, maisters and other officers ymployed in that service, who are to witnes towching manie thinges therin. It pleased yor L. to give ordre to Mr Atye to write for the deliverie of my apparell, and other things, remainyinge at Muscovia howse.[1] wch as I cannot yet receave. So the wante therof is no smale hinderance unto me, having smal meanes and less habilitie to provide new, Besides, they be in effect spoiled by the longe beinge at Sea, and now for wante of lookinge unto. Am therfore most humblie to besech yor good L. that I maie have restitucion therof: otherwaies it wilbe my utter undoing and smale pleasure to any desiering staie of the same: Do crave yor L. pardon for . . . yor L. [humbly to] comande

Edward Fenton

[1] Fenton's personal possessions must have been 'arrested' with the remaining merchandise on board in the interests of the adventurers.

Document 67
Narrative of William Hawkins
6 July 1583[1]

. . . ix of maye 1582 we departed from [Cowes] The seconde of juyn 1582 we departed out of [Plymouth] into wh^{ch} port we came by meanes of a contrary [wind]. Theare the generall wolde have lefte behind hym [Hood &] Blackoller, Pilotts, wth Capiteyn Drake, Willyam [Hawkins] and the barke Frannceys: saying that he had better men wythinborde than anny of those, and that yf neede were [he could] put in wth Falmouth for as good as they. The company sayed, thatt they wold not go to Sea wythout them by [whom they] knewe the voyage must be perfourmed, and made ma[nifest]. Then they seeing the Bark Frauncys coming towards [them] they did cast about.

After my comyng aboorde agayne, becawse I loste Kyrkman from me for querrelling, I had not from that tyme till my comyng home any good countenaunce.[2]

The xvith of Juyn 1582 we had sight of the Canaries

The xxvith of the same monethe we fell with Bonavista, one of the Islands of Cape de Verde wheare we might have watered, but they woolde not staye.

The xxth of Julye 1582 we fell wth the coast of Guynny: the wether heare so fowle as for foure or fyve daies we colde not take the heighthe[3]

---

[1] B.M., Cotton MS Otho E. VIII, ff. 224-8. Abstract in *Cal. S.P., Col., E. Indies, 1513-1616*, no. 231. Hawkins's narrative bears evidence of having been drawn up in relation to the enquiry held on Fenton's return. It is dated July 6, i.e. a week after the *Galleon* anchored in the Downs. The writer's impetuous and boyish character is well brought out. He was one of eleven children of John Hawkins's brother William; and probably about the same age as John Drake. There is an entry in Dr John Dee's Diary (ed. J. O. Halliwell, 1842) for 17 June 1581, 'yong Mr Hawkins, who had byn with Sir Francis Drake, cam to me to Mortlake'. Such a visit would be for the purpose of a horoscope calculated upon the hour and date of the client's birth.

[2] See p. 72.　　　　[3] The latitude by the star or noon sun.

The xth of August 1582 we ankered in Soraleon River at night, and the seconde of Septembre we departed out of this harborough.

The fourthe of Septembre 1582 we came in agayne to the same harborough, the pretence whearof as yet not knowen to me, I was not made acqueynted wyth our comyng yn.[1] All the busisnes wch we did in this place might have been doon in lesse than xxtie daies. Mr Walker preacher, Mr Evans marchaunt, Mr Fayrwether, and Willyam Hawkins, were more envied at than annye of the rest, wth daylie reprowche of spightefull wourdes . . .

The xxvith of Septembre 1582 Master Walker tolde me[2] that he had a matter to let me [know . . . if I] wolde not make it knowen: saying that the voyage [we were come] in was broken cleane, and that from oure first departure [from England] they weare determyned not to proceede in that [voyage we were sent] in: but in an other wch sholde be more profytable (as they [deemed]) and of their owne devising. I answering, said: that [would] be a good voyage of their device wch never weare out of the [sight of their] owne chymbneys, or from their mothers pappes in respect of [voyaging]. In replie wheareof he said, that the generall was determined [to enter] in St Helena, and to possesse the same, and theare to be p[roclaimed] King, promysing great rewardes to all the well-willers [who would] consent to the same: as first to Cap^en: Warde 10,000 li [to Cap. Parker] 5000. To Mr Walker 2000. to Mr Maddocks 2000. [and for] payment of this money he was determyned to have taken the [Portuguese] Armathos[3] if he colde.

I aunswered, will the generall make so light of o^r Artycles as in this ordre, wch weare set downe by so many good, vertuous [men] and those wch we ought wyth all reverence to followe and obey in their [comman]dements for that they are for the benefyte and profyt of the comonweal also oure profyts. Let us travayle thearin as honest men: and

[1] The lieutenant had not his Captain's confidence.
[2] See Walker's Diary (p. 207) and Madox's Diary (p. 184). Hawkins alone gives details of the alleged bribes that Fenton was ready to offer.
[3] The fleet of carracks from the Indies.

[not yield] to the dyscredyt of others that do the contrarye.

Walker (replying) aunswered: well, theare is nowe no remedie, [you] must be content as wee all are: but wth gods assistaunce I [will see] wythin these two daies what I can do wth my Capten toching this matter.

Mr Walker being in great agonye aboute this matter, came to his cap; the daye following[1] being in his Cabyon, and fell downe uppon his knees and besaught hym for god sake that he wolde not geeve his consent to this determination, and with teares made Mr Warde to promyse him he wolde proceede in the voyage we wear sent in, Let the generall do what he wolde, Saied Capt^{en} Warde tomorrowe I will go to the generall & knowe his mynde what he meaneth to do and will tell hym playne my mynde.

The generall being not hable to do this feat wthout Cap^{en} Warde, saied then that he wolde go back agayne to the Islands of Cape de Verd to fetche some wyne: wch was onelye a device to pick & steale . . .

The seconde of Octobre 1582 we departed out . . .

The first of Novembre we passed the equinoctial line.

The first of December we ankered in a Baye in [Brazil] to the Southwardes of the Lyne. Heare our generall [ordered] a Barck to be taken wch we sawe at sea.

The xiith of the same moneth they departed out of that [Bay with] determynacion (in outwarde shewe) of the generall and [Ward] for the Straightes: But in verye deede (as it afterwards [appeared]) nothing at all ment, but dissembled for a further pollicye [so to] blynde their companye. For in truthe this maketh the sayinge of some of our companye [to be] thought true, which said that this honourable voyage (the more [was] the pyttie) was bought & solde by the Spanyards frends, or [by] themselves before oure comyng out of Englande.[2] Wee think that they canne scarce aunswer it at their comyng home wch did it: but some of them care not whether ever they see England.

[1] September 27, according to Hawkins's reckoning. For Fenton's Journal see p. 108. He naturally makes no allusion to his secret plans.

[2] Banister reported this accusation to Captain Fenton at a much later date, 25 April, 1583 (see p. 142).

The xixth of Decembre 1582 we weare in 33 degrees ½.

The same xixth of Decembre the generall called Cap^{en} Warde wth the rest to think what was best to be doon in o^r procedings: the matter being longe before determyned by thre or foure of them, Then casting a doubt of the Spanyshe fleete and of meeting them, being as wee afterwardes understoode to the northewarde of us 150 legues.[1] This they made a suffycyent cawse to breake of the voyage, alleaging also thet they wanted many things the wch they wolde supplye in St Vincents. This color of oure want and to refreshe it was nothing but becawse they wolde go back agayne (as we after found it most true) for traffique for sugar, and being in St Vincents he was not hable longer to deseyv the matter, but it all burst out what myne opynyon was toching oure going back againe.[2]

For my parte[3] (the wants of our victuells every way considered as of water caske, wyne, and other necessaryes) we are inforced with gods assistaunce to geeve thadventure through the straights of Magelan into the Southe Sea, in hoape of a good releefe for our money: whereas going by Cap Bonsperansa or back agayne for Brasel, thear was no hoope to speed for money or love becauwse the country [gives it not] . . . also the chefe time of the yeare: [I think it most meet and by gods good] help, and in his feare to proceed not [knowing any] objection to the contrarye to be alleaged. The [going to Cap] Bonsperansa, or back home agayne I thinke [for leakage] and other defaltes we are neyther waye hable to go.

The names of those wch semed willing [on the 19th] of Decembre to go through the Straights [but] in two dayes weare cleane turned, the [reason] yet to us unknowen; are

[1] In fact they were to the south of the English ships (see p. xlix).

[2] There appears to have been a violent outburst at S. Vicente on January 22, when Fenton demanded that all should sign their assent to coming there; 'about which thing grew foule speeches betweene the Generall and his lieutenant, after the olde custome' (Luke Ward in *Pr. Nav.*, p. 666). See pp. 195, 250.

[3] Here Hawkins is apparently transcribing his own opinion expressed during or following the conference of December 20 (see p. 242).

The Generall	The Edwards two [merchants]
Luke Warde	The M^r of the Ed[ward]
Nicholas Parker	
Richard Maddock, Preacher	
Christopher Hall, M^r of the	

The Generall
Luke Warde
Nicholas Parker
Richard Maddock, Preacher
Christopher Hall, M^r of the
Gallyon.

The names of soch as gave not their consent to go back: becawse they knewe that yf the opoortunity & tyme of the yeare weare neglected: [it was] not possible oure voyage sholde be made for the Molocos: becawse o^r men & victuells wear [continuing] everye daye to decaye

William Hawkins
Thomas Whoode ⎱
Tho: Blackoller ⎰ Pilots
Matthewe Talbuyshe
John Drake
Richard Farwether M^r of the Frauncys

The xxth of Decembre 1582 oure Generall bare up with St Vincents being in heighth 33 degrees ½. The next daye the wynde was contrarye to go to the northwards and so continued there . . .

. . . xi and xii of the clock . . .

The xxth of Januarye we ankered in St Vincent In this harborough the Portingales daylie re[paired to us, but said] that they weare nowe the King of Spayne his subjects, wherefore they durst not neyther wolde they traffique wyth us, Notwythstanding, the Vice Roye promysed us soche loves . . . as sholde be a good refreshing: But this fell out in the [making] but delayes for a further myschief: we had nothing [but one] hogge and a small Bullock.[1]

The xxiiiith theare came into us thre spanysh shippes [who] determyned to have taken us wch afterwardes we understood of there owne menne. Thes Shippes weere sent from Don [Diego Flores] generall of the Spanysh fleete to

[1] The suggestion that the Portuguese were delaying the Englishmen until the arrival of the Spaniards does not appear justified in view of Pedro Sarmiento's narrative. Indeed Lopez Vaz (p. 291) reports that Diego Flores had sent back 'the women and sicke men in all the fleete' in the three ships that entered St Vincent's Bay.

searche the coast, and yf they [should] fynd us to take us.

Theare weare in thes three shippes 670 and odde menne, and they weare in burthen as followeth. The Admyrall 500 tonnes. The viceadmyrall 400. The thirde being in burden 600.[1] They began to fight wyth us aboutes tenne of the clock at night, and contynued verye extreame till the noone of the next daye: Their viceAdmyrall wee did sink: Theare weare of our own menne slayne in bothe shippes six, or eight: and more than twenty hurte. They had of theirs slayne above c[th] menne and manye wounded, This was understoode of at Spirito Sancto of the Portingales when we watered theare.

Being afterwardes at Sea our Generall wrought in soch ordre bearing up before everye winde that blewe: (his mynde was so trobled) that wee weare 25 dayes and more ere wee did get to the northwards 200 legues, w[ch] wolde not have requyred halfe the tyme. He tooke this upon hym for a vayne glorye, being laughed at by every man almost, becawse all knewe that he understoode not what he did.[2]

The xxiith of Februarye wee fell withe Lande being the Lande of Spirito Sancto

The same night we ankered in the mouthe of the River. . . . Dayes after wee weare . . . for King Phillip: yet they spake . . . price of three halfpence the pound. For . . . we had neare, the marchants saied that . . . tymes the valeur, good marchants to bring a . . . When we were reddy to departe they proferred . . . for 500 Roves of Sugar, but no more, w[ch] was [but] pollycye to deseeve the tyme till the Spanyards [should find] us; and some of their companye did tell us as moche that [there] would be thre shippes wythin foure dayes w[ch] sholde come [from the R. of] Januarye. This treacherye was like to that w[ch] they [shewed] us in St Vincent.[3] They also tell us theare was of late killed in St Vincent 100 Spanyards, w[ch] indeed was true, for ourselves had doon it, though we made no boast thereof theare. Sugar

---

[1] See p. 130. Hawkins exaggerates the tonnage.
[2] This is the sailor jeering at the soldier commander.
[3] See p. 137.

was worth in Spirito Sancto 2 ducats the Roove, being for the most part in pouder.

The iiijth of March theare came a Portingale barke [into] the Roade by us wch came [not] from Januarie as they saide, but [came] from Sancta[1] in St Vincents as afterwards they confessed.

The same daye the Generall received two sheetes of paper full wrytten from the ViceRoye of Sancto Spirito subscribed wyth the handes of six or seven severall men wch I judge to be the assistants of the saide Vice Roye: but what it toched I doe not knowe. Albeit the Portingales forewarned us to looke to ourselfes.

The fyveth of Marche in the morning we departed out of Spirito Sancto Roade. Heigthe 20 d. and ⅓.

In this harbrough what our generall did he kept to hymselfe. Manye letters weare sent, receved & aunswered. The second of this marche I craved leave of the Generall to go ashore to the watring place to take the Soone, but he denyed me and at . . .

The xiiijth of Juyn 1583 we arryved in Ireland [and there] stayed ten dayes in Kynsale, and theare was I [kept aboard] being requested by divers noblemen of the contry [to visit] them for the space of one howre: and also wrytten for by [M^r] Sentleger, and required by Cap^en. Bartlet[2] and xiiijen more gentlemen of good credyt.

The xxixth of juyn we Ankered in the Downes wheare I was reserved wyth Irons from the shore[3] least I sholde go to my Lorde with the letter wch I had wrytten to my Loorde in that place opened and kept from sending by the generall. And two dayes before that the generall comyng from the poope commaunded me in his anger to the Bilbowes wythout anny cawse whye: At wch manyfest wronge, shewed, perceiving hym to have no reason in his dealinge, kneeling uppon my knees I appealed to the Queenes Matie, praying

---

[1] Santos.
[2] Warham St Leger and Captain Edward Bartley. See *Cal. S.P., Ireland, passim.* See pp. 147, 148.
[3] This is a point always noted by historians against young Hawkins, but in fact it is a reflection upon Fenton as Captain General.

hym alsso to followe her Ma^ts Commyssion orells I said unto hym that he must Looke to aunsweare this wronge: at wch appeale I called the whole ship to wytnes: whearat he made but a fashe, neyther putting of his cap or using anny other reverence at all: but with vile speches towardes me sayed that if I spake one wourde more he wolde dashe me in the teethe, and called me villeyn sclave, and arrant knave wyth many more vile wourdes, the wytnessing whearof I referre to the whole companye.

The same xxvijth of juyn the generall went into my Cabben and tooke from me all my dagges,[1] one of them being charged uppon occasion of two shippes wch gave us chase in lykelihoode to laye us aborde: commaundement being geven xii howres before both by the generall & Parker that everye man sholde be in a reddynes. The great Ordynounce being prymed & all o^r small shot being reddye.

. . . of his gentrie abusing as good as . . . it was borne. The generall taking the [complaint that I] was more busier than I needed, I awnsered [it was none of] his bussines I do nothing but my dutie, for I [know better what] doth belonge to this voyage than thre soche as he is [and therefore] was I sent in yt. The generall aunswering sayed [I want not] a companion. I know you well enough. I knowe the [way to] make the voyage, and go neyther by Cape Bonesperansa or by the straites of Magelan, and sayed in further choler [that he] had thre strings to his Bowe wch I knewe not of. I said I did knowe one string (yet is it none of yours). Let us [obey] oure comyssion and those directions wch we have to follow [our] Counsell, and wee shall do welynough: but as for your [strings] I feare me they will fall out to be made of rotten stuffe, I think. Nay Sir, saide he: for Sr Frauncys Drake [did] knowe it as well as he hymselfe[2] or anny of you that are [here]. and I knowe that he is not hable to do the like agayne. He played the Pirate and theefe. Do you thinke I will [also]? Naye, I knowe how to make my voyage wythout any of your

---

[1] Weapons, particularly 'a kind of heavy pistol' (*O.E.D.*).
[2] Fenton presumably referred to his planned exploits in the Atlantic Ocean.

advises. Thearto saide I, yf you string that way I care less for your strings: and the sequell showeth that one of [your] imagyned stringes was like to be the dystruction of us [all] if god had not been on oure sides. The Gallyons sides tell of it, and some of our menne are slain and many wounded.[1]

And before that being at the sea, he asked me: What is there at the Molocos? I saied. those thinges we are sent for, all sorts of spices but specyally cloves. Quo he, will you & your Companyons assure me we shalbe hable to lade our shippes when we come thither? Nay, (quo, I) that is more than I was demaunded of in Englande. Quo he, Except you and the rest will insure it me, I will not goe thither. Quo, I, Then doe you not what you weare sent for, and I think that it will not be as easilie aunswered as you make accompt of.

General. Do thies matters troble [you]? Hawkins. Generall your ordre is good, I [have so] made it at the begynnyng: but being doon [now so] neare home it makes the companye in an uproar [for this] is an honorable action overthrowen, yet I thank god it lyeth not in me. But wheare as it is, when wee come home the Counsell will perceive it welynoughe. Gen. Yea it is overthrowen becawse I wolde not play the theefe as in the last voyage. Haw. When God sendeth us home [Sir] Fraunceys and you must ende that matter, for I have [nought] to do wyth it. Howbeit I have more in this Action than perhaps you knowe of, and that maketh me to speake, for I am undoon by the overthrowe of it: but heare for your place [sake] I do reverence you, but when we come home, yf you call [me] Theefe, I will see howe you canne Justifie it: for when we came both fourthe wee weare gentilmen alike. Gen. Thou shalt not be so good as I, so longe as thou lyvest. Hawkins. What make you of me then? Gen: A knave, villayn, and a Boye. Haw: If I weare at home, I wolde not be afearde to followe you in any grounde in Englande: but heare in this place for quyetnes sake I let it passe & will beare every wronge be it never so great. Gen: Wilt thowe so? Haw: Yea trulye. Then the general wolde have drawen his longe knyfe and have stabbed Hawkins, and intercepted of that, he tooke

[1] Hawkins implies that one of the 'strings' was to fight the Spaniards.

up his longe staffe and thearwith was ronnyng at hawkins, but the M^r, Mr Bannester, Mr Cotten and Symin Farnando stayed his furye. Haw. Truly, generall, in this place you [are] a Justice, and this becommeth a governor to be a dysordre to the hole. If you canne fynde anny Just cawse agaynst me, punysh me by yor ordre whiche is prescribed, and let yor weapons passe till wee come in place wheare: for he that cannot holde his handes heare is not wourthie of the place; I knowe this is but yor old quarrell renewed, and so let it go. . . . had for the performance . . . for which speach the general . . . care and whensoever he did see hym . . . to absent himselfe out of the Generals sight for the quyetnes of the hole. As all the company will wytness of my side I doubt not. Written by me Willyam Hawkins this vi [day of July] 1583, wch do not desire of myselfe to be Justefied [and] do willingly reserve myselfe to the reporte of the companyes of the Gallion, and of the other two shipps.

By me William Hawkins.

Document 68

Bernardino de Mendoza to Philip II
16 July 1583[1]

In the ship which I said arrived here after fighting with your Majesty's vessels on the coast of Brazil, and at Fort St. Vincent, here arrived a Portuguese named Juan Pinto,[2] who says he is married at Rio de la Plata. They captured him in a boat with the friars and brought him to London, where the Councillors secretly examined him and begged him to remain in their country and go with English ships to the Rio

---

[1] Abstract. *Cal. S.P., Span., 1580–6*, no. 350.
[2] Pinto was taken aboard the *Edward* of his own free will (see p. 192).

de la Plata.[1] He slipped through their hands and came instantly to inform me. I at once shipped him in a vessel bound for Lisbon and gave him letters for the Cardinal Infante [Viceroy of Portugal] in order that he may give a verbal account of what happened in the combat with the ships as an eye-witness, and thence, if necessary, be sent on to give an account to your Majesty. He positively asserts that the English sent to the bottom the flag-ship of your Majesty's fleet.[2] The Queen has ordered the arrest of the Captain of the ship,[3] and of the Galleon which accompanied her, not to punish them for having attacked your Majesty's ships in your own ports, but for not having continued the voyage. These ships have not plundered, and Drake's going to Plymouth was for the purpose seeing whether they could be sent to serve Don Antonio. All the money spent on this expedition has been lost, and the merchants say the English cannot make the voyage in ships of less than 1000 tons burden, as they have to sail loaded with victuals, considering the way Englishmen eat, and they can only bring half a cargo home for the same reason. Even a cargo of spices will not pay under these circumstances, the voyage being so long . . .

Document 69

Philip II to Bernardino de Mendoza
12 September 1583[4]

Thank you for sending advice about the ships for the Moluccas and the trade with Brazil. If you can learn anything further about Diego Flores de Valdes' flagship let me know,

[1] Edward Cotton sent out a ship for the River Plate in 1583.
[2] This was an exaggerated account of the sinking of the *Begoña*.
[3] This is the only definite news of the arrest of Ward and Fenton for enquiries.
[4] *Cal. S.P., Span., 1580–6*, no. 360.

as we have heard nothing here of her having been sunk, although we know she had fought.[1] Let me know if any other ships are fitted out there for their corsair voyages, and whether the Terceira affair has cooled their ardour.[2]

Document 70

'A Report of the Proceedings of M. John Drake after his Departing to the River of Plate' [by Lopez Vaz][3]

The cause why these English shippes under the conduct of M. Fenton went not to the streits, I know not: but some say that they were put backe by foule weather: other some say that it was from fear of the kings ships.

But the pinnesse of these two ships went from them, in which was Captaine John Drake; the cause why they parted I know not, but the pinnesse came into the river of Plate, and within five leagues of Seale Island, not farre from the place where the Earle of Cumberlands shippes did take in fresh water, shee was cast away upon a ledge of rockes: but the men were saved in their boat, which were in number 18, who went ashore on the Northside, and went a dayes journey into the land, and met with the Savages which are no men-eaters, but take all the Christians they can, and make them slaves.

But the Englishmen fought with them and the Savages slew five of them and took 13 alive, which were with the savages about 15 moneths, But the master of the pinnesse whose name was Richard Faireweather being not willing to

[1] The *San Juan Bautista* had originally been the Admiral of the grand fleet, which may have confused the story.
[2] The defeat of Strozzi's fleet raised to support Don Antonio in the summer of 1582.
[3] *Pr. Nav.*, pp. 673–4.

indure the misery that hee was in and having knowledge that
there was a towne of Christians on the other side of the river,
he in a night called John Drake, and another young man
which was with them, and took a very little Canoa, which
had but two oares, and so passed to the other side of the river,
which is about 19 leagues broade, and were three dayes before
they could get over without meate and comming to land, they
hit upon an high way that went towardes the Christians and
seeing the footing of horses, they followed it, and at last came
to an house where there was corne saved, and there they met
with Indians servants unto the Spaniards, which gave them
meate, and clothes to cover them, for they were all naked, and
one of the Indians went to the towne, and told them of the
Englishmen; so the Captaine sent foure horsemen, who
brought them to the towne behind them.

This Captaine clothed them, and provided lodging for
them, and John Drake dined at the Captaines table, and they
were all very well intreated, the Captaine purposing to send
them for Spaine. But the Viceroy of Peru having newes
thereof, sent for them, and so John Drake was sent to him, but
the other two were kept there because they were married in
the countrey, so that I know no more of their affaires.

Document 71

'An Extract out of the Discourse of
One Lopez Vaz, a Portugal, Touching the
Fight of M. Fenton with the Spanish Ships'[1]

Upon the relation of Pedro Sarmiento concerning the streits
of Magellan, that they might be fortified, and for that the
King heard, that there were ships in England preparing for

[1] *Pr. Nav.*, p. 673.

the same streits, he commanded Diego Flores de Valdes a noble man of Spaine, to passe thither with 23 ships, and 3500 men to stoppe the passage of the Englishmen.

There went in this fleet the governor of Chili, with 500 olde souldiers that came out of Flanders: but this was the unhappiest fleet of ships that ever went out of Spaine; for before they came from the coast of Spaine a storme tooke them, and cast away five of the fleete and in them above 800 men, and the rest came into Cadiz. But the King sent them word that they should proceede: and so there went out on the voyage 16 of the shippes, for two more of their fleet were much spoyled by the storme which they had.

In these sixteene shippes Pedro Sarmiento was sent to the governour in the Straites, and had assigned unto him 500 men to stay there with him, and hee carried with him all kinde of Artificers to make him forts, and other necessaries, with great store of ordinance and other munition.

This fleete because it was late, did winter on the coast of Brasil, in the river of Jenero: and from thence they went when the winter was past, and about the beight of 42 degrees they had a sudden storme, so that Diego Flores beat it up and downe 22 dayes, in which time hee lost one of the best ships he had, which had in her 300 men and 30 women, that went to inhabit the Streits: and in this ship also was most part of the munition which should have been left in the Streits, so in the end the storme grew to be so great, that the ships were not able to endure it any longer, but were put backe into an Island called Santa Catalina; and there he found a barke wherin were some fryers going for the rivir of Plate: which fryers told him of two great English ships, and a pinnesse, which had taken them, but tooke nothing from them, nor did them any harme, but onely asked them for the King of Spaines ships.[1]

Hereupon Diego Flores knowing that these English ships would goe for the Streits, determined to goe thither, although it was in the moneth of Februarie, and choosing 10 ships of the 15 that were left, hee left two ships which were not in

[1] See pp. 231–8.

case to goe to sea at the Island, and into the other three ships which were old, and shaken with the storme, hee put all the women and sicke men in all the fleete,[1] and sent them to the river of Jenero, and he with the 10 other returned again for the Streits.

The three ships in which the sicke men and women were went to Brasil, and there they found within the port of S. Vincent the two ships before mentioned.

They woulde have had the English men to have gone out of the harbour, and thereupon they fell to fight, and because that these three ships were weake with the storme, and the men that they had were the worst in all the fleete, the Englishmen easily put them to the worst, and sunke one of them, and might have sunk another, if the Englishmen would; but they minded not the destruction of any man: for that is the greatest vertue that can be in a man, that when hee may doe hurt, yet he will not doe it.

—So the Englishmen went from this port to Spirito Santo, where they had victuals for their merchandise, and so they went backe for England, without doing of any harme in the Country.

Document 72

Deposition of John Drake
Lima, 9 January 1587[2]

While he was in London a gentleman who was a seaman negotiated with some merchants for making a voyage to China and founding a factory, but as the merchants were for

[1] See p. 269 for Fenton's report.
[2] Extracts, translation. Seville, Archivo General de Indias, 2.5.2/21; Spanish and English text in Lady (E.F.) Eliott-Drake, *The Family and Heirs of Sir Francis Drake* (1911), vol. II, pp. 360–401. The extracts here printed are taken, by permission, from Lady Eliott-Drake's translation (II, 396–8).

giving a similar commission to another man he refused to go. Another gentleman named Edward Fenton offered to make the voyage, but as he had no experience in maritime affairs, the merchants asked the Council, and the Council asked Captain Francis, to give them some of the people who had been with him in his voyage . . .

. . . they took from [the friars] an Englishman who was with them in order to show them the river of La Plata & a Portuguese who of his own free will wished to remain, & go in one of their ships:[1] As Fray Juan de Riba de Neyra told them that at the river of la Plata in Buenos Ayres there was a settlement of Spaniards with plenty of provisions, but who needed what was required to clothe themselves, all the three proceeded in that direction. When about half way on the voyage the General asked the English sailor [Carter] whether they would get into the river of La Plata, and was told sometimes that they could and at other times there were many shallowes, The General did not like to trust himself to the men, and calling a council proposed that as the English merchants had not carried out the agreement to give him provisions for two years, as had been settled, he was equally under no obligation to carry out the agreements he therefore wished to return to Brazil. There were different opinions, and the deponent, with the people in his ship, who were seventeen persons & a boy, decided to proceed to the river of La Plata & to go in since their ship was smaller than the others, and to take provisions for continuing the voyage. Thus they went to the river of La Plata, leaving the Captain, that is to say the General, and the Admiral . . .

[1] Richard Carter and Juan Pinto (see p. 192).

Document 73
Inscription on Fenton's Tomb[1]

Richardus praenobilis comes corcagiensis, uxoris suae patruo B.M.P.—

Memoriae perenni Edwardi Fenton, reginae Elizabethae, olim pro corpore armigeri, Jano O-Neal, ac post eum comite Desmoniae in Hibernia turbantibus, fortissimi taxiarchi; qui post lustratum improbo uasu, Septentrionalis plagae apocryphum mare et excussas variis peregrinationibus inertis naturae latebras, Aº, CIƆ, IƆ, LXXXVIII, in celebri contra Hispanos naumachia, meruit praetoriae navarchus. Obiit Anno Dᴺᴵ. CIƆ, DC, III.

> Cognatos cineres et amicam manibus umbram
> O Fentone, tuis, excipias tumulo.
> Usurum tumuli victuro marmore pensat,
> Et reddit gratus, pro tumulo, titulum.[2]

[*Translation*]

Richard, the noble Earl of Cork to the uncle of his wife B.M.P.—

To the everlasting memory of Edward Fenton, formerly Gentleman of the Guard to Queen Elizabeth, most brave general in the Irish rebellions of John O'Neal and after him the Earl of Desmond, who after traversing by monstrous wastes the unknown seas of northern regions and on various voyages searching the secrets of idle nature, earned a commander's reward as a sea captain in the celebrated

---

[1] In the Church of St Nicholas, Deptford. Transcribed by courtesy of the Incumbent. For help with the translation, particularly of the epitaph in verse, the Editor is indebted to Mr S. J. Arthur.

fight against the Spaniards in 1588. He died in the year 1603.

> O Fenton, may'st thou welcome to thy grave
> Thy spouse's ashes and beloved shade.
> The legend to be cut into the stone
> She weighs and gratefully recites before the tomb.

Appendix I

TECHNICAL DOCUMENTS
(Documents 74–78)

Document 74

Navigation Table of Leagues to Minutes of Latitude[1]

Sowth
$\left\{\begin{array}{l} \text{L} \\ \text{17 \& di.} \quad -60 \\ \text{8.3q}^{\text{d}} \quad\;\; -30 \\ \text{4.1q}^{\text{d}} \text{ \& di} -15 \end{array}\right\}$ 60

Sowth \& by W.
$\left\{\begin{array}{l} \text{L} \\ \text{18} \qquad\; -60 \\ \text{9} \qquad\;\;\, -30 \\ \text{4 \& di} \quad\; -15 \end{array}\right\}$ 60

Sowth S.W.
$\left\{\begin{array}{l} \text{L} \\ \text{19} \qquad\;\; -60 \\ \text{9 \& di} \quad -15 \\ \text{4–3q}^{\text{d}} \quad\, -30 \end{array}\right\}$ 60

S.W. \& by S.
$\left\{\begin{array}{l} \text{L} \\ \text{21} \qquad\;\; -60 \\ \text{10 \& di} \quad -30 \\ \text{5}\tfrac{1}{3} \qquad\;\; -15 \end{array}\right\}$ 60

S.W.
$\left\{\begin{array}{l} \text{L} \\ \text{25} \qquad\;\; -60 \\ \text{12 \& di} \quad -30 \\ \text{6–1q}^{\text{d}} \quad\, -15 \end{array}\right\}$ 60   There is a litle starr accompanied with a

[1] Magdalene College, Cambridge, Pepys MS 2133 (unfoliated). Fenton transcribed this table on a preliminary page of his Journal. It enables the Master to transform distance run on any particular rhumb into change of latitude. As an example of its use, on 5 November 1582 the latitude was 3° 24′, and during the next six days the run was 138 L SSW and 9 L S and by W. The change of latitude, using the table, is 7° 45′, making the ship's position by dead reckoning 11° 9′. The noon altitude of the sun corrected this to 10° 36′ on November 11.

S.W. & by W. $\left\{\begin{array}{l}\text{L} \\ 31 \\ 15\ \&\ \text{di} \\ 7\frac{1}{2}\end{array}\right.$ $\left.\begin{array}{l}-\ 60 \\ -\ 30 \\ -\ 15\end{array}\right\}60$ litle white clowde to the Sowth wardes of the Lyne, whose ellevacion is 10 degr. from the Pooll and is in Rule at the S.[1]

W.S.W. $\left\{\begin{array}{l}\text{L} \\ 47 \\ 23\frac{1}{2} \\ 11\frac{1}{3}\end{array}\right.$ $\left.\begin{array}{l}-\ 60 \\ -\ 30 \\ -\ 15\end{array}\right\}60$

W. & by S. $\left\{\begin{array}{l}\text{L} \\ 88 \\ 44 \\ 22 \\ 11\end{array}\right.$ $\left.\begin{array}{l}-\ 60 \\ -\ 30 \\ -\ 15 \\ -\ 7\frac{1}{2}\end{array}\right\}60$

W. $\{$ $-\ 0$

Document 75
A Translation of a Portuguese Sea Manual[2]

This rulle searveth to knowe what Declination the stare of the northe doth marke from the polle[3]

When you tacke the altitude of the polle marke in what place

[1] Mr W. A. Scott, of H.M. Nautical Almanac Office, writes: 'A possible identification of the "litle starr" is that it is λ Hydri, which is situated just south of the Lesser Magellanic Cloud; but, in view of the meagre data given, this must not be taken as a definite identification.' A star was said to be 'in rule' when on that bearing that the observation should be made. The Pole Star was 'in rule', i.e. at the elevation of the Celestial Pole, when the Guards lay approximately SE and by E or NW and by W (see p. 299).

[2] Extracts. B.M., MS Harl. 167, ff. 39–72. The extracts have been taken from what is an ill-arranged translation of a contemporary Portuguese sailing manual with English addenda.

[3] This table gives the number of degrees and minutes to be added to or

the guardes be in and then you shall knowe whether that the northe starre be benethe polle or above the polle etc.

					D.	M.
The guardes beinge in the NW then ys the starre				benethe polle	oo.	40.
,,	,,	,,	,,	NW and by W ,, ,,	oi.	20
,,	,,	,,	,,	NNW	oi.	57
,,	,,	,,	,,	N and by W	02.	28
,,	,,	,,	,,	N	02	53
,,	,,	,,	,,	N and by E	03	13
,,	,,	,,	,,	NNE	03	24
,,	,,	,,	,,	NE and by N	03	30
,,	,,	,,	,,	NE	03	24
,,	,,	,,	,,	NE and by E	03	13
,,	,,	,,	,,	ENE	02	53
,,	,,	,,	,,	E and by N	02	28
,,	,,	,,	,,	E	oi	57
,,	,,	,,	,,	E and by S	oi	20
,,	,,	,,	,,	ESE	oo	40
,,	,,	,,	,,	SE and by E then ys the north stare equalle with the polle etc.	oo	oo

When you wolde know by the heighth of the sonne in what degre or Latitude youe be in youe shall first tacke the heighth of the sonne w^t youer astrolobe or quadrant or ballestila.[1]

Youe shall understande ther be thre kynde of martills belonginge to your ballestella. the firste ys frome fyve to fyftine, the seconde from fyftine to thyrtie and the thyrde ys from thyrtie to nynetie [degrees]. and thys accompte

subtracted from the observed height of the Pole Star when it was not 'in rule'.

[1] The three instruments in common use were the mariner's astrolabe, the mariner's quadrant, and the *balestilha* or cross-staff. The latter had (as the next paragraph explains) three separate cross-pieces to be used according to the height of the heavenly body observed.

begynneth from the equynoctiall Lyne to the northewarde and when youe will tacke your altitude of the northe stare youe muste [hold] youer staffe by youer eye and close youer other eye on the other syde from your staffe & bringe youer martille straight that youe maye see the stare direct over youer martille. I saie of the hyther parte of youer martill and youer clossinge of the ellament or skey to the matter [i.e. horizon] under the loware parte of the ende of youer saide martille and principallie tacke youer altitude whan the guardes be in the northweste,[1] notwithstandinge youe maie tacke the stare in anye of the poyntes of the compase but usuallie those mentioned in the compas on the other side [i.e. the diagram] provided that when youe doe tacke the stare see that you take the stare Juste w^t the upper parte of youer martill and a verie littell space betwen youer parte of youer martill, I saie the lower parte therof, and the skeye from the matter [horizon] the smaller that you leave the skey betwen the matter and the martille the better yt ys and the Juster youe shall tacke yt.

A rulle for to knowe howe to use the
Crossiers wch are to be used of those that
Saille to the sowthwarde of the Lyne Equinoctial

When you wille tacke the altitude by the crossiers you shall tacke the Lower stare that ys the fotte of the saide starres and se youer straighte you shall understande that Lowke howe muche youe tacke the saide stare in a bove 30 so muche are youe to the southwarde of the Lyne Equinoctiall, and so muche as youe shall fynde or tack the Stare in under or les than 30 so muche shall youe be to the northwarde of the lyne Equinoctiall and yf so be that youe take the said stare juste in 30 then ar youe ryght under the Equynoctiall lyne etc.

[1] I.e. approximately 'in rule'.

[*Table for the nocturnal*][1]

The nyntine of Apprell the guards at north ys mydnyghte
The twantie and towe of october the guardes at
south „ „
The Seconde of Marche the guardes at northeast „ „
The thyrteenth of Januarie the guardes at easte „ „
The fourthe of December „ „ „ sowth
easte „ „
The fyrste of september „ „ „ sowth
weste „ „
The seventinthe of Julie „ „ „ weste „ „
The thirde of June „ „ „ north
weste „ „

[*The coast of Guinea*]

The distances of leages from place to place	Leages.	The heighths from Cape S. Vincent southwards	D. M.
		Cape Sante Vincent standethe in	37.00
from Cape sante Vincent to Tenerife ys	190	the Iland of Tenerife standeth in	28.0⅓
from Tenerife to the Ile of Palme ys	018	The Ile of palma in	28.0⅓
from Tenerife to forteventura ys	046	Fortaventura in	28.
from ye wester parte of Tenerife to cap blanke	119	Cape blancke in	20.0½ [2]
from cap blancke to bonavista ys	112	Ile of bonavista in	16.
from bonavista to mayo ys	020	the Ile of mayo in	14.50
		The Iland of santiago in	14.50
from santiago to fogo ys	014	The Isle of Fogo in	14.20
from the Iland of Santiago to cabo Verde ys	102	Cape Verde standeth in	14.00

[1] The Nocturnal was an instrument used to obtain a rough estimate of the time at night by marking the bearing of the Guards in relation to the given midnight position at the date of observation.

[2] The fractions indicate parts of degrees, i.e. o⅓ means 20 minutes.

Leages.			*D. M.*
from cabo Verde to Cap. Roxo			
ys	053	Cape Roxo standeth in	11.55
from cap. Roxo to serra liona			
ys	038	Serra Liona standeth in	08.00
from ye shole of sera liona		Cape de monte standeth	
to cap. de Monte	048	in	06.00
from cape de monte to C. de		cape de palmas standeth	
palmas is	076	in	04.00

The Courses upon the coaste of Guynea

Cape sante vincent and tenerife lyeth SW & be S, NE & be N[1]

forteventura & tenerife lyeth E & W

the wester parte of tenerife and Cape blancke lyeth S & W

Cape blancke & bonavista lyeth S & N

The ester parte of bonavista and the Ile of maye lyeth
SW & NE

Santiago & the Ile of Fogo lyethe SW & be W, NE & be E

The northern parte of the Illand of santiago & Cabo Verde
E & be S, W & be N

Cabo verde and cape roxo lyethe sowthe easte somewhate to
the southwarde.

Ryo Grande lyethe in and oute easte & be N, W and be S to
goe clere of a shole that lieth in the mouthe rio grande youe
muste rune southwest of 20 leages and tacke heed of a rocke
lieth in yor weye 7 or 8 leages of.

When you are 20 leages of a sea boarde cape roxo
sowtheweste of then yor course to sera lyona ys SE & be E,
NW & be W.

To goe clere of the sholde that lieth to the sowthwarde of
sera Liona youe muste runne of sowthe and be weste 25
leages. This shold standeth in 6 degrees 40 mynettes.

Sera Liona and Cape de monte lyeth E & be S, W & be N.

Cape de monte and Cape de palmas lieth SE & by E, NW
& by W.

Cape de Palmas and cape des tres pountes lyeth easte and a
lyttle northerlye.

[1] The bearings to and fro are given.

La costa de brassill

	Leages		D. M.
from Rio dos Pontos to Isleos ys	004	Isleos standeth in	15.00
from Isleos to rio grande ys	020	Rio Grande standeth in	16.00
from rio grande to porto seguro ys	015	Porto seguro standeth in	16.00
from porto seguro to cape dos Baxos ys	020	Cape dos Baxos standeth in	18.00
from cape dos baxos to rio dolce ys	020		
from rio dolce to spirito santo ys	018	Spirito Santo standeth in	20.30
from spirito santo to perojyba ys	020	Perrojba in	21.30
from perojyba to baya de San salvador ys	015		
from bayo salvador to Cape Frio ys	022	Cape frio standeth in	23.00
from Cape Frio to rio jeneiro ys	019	The rive of Janewary	23.00
from rio Jeneiro to gangro dos ries ys	018		
from rio Jeneiro to sante Vincent ys	045	Sant vincente	24.00
		San Sebastian Iland in	24.0½
from sante Vincente to Cananea ys	034	Cananea standeth in	25.45
from Cananea to rio das deabos ys	028		
from Rio das deabos to rio de pateos	028	Rio de pateos in	28.40
from rio demtina to cape Sant Marie	080	Cape santa maria in	35.00
from cape sant marie to ye sother cape of ryo de plat	028	ryver of plate standeth in	35.0½
from y same sother cape to porto santa Antonio	018	Souther cape of ryo de plate	36.00

from sant antonio to ponta de baxas	205	Pounta de las baxas in	45.50
from ponta de baxas to porto Cruze	060		
from porta cruz to porte sant Julians	017	Sante Julians stands in	49.50
from ye southe cape of port sant Julians and Cape de las virgenes are distant	055	The next head land to the southere of Sant Julians cape de las Virgenes in	50.35 52.0½
from cape de las virgenes to the souther cape of y straight of magilan	044	Cape del estrecho in	53.0½
from the souther cape to sajda del canall	047		
from Cape de las virgenes to sajda de canale	082	the mouth of the Strait	52.00
from sajda del canal to sera alta	095	the headeland of sera alta	48.0½

The Courses

Ryo das Pontas and Isleos lyethe S & N
from the Bayia to Isleos your course ys S and N
Isleos & Rio Grande lyeth S & be W, N and be E
Rio grande and porto Seguro lyeth S & By E, N and be W
from Isleos to port seguro your course ys S and N
Porto seguro & Capo dos Baxos lyeth S & by E, N & be W
cape de baxos & rio dolce lyeth SW & by S, NE & be E
Rio dolce & spirito Santo lyeth S & N
Spirito santo & perojba lyeth SSW & NNE
Perojba & baye de salvador lyeth S & be W, W and be E
Baye de salvador & cape frio lyeth S & be E, N and be W
Cape frio & rio de Janeyro lyeth W & be S, E and be N
Rio de Janeiro & gangro dos reis lyeth W & be S, E and be N
Gangro des reys & the illande of san sebastians lyeth SW & be
S, NE & be N

San sebastians and the baye of saynte Vyncent lyeth W & to the northwarde and E and to the sowthward

Sant vyncent and Cananea lyeth sowthe weste and somewhat to the westward

Cananea and rio das deabos lyeth S & by W, N & be E

Rio das deabos and rio de puteos lyeth SSW and NNE

Ryo de puteos and rio demtynå lyeth SSW and NNE

Ryo demtynå and sant marie lyeth SW & be S NE and be N

Cape sant marye and the souther cape of the ryver of platte lyethe SSW & NNE

The sowthe Capo and porto da sancte antonyo lyeth sowthe west and be sowthe and northe easte and be northe.

Saint antonio and ponta de baxas lyeth SW and be S and NE and be N, *but in this course beware of a shole that lyeth a 20 leages of [f] of Cape de las haenas wch ys to the southwarde of cape sant antonye 40 leages.*

Ponta de baxas and porta cruz lyeth SSW and NNE and of[f] the headlande next to porta cruz to the northward lyeth certaine Illands a bowte fyve leags of the mayne and lyeth WNW and ESE and are in number 9 and lyeth in length 21 leags WNW and ESE

Porta cruz and porta sainte Julyans lyeth WSW and ENE

The sowther Cape of porte sainte Julians and Cape de la virgenes lieth SW and be W, NE and be E

Cape de las virgenes and cape del estreche one the sowth syde of the straighte lieth WSW and ENE and so youe go cleer leavinge all the Illands one yor starboarde syde

Cape de lestrecho one the sowth syde and the norther one the wester end of the sayd straight of magylans caled sayda del canal lyeth NW and be W, SE and be E.

Sajda del canal and sera alta lieth NW and SE and so shold you fall 5 or 6 leages w^{t}in the sayde head lande

Sera alta and the head land of ryo de coantie lyeth north west and be west SE and be E.

The Portingalls when they go from the brassill to Portingall they never hall of to sea above 70 or 80 leages at the moste, yf a 100 leages that ys verye muche and one in 7 years that will rune so fare of as a pylate of that country told me.[1] And when they come to Brasyll [ie. from Portugal] they will then halle up as nere as they can to santyago [Cape Verde Is.] and then the[y] rune SSE or lytle other for yf a man covet to nere the coste of guynea then he shall have calmes.[2] therefore yt ys good to kepe a good course to come not to nere yt.

Abrolios a sholde that lyethe uppon the coste of brasyll 30 leagues lytle more or less in to the sea from the mayne and ys in length 19 leagues.

He that ys bounde to saynte Vincents in brasill so sonne as he fyndeth hymselfe in the heyght of Spiritus santo [20°S] let hime presently seke the lande because the corrent and the wynde bothe dothe sett hyme of all to the southwarde to the Ryver of Platt which muste be consydered.

Document 76

A Letter Written from Goa . . .
by One Thomas Stevens . . . An. 1579[3]

The fourth of April five ships departed for Goa, . . . such evil weather we had until fourteenth of May, that they despaired to compasse the Cape of Good Hope that yeere. Nevertheless, taking our voyage between Guinea and the islands of Cape Verde, without seeing of any land at all, we arrived at length unto the coast of Guinea, which the Portugals so call, chiefly that part of the burning zone, which is from the sext degree unto the Equinoctiall, in which parts they suffered so many inconveniences of heats and lack of

---

[1] This appears to be an interpolation of the translator.
[2] A warning which Fenton disregarded.
[3] *Pr. Nav.*, pp. 160–2. It contains a landsman's observations of the navigation methods used on the Cape of Good Hope route.

windes, that they thinke themselves happy when they have passed it: . . . The thirtieth of May we passed the Equinoctiall . . . You shall understand, that being passed the line, they cannot straightway go the next way to the promontory: but according to the wind, they draw alwayes as neere South as they can to put themselves in the latitude of the point, which is 35 degrees and an halfe, and then they take their course towards the East, and so compasse the point. But the wind served us so that at 33 degrees we did direct our course toward the point or promontory of Good Hope.

You know that it is hard to saile from East to West or contrary, because there is no fixed point in all the skie, whereby they may direct their course, wherefore I shall tell you what helps God provided for these men, There is not a foule that appereth, or signe in the aire, or in the sea, which they have not written, which have made the voyages heretofore. Wherfore, partly by their owne experience, and pondering withall what space the ship was able to make with such a winde, and such direction, and partly by the experience of others whose booke and navigations they have, they gesse whereabouts they be, touching degrees of longitude, for of latitude they be always sure: but the greatest and best industry of all is to mark the variation of the needle or compasse, which in the Meridian of the Iland of S. Michael, which is one of the Azores in the latitude of Lisbon, is just North, and thence swarveth towards the East so much that betwixt the Meridian aforesaid and the point of Africa it carrieth three or four quarters of 32. And againe in the point of Afrike, a little beyond the point that is called Cape dos Agulios (in English the needles) it returneth againe unto the North, and that place passed, it swarveth againe toward the West, as it did before proportionally.

Document 77

Observations of Compass Variation and Some Astronomical Notes by Richard Madox in 1582[1]

[(i)–(iv) *are translations from Latin*]

(*i*) September 15. I have often found by experiment that the magnetic needle which in England varies from the north by at least [eleven] degrees towards the east, here does not turn more than three degrees from the arctic pole . . .

(*ii*) November 7. We have established the true magnetic pole:[2] sunset according to the magnetic compass was 27 degrees from the west towards the south, when the distance should have been 19 degrees, for the sun was 24 degrees in Virgo and we were 6 degrees south from the equator, not far from the coast of Brazil, Hence I conclude that the true north pole is 8 degrees from the north of the magnet. And today, Thursday 8th, carefully investigating the sunrise with the same instrument, I found it after close scrutiny nearly 20 degrees from the east, which at setting had been observed 19 degrees south from the west, I conclude therefore that the declination of the needle from the arctic pole has been proved with great exactitude to be 7 degrees and 30 minutes more or less towards the [west]. Yet in England it is 11 degrees towards the east.

(*iii*) November 15. Hall told me as a certainty that when they were in the north-west, they passed close to the coast commonly called Labrador, in lat. 63°, they found the noon sun two points from the compass, whence I gather that the

---

[1] (*i*) B.M., Cotton MS App. XLVII, f. 48v; (*ii, iii, iv, v*) B.M., Cotton MS Titus B. VIII, ff. 197v, 200, 212v, 181r.

[2] I.e. established the local compass variation. The true bearing of sunrise or sunset for any latitude can be calculated from the *Ephemerides* or obtained from the celestial globe, the sun's position in the zodiac being known.

needle deviates 22 degrees to the west, which if it is true that it is so great suggests to me that the rule is the nearer the pole the greater the deviation of the needle etc. I do not know, however, by what hidden force it is impelled.

November 16. Today having observed at sunset, I find it sinking below the horizon at a distance of 3 degrees from the west toward the south, and when it had run its accustomed course, [it rose] 21 degrees south [of east], having entered the 4th degree of Sagittarius. And so, according to this, the magnetic needle varies 12 degrees from the north. But in fact on the 17th we saw that it was 7°.[1]

v) December 14. The sun rose 15 degrees to the south of east when on the previous night it had set 35 degrees south of west. From which we calculated that the variation of the needle is nearly a point[2] to the west. Thus, when actually navigating southward we assume that we are bending westward which may be why the shores of America in fact run more to the west than they appear to do on sailors' charts and maps. All this squares and agrees with what I have found out by my own exertions and have been told by Francisco de Verra[3] & others.

[1] The bearings of sunrise and sunset within any 24 hours should be approximately equidistant from true South. Madox has taken the sum instead of the difference between the two readings. His corrected observations give 9° E, not very different from the rough result of 7° E that was obtained by pointing the compass to the sun at noon on November 17.

[2] $(35° - 15°) \div 2$ gives 10° W variation, or nearly a 'point', i.e. $11°\frac{1}{4}$.

[3] The young Spaniard in the friars' bark. See p. 120, n. 3.

(v) ταισνερος. Ratione solis luna et hora in caelo punctorum augmenturorum aquae itaque ♂ et o–o ebullitionem faciunt maximam.

[*transl:* Taisnier. According to the rule of the sun, the moon and the hour in the heavens of the augmenting points of water, conjunction and opposition make the maximum upheaval.]

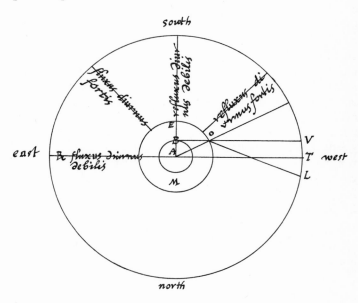

bi the thickness of the aire the star that is yet in L under the horizon may be seen in V above the horizon by the lyn BOL because the ayr betwyxt B and O is thik & moyst

[*Editor's note:* Madox's diagram above (redrawn from Cotton MS Titus B.VIII, f.181) illustrates the effect of atmospheric refraction which raises a heavenly body L from a position below the horizon of an observer at B to an apparent position, V, upon his horizon. The diagram also illustrates the occurrence of spring and neap tides. Taking the outer circle as representing the 30 days of the moon's cycle they follow one another at 15 day intervals. Taking the circle as 24 hours, the neap high tide (R) is followed six hours later by the neap low tide (E), the spring high tide (*fluxus fortis*) by the spring low tide (*refluxus fortis*).

Jean Taisnier of Hainault (b. 1508) was a prolific writer on mathematics, technology and the occult arts. His *Opusculum . . . de natura magnetis* (Cologne, 1562) was translated into English by Richard Eden in 1579 under the title *A very necessarie and profitable Booke concerning Navigation . . . named a treatise of continuall Motions.* The fourth section of the English version, 'Of the Flowing, and Reflowing, (that is) increase and decrease of the Sea, with the causes therof', is the source of Madox's note. On sig. Bi^v Eden gives a tide diagram (not in Taisnier's original edition), from which Madox's is plainly derived, although Eden omits the refraction data. Cf. also the passage, on sig. Ciiii^v: 'The greatest concourses and motions of waters, are when the Moone is in coniunction with the Sunne, and also the greatest flowynges and reflowynges. Lykewyse in opposition of the Moone with the Sunne . . . ']

Document 78
Note by Richard Madox on Longitude at Sea[1]

[March] 10. In casting for to fynde owt a perfet longitude in sayling, I considered y^t al Ephemerides wch are calculated according to ye latitude of any place, have certenty of truth noe wher but in the same longitude wher ye observation was taken, wch is a note not ether heeded, or not as I knoe by any yet published, the evident proof hereof is this. Suppoze ye ephemerides be calculate for ye meridian of Compostella in

An observation of longitude

---

[1] B.M., Cotton MS App. XLVII, f. 8. The method of lunar distances was sound in principle, but useless in practice until precise time-keeping was possible and precise lunar-tables were obtainable, which was not until the latter part of the eighteenth century. Madox was mistaken in thinking the method had not previously been described. It had even been attempted by Vespucci in 1499.

galizia wch is about 44 degrees in latitude, or 14 in longitude. in erecting a figure ryght at noone I fynd ye moon to be just in the angle of ye east, 5 degrees beyond ye buls eye. now if I wold, by ye same book erect a figure for ye same noontyde at constantinople, wch is of the same elevation, I shal find moon somewhat w^tin ye angle of ye East, but 3 degrees & 30 minutes overpast ye buls eye, & this in medio motu luna, because Constantinople being at 59 degrees in longitude, y^t fawleth to be 3 a clock at Constantinople, when yt is noone at Compostella, so y^t in those 3 howrs, Moon according to hir mydle motion passeth a degree & a half, & so at noon in compostella is 5 degrees past ye buls eye. Hens may be gathered this instruction: Suppose yt be fownd by observation y^t 20 sept. 1582 ye ful moon rising in ye East angle, be 3 sygnes & 20 degrees behind ye hart of ye scorpion, at ye general meridian, wch is ye beginning of longitude, and ye latitude of 40 or 50 or so furth, yt muche mattereth not, now yf ye same second day of sept. I trend an unknown place, & ther fynd y^t ye moon rising in ye east angle be 3 sygns & but 17 degrees behind ye hart of ye scorpion, & in hir mid-motion, I pronownce y^t I am risen eastward 90 degrees in longitude from ye general meridian, wch is my first observation, wherunto applying my latitude, I fynd ye exact poynt of ye yerth wher I am. but yf ye moone rising be 3 sygnes or 23 degrees behind ye hart of ye scorpion than am I fawlin to ye west of my general meridian & so am at 270 degrees of longitude & by this proportion judge of al other. And this is an observation as I think never publyshed.[1]

[1] The difference in longitude between Constantinople and Compostella is 45°, equivalent to 3 hours (45 ÷ 15) difference in local time. Taking the moon's 'mean motion' as half a degree an hour, she alters her position by $1\frac{1}{2}°$. If therefore her position at a certain moment (here at her rising) is found in the Ephemerides and observed at an unknown place, the difference between the readings gives the difference of local time and hence the longitude. In the case cited she is 3° before or behind the Ephemerides, equivalent to 6 hours time difference or 90° longitude east or west.

Appendix II

RICHARD MADOX AND HIS DIARY
(Documents 79–80)

Document 79

Autobiographical Note by Richard Madox[1]

Natus sum 11 novemb. 1546

Ad oxonium me contuli 24 jan. 1567

Ad lectionem logices admissum Nov. 1571, 4 annos [et 10 menses] post adventum

Incepi octob. 24, 1575. 3 an. et mens. 11 post baccalaureate

In commitijs steti 9 Julii 1576

Ad Dorcestriā veni 15 julii 1576, ibi permensi 2 an. et mens. 9

Ad parisios ibam Julii 1579. sequenti oct. versus dorcestriam

Prelector factus novemb. 1580 10 menses post reditum dorcestri

Sacris initiatus nov. 24 1580 ♃ et minister ♀ 25

Ad mare me contulit 1582 Apl. 1°

Nix alta

Insurrectio borealis

Dux decollatus

Pyramis pauli exusta

pestilentia Londinensis

Veneris concio dorcestrie 1580 1° Aprilis

probationarius admiss. Januarij 16 1572 ☿

sodalis Januarii 18 1573

. . . tuli petiti sodalitij Nov. 1570 Opus huibrarum[2]

. . . rator factus Ap¹. 5 1571 ☿

[*Translation*]

I was born 11 November 1546

I went to Oxford on 24 January 1567

---

[1] B.M., Cotton MS Titus B. VIII, f. 221.
[2] This word has not been elucidated.

315

I was admitted to read Logic [i.e. admitted B.A.] November 1571, 4 years and 10 months after coming up

I commenced [i.e. admitted M.A.] October 24, 1575, 3 years and 11 months after my B.A. degree

I disputed before the Comitia 9 July 1576

I came to Dorchester 15 July 1576, where I remained 2 years and 9 months

I went to Paris July 1579, the following October back to Dorchester

I was made Lecturer November 1580, 10 months after my return from Dorchester

I took orders Thursday November 24, 1580, and became minister Friday the 25th

I betook myself to sea 1582, April 1

Deep snow

The Rebellion of the North [1569]

The Duke beheaded [the Duke of Norfolk, 1572]

St. Paul's steeple burned down [struck by lightning, 1561]

The plague of London [1563]

I excite love at Dorchester 1580 April 1

Admitted a probationary Fellow January 16, 1572, Wednesday

A Fellow January 18, 1573

Petition for a Fellowship [refused?] Nov. 1570

Work of [?]

I was made [Moderator?] April 5, 1571, Wednesday

[Madox died at Spirito Santo, Brazil, on 27 February 1583.]

[*Editor's note:* Nothing positive has been learned about Madox's family and origins except that he had an elder brother, Thomas Madox, who was a Merchant Taylor. According to a note communicated by the Clerk of the Company, Thomas was made Free by Servitude to the relict of Bartholomew Beaston, 26 May 1564. Richard assigned to him all his personal possessions before embarking on his voyage.

No evidence has been found to support the assertion in George

Walker's biography of Madox (*Puritan Salt*, 1935) that the chaplain was born in Dorset.

The account of Madox's university career given in Andrew Clark, *Register of the University of Oxford*, II (1889), reads as follows: 'Richard Madox, suppl. B.A. 26 Ap., adm. 1 Dec. 1571, det. 1571/2, suppl. M.A. 10 Oct., lic. 25 Nov. 1575, inc. 1576, suppl. lic. to preach 8 Feb. 1581/2, Fellow of All Souls in 1571.' Strictly speaking, Madox did not take his M.A. degree until he had disputed before the *Comitia* on 9 July 1576. Another Richard Madox (conjectured by Walker to be a relative) had taken his B.C.L. degree from All Souls in May 1563.

The fact that Madox obtained his Fellowship in 1573 and went to Dorchester in 1576 implies an official appointment, since conditions of residence were enforced upon Fellows. This appointment may have been in Leicester's service; on 1 May 1582 (Document 33) Henry Oughtred refers to him as 'your honours [i.e. Leicester's] chaplain'.]

Document 80

The Cipher and Nicknames Used in Madox's Diary

The Cipher

The use of a cipher was no novelty in Madox's day, and all three statesmen who were most concerned with Fenton's voyage, namely Burghley, Walsingham and Leicester, had their systems of 'hidden writing'. Some of them are found in three volumes in the Public Record Office (State Papers, Foreign, Ciphers, S.P.106/1–3), which contain 187 ciphers of the Elizabethan period.[1] None of these corresponds in detail to Madox's system; but familiarity with contemporary

---

[1] See also A. J. Butler, 'Some Elizabethan cipher-books', *Trans. of the Bibliographical Society*, vol. VI (1903), pp. 127–37.

Letter Symbols

a	γ	i,y	4	s	X
b	β	k	℃	t	γ
c	℃	l	ᴧ	u,v	ϙ
d	7	m	σ	w	φ
e	z	n	ν	x	x
f	ᴪ	o	ℓ	th	y
g	ㅍ	p	+	sh	⅄
h	ʒ	r	η	st	⅄

Vowel Symbols

(below the line)		(above the line)			
a	..	o	.	au,oo	⊢
e	:	u,v	.	ea	⋀
i,y	.	ai,ay	＼	ee	⌄
		oi	c	ar,er	<

Word Symbols

and	γ	that	ⱦ
in	4	which	ℋ
of	ℓɟ	with	⧺

master σᵏ

318

ciphering methods is suggested by his use (albeit with his own equivalents) of cryptograms commonly found in ciphers employed by Elizabethan statesmen and their agents. If Madox had indeed been in Leicester's service as chaplain or secretary, he might well have become familiar with the ciphers used by the Earl in his secret correspondence. Private diarists as well as statesmen employed ciphers: John Dee, for example, transliterated the more intimate passages of his Diary into the Greek alphabet.[1] Madox, too, used a simple substitute alphabet which included several Greek letters, besides a number of astronomical symbols, and some symbols arbitrarily invented. (See the key on p. 318.)

In a complete alphabet of 23 symbols, hard *c* and *k* were not distinguished while soft *c* was represented by the same symbol as *s*. A separate symbol was devised for *th*, while *sh* and *st* had compound symbols. An alternative system of vowel symbols, including single and paired dots for the short vowels, and diacritical marks for the long vowels, helped to make reading more difficult. In particular the dots are very inconsistently placed in relation to the consonant symbols. Half a dozen short words have their own symbols, as does the frequently used 'Mr.'

A beginning was made in decoding the 'secret' passages by means of four code words which occurred before an entry of £16 in the diarist's monthly accounts. He had previously mentioned sending £16 to his brother, and since the fourth and longest word began with Greek 'beta', it was assumed that this represented *b*, and that the whole phrase was 'Sent to my brother'. This proved correct and not only gave the reader half a dozen consonants, but revealed the meaning of the dots above and below the line. Patient trial and error opened the rest of the alphabet. In point of fact only *beta* and *nu* are direct transliterations, nor did the present writer at first notice that the borrowed astronomical symbols for Aries, Taurus and Libra (the last usually incomplete) all indicated the initial letters of these signs of the zodiac, i.e. *a*, *t*, and *l*. The fact that the symbols are used phonetically has created

[1] *The Private Diary of Dr John Dee*, ed. J. O. Halliwell (1842).

some difficulties of interpretation, especially as Elizabethan vowel sounds were broader than is the mode today. It may be suspected besides that Madox deliberately mis-spelt a word that he had special reason to make indecipherable.

From the fact that Madox used the cipher in the 'domestic' part of the Diary which preceded the story of the voyage, it is clear that it was not invented especially for ship-board use. Only, however, when the dishonest intentions of his companions became self-evident did he write lengthy passages in cipher. And he hoped it would be imagined that he wrote in Greek!

A typical ciphered passage in the Diary is reproduced as Plate XV (opposite); the transliteration of this passage will be found on p. 185.

The Nicknames

Madox's choice of nicknames for his companions was eclectic and deliberate, and he selected them with care for their aptness, as his note characterizing the eponyms suggests (above, pp. 183–4). The following list includes the names which he applied to Fenton and his officers, and a few other names which occur in the passages of the Diary here printed. Identifications and sources are added where they have been determined.

Clodius (= Fenton). Publius Clodius, tribune of Rome, noted for licentiousness and ambition. He banished Cicero from Rome, and was murdered by T. Annius Milo.

Milo (= Ward). Titus Annius Milo, defended by Cicero (*Pro Milonem*) at his trial before the Roman senate for the brutal murder of Clodius.

Hypothalasticus, Hyponauticus (= Ward). Coinages, concocted from Greek words, as equivalents for 'vice-admiral', 'under-captain'.

Glaucus (= Hawkins). A Greek hero in the Trojan war. Represented by Homer as ingenuous, bold, and impetuous.

Pyrgopolinices (= Parker). The braggart captain in Plautus' comedy 'Miles Gloriosus'.

XV. A passage of Madox's Diary, 30 September–1 October 1582

B.M., *Cotton MS Titus B. VIII, f. 186. (Transcribed on p. 185)*

Palinurus (=Hall). The pilot of Aeneas' ship (Vergil, *Aeneid*, bk. 3).

Verres (=Ferdinando). The oppressive and arbitrary Roman governor of Sicily who was indicted before the senate by Cicero (*In Verrem*). Also, as a common noun, means 'boar' or 'swine'.

Cornicola (=Ferdinando). Perhaps intended for Annius Cornicola, a flatterer of the Roman emperor Gallienus.

Hegemon (=Hood). A Thracian poet in the age of Alcibiades. (The relevance is not obvious.)

Hypogemon (=Drake). Meaning and allusion not discovered.

Podalirius (=Banister?). A physician, son of Aesculapius; served with the Greeks in the Trojan War.

Hypocritas (=Banister? or Cotton?).

Jennarius (=Taylbois? or Cotton?). The allusion is perhaps to Janus, the two-faced god.

Colax, 'a sort of parasite who hated everything and everyone' (Madox). This description seems to fit Madox's characterization of Cotton.

Quintus Martius, an augur. Not identified.

Anas (=Sir Francis Drake). Latin word for 'duck'; *anas mas*, 'drake'.

ADDENDUM

Document 81

Interrogatories at St Vincent
8–9 February 1582/3[1]

1. If they know the said Andres de Eguino and have heard of the part of his Majesty's fleet which came to this port of Santos, and of the two English corsair galleons which were here?

2. If they know that on Sunday, the twentieth of January past of this year 83, two English corsairs entered into this port of Santos and took possession of it?

3. If they know that on several occasions the said English corsairs sent word to Sᵣ Jeronimo Leitão, Governor and Captain of this Captaincy of São Vicente, to ask him to grant them leave to land and erect a forge, saying it was to repair their ships, the which it seems likely was in order to build a fort in the said town?

4. If they know that during the first days the English sent to Jeronimo Leitão many polite words and offers so that he might grant them the said permission and as he did not wish to grant it they offered him threats if he did not decide in a very short time to do as they wished?

5. If they knew that through fear of the said English corsairs the inhabitants of this town of Santos and those of São Vicente sent to their farmsteads and clearings in the hinterland their womenfolk and children and their belongings, two, four and six leagues away and further. And some, thinking themselves not safe in the farmsteads, left them and took themselves into the depths of the mountains. And that also they hid the church ornaments with which is celebrated the Holy Sacrifice and the ministry of the Altar and the images, from the enemies of the Catholic Church?

6. If they know that although the captain Jeronimo Leitão took all the measures he could as a good and faithful vassal of His

---

[1] Extracts, translated. Seville, Archivo General de Indias, 2.5.2/21. These leading questions were put to the six witnesses at the inquiry before the Governor of S. Vicente (see p. 252).

Majesty, he could not have resisted the enemy, being weaker than the force they had with them, nor could he defend the land?

7. If they know that if the said Andres de Eguino had delayed a few days more and the enemy had raised some fortifications, to which end he had wished to erect the forge, and placed in it half a dozen pieces of artillery : with them and with the two galleons he could have defended the port against a large fleet and been master of the country?

8. If they know that the said Andres de Eguino arrived at this port on Thursday the twenty-fourth of the aforesaid month of January, and if they know, saw, or heard say that it is public and notorious that from early night until the following day at two in the afternoon, when the enemy fled from this port, he fought with them with artillery, arquebuses and musket?

9. If they know that the flagship of Andres de Eguino, at the time the enemy fled, because of the great number of shot-holes, the rigging all cut away and the many openings along the water-line from one side to the other, was in such a condition that if it had made sail and left the port it would have sunk?

10. If they know, saw, and heard say and it is public and notorious that in all that night, although the battle continued throughout, the ship *Concepcion* which is the biggest and newest ship and the one with the best artillery and a large crew, did not fight nor help the flagship because it was sheltered and hidden behind her, so that it did not come out (of shelter) until the following day at 9 o'clock when it fired its first shot?

11. If they know, believe and hold it true that if the said ship *Concepcion* had helped against the enemy in compliance with the orders which had been given to her captain Francisco de Cuellar, the ship *Begoña* would not have been lost nor the English have escaped?

12. If they know that although the ship *Begoña* was lost, yet much was gained and his Majesty well served in having chased the English from this port, seriously damaged and with many of his men killed, according to reports received that the bodies of many Englishmen have been found along the coast?

13. If they know that this port is the most convenient one on the coast for the evil purposes of the English, which are to terrorize this land of Brazil and set out to attack the ships from India, Angola, Rio de la Plata, and the Magellan Straits?

14. If they know that all the above said is common knowledge and report?

INDEX

325